INTRODUCTION TO LITERARY CONTEXT

Plays

INTRODUCTION TO LITERARY CONTEXT

Plays

SALEM PRESS

A Division of EBSCO Information Services, Inc.
Ipswich, Massachusetts

GREY HOUSE PUBLISHING

Publisher's Cataloging-In-Publication Data

Introduction to literary context. Plays / [edited by Salem Press].—[First edition].

   pages; cm

  Includes bibliographical references and index.
  ISBN: 978-1-61925-715-3

1. Drama—History and criticism. I. Salem Press. II. Title: Plays

PN1811.I587 2014
809.2

First Printing

PRINTED IN THE UNITED STATES OF AMERICA

CONTENTS

PUBLISHER'S NOTE

Introduction to Literary Context: Plays is the newest title in Salem's *Introduction to Literary Context* series. Other titles in this series include *American Post-Modernist Novels, American Short Fiction, English Literature*, and *World Literature.*

This series is designed to introduce students to the world's greatest works of literature – including novels, short fictions, novellas, plays, and poems – not only placing them in the historical, societal, scientific and religious context of their time, but illuminating key concepts and vocabulary that students are likely to encounter. A great starting point from which to embark on further research, *Introduction to Literary Context* is a perfect foundation for *Critical Insights,* Salem's acclaimed series of critical analysis written to deepen the basic understanding of literature via close reading and original criticism. Both series – *Introduction to Literary Context* and *Critical Insights* – cover authors, works and themes that are addressed in core reading lists at the undergraduate level.

Scope and Coverage

Plays covers 31 plays written by authors from around the world, published between the 17th and 20th centuries. The playwrights in this collection represent a variety of ages, life styles, and political beliefs, including those whose work has been banned, burned, and revered. Their work is based on personal experiences and struggles, as well as societal issues of the time.

With in depth analysis of works by the likes of Tony Kushner, Tennessee Williams, Arthur Miller, Henrik Ibsen, T. S. Eliot, Oscar Wilde and Bernard Shaw, *Introduction to Literary Context: Plays* offers students the tools to grasp more firmly and dig deeper into the meanings of not only the works

covered here, but literature as it has been created around the world.

Organization and Format

The essays in *Plays* appear alphabetical by title of the work. Each is 6–8 pages in length and includes the following sections:

- Content Synopsis – summarizes the plot of the play, describing the main points and prominent characters in concise language.
- Historical Context – describes the relevance to the story of the moods, attitudes and conditions that existed during the time period that the play took place.
- Societal Context – describes the role that society played within the play, from the acceptance of traditional gender roles to dealing with mental illness.
- Religious Context – explains how religion – of the author specifically, or a group generally, influenced the play.
- Scientific & Technological Context—analyzes to what extent scientific and/or technological progress has affected the story.
- Biographical Context – offers biographical details of the author's life, which often helps students to make sense of the play.
- Discussion Questions – a list of 8–10 thoughtful questions that are designed to develop stimulating and productive classroom discussions.
- Essay Ideas – a valuable list of ideas that will encourage students to explore themes, writing techniques, and character traits.
- Works Cited

Introduction to Literary Context: Plays ends with a general Bibliography and subject Index.

ABOUT THIS VOLUME

"The play's the thing," declares Hamlet, a statement that not only serves as a vehicle to propel the plot of Shakespeare's most wordy drama, but a sentiment that also is indicative of the historic role theater has played in society from ancient Greece through modern times. The works analyzed in this collection date from the 17th through the 20th centuries and reflect the evolution in scope, concept, and purpose that plays have experienced in only a few hundred years.

Theater was among the very earliest forms of mass entertainment and remained at the forefront until the advent of moving pictures in the early 20th century. Many early films followed the format of plays and featured single locations and settings and simple scenery until the full potential of that art form was developed. It is fitting that in today's high-tech world where music and movies are consumed on a global scale through television and the internet that plays endure and that a small audience gathered in the intimacy of a theater for a live performance ranks as a higher form of entertainment.

While the early plays coming from Greece often were stern morality tales, English language plays put a twist on that concept by couching a moral lesson in comedy with characters scuttling around on stage in exaggerated situations to induce laughter while the villains, ultimately, were punished before the curtain was drawn. To put the past on a par with the present, romantic comedies and action were dominant on the stage as they are currently in film and television. Humanity's desire to be thrilled and titillated remains intact.

Bawdy sex romps featuring characters pursuing carnal desires in a comedic fashion were popular with pre-Victorian audiences. Ben Johnson's *Volpone* (1606), featured in this collection, is a perfect example of the variety of plays that found a large, appreciative audience for many years. Featuring and exotic setting (Venice) and characters of noble birth who are lecherous in their desires and succumb to their feelings of avarice and lust, the play satirizes both greed and sex, two venerable human foibles than any audience member can understand. Title character Volpone uses the allure of his wealth to trick merchant Corvino into pushing his luscious wife Celia into bedding him so that Corvino will be named heir to the rich Venetian's vast fortune. Volpone feigns a deadly illness in order to season his ruse, which widens to include wrangling gifts out of two other men who also desire to be his heir.

The play also features the character Mosca, Volpone's servant, who, although a common man, manipulates the noblemen, making them targets of the equally common-man audience's disdain and laughter. Johnson's play also includes another important and common element present in many works of its tenure; namely characters disguising themselves in order to manipulate the players and be a fly on the wall. Characters masking themselves to play dual roles has been a successful ploy from the 1600s on up to comic book superheroes of the 20th century who don a simple pair of eyeglasses to go unrecognized as the caped champion of good. Besides manipulating the plot it draws in the audience making them insiders to the character's deceit.

Although written well more than 170 years after *Volpone*, Irish playwright Oliver Smith's *She Stoops to Conquer* (1773) also sports upper-class characters employing alternate identities in order to achieve their goals. The plot finds wealthy Charles Marlowe pursued by Kate Hardcastle and her scheming father who desire that she and Marlowe should marry. The London lad, however, is shy and falls to pieces around upper class women while being thoroughly comfortable around those of the lower class. In order to attract Marlowe (and his father's fortune), Kate must disguise herself as a servant girl. Furthermore, Kate's cousin tricks Marlowe into believing that the Hardcastle's home is an inn, leading Marlowe to treat his potential future in-laws like common servants.

A subplot of the play involves two other would-be lovers—Marlowe's friend George Hastings and Constance Neville—whose romance is thwarted by Mrs. Hardcastle's desire for Constance to marry her son in order for the young woman's Volpone forthcoming inheritance to Hardcastle money. Although a light comedy of errors—and romance—the underlying theme, as in Johnson's *Volpone* is greed. Although playwrights Johnson and Smith are separated by hundreds of miles and as many years, the two works share numerous similarities.

Deal with the Devil

While the English busied themselves with sex-romp morality tales that would titillate large audiences, playwrights in other nations pursued a darker approach to their craft, although, again, common threads abound. German Johann Wolfgang von Goethe published the first part of his epic *Faust* in 1808. Far from wealthy noblemen trying to seduce young lovelies while others scramble about like hounds trying to sniff out fortunes, protagonist Dr. Faust seeks the riches of knowledge as he pursues the study of the universe. In order to secure the treasures of the natural world, Faust turns towards the supernatural. On a bet with God, Mephistopheles partners with Faust in order to win his soul.

Faust makes a deal with the devil in which Mephistopheles will serve him during his life and become his master after death. A witch's conjuring morphs Faust into a young, attractive man who proves alluring to women, especially a fetching lass named Gretchen with whom the transformed Faust becomes smitten. Here again is the concept of a character in disguise, although unlike in *Volpone* and *She Stoops to Conquer* where players simply donned costumes to switch personas, Faust is physically transformed through black magic. As the alluring young man, Faust is able to win Gretchen, a feat that would have been impossible in his natural form. Goethe then submerges *Faust* into darkness as a pregnant Gretchen accidentally kills her mother and Faust and Mephistopheles kill her brother in a sword fight. The woman's grief is so great that she freefalls into insanity and murders her baby, an act for which she is to be executed.

Kill the Messenger

Norwegian playwright Henrik Ibsen's *An Enemy of the People* (1882) was one of the early theater works to focus on the social conscience. Protagonist Dr. Thomas Stockmann has damning evidence that the local health baths have been contaminated by a tanning works and feels that the citizenry must be apprised of the great risks involved in their use. The baths and the tanning operation, however, are the backbone of the area's economy and closing them would bankrupt the town and financially devastate most of the populace. The doctor's discovery initially is met with great interest by the press, which is anxious to publish his findings.

Stockmann shares the information with his brother, the town's mayor, who immediately debunks the findings and plots to discredit his brother in favor of saving the town from financial ruin. The press also reverses its support and sides with the mayor. Stockmann decides to address the population directly in order to save them from possibly becoming deathly ill. He reveals his findings at a town meeting, but his brother immediately assassinates his character and turns the crowd against him. Even though he is trying to save their health, Stockmann and his family become outcasts; they lose their jobs and their home. Knowing that he is right, however, Stockman decides to remain in the town.

At its core, *An Enemy of the People,* like *Volpone* and *She Stoops to Conquer* centuries before, is a morality tale about greed. Reasonably, the mayor, the publishers, and the town's people know that Stockmann is trying to help them and that allowing the tannery and the baths to remain in operation conceivably could kill them, yet they're willing to risk it because they are more frightened by the thought of having no money than being sick. The baths *might* make them ill, but closing them *will* make them poor. The play also is the ultimate "kill the messenger" story. Rather than simply ignore Stockmann's findings or try to censor the man, the people—including his brother—destroy him for bringing the situation to light even though he does so for their benefit. Even the press, which should serve as the unwavering and incorruptible defender of the people, turns on Stockmann in favor of preserving the baths: no baths/factory equals no populace and no populace equals no need for a newspaper.

The play also serves as a commentary on the industrialized society of the late 19th century. Ibsen wasn't the only author to observe that in an economy fueled by factories, workers became less valuable than machinery and the goods they produced for sale. This advent is all the more shocking because it transpired in a society that in living memory had overthrown kings and shucked the yokes of nobles who treated the common people like worthless possessions. Captains of industry were replacing nobility in using the masses like beasts of burden who were disposable and easily replaced.

Family Affair

Eugene O'Neill arguably is the 20th century foremost American playwright and one of the pillars of that form regardless of age and nationality. *Long Day's Journey into Night* was published after his death, as he didn't want the revelations of the auto-biographical play to be revealed to the public while he and his family members lived. Although *Long Day's Journey into Night* was written towards the end of his sterling career after he had received the Nobel Prize and several Pulitzers, his experimental fledgling efforts are no less distinct. Even in his early one-act creations, O'Neill's strove unflinchingly to create art. When applying to Harvard University to attend George Pierce Baker's playwriting course, O'Neill stated that his goals was to become "a great artist or nothing." Despite leaving the university without completing the course, O'Neill succeeded.

The son of noted actor James O'Neill, who won world renowned for his portrayal of *The Count of Monte Cristo,* Eugene spent a good portion of his earliest childhood in theaters, which instilled both a love of drama and a loathing for vapid productions substituting romance and action for meaningful plots. James also showed great promise as a young actor and may have become one of the great artists of the stage but instead chose to purchase the rights to Alexander Dumas's *The Count of Monte Cristo,* which he played for easy money for the remainder of his career. O'Neill progressed from one-act shorts to behemoth multi-act productions running nearly six hours. *Long Day's Journey into Night* follows a single day in the life of the Tyrones—father James, mother Mary, and sons Jamie and Edmund—and several servants at their Connecticut home. The Tyrones are thinly veiled carbon copies of the O'Neills and the plays setting is a duplicate of the family's house in New London, Connecticut.

The drama unfolds through the slow revelation that Mary became addicted to morphine after a difficult birth when delivering Edmund and has been a full-blown morphine addict for more than 20 years. Although the father has kept this dark secret for decades and Jamie long has suspected the truth, the disclosure hits Edmund like a heavy blow and the knowledge that his mother's torment was caused by his birth nearly is more than he can bear. O'Neill laces the play with sharp irony as James and his two sons chastise the wife/mother for her addiction to "that poison" while all three men refuse to acknowledge they are alcoholics. James keeps his liquor under lock and key and when the maid puts out a bottle of bonded bourbon so he can embark on his nightly ritual of drinking before dinner, the sons each take drinks and refill the bottle with water to hide their theft before their father enters.

Like Ibsen's characters, The Tyrone's ignore the truth in hopes that the problem of Mary's addiction simply will go away. The family's inability to face the truth climaxes when Edmund announces that he has tuberculosis. His mother immediately accuses him of lying to get attention, although later she expresses fear to her husband that Edmund will die. Mary also hopes that she will overdose accidentally and end her own drug-fueled existence. Like the mayor accusing Dr. Stockton of lying about the baths in *An Enemy of the People*, so Mary Tyrone refuses to face the truth even if it results in the death of her own son (all the more horrible as she already had lost a baby—Eugene—in childbirth prior to Edmond).

An overriding theme of the play is guilt (a recurring theme in O'Neill's canon). James Tyrone feels guilty that he took the easy road for money and fame rather than work hard to live up to his potential as a great artist; Mary wallows in guilt over her drug addiction rather than seek help; Jamie feels guilt over having decayed into a drunk who will stab anybody in the back; and Edmund feels guilt for even being born because it made his mother a junkie and ruined the family. Where the others have accepted their fates, Edmund, like Dr. Stockmann, refuses to submit and accept the lies as truth. Rejecting the shield of ignorance his family wields to protect itself, Edmund tells his father that

he will be a great artist. Although all seems bleak, Edmund and Dr. Stockmann's willingness to stand alone in accepting the truth leaves the audience with the smallest ember of hope.

Shattered

The Glass Menagerie is Tennessee Williams' entrée into autobiographical theater. Protagonist Tom Wingfield is a thinly disguised version of himself. Like *Long Day's Journey into Night*, *The Glass Menagerie* offers a dysfunctional family at odds with one another. Tom is a factory worker with aspirations of becoming a famous poet. Although he supports his mother and handicapped sister, he secretly plans to join the merchant marines and abandon them. Mother Amanda desires only to marry off her daughter Laura, but the girl's damaged leg and equally crippling shyness prevents her from meeting men. Tom brings home Jim O'Connor, a coworker from the factory, as a potential suitor for Laura and the two seem attracted to each other—they dance and share a kiss—but Jim reveals that he is engaged to be married and must leave. Laura is crushed by the news of Jim's engagement and Amanda scolds Tom for bringing him home as a suitor. Tom separates himself from the women who don't know that he lost his job and, like his father before him, is abandoning the family to pursue his own interests.

Like O'Neill's Tyrones, William's characters refuse to face reality. Amanda fantasizes that Laura will find a loving husband, when, in reality, the young woman is physically *and* emotionally dysfunctional and destined to live her life alone. Tom truly *is* the self-centered dreamer that Amanda accuses him of being and rejects his responsibility to his mother and sister, leaving them to somehow fend for themselves. Even Jim seemingly leaves his responsibility to his fiancé at the Wingfield's front door when kissing another woman. Laura, too, refuses to look the truth in the eye: her mother enrolls her in business school in order to ensure that the girl will have a means of supporting herself as well as the possibility of meeting a suitor. Laura, however, succumbs to her own shyness and quits school without a thought to how she will survive in life.

Passing the Blame

David Mamet's *Oleanna* (1992) also examines the notion of truth. It also is a knife-to-the-throat denunciation of the political correctness that gripped—and, perhaps, strangled—late 20th century society. The brief work offers the interaction between John, a 40-something college professor and Carol, a 20-year-old student. The student comes to the professor in a state of distress over her inability to understand any of the work involved in his class—she comprehends neither the class discussions by other students nor the material in the textbook, which was written by John.

Although sympathetic, John is distracted by numerous phone calls from his wife regarding a house they will purchase with the bonus money he'll receive if the college awards him tenure. Carol is near hysterical and rises to leave but John puts a comforting arm around her and attempts to calm her fears by declaring that much of what is taught in college is meaningless academic rhetoric that is difficult to understand. At a follow-up meeting, Carol returns a pillar of confidence and strength and is unrecognizable as the same distraught woman. She stuns John with the information that stemming from his conduct at their initial meeting, on the advice of an unnamed "group" she has filed a formal complaint of sexual harassment and battery against him, jeopardizing his tenure.

John attempts to explain that his physical contact and verbal interaction with her was the universal act of one human being trying to comfort another in distress and fully nonsexual. Carol rejects his explanation asserting that unlike what is taught in classrooms, her accusations are facts not theories. The third act finds John packing his office after losing tenure and being terminated. Carol offers to withdraw her complaint against him allowing him to keep his job on the condition that he alter the class to replace certain materials with others prescribed by her and the "group." Among the materials to be excised is John's own book. Essentially, the "group" will determine what will be taught in his class. The two again are interrupted by a phone call from John's wife informing him that in addition to losing his job, a rape charge may be lodged against him. During their conversation, John calls his wife "baby," and Carol immediately orders him to stop using that degrading term, causing John finally to lose control and physically assault her.

Although exaggerated, Mamet offers a raw look at how the fabric of society is being unraveled by nameless, faceless bodies like the "group" in order to foist their own agendas on a public that is no longer willing to accept responsibilities for its actions. Unlike O'Neill's Tyrones, who realize their own shortcomings but choose to ignore them, Mamet's characters fully refuse to accept the possibility that they are responsible for their problems.

The plays discussed above along with the others in this collection span several centuries and originated in numerous diverse countries, yet they share many themes and grapple with identical problems, proving the universal importance of the play as a reflection of society and as a chronicle of the human condition.

Michael Rogers
Freelance writer and former
Senior Editor, *Library Journal*

American Buffalo

by David Mamet

Content Synopsis

Act 1 of this two-act play opens on a Friday morning in Don's Resale Shop, a junk shop owned by Don Dubrow. Don is talking to Bob, his young gofer, and trying to guide him in the way of certain matters. Bob was supposed to watch somebody and failed to keep an eye on him, and Don is lecturing Bob on the matter. He takes a fatherly stance, telling Bob of the importance of eating a good breakfast and taking care of oneself. In the midst of their conversation, Teach enters the shop, ranting about how Ruthie suckered him into paying for their breakfast at the diner, the Riv, across the street. Bob leaves for the Riv to get coffee and food for the three men. Teach and Don talk about the previous night's poker game, and how well Fletch did.

Bob returns with their order, and tells Don that he saw "him" leaving the Riv with a suitcase, suggesting that he's taking a trip and won't be home that evening. The restaurant forgot to include Don's coffee, so Bob goes back to get it. After he leaves, Teach probes Don for information about his conversation with Bob. Don tells him that a man came into the shop and took interest in a coin, an old buffalo head nickel, and offered Don $50 for it. Don bargained with the guy, and sold it for $90 but could tell it was worth much more. The next day, the guy returned and gave Don his card in case he comes across more coins to sell. Don tells Teach

that this man must be a big coin collector and that he and Bob are planning to break into his house to steal his valuable coins.

Teach tries to convince Don that Bob is not ready for this type of job and that Don should instead trust Teach with it. When Bob returns, he tries to get Don to give him some money upfront for the job. Instead, Don offers him $25 to forget about the job. Bob leaves with $50 under the agreement that he will pay Don back $25 in the future. Don and Teach try to plan out the job, but Teach does not seem any more prepared than Bob, and Don decides to include Fletch as an extra lookout. Act I ends as Teach leaves to take a nap. He agrees to come back at 11 pm.

Act 2 opens at 11:15 pm in Don's shop. Don, frustrated, is hanging up the phone as Bob enters. He tells Don that he needs money and has a buffalo nickel to sell him. Teach walks in, and Don yells at him for being late. Teach wants to know why Bob is there, and he offers to pay Bob for the coin in order to get him out of there. Bob wants $50, but Teach gives him $5 and tells him to keep the nickel for now. He tells Don to give Bob some more money, which he does, and Bob finally leaves. Teach wants to know where Fletcher is, and Don assures him that Fletcher will be there. Teach tries to convince Don that Fletcher is not to be trusted and they should just go do the job without him before it is too late. Teach then takes out a gun and, despite

Don's objections, says he is bringing it with them just in case the robbery goes awry.

Bob returns and tells them that Fletch is in the hospital with a broken jaw after getting mugged. Teach does not believe him and accuses Bob and Fletch of being disloyal and attempting to execute the robbery on their own. Bob denies this but gets the hospital name wrong so that, when Don and Teach call it, they are told that Fletch is not there. Teach then viciously beats Bob with an object from the store. Moments later, Ruthie calls and tells Don the correct hospital. Don calls the hospital and verifies that Fletch is there with a broken jaw. Bob is seriously hurt, and they agree to take him to the hospital. Bob then admits that he bought the buffalo nickel from a coin store to impress Don and that he also lied when he said he saw the man who bought the coin leaving the Riv with a suitcase. Teach lashes out in anger and trashes the junk shop because he knows the job will never happen. In a moment of comic relief, Teach makes a paper hat out of a newspaper and puts in on. He then leaves to get his car to take Bob to the hospital. The play ends as Bob, who is in and out of consciousness, apologizes to Don who assures him that it is all right.

Symbols & Motifs

A recurring motif in "American Buffalo" and many of Mamet's plays is to parody the quest for the American Dream. All three men want a better life for themselves but do not seem to know how to get it. The coin, a symbol of wealth, represents a shot at a different kind of life. Their quest involves breaking the law in order to succeed, and the men cannot even succeed at that.

According to Don, Teach, and Bob's image of him, the man they plan to rob is wealthy, married, and has a valuable coin collection stowed in a safe in his house. The man embodies their dreams; he is a symbol for what they could become if they just had a chance. The fact that Bob never saw him when he said he did forces the men to face the grim reality that their plan was never meant to be. It was merely an illusion.

Teach's name serves as an ironic symbol because he is the character who is constantly trying to give Don advice. He thinks he knows best and convinces Don not to trust Bobby or Fletcher or anybody but him. His assumptions about people and his rash actions, however, prove that Teach is the one who should not be trusted. At the end of the play, the gesture of Teach making and putting on a paper that reveals him for the silly old man that he is.

Historical Context

"American Buffalo" premiered on November 23, 1975 at the Goodman Theater in Chicago. It starred William H. Macy as Bob, Bernard Erhard as Teach and J. J. Johnston as Don. It was directed by Gregory Mosher. In February of 1976, the play was performed at St. Clement's in New York, and one year later, it opened on Broadway at the Ethel Barrymore Theatre.

The play was nominated for two Tony awards and Four Drama Desk Awards (Theatre Database). A Broadway revival opened in 1983 and in 1984, J. J. Johnston won Theatre World Award for his reprisal of the role of Donny (Theatre Database). In 1996, Michael Corrente directed a film version of the play starring Dennis Franz as Don and Dustin Hoffman as Teach.

Societal Context

David Mamet is known for his unique dialogue in his plays and films. He tries to recreate natural speech and has his characters speak quickly, stutter, and not complete their sentences. In "American Buffalo," Mamet's style adds a realism to the down and out characters he aims to depict. Their conversions are often terse and vague, lending to the notion that these men are unable able to effectively communicate with one another. By the end, they seem to come together in other ways, as shown by Don assuring Bob that he "did good" despite his lies and deception, but they are still faced with the lonely reality that they live in a world where their wants and needs are never fully understood. Mamet makes it clear that there is a big difference between talk and action.

The play mocks America's obsession with money. In an essay in "Twentieth Century Literature," Jon Dietrick states that, "Mamet reveals the philosophical dilemmas raised by money as the primary concern." This issue, which became a common theme in Mamet's work, was especially timely at the play's inception. In 1975, President Nixon signed an order allowing the trade of gold on the free market (Dietrick). Free enterprise is a concept that Don, Bob, and especially Teach, espouse in the play. Teach insists that he has the right to make money however he sees fit and that this is the American Way (Novick). Otherwise, Teach insists, "we're just savage shitheads in the wilderness." (Mamet). Through the selling of the buffalo nickel at one price and the characters' attempts to steal back the coin to sell again at a higher price, Mamet makes the point that whether it is paper, coin or gold, the value of money is never a constant. He also makes the point that societies founded on greed and materialism are indeed savage and destined to crumble.

Religious Context
"American Buffalo" does not have a specific religious context. The characters lack any sense of spirituality and their existence seems to revolve around the acquisition of wealth and material goods. The setting of the junk shop accentuates this emphasis on things rather than people or relationships. Even after hours, the men spend their downtime in the shop playing cards and gambling.

Scientific & Technological Context
"American Buffalo" does not have a specific scientific or technological context.

Biographical Context
David Mamet was born in Chicago, IL on November 30, 1947. He attended Goddard College in Vermont and the Neighborhood Playhouse School of Theater in New York. He is married to actress Rebecca Pidgeon, and they have two children. He also has two children from a previous marriage. His first successful play was "Sexuality Perversity in Chicago" in 1974. When "American Buffalo" came out in 1975, Newsweek dubbed Mamet the next "hot young American playwright" (Grove Press).

Mamet won the Pulitzer Prize in Drama for "Glengarry Glen Ross" in 1984 and was also nominated for a Tony Award. "Speed the Plow" was nominated for a Tony in 1988.

In addition to playwriting, Mamet also writes for the screen and occasionally directs. His first big onscreen success was as the screenwriter for the film The Untouchables. He later received an Oscar nomination for his screenplay Wag the Dog.

Jennifer Bouchard

Works Cited
"David Mamet." 20th Century Theatre. Theatre Database. 28 May 2009. <www.theatredatabase.com/americanbuffalo.html>.

Dietrick, Jon. "Real Classical Money, Naturalism, and Mamet's American Buffalo." *Twentieth Century Literature*. 52.3 (Fall 2006): 330–346. Academic Source Complete. EBSCO. 3 June 2009. <http://search.ebscohost.com/login.aspx?direct=true&db=s8h&AN=24831626&site=ehost-live>.

Filmmakers.com. 20 October 2008. <http://www.filmmakers.com/artists/mamet/biography>.

Mamet, David. "American Buffalo." New York: Grove Press, 1976.

Novick, Julius. "Theater." Nation 231.16 (15 Nov. 1980): 521–522. Academic Source Complete. EBSCO. 6 June 2009.

Discussion Questions

1. Which character did you most like?
2. Which character did you like the least?
3. Discuss the way the characters communicate with one another.
4. Who is the hero in the play? The villain?
5. What does the nickel symbolize to each of the men?
6. Describe Teach. Is his nickname appropriate?
7. What are the roles of the characters that never set foot on stage, namely Ruthie and Fletcher?
8. What is the theme of the play?
9. Reflect on the title of the play.

Essay Ideas

1. Develop a formal argument, supporting with text evidence, what you consider is the main statement or theme of the play.
2. Discuss the role of morality in the play. Evaluate whether you think the characters are immoral or whether the business makes them so.
3. Compare and contrast Don and Teach. Discuss their approach to business as well as their approach to life.
4. Write an extended ending or follow up to the play in which you address how these characters go on with their lives.
5. Compare and contrast "American Buffalo" to another work of literature that addresses the failure of the American Dream.
6. Write an essay in which you analyze the relationship between Don and Bob.

Angels in America

by Tony Kushner

Content Synopsis

Part I, Act I

It is 1985, and Louis Ironson is going to the cemetery to bury his grandmother. His lover, Prior Walter, reveals that he has AIDS. Rather than being able to offer emotional support to Prior, Louis needs his comfort and reassurance.

Roy Cohn offers Joe Pitt, a clean-cut Mormon and dedicated conservative, a job in the Reagan Justice Department. Joe is flattered and eager to accept the offer, but must consult his wife. Roy hides his disappointment and encourages him to speak with her. Joe's wife, Harper, is addicted to valium and prone to hallucinations. One involves an imaginary travel agent, Mr. Lies, who promises to take her to Antarctica. She is concerned about the hole in the ozone layer. After swallowing a number of valium, Harper hallucinates her way into a dream that Prior is having.

Prior sits before a mirror in drag, applying make-up. He tells Harper her husband is homosexual. She tells Prior that despite his terribly diseased condition, deep within he is clean and healthy. Harper vanishes. Prior hears a voice telling him to look up. He sees a feather fall from the ceiling.

Harper tells Joe she will not go to Washington and that she is afraid a man with a knife is hiding in the bedroom.

Louis tells the rabbi burying his grandmother that he cannot stay with Prior: he cannot cope with illness, blood, vomit, and all the signs of the body's decay. Louis asks Prior if he will hate him if he leaves him; Prior says yes.

Louis and Joe first meet in the men's room of the Federal Courthouse. Lewis is a word processor; Joe, chief clerk to a judge. Louis explains that his friend is ill and alludes to his own homosexuality. Joe offers comfort. When Louis notes that he is the first of the several lawyers who have come upon him crying to show any concern, and characterizes the others as heartless, macho, right-wing, Reagan Republicans, Joe says that he voted for Reagan, twice. Louis retorts that he did not know there were gay republicans. Joe denies being gay and Louis teases him. As Louis leaves, he kisses Joe on the cheek.

Harper asks what Joe does when he walks alone at night. He refuses to admit that he is looking for sexual encounters with men. She says that she hates having sex with him and asks him if he is "a homo." Joe begins to ask, "what if I were," and then denies that he is.

Roy's doctor tells him he has AIDS. Roy refuses to accept that designation for his illness since only homosexuals have AIDS and he denies that he is homosexual: he has "clout," and homosexuals do not; he is a heterosexual man who has sex with men. He says he has liver cancer.

Act II

Prior is in pain, feverish, spitting blood, unable to walk. Louis calls an ambulance.

Joe returns home, finds Harper sitting in the dark, afraid to go into the bedroom. She asks what Joe prays for. He says for God to crush him. He recalls that the picture in the Bible of Jacob wrestling with the angel, portrayed as a beautiful man, fascinated him as a boy. Harper tells him he is the only person she ever loved but that she is going to leave him.

Prior is asleep in the hospital. Louis leaves, tells Prior's nurse to say "Goodbye" when Prior wakes.

Roy encourages Joe to accept the job in Washington and not to let his wife hold him back. He is attracted to Joe and wooing him, but keeping his guard up. Joe promises Roy he will think about Washington. Roy says that he wants Joe to be like his family. He tells Joe that he is dying of cancer.

Louis meets a leather man cruising Central Park. They have brutal anal intercourse. The man says he thinks the condom he is using has broken. Louis says it does not matter: he wants to get infected. The man leaves.

Belize, former drag queen and once Prior's lover, now a nurse, visits Prior in hospital. Beneath his campy cynicism, Belize is sweet, tender, loyal, and generous. Prior says he wants Louis, that his medication is disorienting, that he hears a voice, and it arouses him sexually. Belize leaves. Prior hears the voice promise to return soon in its fullness.

Roy, Joe, and Martin, a senior member of the Reagan administration, are dining at an exclusive restaurant. The two are trying to convince Joe to accept the position in Washington. Roy repeats his own anti-communist credentials and Joe restates his esteem for Roy. Roy explains that he needs Joe in Washington in order to represent his interests. Roy shows Joe a letter announcing the start of disbarment proceedings against him because of his having borrowed half a million dollars from a client and failed to return it. He needs Joe in Washington in order to bring pressure against his foes. Politics, he says, is not about being ethical or being nice but about wielding power. Shaken, Joe says he will "think about it."

At lunchtime, outside the federal building, Joe runs into Louis. Their flirtatious conversation roams through politics, Reagan family dynamics, and the conflict between desire, love, and responsibility. Louis tells Joe he has left Prior. Joe complains that his world has become destabilized. Louis recommends that Joe stop conforming to the expectations that others have of him, but warns that freedom is fraught with anxiety.

That night, drunk, Joe calls Hannah, his mother, in Salt Lake City. He asks her if his father loved him and tells her that he is "a homosexual." She reproaches him for being drunk, tells him to stop his nonsense, and go home to his wife, and to call her from home. Then she hangs up on him.

Louis visits Prior, says he has moved out and promises to visit him regularly. Raging, Prior condemns Louis's inability to love, and demands Louis leave.

Joe tells Harper that although he loves her like a buddy, he has no sexual desire for her, and continually fights off his desire for men. She summons Mr. Lies, and he transports her to Antarctica.

In Utah, Joe's mother puts her house up for sale and sets off for New York City.

Act III

Prior sees the ghosts of two of his ancestors, one from the thirteenth century, one from the eighteenth. Both died in the plagues of their eras. They tell him they come to announce the arrival of a messenger and that he is a prophet.

In a coffee shop with Belize, Louis talks compulsively about democracy, freedom, AIDS, and gay liberation, of the importance of a group to have power, not just to be tolerated, and argues that although there are racial disparities in America, the cause of discrimination is not racial but economic.

Belize, who is black, objects to his denial of racial injustice in America and condemns him for how out of touch with reality and how theoretical he is. He reproaches Louis for his self-pity regarding Prior and tells him the terrible condition Prior is in. Louis complains that he might be sick, too, that he is wretched, that he feels like Judas. Belize refuses to sympathize with him. It begins to snow.

The nurse tells Prior that he is making progress. As she speaks, her words become garbled to Prior; she seems to be speaking something like Hebrew. As she fills out his chart, Prior sees the floor split open. A great book appears, the Hebrew letter Aleph bursts into flame; then the book shuts and disappears under the floor. The nurse sees none of this.

Harper appears in her imaginary Antarctica with Mr. Lies, excited and happy. She wants to meet an Eskimo, plant a forest, and stay forever. Mr. Lies tells her there are no forests in Antarctica, nor Eskimo, nor forever, since ice melts. An Eskimo appears.

Hannah Pitt arrives in New York City. Lost, she wanders around the Bronx, searching for Brooklyn. She asks a psychotic homeless person by a garbage-can fire drinking soup from a paper cup for directions. When Hannah forces her to take deep breaths and focus, the street person directs her to the subway.

After two days of being hospitalized with a bleeding ulcer, Joe goes to Roy's townhouse: he turns down the job in Washington. After seeming to take Joe's news calmly, Roy explodes with anger, shouts at Joe that he [Roy] is not nice, that to be effective the way he has been, one cannot be nice. He makes his point by telling Joe how he was in daily contact with Judge Kaufman, who presided over the trial of the Rosenbergs, and that it was because of his intervention that Ethel Rosenberg was executed. Joe is shocked at this criminal behavior but tries to excuse Cohn's rant by reflecting that Cohn has cancer. Cohn denies he is sick. He pulls Joe towards him and explodes in fury again. Joe just manages to restrain his impulse to beat Roy up and leaves.

Roy collapses and calls for his house servant. Instead, the ghost of Ethel Rosenberg appears. He defies her to frighten him. She taunts him and calls an ambulance for him.

In Prior's bedroom, his ancestors announce that the messenger is arriving. Scared, he tries to scare them away, but they stay. The specter of Louis enters and he and Prior dance until Louis disappears and Prior falls to the floor. He feels the angel's approach.

Louis sits on a bench in Central Park. Joe has followed him, feeling damned because of his desire. He asks to touch Louis. Louis kisses him and invites him to go home with him.

Prior hears a sound like a big bird flapping its wings. The plaster of the ceiling cracks; the ceiling falls in; the angel descends and greets Prior as a prophet.

Part II, Act I

"The oldest living Bolshevik," addressing a Communist Party congress about the dialectics of progress, admits that change and restructuring [Peristroika] are necessary, but argues that they are impossible and worthless without a great guiding theory. The scene shifts to Prior's bedroom and the final event of Part 1 is repeated. The angel comes crashing through the ceiling.

Harper and Mr. Lies are in Harper's imaginary Antarctica. Cold, dressed in the clothing she left home in rather than her beautiful imaginary snowsuit, she is dragging a small pine tree and begins to make a fire. Joe appears in the distance, an Eskimo. He says he is having a scary adventure but that she cannot go with him. The scene changes into a section of Prospect Park in Brooklyn. The police have arrived and arrest Harper.

Hannah arrives at Joe and Harper's apartment, where the superintendent lets her in. She answers the ringing phone. The police tell her they have Harper. Hannah says she will take a cab to the police station and not to put Harper in the hospital.

Belize, on night duty, is on the phone with Prior, who tells him of the angel's appearance. Roy's doctor brings Roy's medical folder to Belize and tells him he is a new admittance. Belize notes that liver cancer patients are on a different floor but the doctor asserts that, no matter what the folder says, Roy is on the right floor.

Roy insults Belize, insists on having a white nurse. Belize holds his own and despite his dislike for Roy advises him not to let the doctors give him radiation treatment because it will further damage his immune system. If he wants to be sure he is getting real AZT medication and not a placebo, Belize tells him to get his own supply. Roy calls Martin and threatens him with scandal if he does not get him the medication.

Louis and Joe arrive at Louis' apartment and after Joe's initial vacillation, have sex together.

Act II

After the funeral of a glamorous drag queen, Prior tells Belize about the angel's visit. He tells of a book hidden under the tiles in the kitchen and of how she took Prior in a violently ecstatic sexual embrace and afterwards told him that God disappeared from heaven in 1906 on the same day as the great San Francisco earthquake. Influenced by mankind, God became hungry for change, something human beings pursue along with thought, imagination, and exploration. Change causes undesirable upheavals. Heaven, the angel explained, is a place of stasis; time is a virus and humanity must stop moving.

Belize says the dream is about how Louis abandoned Prior and how Prior wishes he could have stopped time before he became ill. Prior acknowledges that but insists the encounter with the angel was real.

Act III

Hannah and Harper prepare to go to the Mormon Visitor's Center where Hannah is a volunteer worker and Harper spends her days. Harper both longs for Joe and wishes him dead.

Joe wakes in Louis' bed and tells him that he is a Mormon.

From his hospital bed, Roy shouts at someone on the phone about defending himself against disbarment proceedings. Ethel Rosenberg keeps appearing and disappearing, haunting Roy. Belize, seeing Roy's stash of AZT, demands some for his friends. Cohn refuses, but Belize pockets some. Cohn curses him, shouting obscenities and racial epithets. Belize returns the insults and gains Roy's respect.

Harper, sprawled on a seat in a small theater, on stage, a diorama of a Mormon family, inside the Mormon Visitors Center, eats junk food. The father looks like Joe. They are crossing the plains to Utah in a wagon. Hannah enters with Prior. He wandered into the Center to see if he could learn anything about angels. Harper and Prior listen to a taped narration about the Mormon trek. Spectral Louis appears and converses with the figure of Joe about how strange it is that Joe is a Mormon. Prior is distressed to see Louis in this hallucination. Louis senses Prior's presence. He leaves with the diorama Joe. When Hannah returns to the theater, the father dummy is back on the buckboard. Prior leaves and Harper speaks to the Mormon mother dummy asking her what crossing the plains was like.

It is a cold winter day. Louis and Joe walk along the shore at Jones beach. Joe tells Louis he loves him. Louis says that he wants to see Prior again.

High from morphine, Roy expresses sexual longing for Belize. He asks him what it is like after death. Belize describes heaven as a city like San Francisco, multicultural, glamorous, and sensual. Roy considers it a description of hell.

Harper asks the Mormon mother how people change. She describes a wrenchingly painful experience of the hand of God ripping the body open, rearranging the innards, and leaving the person alone to stitch the tear back up.

Prior gets a phone call from Louis saying he wants to see him.

Act IV

Joe visits Roy in hospital. Roy boasts about his importance to American Conservative politics. He gives Joe a blessing. When Joe tells him that he has left his wife and is living with a man, Roy becomes furious, rushes out of bed, pulling the drip tube attached to him out of his arm, and bleeds profusely. Belize rushes in, pulls on latex gloves, and gets Roy back into bed. Roy screams at Joe to leave and to go back to his wife. Roy complains that everything he ever wanted has been taken from him: Ethel Rosenberg reappears.

Louis sits on a park bench with Prior, hoping to reestablish a connection. Prior thinks that Louis wants to come back to him. But Louis says he does not want that. Prior intuits that Louis has a boyfriend. Louis denies it, but finally admits he does and justifies himself by saying that he had to have companionship. Prior responds with bitter irony considering that Louis has abandoned him to solitude at a time of his great need. Louis argues that he is in pain, too, and has internal wounds. Prior tells him to go away and come back when his wounds are visible.

After Prior finds out that Louis's boyfriend is a Mormon Republican who works in the Federal building, he drags Belize there to see Joe for himself. Prior looks into Joe's office and shouts angry reproaches at him. When Belize looks in, Joe

recognizes him as Roy Cohn's nurse. Joe comes out into the corridor and tries to confront the two; they flee.

Belize and Louis meet by the Bethesda fountain in Central Park. Belize tells Louis that Joe is in a relationship with Roy Cohn. Louis becomes hysterical.

At the visitor's center, Joe tells his mother he cannot find Harper and that she [Hannah] ought not to have come to New York. When he leaves Prior appears and asks Hannah if Joe is her son because he wants her to warn him against Louis, that Louis cannot stand the flesh and that when Joe starts to show age and signs of bodily deterioration, Louis will leave him. Hannah acknowledges that Joe is homosexual and asks Prior if he is. He says he is and collapses. He tells her to get him a cab to the hospital; she takes him there herself.

Joe finds Harper on the promenade in Brooklyn looking out at the river. He says he has come back and they go home.

The hospital nurse scolds Prior for exhausting himself when he was recovering. Prior tells Hannah about having seen the angel. She tells him having such a vision is not strange, that the Mormon leader Joseph Smith saw an angel. Prior asks her to stay with him when he feels the angel approaching because she gives him courage. She stays.

Harper asks Joe if he imagines men when he makes love to her. He does. She says that she thought he was real for her but now understands that he was a dream and that she is nothing to him. Joe goes to Louis' place expecting to be received warmly, but Louis rages against him because of his association with Roy and because of the reactionary legal decisions Joe wrote for the judge whose clerk he is. When Louis pushes Joe, Joe loses his self-control and beats Louis until his rage is spent. Louis lies bruised and bloody on the floor.

Ethel Rosenberg returns to Roy's hospital bedside and tells him that he has been disbarred. He tricks her into singing him a Yiddish lullaby and thinks that he has won a victory over her by eliciting her sympathy, but realizes that it is happening only in his imagination and that it means that he wishes for her loving forgiveness. With a sense of defeat, he dies.

Act V

Prior asks Hannah what to do when the angel reappears. Referring to the biblical story of Jacob and the angel, she says he must wrestle with the angel and demand a blessing. Prior overcomes the angel, a great, flaming ladder appears, and he ascends to heaven. Before the angel leaves, she takes Hannah in her arms and brings her to explosive sexual ecstasy. She then returns to heaven and greets Prior as he comes before a panel of angels to return the book: he does not wish to be a prophet; he does not wish to stop moving and embrace death. Even if life is fraught with terror, tragedy, and pain, he wants more life. The angels release him with a blessing. In heaven, he meets the rabbi who presided over Louis's grandmother's funeral with his grandmother. The rabbi recites an incantation that allows Prior to return to earth and Louis's grandmother says Louis ought to have visited her, that he had been confused since his childhood, and that the task of a Jew is to struggle with God.

Belize has called Louis to come to Roy's hospital room in order to take the jars of AZT out of the hospital and to say the mourner's Kaddish, the Jewish prayer for the dead, over Roy's body. Louis, bruised, tells Belize he is a secular Jew and does not know the Kaddish, but as Ethel Rosenberg says it behind him, he hears it, and repeats it perfectly.

Prior wakes in his hospital bed, his fever broken, Belize sitting by his bedside. Hannah emerges from the bathroom. A bond has been forged between them. Louis enters with the AZT. Hannahand Belize leave and Louis apologizes to Prior, admits his failure and his continuing love. He says he has returned because he now has visible bruises. Prior

tells Louis that he does love him, but that Louis may not come back as his partner, ever.

At home, Harper tells Joe she is leaving him, demands his credit card until she can support herself, slaps him, gives him some valium to take, and advises him to "get lost." From inside an airplane, she relates her vision of how the rising souls of the dead fill in the hole in the ozone layer.

Epilogue

Five years have passed. Hannah, Belize, Louis, and Prior gather by the fountain under the statue of the angel Bethesda in Central Park to celebrate Prior's birthday. He walks with a cane but has survived. As the other three discuss the political changes that are taking place in the world, Prior addresses the audience speaking of the beauty of the place and of his hope for a healthy and just future.

Symbols & Motifs

Disease is a recurring motif, whether as the AIDS virus or the virus of change of which the angel speaks. Change itself is also a motif, beginning with Louis's grandmother's immigration to America and continuing throughout the play. Most of the characters experience profound changes in their lives because of the effects of the plague-like spread of AIDS. Ethereal spirits, too, whether ghosts or angels or spectral and hallucinatory revelations, also serve as a recurring motif symbolizing the hidden depths of human perception and experience.

Loyalty recurs as a central theme, too, whether it is Louis's disloyalty to Prior or Roy's betrayal of the law or the conflict Joe and Harper face regarding loyalty to Mormon strictures.

Historical Context

Written at the end of the 1980s and the beginning of the '90s, "Angels in America" is concerned with the effects of the first wave of the AIDS epidemic on gay men in New York City. It was a time when a number of preconceptions about sexual encounters and relationships were called into question by the outbreak and rapid spread of the deadly epidemic and when relationships and values were challenged and tested.

The period between the historic Stonewall riots of 1968, when a group of homosexual men, lesbians, and drag queens resisted a police raid on a Greenwich Village gay bar, the Stonewall, and 1980 or so, when the world realized that AIDS was a serious problem, represented a kind of rebirth of homosexual culture, when gay men could be relatively open about their sexuality and promiscuous encounters were easy and plentiful. The onset of AIDS changed that.

Roy Cohn, an actual historical figure, had been chief counsel to Senator Joe McCarthy, 1908–1957, in senate, 1947–1957, notorious for his crusade against alleged American communists in the early 1950s. Cohn was instrumental in securing the execution of Julius and Ethel Rosenberg, accused of stealing the secret of the atom bomb and giving it to the Soviet Union.

Societal Context

Despite the comparative freedom of homosexual activity in special enclaves, like New York's Greenwich Village, homosexuality was considered a socially deviant sexual behavior and by many as sinful and psychologically sick. While some homosexuals began to "come out" and publicly admit their homosexuality, a great number remained "in the closet," keeping their sexuality secret.

The advent of AIDS forcibly brought the secret of many closeted people out into the open. Consequently, gay people were faced not only with a deadly disease but with intensified social vilification.

The 1950s were a time of widespread political trials in the United States aimed at uncovering alleged communist conspiracies. Roy Cohn achieved notoriety during that period as Senator

McCarthy's legal counsel when McCarthy's investigation of alleged communists in the United States military was televised.

Religious Context

The condemnation of homosexuality often took on a religious dimension and certain fundamentalist religions publicly proclaimed that AIDS was God's punishment for homosexuality. Homosexuality was often referred to, backed up by quotations from scripture, as an abomination.

While "Angels in America" traces some religious attitudes towards homosexuality and incorporates Mormon, Jewish, and Christian religious teachings and practices, its spiritual center relies on a faith in the goodness of which the human spirit is capable outside formal religious contexts and when the fundamental humanity of each person is appreciated.

Scientific & Technological Context

"Angels in America" incorporates both the strengths and the weaknesses of medical science and technology. AZT, a new drug meant to fight AIDS, could do some good but could also, Prior argues, negatively affect the organism. Medical science and technology can uncover the existence of AIDS but is relatively powerless, in 1986, to control or eradicate the disease.

There is in the play a strong anti-scientific, anti-technological assertion of fantasy, dream, vision, and intuition. These unscientific ways of knowing allow people to communicate with each other as creatures who share a common vital environment and a humanity that interlinks everyone.

Biographical Context

Winner of the Drama Desk Award twice, the Pulitzer Prize for Drama, two Tony awards, an Emmy Award, the Laurence Olivier Award, and the Steinberg Distinguished Playwright Award, Tony Kushner is one of the most lauded living

American playwrights. He was born in Manhattan on July 16, 1956 and grew up in Louisiana. His parents were both musicians. Kushner earned a B.A. from Columbia University in Medieval studies and studied directing at New York University. His work reflects his secular Jewish upbringing, his socialist politics, his literary education, and his concern for issues confronting gay men. "Homebody/Kabul, The Intelligent Homosexual's Guide to Capitalism and Socialism with a Key to the Scriptures," and "Caroline, or Change" are among the plays he has written besides "Angels in America." He has also translated several plays of the twentieth-century German playwright Bertolt Brecht, and collaborated with Maurice Sendak on "Brundibar," an opera, and on several films with Steven Spielberg.

Tony Kushner is married to Mark Harris, author of "Pictures at a Revolution – Five Movies and the Birth of the New Hollywood" and an editor of "Entertainment Weekly."

Neil Heims, Ph.D.

Work Cited

Kushner, Tony. "Angels in America". London: Nick Hern Books, 2007. Print.

Discussion Questions

1. Do Kushner's characters seem real to you? If they do, which aspects of the characters make them seem real? If they do not, why not? What prevents them from seeming real?

2. What part do politics play in "Angels in America"? Do you often see political issues and concerns being incorporated into a play? What is the effect on the play of the introduction of social and political issues into the plot?

3. What is the role of religion and of faith in the play? What is the vision of God that the play presents and what role does "Angels in America" suggest that God plays in shaping or directing the events of the world?

4. Discuss the value judgments that the characters in "Angels in America" make about each other and about themselves, implicitly or explicitly.

5. Do the dynamics and psychology of homosexual relationships as presented in "Angels in America" seem particularly different from those of heterosexual relationships?

6. Focusing on individual characters, discuss how Kushner combines virtues and faults in his characters.

7. Do you agree with the angel's assertion that mankind's problem is that people are too busy pursuing progress and change? Why or why not?

8. By the end of the play, every character seems to be accounted for except Joe. We know what each one moves on to, except Joe. How do you account for that as a dramatic strategy? What does it say about the character of Joe and about Kushner's attitude towards him? If you were to write a sequel what would you do with Joe?

Essay Ideas

1. Analyze the role of the supernatural in "Angels in America."

2. Examine the themes of optimism and pessimism and the conflict between progress, tradition, and reaction in "Angels in America."

3. Analyze the dramatic techniques Kushner uses in "Angels in America" to tell a complex story and to make visible each character's personality.

4. Discuss the importance of politics and ideological beliefs to the characters in the play and to the meaning of the play.

5. Although "Angels in America" is a serious play that deals with serious, even tragic issues and circumstances, it is a very funny play. Discuss the use of comedy in the play, how Kushner achieves its comic effects, and how the use of comedy affects the drama and verisimilitude of the play.

Playwright Tony Kushner. His play, "Angels in America," featured on page 5, comments on the effects of the AIDS epidemic in New York City. Photo: Commonwealth Club from San Francisco, San Jose, United States (by Ed Ritger)

Arcadia

by Tom Stoppard

Content Synopsis

"Arcadia" is a drama in two acts and seven scenes with a dual time-scheme alternating between the present and the early nineteenth century—April 1809 and June 1812, to be precise. In the final scene, present and past coalesce. The play's cast numbers thirteen characters, eight of them nineteenth-century, the remainder contemporaries. The principal characters from the past are Thomasina Coverly and her tutor, Septimus Hodge, and, in the present, Hannah Jarvis and Bernard Nightingale.

"Arcadia" is set on the Sidley Park estate in Derbyshire, a setting both significant and symbolic. Stoppard originally intended to entitle the play "Et in Arcadia Ego," not simply "Arcadia" had he done so, Death, which overshadows the play, would have loomed larger (Nadel 428). There is no doubt the playwright had in mind Nicolas Poussin's famous painting "The Arcadian Shepherds," in which this Latin motto appears, signifying Death announcing his presence even in "Arcadia," a type of earthly paradise.

As the play opens, Lady Croom is having her estate remodeled by Richard Noakes, who resembles such celebrated English landscape gardeners as Capability Brown and Humphrey Repton. This remodeling, like the clash between Hannah Jarvis and Bernard Nightingale, dramatizes the conflict between classicism and romanticism, the major theme, but "Arcadia" also dramatizes related conflicts between science and art, order and chaos, determinism and free will, head and heart.

Although the drama takes place indoors, we are aware from first to last of the out-of-doors, of Nature. Set in a single room, this drama ranges over the cosmos. The set is spare and elegant, with French windows letting in "light and air and sky." In his stage directions, Stoppard prescribes how everything on the table and in the room should belong to both the past and the present. Setting and props are handled interestingly throughout. Some props appear identical. For example, a tortoise named Plautus that Septimus Hodge, Thomasina's tutor, uses as a paperweight also appears as Valentine's "Lightning" in the present. The apple given by Gus to Hannah is replicated in the one Septimus munches as he listens to Thomasina translating. This apple recalls both the fruit of the Tree of the Knowledge of Good and Evil that Eve proffered Adam and the proverbial apple that fell on Newton's head inspiring thoughts of Gravity. In the final scene, the present-day Coverlys, dressed in Regency costume for their annual ball, resemble their nineteenth-century forebears. Up to this point, appearance and speech have been the sole means of distinguishing nineteenth- from twentieth-century characters. Aural motifs such as piano music, pistol shots, and the sound of a steam engine punctuate the action.

Thomasina's opening question, "What is carnal embrace?" announces the erotic theme of the play. Septimus answers her, first evasively, then scientifically, then more thought-fully. About to turn fourteen, Thomasina asks this question because of gossip among the servants, who have seen Septimus making love to Charity Chater, wife of the minor poet, Ezra Chater, in the gazebo. (Thomasina is falling in love with Septimus herself). Ezra Chater promptly challenges Septimus to a duel. He at first succeeds in putting this off by offering to write an appreciation of Chater's poem "The Couch of Eros," whereupon the vain and fatuous poet inscribes Septimus' copy of the poem, "To my friend who stood up and gave his best on behalf of the Author." (Chater does not realize Septimus trounced his previous poem, "The Maid of Turkey.")

This first scene also introduces scientific themes explored by the play: Thomasina is trying to solve Fermat's theorem and there are also references to the Newtonian universe and to determinism and free will. Thomasina's mind works on a cosmic scale. She speculates: "If you could stop every atom in its position and direction and if your mind could comprehend all the actions thus suspended; you could write the formula for all the future" (I. i. 30–33).

The second scene presents a flamboyant literary scholar, Bernard Nightingale, calling on Hannah Jarvis at Sidley Park. Hannah, a rather prim bluestocking, is studying English landscape gardening from 1750 to 1834. She has published a book on Lady Caroline Lamb, one of Byron's lovers, which has been successful, and now contemplates another on "The Hermit of Sidley Park." Bernard is researching Lord Byron and the minor poet Ezra Chater. Based on three notes he has discovered in Chater's "The Couch of Eros," Bernard becomes convinced that Byron killed Chater in a duel at Sidley Park. Chloe, present-day daughter of the house, introduces the scholars. Her brothers, Valentine, a mathematician, and Gus, a mute, are also present. (Valentine refers to Hannah as his

fiancé and Gus mutely adores her). Bernard asks Hannah for "leads" and in his enthusiasm over his Byronic theory (which Hannah finds half-baked), he kisses her. At first, he pretends his name is Peacock, not Nightingale, but Chloe addresses him by his real name, and then the fat is in the fire, for Hannah recalls Bernard Nightingale gave her book a lukewarm review. The interplay between these two academics shows Bernard to be a devotee of Romanticism, Hannah an adherent of classicism and the Enlightenment. Apparent in their dress and behavior, this conflict is expressed in Hannah's denunciation of the "whole Romantic sham," which she dismisses as "the decline from thinking to feeling" (I. ii. 38).

The third scene opens with Thomasina haltingly translating a Latin passage about Cleopatra. (It is Enobarbus' speech from Shakespeare's "Antony and Cleopatra" describing Cleopatra on her barge going to meet Antony.) Although a prodigy in mathematics, Thomasina appears not to excel in humanities. She tells her tutor she has seen Lord Byron with her mother in the gazebo and believes her mother to be in love with the poet. (As Thomasina works, Septimus is writing a letter that is later revealed to be a farewell note written in case he is killed in the forthcoming duel). Mr. Brice presents himself as Chater's "second," and Lady Croom recommends Septimus select his school-friend, Byron, as his second. She also urges Septimus to make Byron stay on at Sidley Park, for the poet threatens to leave England.

Scene IV opens with Hannah questioning Valentine about Thomasina's primer, in which she has found examples of iterated algorithms, part of Thomasina's "New Geometry of Irregular Forms." Valentine confirms his ancestress was a mathematical prodigy who anticipated contemporary statistical techniques. He himself is studying the grouse population on the Sidley estate. Valentine explains: "The unpredictable and the predetermined unfold together to make everything the way it is. It's how nature creates itself, on every scale, the snowflake, and the snowstorm" (I. iv. 29–32). He adds that, though relativity and quantum theory can account for the very large and very small, neither explains phenomena in the midrange of human experience, which remains mysterious and inexplicable.

Bernard continues evolving his theory that Byron killed Chater and fled England. Hannah pooh-poohs this, but Bernard insists gut instinct is never wrong.

Act II's first scene opens with Bernard declaiming his thesis, "the most sensational literary discovery of this century," that Byron made love to Chater's wife, panned his latest poem, and then killed him in a duel. He plans to present this theory before London's Byron Society. Bernard's present audience (Chloe, Valentine and Hannah), however, is critical and unruly. Valentine terms Bernard's arguments superficial and unscientific, finding the cult of personality in which Bernard indulges contemptible. Hannah remarks scathingly that Bernard has gone "from a glint in your eye to a sure thing in a hop, skip, and a jump." Bernard counters, "Is it likely that the man Chater calls his friend Septimus Hodge is the same man who screwed his wife and kicked the shit out of his last book?" (II. v. 9–11).

Bernard attacks science, upholding art as more valuable because it instills self-knowledge, the most valuable kind of knowledge. He quotes Byron to indicate the beauty and power of poetry. Then he propositions Hannah, who remarks that Bernard's mind is filled only with sex and literature. Bernard tells Hannah he has found a book describing her hermit as a lunatic who, for twenty years, lived alone in the Sidley Park hermitage with only a tortoise. By comparing birth and death dates, Hannah deduces her hermit to have been Septimus Hodge. Prompted by the hermit's sad fate, Hannah and Valentine discuss entropy.

Scene VI, set in the past, opens with Septimus entering at dawn with pistols. He has shot a rabbit

for Thomasina, who is fond of rabbit pie. The butler, Jellaby, reveals to him that the Chaters have left in a carriage with Mr. Brice and that Lord Byron departed separately. Lady Croom has been looking for Septimus in his room. She enters to reveal she sent the other guests packing because she found Mrs. Chater coming out of Lord Byron's room. (It is further revealed that Ezra Chater is still alive and will become the botanist on Brice's expedition to the Indies, chiefly because Brice dotes upon Chater's wife.) Lady Croom carries two opened letters, both written by Septimus—one to her, one to Thomasina—that she found in his room. Jellaby delivers a letter from Lord Byron, which Septimus burns. In repartee with Septimus, Lady Croom proves herself the soul of wit. Though angry with Septimus for making love to Mrs. Chater, he pays her such a deft and unusual compliment that she invites him to her room.

In the final scene of the play, past and present come together, historic and contemporary characters mingling and examining the same topics. As Chloe and her brothers don Regency costumes for the annual ball at Sidley Park, Chloe, like Thomasina, asks Valentine if she's first to think that "the future is all programmed like a computer." Chloe asserts that, even if the universe is mechanistic and deterministic, as Newton believed, what makes it unpredictable is sex—people fancying people who aren't supposed to be in that part of the plan (II. vii. 22–23).

Hannah reveals that Thomasina died in a fire the night before her seventeenth birthday. Bernard and his Byronic theory are still a topic of conversation; Hannah acknowledges that all topics of inquiry may appear trivial in the grand scheme of things, but "It's wanting to know that makes us matter. Otherwise we're going out the way we came in" (II. vii. 28–29).

While Hannah studies garden books, Valentine, at the computer, inputs Thomasina's equations, producing "islands of order" in "an ocean of ashes."

At this point, the past breaks in on the present as Thomasina and her brother, Augustus, come romping into the room with Septimus following. While Hannah and Valentine discuss entropy, Thomasina asks her tutor if he thinks she will grow up to marry Lord Byron. Septimus thinks not because "he is not aware of your existence" (II. vii. 24).

Thomasina reveals she has confided to her brother that her tutor kissed her the day before-Septimus claims not even to remember doing so. Thomasina then entreats her tutor to teach her the waltz, the new dance just imported from Germany. Septimus draws her attention to the book he is reading by a scientist who claims atoms do not behave as Newton proposed, particularly when subjected to heat. Thomasina points out that "heat goes only one way"—once energy has been expended, it is no longer there. (She draws a diagram to demonstrate this.)

Bernard returns to find his Byron theory proven false by an entry in one of Lady Croom's garden books about a dahlia named after Mrs. Chater, whose husband survived after all, only to die of a monkey bite in Martinique. Bernard is mortified to discover Byron could not have killed Chater. Hannah, who uncovered the evidence, offers to write a "gloat-free" letter to "The Times." Meantime, Lady Croom protests about Culpability Noakes' transformation of her estate and his "cowshed," which he terms a hermitage, asking where is the hermit who will inhabit it.

It is the eve of Thomasina's seventeenth birthday. She visits Septimus in her nightgown, carrying a candle. Thomasina kisses him and begs him to dance with her as he peruses one of her essays.

At once, Valentine and Septimus pore over a diagram of the steam engine Thomasina has drawn, deducing the same lesson of entropy. Septimus says, "When we have found all the mysteries and lost all the meaning, we will be alone, on an empty shore." Thomasina responds resolutely, "Then we will dance," and Septimus finally kisses her (II. vii. 9).

Bernard is caught kissing Chloe, who offers to leave Sidley Park with him, but Bernard rejects her-as Septimus will decline to make love to Thomasina. Bernard then apologizes to everyone, even wishing Hannah well.

Septimus gives Thomasina her candle, warning her to be careful of it as she goes to bed. She replies that she will wait for him, but he responds that he will not come. Thomasina entreats one more waltz to celebrate her birthday. As Septimus again waltzes with Thomasina, Gus invites Hannah to dance-which, being no dancer, she does awkwardly. This dark but sparkling comedy ends with a dance of atoms that is also the dance of the cosmos.

Historical Context

One of "Arcadia's" most significant and seductive features is its dual time frame. The central plot involving Thomasina, Septimus Hodge, Lady Croom, and others at Sidley Park in the early nineteenth century demonstrates the conflict between Neoclassicism and Romanticism that is at the play's heart. This clash of taste and temperament may be examined in the art, literature, architecture, and landscapes of the period that witnessed the decline of Neoclassicism and the rise of Romanticism. To give just one example, Lady Croom's garden is undergoing a transformation from Neoclassical regularity and order to Romantic wildness and disorder under Culpability Noakes. Hannah's comment that "English landscape was invented by gardeners imitating foreign painters who were evoking classical authors" illustrates how art and nature, history and myth are seamlessly interwoven in "Arcadia" (I. ii. 28–29).

"Arcadia" reflects the intellectual preoccupations of two different societies. The age-old conflict between the arts and sciences is a larger example of the dichotomy between Neoclassicism and Romanticism. Interest in mathematics and science during Newton's lifetime (1642–1727), overlapping this period, was as keen as it is today. The early nineteenth century was about to witness upheavals attendant on the Industrial Revolution that transformed a rural and agricultural society into an urban and industrial nation. Hence the interest in the laws of thermodynamics—particularly the second law that governs transactions among machines, heat, and energy.

Stoppard has acknowledged the Bernard Nightingale/Hannah Jarvis subplot was inspired by A. S. Byatt's best-selling novel "Possession," featuring a male and female scholar vying with each other to uncover the secrets of a Victorian poet and poetess who resemble Elizabeth Barrett and Robert Browning (Nadel 428). Other suggestions have been made for models-that Stoppard may have read and been influenced by Thomas Love Peacock's novel "Headlong Hall," set on a country estate filled with "disputatious writers, scientists and landscape architects." (This novel is mentioned in "Arcadia"—see p. 26. There are also resemblances to Lindsay Clarke's "The Chymical Wedding"). Interestingly, Byron's daughter Ada, like Thomasina, was a mathematical genius at a tender age; however, Stoppard denied he modeled his heroine on her (Nadel 428–29). (Naming his heroine Thomasina is perhaps an authorial inside joke—Thomas/Thomasina).

"Arcadia's" past and present plots mirror each other. Bernard, Hannah, and the present-day Coverly's are trying to unravel and interpret the past. The play's audience has the advantage over them of having seen that past enacted; hence, this is a play full of dramatic irony.

Societal Context

Part of "Arcadia" is reflective of contemporary British society, namely the plot-taking place in the 1990s involving the present-day Coverly family. The dominant impression, if one compares Septimus, Thomasina, Lady Croom, and affairs at Sidley Park between 1809 and 1812 with those of the

present generation of the family, is one of entropy. Energy seems to have dissipated; vitality seems to have been watered down. The early nineteenth-century scene is still Edenic, even if impregnated with eroticism, whether one focuses on Septimus, his pupil, or Lady Croom. In the latter-day scene, eroticism is diluted, whether one examines relations between Bernard and Hannah, Bernard and Chloe, or Chloe's brothers with Hannah. Chloe fancies Bernard, who is a philanderer—much less a "body in heat" than Lord Byron. Chloe's brothers, Valentine and Gus, admire Hannah. Bernard and Hannah spend more energy examining others' lives than living themselves. Nevertheless, even if the present-day Coverly's live at a lower temperature than their forebears are, love is still what makes the world go round. As Chloe observes in the final scene, "The universe is deterministic all right, just as Newton said: "—it's trying to be—the only thing going wrong is people who aren't supposed to be in that part of the plan" (73).

Examining the play's reception yields interesting insights into today's society on either side of the Atlantic. Though a commercial and critical success in England, "Arcadia" did not translate well to the American stage, probably because the American actors appeared overawed by the English context. In its initial London run, "Arcadia" played for 350 performances. It won both the Evening Standard Award for best play and the Olivier Award in 1993. More surprisingly, the first print edition of the play sold 6,000 copies within three weeks of publication, which may be attributed to its superb literary quality (Nadel, 447).

Religious Context

Does this thoughtful play demonstrate its author's beliefs? Stoppard takes a relativistic view of the universe and owns to a lack of certainty about just about everything. He appears to be a skeptic, which does not prevent his being a moralist, however. Paul Delaney quotes Stoppard as saying,

"I subscribe to objective truth and to absolute morality" (Delaney 2). Paraphrasing a speech in "Arcadia" by Valentine about how exciting physics is nowadays, Paul Edwards observes:

> There is a straight ladder from the atom to the grain of sand, and the only real mystery; is the missing rung. Below it, particle physics; above it, classical physics; but in between, metaphysics. All the mystery in life turns out to be this same mystery, the join between things which are distinct and yet continuous, body and mind, free will and causality (Edwards 182; cf. "Arcadia", sc. iv, 2–6, p. 48).

Fred Bilson believes the universe of Stoppard's plays is one that demonstrates "an order that is not governed by the remorseless determinism of Newtonian physics but by the organic order that emerges from chaos" (Bilson 36). John Fleming holds that "Stoppard is a deeply romantic writer," the heart of whose dramas lies in "what cannot be articulated directly" (quoted in Edwards 172). Fleming detects in the structure of many Stoppard plays an "apparent randomness" accompanied by an "underlying order" reflective of the author's worldview, "in which there is a high degree of relativity yet also moral absolutes" (Fleming 192). The conflict between absolute morality and moral relativism is dramatized most directly in "Jumpers" (1972).

Scientific & Technological Context

"Arcadia" evinces Stoppard's interest in the latest scientific developments in math and physics. Stoppard is an avid reader with eclectic tastes; his reading of James Gleick's "Chaos: The Making of a New Science" (1987) was just one inspiration for this drama, whose characters include three mathematicians (Septimus Hodge, Thomasina Coverly, and Valentine, a descendant). During the course of the London production, the playwright and actors playing Thomasina and Valentine visited the Oxford lab of chaotician Robert May, who also gave a seminar for the remainder of the cast on chaos theory (Nadel 441).

Following are capsule explanations of scientific ideas appearing throughout the play.

Sir Isaac Newton (1642–1727), inventor of Calculus, discovered the three Laws of Motion and that of Gravity, as well as invented the modern telescope and making important discoveries in optics. As "Arcadia" makes clear, the Newtonian universe is essentially deterministic; it does not permit randomness or the exercise of free will. (See Septimus' and Thomasina's discussion in the first scene, and Valentine's in the last pp. 5 and 73).

Chaos theory—Whereas the Newtonian universe is essentially mechanistic and deterministic, chaos theory posits a universe that exhibits apparent pockets of randomness and unpredictability: "There is order in chaos—an unpredictable order, but a determined order—" (Fleming 194). If determinism is the warp of the universal fabric, "Arcadia" suggests it is chance that spins the weft or woof. Human beings are subject to choice and chance, free will and determinism.

Fermat's Theorem—In the play's opening scene, Septimus sets Thomasina to solve Fermat's Theorem (2–3), which, interestingly, was finally solved after "Arcadia" appeared on the London stage by Andrew Wiles of Cambridge University, in 1994. This theorem dates back to the third century A.D., however, and bears on Pythagoras' theorem that the sum of the squares of the two sides of a right-angled triangle equals the square of the hypotenuse (Effinger). French mathematician Pierre de Fermat claimed, in a marginal note in 1637, to have proved that, if x, y, and z are whole numbers raised to the power of n, the sum of the first two can never equal the third if n is greater than 2.

Iterative algorithms entail beginning with a number or point, then calculating a new number or point, which, after being recorded, is fed back into the process. "Arcadia" shows several examples of this in Thomasina's attempts to plot a natural form, such as a leaf, through numbers, and in Valentine's calculations of fluctuations in Sidley Park's grouse population with the aid of a computer (scenes I. iii. and II. vii. 37, 43, 75–76).

Population biology-Valentine uses iteration theory, dating from the 1970s, to trace fluctuations in grouse on the Sidley Park estate. This is a mathematical process (outlined above) that uses feedback and is enormously aided by the computer; it takes the solution to an equation, then plugs it back into the equation to generate further solutions.

The science of fractals (also dating from the mid-1970s) is concerned with modeling irregular natural forms. Fractals are visual objects resulting from plotting shapes through iterated algorithms. They appear similar across different scales and echo Thomasina's "new Geometry of Irregular Forms" (Effinger). A subset of fractals, "the butterfly effect" refers to the sensitivity of systems to initial conditions and to their showing dramatic changes; such effects are manifested in weather and in the way populations behave.

The Laws of Thermodynamics and Entropys— As the name implies, thermodynamics concern transfer of energy in the form of heat from one body to another. The First Law of Thermodynamics, the Law of Conservation of Energy, states that matter can neither be created nor destroyed. The quantity of energy in the universe remains constant. An expression of this is Einstein's equation $e = mc^2$, which indicates that energy and matter are interchangeable.

The Second Law of Thermodynamics foreshadows the heat death of the universe in stipulating that heat cannot pass from colder to hotter bodies. Natural processes entailing energy transfer are therefore irreversible-as time is-and tend toward entropy, which is a measure of the amount of randomness, chaos, or disorder present in a system. The Third Law of Thermodynamics posits an "absolute zero" which would be reached if all energy in the universe dissipated, leaving inert matter distributed randomly across space.

Key scientific names in thermodynamics are Joseph Fourier (1768–1830), R. J. E. Clausius (1822–88), J. P. Joule (1818–1889), Hermann von Helmholtz (1821–1894), and Lord William Thomson Kelvin (1824–1907).

"Arcadia" dramatizes the above ideas in modest but brilliant ways. In the first scene, Thomasina points out to her tutor that, when she stirs jam into her rice pudding, the red blends into the white, making pink, but "if you stir backward, the jam will not come together again" (I, i, 2, p. 5): the process is irreversible. Similarly, in Act II, scene vii, Valentine points out Hannah's tea is cooling; without outside help, it cannot be reheated. Valentine adds, "What's happening to your tea is happening to everything everywhere" (78). Entropy has set in, in other words.

Biographical Context

Tom Stoppard was born Tomáš Straussler in Zlin (now Gottwaldov) in what is now the Czech Republic, on July 3, 1937. His father was killed by the Japanese in Singapore during World War II; he, his mother, and brother were evacuated to India. In 1945, his mother married Major Kenneth Stoppard. The future playwright was educated at an American school in Darjeeling and at British public (private) schools in Nottinghamshire and Yorkshire. He became successively a journalist/reporter, a drama critic, and then a playwright. He has been married twice and has four sons. Stoppard writes for stage and screen, radio and television.

As a displaced person who has lived on several continents and in different countries, Stoppard has a cosmopolitan, relativistic, and skeptical perspective. His belief that "truth is a matter of perspective," relative to its context, is compatible with his youthful experience of being bounced about the world (Bigsby, 445). A thoughtful man, world traveler, and avid reader, Stoppard seems able to engage any subject, no matter how large or complex. His dramas are truly cosmic in scope and concern themselves with the stage, politics, mathematics and science, art, and love. His first notable success came at the age of twenty-nine with "Rosencrantz and Guildenstern are Dead" (1967). Starting out by writing what he calls "nuts-and-bolts comedies" or farces, Stoppard has evolved into an intellectual playwright producing dazzlingly complex comedies of ideas. His most important plays, besides "Rosencrantz and Guildenstern are Dead," are "Jumpers" (1972), "Travesties" (1975), "The Real Thing" (1982), "Arcadia" (1993), and "The Invention of Love" (1997).

"Arcadia" is Stoppard's most English play, and some think his most perfect because of its clarity and unity. When he came to England at the age of eight, Stoppard says he immediately embraced the country, loving English landscape and feeling completely at home. One of his schools was temporarily relocated to Derbyshire, possibly inspiring the choice of "Arcadia's" setting. The dialogue between Thomasina and her tutor, Septimus, shows a quality of affection unusual in a dramatist who is considered cerebral rather than emotional. The "teacher taught" relationship between Septimus and Thomasina recalls that between father and daughter in "The Real Thing."

Doris L. Eder, Ph.D.

Works Cited

Bigsby, C. W. E. "Tom Stoppard," in *British Writers, Supplement I*: 437–454. New York: Charles Scribner's Sons, 1987

Bilson, Fred. "Tom Stoppard's Arcadia,' in *British Writers Classics*. Vol. 1: 23-29. Ed. Jay L. Parini. New York: Charles Scribner's Sons, 2003

Delaney, Paul. *Tom Stoppard: The Moral Vision of the Major Plays*. New York: St. Martin's Press, 1990

Edwards, Paul. "Science in Hapgood and Arcadia," in *The Cambridge Companion to Stoppard*. Ed. Katherine E. Kelly. New York: Cambridge Univ. Press, 2001

Fleming, John P. *Stoppard's Theatre: Finding Order amid Chaos*. Austin, TX: University of Texas Press, 2001

Nadel, Ira. Double Act: A Life of Tom Stoppard. London: Methuen, 2002.

Stoppard, Tom. "Arcadia". London: Faber & Faber, Inc. /New York: Farrar, Straus & Giroux, 1993. (All page references are to this edition.)

Effinger, Gove. "Two Mathematical Ideas in Arcadia." http://www.skidmore.edu/academics/theater/productions/arcadia/math.html>

Jackson, Allyn. "Love and the Second Law of Thermodynamics: Tom Stoppard's Arcadia." November 1995 <http://plue.sedac.ciesein.org/geocorr/doc/arcadia.html>

Liaugminas, Andrew V. "What Is a Simple Definition of the Laws of Thermodynamics?" <http://www.physlink.com/Education/AskExperts/ae280.cfm>

Moss, Stephen. "The Arcadia Archive." <http://www.cherwell.oxon.sch.uk/arcadia/outlineO.htm>

Stone, John David. "Arcadia." November 6-14, 1997 <http://www.math.grin.edu/stone/events/arcadia>

Discussion Questions

1. Discuss the significance of any of the following motifs: "Arcadia," the apple; the hermit in the garden, Thomasina's rice pudding that turns pink and cannot be stirred backward.
2. Consider how many letters are written in this play. By whom, to whom, and why are they written? What becomes of them?
3. Who wins in the face-off between Bernard Nightingale and Hannah Jarvis, and how?
4. Discuss "Arcadia" as a satire or parody on academe.
5. What is dramatic irony? Discuss the prominent role played by dramatic irony in Stoppard's "Arcadia."
6. "Arcadia" shows several of its characters engaged in the pursuit of knowledge. Both Septimus and Hannah make eloquent speeches on the subject. Why do this play and its author prize knowledge?
7. Stoppard is a playwright admired for his wit and brilliance but often criticized for lack of emotion. Do you find "Arcadia" lacking in feeling? If not, which characters, activities, or events are invested with emotion?
8. Stoppard's dramas are full of doubling and twins. Discuss "doubling" in "Arcadia."
9. Stoppard's intricately constructed dramas often layer past and present, and feature plays-within-plays. What examples of the past juxtaposed with, or superimposed upon, the present do you find in "Arcadia?"

Essay Ideas

1. What is the principal plot of "Arcadia?" What becomes of Thomasina and her tutor and why?
2. What is the subplot of "Arcadia" and how does this track, reflect, and modify the main narrative?
3. Examine either the conflict between classicism (Neoclassicism) and romanticism in Stoppard's "Arcadia" or that between science and the arts and humanities.
4. Take any of the scientific ideas explored in "Arcadia—chaos theory, Fermat's theorem, iterated algorithms, fractals, population biology, or entropy and the Second Law of Thermodynamics. Explain the ideas behind the theory. How are these ideas integrated into the play? 5. The term "fractals" implies both "self-similarity" and symmetry across scale, as well as irregularity. Demonstrate how "Arcadia" employs similarities in situation, character, dialogue, setting, costumes, props, and sound effects throughout, and how these are subtly varied as well.
5. Compare and contrast plot, theme, and characterization in any of these pairs of Stoppard plays: "Arcadia" and "Hapgood"; "Arcadia" and "The Invention of Love": "Arcadia" and "The Real Thing."

Tennessee Williams, author of "Cat on a Hot Tin Roof," featured opposite. Another Williams play, "A Streetcar Named Desire" is featured on page 187. Photo: Library of Congress, Prints & Photographs Division, LC-USZ62-115075

Cat on a Hot Tin Roof

by Tennessee Williams

Content Synopsis

"Cat on a Hot Tin Roof," by Tennessee Williams, is a drama about the hidden secrets of a rich Southern family. The play is set on the 65th birthday of the family's patriarch, Big Daddy Pollitt. Big Daddy is the owner of the largest estate in the Mississippi Delta, with over 28,000 acres of fertile land and more than $10 million in cash and blue chip stocks to his name.

The Pollitt Family consists of Big Daddy; his wife, Big Mama; and their two sons, Gooper and Brick. Other characters in the play include Gooper's wife, Mae; Brick's wife, Margaret (Maggie); a reverend; a doctor; and the five young children of Gooper and Mae.

The play takes place on a continuous basis over the course of one summer evening in the Pollitt home. Nearly all of the action takes place in a bed-sitting room of the home, mainly because Brick is confined to this room after breaking his ankle while drunkenly trying to jump hurdles the night before.

For Big Daddy and Big Mama, the birthday party is cause for extra celebration. Up until this day, most of the family thought that Big Daddy was suffering from terminal cancer. However, after a thorough medical examination at one of the best clinics in the country, Big Daddy and Big Mama have just been told that the only thing wrong with

him is a spastic colon. The problem is that this diagnosis is not a truthful one. Big Daddy does in fact have cancer, and it is almost surely fatal.

Gooper, Mae, and Margaret are all aware of the truth and are busy concocting schemes to get their hands on the inheritance that Big Daddy will leave behind. Brick, a withdrawn and indifferent alcoholic, is seemingly only concerned about getting his next drink.

Act I

The first act of the play deals primarily with the relationship between Maggie and Brick. Maggie informs Brick that Big Daddy is in fact dying of cancer, and we see how desperate she is to carve out a share of the inheritance that will be left when Big Daddy dies. We can also see that Maggie is directly at odds with Gooper and Mae, who have their own designs on the inheritance.

In addition to craving financial security, we also learn that Maggie is desperate to reconnect with her husband on a physical and emotional level. But Brick holds her at a distance. He is no longer willing to sleep with her, barely engages her in conversation, and even suggests that she take a lover to satisfy her unmet needs.

We later find out that Brick holds Maggie responsible for the death of his best friend, Skipper. Skipper died from a drug and alcohol overdose, but

Brick thinks that his friend entered into a downward spiral only after Maggie suggested to him that he had homosexual feelings for Brick.

Act II

The second act of the play deals primarily with the relationship between Brick and Big Daddy. The act begins with the entire family coming upstairs and into the bed-sitting room so that Brick can take part in the birthday celebration.

Big Daddy enters the room on an emotional high, still under the misconception that the only thing wrong with him is a spastic colon. After clearing the room so he can have a conversation with Brick, Big Daddy tells Brick how relieved he is to know that he is not dying and admits that he was paralyzed by his fear of a fatal diagnosis. Now that he has a new lease on life, Big Daddy is eager to take advantage of the spoils of his wealth. He tells Brick that he plans to get a young mistress and smother her with diamonds and furs.

Big Daddy also vows to take a more direct role in Brick's life and tries desperately to reconnect with his son during their conversation. Big Daddy is especially concerned about Brick's problem with alcohol. He tries to get Brick to tell him why he drinks so much.

Brick is reluctant to discuss the subject, but finally tells Big Daddy that he drinks out of "DISGUST" (78). He says he is disgusted with all of the lying and dishonesty in the world. He is also disgusted by the way that Maggie interfered in what he describes as his platonic relationship with Skipper.

Big Daddy raises some questions about the accuracy of Brick's story, however. He points out that there was one last phone call between Skipper and Brick before Skipper died. In this phone call, Skipper may have admitted his true feelings for Brick. Big Daddy suggests that Brick's rejection of Skipper during that phone call may have had more to do with Skipper's death than anything that

Maggie did. It is this statement that finally breaks Brick out of his cool detachment, and for the first time we can see there is a deep mental anguish buried inside him.

Brick then tells Big Daddy something with similar emotional impact: that his father is, in fact, suffering from terminal cancer. Big Daddy is shocked to hear the news and departs from the room, loudly cursing his family for lying to him.

Act III

Note: Most published versions of the play include two versions of Act III; the original version as written by Williams and a version that Williams revised after conversations with the play's original director, Elia Kazan. The differences between the two versions of Act III are discussed after the plot summary.

The third act of the play revolves around the battle between Gooper and Mae, on one side, and Maggie, on the other, for Big Daddy's estate. While Brick is still a part of the scene, he does his best to reclaim the detachment he lost during his conversation with Big Daddy in Act II. He refuses to participate in the discussion about Big Daddy's health or take a side in the battle for the inheritance.

The act begins with Gooper, Mae, and Maggie telling Big Mama the truth about Big Daddy's condition. Gooper then tries to get Big Mama to sign an agreement that will establish him as the trustee for the estate. However, Big Mama refuses, saying she will not sign any such agreement while Big Daddy is still alive. Gooper angrily vows to get his fair share of the estate. He says that Big Daddy cannot possibly leave it in the irresponsible hands of a childless alcoholic like Brick.

Maggie battles back by announcing to the room that she is pregnant with Brick's child. The family (with the exception of the naïve Big Mama) greets the news with skepticism because they have overheard conversations between the couple and know they have not been sleeping together.

Ultimately, Gooper and Mae are unable to get Big Mama to sign the trustee agreement and leave in frustration. Big Mama leaves the room to tend to Big Daddy.

With her and Brick left to themselves, Maggie gets rid of all the liquor that is left in the house. She promises to get Brick more liquor if he will sleep with her so she can make good on her pregnancy claim. The play ends with her trying to draw him into bed.

Alternate Act III

Before the play's Broadway premiere, Williams rewrote the third act to incorporate feedback he received from director Elia Kazan. Kazan had three major suggestions for Williams: he wanted to see Big Daddy return in Act III of the play; he wanted Brick to show more of a change in his character following his conversation with Big Daddy in Act II; and he wanted Maggie to be a more sympathetic character.

Of the three suggestions, Williams admits that he was only in favor of making Maggie a more sympathetic character. But out of respect for Kazan, he did incorporate elements of all three suggestions into the rewritten third act.

In the revised Act III, Big Daddy returns to the room in time to hear Maggie make her pregnancy announcement. He declares that Maggie does indeed have a child in her belly and then departs from the room with Big Mama so they can watch a storm roll in.

Brick also plays a more active role in Maggie's deception in the revised Act III. In this version, he actually argues that it might be possible for Maggie to be pregnant, and he hints that the two of them might be sleeping together.

Symbols and Motifs

There are numerous themes and motifs in "Cat on a Hot Tin Roof." Few of the characters can communicate well or be truthful, and a number of them are overwhelmed by feelings of disgust and a fear of death.

There are numerous examples of miscommunication or a lack of communication in the play. Maggie and Big Mama are the only characters who seem to be truly capable of saying what they are feeling. Maggie, desperate to reconnect with Brick and get a share of Big Daddy's fortune, openly admits that the stakes are too high for her to play nice. During her conversation with Brick in Act I, she confesses that she is willing to do whatever it takes to get what she wants. "The rich or well-to-do can afford to respect moral patterns, conventional moral patterns, but I could never afford to, yeah, but—I'm honest" (45). The buffoonish Big Mama, on the other hand, seems to be too simple to say anything other than what she means.

Mae and Gooper seem to say all the right things during the play. They fall all over themselves to create a portrait of the perfect, loving family. But they mean none of what they say and use hand signals and gestures throughout to communicate their true feelings. Their only goal is to secure a part of the inheritance. The two only truly start to speak their minds at the end of Act III, when their bid to secure control of Big Daddy's fortune fails. It is then that Gooper says that he knows Big Daddy never loved him and admits that he has always resented Brick for being the favorite son (113).

Big Daddy tries harder than any other character to get across what he is feeling, but even he has a hard time putting his thoughts into words. He talks and talks and talks, but never really gets his point across.

Brick tries at all costs to avoid talking about his true feelings. He hides his emotions through his alcoholism and by feigning indifference. Whenever a conversation threatens to become too personal, he tries to diffuse it by talking about how much he wants his next drink, changing the subject, turning on the radio, or hobbling out of the room and onto the gallery.

Maggie addresses Brick's attempts to hide his feelings through silence and deflection early on in the play. She tells him that avoidance is not helping him solve his problems. "It's just like shutting a door and locking it on a house on fire in hope of forgetting that the house is burning. But not facing a fire does not put it out. Silence about a thing just magnifies it. It grows and festers in silence, becomes malignant" (25).

The theme of miscommunication comes to a head during the conversation between Brick and Big Daddy in Act II. The act begins with Big Daddy sending everyone but Brick out of the room so he can have a one-on-one conversation with his son. Their talk is immediately strained, which leaves Big Daddy wondering, "Why is it so damn hard for people to talk?" (64). Brick responds by telling him that as much as he may want to have a talk, the two of them are not capable of having a conversation. "Nothing is said. You sit in a chair and gas about this and that and I look like I listen. I try to look like I listen, but I don't listen, not much" (67). As their conversation continues, Brick gets increasingly frustrated with their lack of progress. "We talk—you talk, in—circles. We get nowhere, nowhere! It's always the same, you say you want to talk to me, and don't have a ruttin' thing to say to me" (76).

Much of the difficulty that the characters have in communicating with each other is due to the fact that they are unable to share their true feelings. The pressures of polite Southern society have forced them to act a certain way, even if they do not believe in what they are doing. Brick pretends not to care about anyone or anything, even though he is hurting inside. Gooper and Mae pretend to be the devoted son and daughter-in-law of Big Daddy, even though Gooper knows that Big Daddy has never loved him and resents his father for playing favorites. Big Mama pretends that Big Daddy's insults are only his way of showing affection for her. The Reverend pretends to care about

the family, but his only interest is in securing a sizable donation for his church. Even Big Daddy, who is notable for his blunt manner of speaking, admits that his life is filled with lies. He tells Brick he cannot stand Gooper, his grandchildren, his wife, or his religion. "Church!—it bores the Bejesus out of me but I go!—I go an' sit there and listen to the fool preacher!" (80).

The characters in the play are disgusted with themselves for all the lying and pretending they have to do to maintain appearances. As evidenced by this exchange between Brick and Big Mama in Act III, "crap" is catchall phrase that the characters use to express their disgust:

Big Mama: I say—what is it Big Daddy always says when he's disgusted?

Brick [from the bar]: Big Daddy says "crap" when he's disgusted.

Big Mama [rising]: That's right—CRAP! I say CRAP too, like Big Daddy (116).

During his conversation with Brick in Act II, Big Daddy blames his medical condition (what he still thinks is a spastic colon) on the disgust he feels for himself and his relationship with Big Mama. "I've had the goddam exploratory operation, and nothing is wrong with me but a spastic colon—made spastic, I guess, by disgust. By all the goddam lies and liars that I have had to put up with, and with all the goddam hypocrisy that I lived with all these forty years that we've been living together" (58).

The source of Brick's disgust is harder to pinpoint. He tells Big Daddy that he is disgusted with all of the lying and liars in the world. But Big Daddy suggests that Brick is disgusted with himself for not being able to admit his true feelings. He tells Brick that by blaming Maggie for the death of his friend, he has been passing the buck. "This disgust with mendacity is disgust with yourself. You!—dug the grave of your friend and kicked him in it—before you'd face the truth with him." (92)

Williams himself is content to let the source of Brick's disgust remain a mystery. After Big Daddy tells Brick that he is disgusted with himself for rejecting Skipper, Williams breaks out the play to talk directly to the reader as the author. He wants to make it clear that there are no easy answers:

> The thing they're discussing, timidly and painfully on the side of Big Daddy, fiercely, violently on Brick's side, is the inadmissible thing that Skipper died to disavow between them. The fact that if it existed it had to be disavowed to 'keep face' in the world they lived in, may be at the heart of the mendacity that Brick drinks to kill his disgust with. It may be at the root of his collapse. Or, maybe it is only a single manifestation of it (85).

Mortality is another strong theme in the story and a primary concern for Big Daddy, who believes that he has just cheated death and is determined to stay alive for as long as he can. He tells Brick "Life is important. There is nothing else to hold onto" (63). and later goes on to say that animals are lucky in that they are born with an ignorance of their own mortality. "A man don't have that comfort, he's the only living thing that conceives of death, that knows what it is. The others go without knowing, which is the way that anything living should go" (68).

Big Daddy is eager to stay alive because he is convinced that there is nothing waiting for him in the afterlife. After he tells Brick about the tremendous relief he felt when he heard that he was only suffering from a spastic colon, Brick—who knows the true diagnosis—asks Big Daddy if he was not ready to "go" yet. Big Daddy responds incredulously:

> "GO WHERE? When you are gone from here, boy you are long gone and nowhere! The human machine is not no different from the animal machine or the fish machine or the bird machine or the reptile machine or the insect machine! It's just a whole lot more complicated and consequently more trouble to keep together" (75).

Social Context

Money and social status are intrinsically linked in this play. Maggie grew up in a unique situation as her family was poor but still a part of polite society. Much of her early life was spent struggling to present the appearance of wealth where there was none. She knows that her key to solving her money problems is to stay married to Brick and ensure that Brick gets his share of his inheritance from Big Daddy. However, she also can see that Brick no longer loves her and does not seem to care that Gooper and Mae are trying to cut him out of the inheritance.

She compares her struggles to stay afloat in this uncertain world to that of a cat on top of a hot tin roof. "What is the victory of a cat on a hot tin roof? I wish I knew. Just staying on it, I guess, as long as she can" (25). During their conversation in Act I, Maggie describes her childhood to Brick as one where she "[a]lways had to suck up to people I couldn't stand because they had money and I was poor as Job's turkey. You don't know what that's like" (41). She goes on to define the worth of a person in two ways—age and wealth. "You can be young without money but you can't be old without it. You've got to be old with money because to be old without it is just too awful" (42).

The conflict between Maggie and Mae is a battle for status as much as it is for money. The two women belittle each other and their families. Maggie tells Brick that Gooper "still cherishes the illusion he took a giant step up on the social ladder when he married Miss Mae Flynn of the Memphis Flynns" (20). She adds that the Flynns "never had a single thing in the world but money, and they lost that. They were nothing at all but fairly successful climbers" (21). Later, as the two women square off, Mae refers to Maggie's father being an alcoholic (110) and makes condescending remarks about Maggie having a childless marriage (113).

The second major social theme in the play deals with what behavior is acceptable in polite society. It is not clear from the play if Brick is gay, but it is clear that Brick does not think he lives in a society where one is free to be gay. He tells Big Daddy how unacceptable homosexuality is to society during their conversation in Act II: "Don't you know how people feel about things like that? How, how disgusted they are by things like that?" (88). Brick goes on to tell Big Daddy about a student pledge at his college fraternity house who attempted to engage in a homosexual act: "We not only dropped him like a hot rock!—We told him to git off the campus, and he did, he got!" (88).

Ironically, it is Big Daddy who seems to be more tolerant of homosexuality than his son. When he asks Brick about his drinking and his relationship with Skipper, it seems to be out of a genuine concern for his son's wellbeing, not an effort to scorn or shame him.

Religious Context

Williams is fairly clear on his views about religion in the play. For him, it is not a source of comfort for a dying man. Instead, religion and religious figures are portrayed as fraudulent and insincere.

This view is personified by the grossly inappropriate figure of Reverend Tooker. Although he has presumably been brought to the house to minister to the sick, the Reverend makes no effort to offer Big Daddy any spiritual comfort. He instead spends his time at the house trying to solicit a memorial donation for his church.

The Reverend first enters the play at the beginning of Act II and is already talking to Gooper about the donations that other prominent families have made to the church (48).

Big Daddy is wise to the true nature of the preacher, however, and does not hesitate to call him out for his lack of tact. "Hey Preach! What's all this talk about memorials, Preach?" (49). Big Daddy also makes it clear how little respect he has for the preacher. While the family is gathered in the bed sitting room at the beginning of Act II, Big Daddy tries to find out how Brick injured himself the night before. He asks Brick in graphic terms if the injury happened during a sexual liaison. When Big Mama tries to stop him from talking that way in front of the preacher, Big Daddy responds, "Rut the goddamn preacher" (58).

Williams himself describes the preacher in condescending terms. When the Reverend Tooker reappears near the end of Act II—temporarily interrupting the heated, emotional conversation between Brick and Big Daddy—Williams describes his practiced clergyman's smile as "sincere as a bird-call blown on a hunter's whistle, the living embodiment of the pious, conventional lie" (86).

Historical Context

There is no significant historical context to this play, though it is helpful to understand what the social mores regarding homosexuality were at the time that it was written.

The play was written in the 1950, and performed for the first time in 1955. This was well before the gay rights movement and the legalization of same-sex marriages or civil unions in some states. Williams himself did not acknowledge his own homosexuality until some twenty years later.

Scientific and Technological Context

The gigantic console in the bed sitting room that serves as a combination bar, radio, and television is the one significant element of technology that appears in the play.

Williams thinks of technology, like religion and liquor, as an aspect of modern life that can offer no true comfort to the characters in his play. It is merely a way for them to temporarily distract themselves from the struggles of their everyday lives.

He explains as much in the notes for the set director at the beginning of the play: "This piece of furniture (?!), this monument, is a very complete and compact little shrine to virtually all the comforts and illusions behind which we hide from such things as the characters in the play are faced with" (xiv).

Biographical Context

Tennessee Williams was born in Columbus, Mississippi on March 26, 1911. His given name was Thomas Lanier Williams.

By most biographical accounts, Williams had a difficult childhood. His father was a traveling salesman who was distant and abusive to his children, and his mother was a harsh woman who was obsessed by fantasies of traditional Southern living.

William's older sister, Rose, suffered from mental illness. She was eventually given a lobotomy and spent the rest of her life in a mental institution. Williams' younger brother, Dakin, was supposedly the favorite son of his father (much like Brick is the favorite son of Big Daddy).

Many critics believe that Williams incorporated much of his difficult family life into his dramatic works. Over the course of his career, Williams wrote more than thirty full length plays. Nearly all of the plays were set in the South, and many explore the same themes of mortality, greed, sexuality, and Christianity.

Brian Burns

Works Cited

"Tennessee Williams 1911–1983." *The Moonstruck Drama Bookstore*. 12 May 2009. <http://www.imagination.com/moonstruck/clsc9.htm>

"Cat on a Hot Tin Roof: Introduction." *Drama for Students*. Ed. Marie Rose Napierkowski. Vol. 3. Detroit: Gale, 1998.

Cash, Eric W. "Tennessee Williams 1911–1983." 19 Nov. 2007. *The Mississippi Writers' Page*. University of Mississippi English Department. 6 May 2009. <www.olemiss.edu/depts/english/ms-writers/dir/Williams_tennessee>

Haley, Darryl E. "'Certain Moral Values': A Rhetoric of Outcasts in the Plays of Tennessee Williams." 1997. East Tennessee State University. 12 May 2009. <http://www.etsu.edu/haleyd/Prospectus.html>

Discussion Questions

1. Who are the most sympathetic characters in the play?
2. Who are the least sympathetic characters?
3. Describe Big Daddy's relationship with Big Mama. Why do you think he stayed married to her?
4. Why does Brick stay married to Maggie?
5. What role does religion play in the lives of the characters?
6. Describe the three central relationships in the play. How does the relationship between Brick and Maggie reflect that of Big Daddy and Big Mama? That of Gooper and Mae?
7. Discuss the role of the gigantic bar-television-stereo console in the play. What does Brick use it for? What role does it serve in the set design?
8. Why do you think Williams chose to have Brick be injured for the duration of the play? How does his injury reflect on his circumstances?
9. How is sexuality treated in the play? Talk about the different expressions of it.
10. What do you think of Williams' original decision not to have Big Daddy return to the stage in the third act of the play? Does his presence off screen impact what happens on stage?

Essay Ideas

1. Discuss Williams' decision to interject his voice at a key moment of the play. How does his explanation of Brick's feelings and motivations influence your reading of the play? Would your reading of the play be different without his interjection?
2. Describe the relationship between Brick and Big Daddy. How do they feel about each other? What evidence is there that they respect each other? Is there any evidence that they love each other? Are they at odds during the play?
3. What is Maggie's role in the play? How does her position as an outsider affect her thoughts and actions? How does her physical appearance play into her character?
4. Describe Brick's progression as a character throughout the play. How do the events of the second act affect him in the third?
5. What does the play's title mean? Which characters admit to being cats? Which characters are described by others at cats? Who else besides Maggie can be considered a cat on a hot tin roof?

The Cocktail Party

by T. S. Eliot

Content Synopsis

Eliot's third full-length play, "The Cocktail Party," is the poet-playwright's attempt to meld the conventions of the stage comedy with a story of religious vocation and martyrdom. It is, at times, an unstable amalgam, but Eliot's verse, modulating subtly from colloquial parlor talk to the prophetic utterances of the play's quasi-divine "guardians," ultimately binds the work together and lends it coherence. Like his previous dramas, "Murder in the Cathedral" (1935) and "The Family Reunion" (1939), "The Cocktail Party" is a play in verse. Yet whereas the latter two works employed deliberate artifices such as a tragic chorus, "The Cocktail Party" finds Eliot creating a more conventional surface to his play. Not only are there none of the non-naturalistic elements of the earlier works, but the language itself is restrained, brought closer to the rhythms and cadences of conventional speech. The play's generic subtitle, "A Comedy," further reinforces this air of conventionality. Yet Eliot invokes the generic conventions of the farce or parlor comedy only to subvert them, and although "The Cocktail Party" may initially put one at ease, it moves towards a radically unconventional conclusion, ending not with the heroine Celia Coplestone's marriage, but with her violent martyrdom.

The play opens in the middle of a party that Edward and Lavinia Chamberlayne are hosting in their London flat. Lavinia is not to be found, however, and Edward must play an awkward host to their mutual friends. When Julia Shuttlethwaite, a gossipy spinster, makes repeated and incisive inquiries into Lavinia's whereabouts, it becomes apparent to Julia and the audience alike that Lavinia has left her husband. The guests, Edward will later confide, "Were only the people I couldn't / Because I couldn't get at them in time" (303). One guest lingers after the others leave, and Edward invites him, admitting he does not know his identity, to have another drink. This "unidentified guest," who will later be identified as Sir Henry Harcourt-Reilly, speaks with a startling, prophetic directness of Edward's marriage and future. He says, "I know you as well as I know your wife; / And I knew that all you wanted was the luxury / Of an intimate disclosure to a stranger" (306). As a stranger, the guest is in a position to hear Edward's confession and to anatomize his marriage. Yet, he cautions Edward that "to approach the stranger / Is to invite the unexpected, release a new force, / Or let the genie out of the bottle" (306). The genies, in this case, are three characters who term themselves guardians. Seeming sometimes like bureaucrats and other times like angels, they walk among mortals (although they may well be mortal themselves; their exact nature is unclear) helping them to "accept their destiny" (368). Reilly, of course, is one of the guardians. The busybody Julia and the bon-vivant Alex are guardians, too, although their comic, befuddled manners mask their divine mandate.

Two plots are set in motion during Reilly's interview with Edward. One is the love triangle of a conventional farce: Edward loves the young poet Celia, while Lavinia loves the young filmmaker Peter Quilpe. Yet when Lavinia leaves Edward, he suddenly realizes that his love for Celia was illusory. Peter, meanwhile, confesses to Edward his love for Celia. One sees the wheels of the plot beginning to turn, then, toward a happy ending in which the married couple is reunited and the younger lovers marry each other. A second plot will subvert this happy ending, however, for the guardians will help to guide Celia down a radically different path. Celia feels "an awareness of solitude" which she suspects renders her unable to have a relationship with Peter, Edward or anyone else (360). She tells Reilly: "No—it isn't that I want to be alone, / But that everyone's alone—or so it seems to me" (360). Celia is being called to something other than the marriage plot: "You see, I think I really had a vision of something / Thought I don't know what it is. I don't want to forget it. / I want to live with it" (364). This divine calling will take Celia far from London, on what Reilly cautions her "is a terrifying journey" (364). Although the guardians help guide her way, the decision to follow a sainted path is Celia's own.

The play concludes with a second cocktail party, two years later, to which the reunited Edward and Lavinia have invited all the same guests. During this party, Alex breaks the news that Celia is dead, crucified on an island called Kinkanja, where she was helping victims of a plague. Her fate stands in a sharp contrast to the orderly lives of Edward, Lavinia, and Peter. Faced with the martyrdom of their former friend and lover, a martyrdom which Reilly assures them is "triumphant," the partygoers must reevaluate their own lives. As Edward puts it, "But if this was right—if this was right for Celia— / There must be something else that is terribly wrong, / And the rest of us are somehow involved in the wrong" (385).

Historical Context

Eliot's immediate purpose in juxtaposing the martyrdom of Celia with the pedestrian lives of the play's other characters is a religious one: he means to show how the extraordinary life of the saint might light a way for the ordinary sinner to live with a greater degree of spirituality. Celia's fate moves Edward, Lavinia, Peter, and the others to engage in spiritual self-examination. Yet one might also read this juxtaposition of the orderly English parlor and the wild South Seas Island as a reflection of English and American attitudes toward empire. Celia's death demonstrates that the state of affairs on a place like Kinkanja can have ramifications for the people of England. The play subtly critiques imperial or colonial practices by implying that the English have not yet learned how to put their own house in order, and therefore are doomed to fail in their attempts to order that of another people. The conclusion of "The Cocktail Party" seems to anticipate that England would soon lose its hold on its once-vast empire.

Alex tells a story of civil unrest on the island of Kinkanja which, while ridiculous, resonates with the larger themes of the play. Most of the island's inhabitants are "heathens" who hold monkeys in veneration but cannibalize their neighbors (374). While there are some Christians converts among the people, they are always tempted to relapse "into heathendom" to avoid being eaten themselves (375). Then Europeans bring to Kinkanja not order, but disease, political infighting, and bureaucracy (375, 380). Asked what his commission accomplished during their visit to the island, Alex says in an ironic understatement, "We have just drawn up an interim report. Eventually, there may be an official publication" (375–376). The English colonial administrators only make the situation on Kinkanja worse, because they have no spiritual capital to export to the island. The English themselves, the play implies, are cannibals and heathens in spirit. Indeed, Celia's impact on the people of Kinkanja stands in contrast to Alex's impact. Where Alex moved in official circles and drew up a report, Celia nursed plague victims and was killed in an insurrection. The grassroots work of the missionary is held up as valuable, the paperwork of the colonialist is not.

Eliot wrote about a "cannibal isle" once before, in his 1927 fragment of a play, "Sweeney Agonistes." There the island represents an escape from English society—and is, indeed, represented in a wholly escapist fashion. There are only three things on the island, Sweeney says: "Birth, and copulation, and death. / That's all, that's all, that's all, that's all" (80). In returning to the island in 1949, Eliot seems to see much more there than he had two decades earlier. The cannibal island of "The Cocktail Party" is at once an allegory of English society and an independent entity that the English cannot hope to govern. Sometime between 1927 and 1949, Eliot's vision has become post-colonial.

Societal Context

After his 1927 conversion to Anglicanism, Eliot became increasingly concerned with the social utility of the poet. Many of his essays of the 1930's are works of social rather than literary criticism. "After Strange Gods" and "The Idea of a Christian Society" are perhaps the two best-known and provocative examples of Eliot's new brand of social criticism. There is always interplay between Eliot's criticism and his poetry, and one can see the germination of "The Cocktail Party" in some of the essays of the 1930's and 1940's. In a 1936 essay, for example, Eliot writes of the corruption wrought upon the people of Papua, New Guinea, by Christian missionaries and colonialists (Ackroyd 242). England should not offer "helping hands," he argues, if those hands are in fact leprous (242). In many other ways, as well, "The Cocktail Party" finds

Eliot dramatizing concerns that were central to his critical enterprise during the preceding twenty-odd years. In particular, the play centers on the question of how one might live a Christian life in the midst of modern culture. The stage allowed Eliot to bring his social criticism to a wider audience than might his essays. Writing a comedy likewise seems a ploy to draw in a mainstream audience (rather, say, than the specifically Christian audience that might have gravitated toward "Murder in the Cathedral"). Whereas his previous play, "The Family Reunion," had employed a Greek chorus and other elements of classical tragedy, "The Cocktail Party" draws on the conventions of the popular stage play in order to present a less imposing surface to the casual theatergoer.

Eliot believed that the theater might serve yet another social good: it might allow, as it had in the past, everyday people access to poetic language that would otherwise be unavailable to them. Again, this is a recurring topic of the essays of the 1930's and 1940's. For Eliot, this shared experience of spoken poetry was a hallmark of Elizabethan and Jacobean culture. During Elizabeth's reign, the poetic drama became a unifying social force that cut across lines of class and education to create and express a shared culture. Eliot's various attempts to write a popular poetic drama must be read in light of his fascination with the Elizabethan stage and culture. If in "The Waste Land," Eliot characterized modern culture as being fragmented, in the plays of the 1930's and 1940's he marshals poetic drama and Christian symbolism as a means of unifying that culture.

Religious Context

Like Eliot's earlier plays, "The Cocktail Party" is overtly Christian in theme. Eliot had been raised a Unitarian, but he abandoned this liberal, humanistic, socially-conscious denomination as a young man. When he returned to Christianity in middle age, it was to a far more orthodox brand of faith: he was baptized into the Church of England in 1927. Eliot seemed to require a Christianity that recognized the existence of sin and evil and which laid out the means by which one could expiate one's sin. The Catholic writers who were most important to Eliot, including Dante and St. John of the Cross, were concerned with the means by which a sinner might make atonement both for his own sins and for the original sin into which all people are born. In "The Cocktail Party," Celia finds means for such atonement by renouncing the easy path of the romantic heroine and taking instead the "terrifying journey" that Reilly offers her (365). Her crucifixion on Kinkanja takes this religious vocation to its logical end, as she approaches the life and death of Christ literally rather than figuratively.

Scientific & Technological Context

"The Cocktail Party" repeatedly invokes psychiatry and psychology as analogues to spirituality. Reilly, who first appears as the Unidentified Guest, eventually reveals himself to be a famous psychiatrist. At various points in the play, Reilly's acuity and the authority with which he makes his gnomic pronouncements is ascribed to his training in psychology. His practice of psychology is also a comic device, one which produces some of the complications of stage comedy. Those scenes that are not set in the Chamberlayne's drawing room are set in his consulting room. He arranges for Lavinia and Edward to make appointments with him for the same time, thereby bringing the estranged couple together. Yet Reilly's psychological practice is a cover story, and he uses his patients' faith in psychotherapy to lead them to a deeper faith in God.

All of the characters have some familiarity with psychology: they know its forms and litanies, as if it were an ersatz religion. At Reilly's office, it is Edward rather than Reilly who seems eager to engage in Freudian psychoanalysis. Edward begins to say, "I remember, in my childhood" Yet Reilly cuts him off, declaring, "I always begin from the immediate situation / And then go back as far as I find necessary" (348). Reilly has little patience with either childhood memories or dreams, two of the mainstays of Freudian analysis. He argues that Edward's memories of childhood now would be "largely fictitious; and as for your dreams, / You would produce amazing dreams, to oblige me" (348). Reilly actively combats his patients' faith in psychotherapy; he seems, indeed, annoyed by their readiness to accept wholesale the premises and promises of analysis. For example, Edward and Lavinia each suggest, independently of each other, that they be sent to a sanitarium. It is the doctor, and not the patients, who remains skeptical of such a treatment. For Reilly puts his own faith not in Freudian psychoanalysis, but in Christian spirituality.

Celia is the only patient who seems unsatisfied by the solutions which psychotherapy offers her. Unlike Edward and Lavinia, she does not suggest that she be sent to a sanitarium. When Reilly, slipping on the mask of the conventional psychotherapist, makes the suggestion himself, she responds, "Oh, what an anti-climax!" (365). Celia is looking for something more than the easy reassurances of therapy. She wants to confront some great truth located outside herself rather than a subjective one based on her childhood and her dreams. People who go to the sanitarium eventually return, she notes, "to everyday life" (365).

Everyday life is no longer enough for Celia. Over the course of the play's second act, she moves from ordinary life to the life of religious vocation. Set in Reilly's office, the act begins with the banalities of a doctor's waiting room and ends with Alex, Julia, and Reilly blessing Celia in the cadences of a liturgy. Reilly's interviews with Edward, Lavinia, and Celia therefore modulate from the psychological to the spiritual to the liturgical. Reilly sees religion as a neglected truth and psychology as an accepted bastardization of that truth.

It might be worth noting Peter's relationship to truth and illusion, for it is the inverse of Reilly's. As a filmmaker, Peter has embraced illusion at the expense of reality. In Act III, Peter has returned to England in order to study the decayed mansion Boltwell. He says, "We've got a team of experts over / To study the decay, so as to reproduce it. / Then we build another Boltwell in California" (378). In his film about English life, all the principal parts will be played by Americans, although "the director is "looking for some typical English faces— / Of course, only for minor parts" (378). Film, as a medium, approximates the appearance of things rather than getting at a deep truth which lies beneath appearances.

Both psychoanalysis and film, two late nineteenth and early twentieth century innovations, offer surface approximations of real life, rather than revealing the deep truths of religion. Reilly speaks of "the final desolation / Of solitude in the phantasmal world / Of imagination, shuffling memories and desires" (365). Psychology and filmmaking, modernity's practices for recording the inner and the outer life, leave one alone in this "phantasmal world."

Biographical Context

Born into a prominent St. Louis family in 1888, T.S. Eliot was raised a Unitarian. He attended Harvard and in 1914 moved to England, where he studied philosophy at Oxford University. The next year he married an Englishwoman, Vivienne Haigh-Wood and began pursuing a rigorous program of writing criticism and book reviews. He worked as a middle school teacher, as an extension lecturer at University College, and as a clerk at Lloyd's Bank before eventually moving into editing and publishing. In 1922, he became editor of "The Criterion," while in 1925 he left the bank to take a position with the publishing House Faber & Gwyer. Their marriage would be a fraught one, ending in the 1930's with their separation and with Vivienne's commitment to a mental asylum.

Conventional wisdom would break Eliot's life and career into two parts. In the first phase, Eliot creates through his essays and poetry—particularly with the 1922 publication of "The Waste Land"—the movement that would come to be called Modernism. The second phase begins in 1927 with his conversion to the Anglican faith, after which he writes poems and plays which are of a more explicitly religious nature and which in some ways fly in the face of his Modernist contemporaries. "Ash Wednesday," "Four Quartets," and Eliot's plays are all the products of the post-conversion.

In 1927, Eliot was baptized into the Church of England. Later that same year, he became a British citizen. Much of his poetry after his conversion dealt with religious themes. "Journey of the Magi" (1927) and "Ash Wednesday" (1930) are two such overtly Christian poems. In the 1930's Eliot turned his attention to drama, writing "Choruses from the Rock" and "Murder in the Cathedral," both for the stage.

"The Cocktail Party" is a play about religious conversion and martyrdom, but it does not follow that Eliot's interest in such explicitly religious topics began around the time of his own conversion. In fact, Eliot seems always to have had a fascination with the lives of the saints and martyrs. In "The Love Song of J. Alfred Prufrock," Prufrock compares himself to a beheaded John the Baptist. Parts of "The Waste Land" grew out of an earlier poem titled "The Death of Saint Narcissus." However, perhaps the most disturbing of Eliot's early martyrdom poems is "The Love Song of Saint Sebastian," which was not published in the poet's lifetime. The poem's speaker describes to a woman he loves his own self-mutilation: "I would flog myself until I bled / Then you would take me in / Because I was hideous in your sight" ("Inventions of the March Hare" 78). In the second stanza, he reverses the action, and describes his mutilation of the woman: "You would love me because I should have strangled you / And because of my infamy; / And I should love you the more because I had mangled you" (ibid). The "martyrdom" of the speaker and his beloved is of a sadomasochistic nature. Violence and torture become a substitute for the sex act.

"The Love Song of Saint Sebastian" may therefore provide some insight both into the fate of Celia and into Eliot's tendency to associate sexual desire with religious martyrdom. If Eliot's play is, as his subtitle proclaims it, "a comedy," then Celia is its ingénue. She has two suitors for her hand—Edward and Peter. One might expect "The Cocktail Party" to follow a conventional marriage plot. Yet Eliot frustrates this plot, for Celia elects to follow a "vision" which will take her away from the parlor in which this comedy is set, and also away from the marriage bed onto which one of the parlor's doors might open. Celia chooses a cross over a wedding band, and there is perhaps no clearer conflation of sex and religious martyrdom than in her fate on Kinkanja.

In this respect, one might read Celia as a stand-in for Eliot himself. The poet twice during the 1930's and 1940's broke off relationships that seemed likely to end in marriage. During the 1930's, Emily Hale, whom Eliot had loved as a young man in Boston, visited England nearly every summer to visit the poet. Although Hale and many of Eliot's friends seemed to assume they would be married upon the death of Eliot's first wife, Vivienne, Eliot instead broke off the relationship. Later, in the 1940's, he followed much the same progression with his friend Mary Trevelyan.

Nor is it only in the conflict between religious and romantic love that Eliot has drawn on events or preoccupations from his own life. Edward, Lavinia, and Celia all talk of visiting a sanitarium, and Edward in particular argues that he may be suffering from a nervous breakdown. Eliot himself suffered from what might have been a nervous breakdown in 1921 and spent time in a sanitarium in Lausanne (where he finished writing "The Waste Land"). Of course, Eliot was also familiar with sanatoria on account of his wife Vivienne, who spent the last decade of her life in a mental hospital. It may in part be out of guilt over his wife's commitment that Eliot, through Reilly, invokes the sanatorium as a metaphor for the world at large. In "East Coker," one of the "Four Quartets," Eliot offers a similar comparison: "The whole earth is our hospital / Endowed by the ruined millionaire" (128). If the world itself is a sanitarium, there is less guilt in having one's wife committed to one.

Celia's conversion and martyrdom must therefore be read in dialogue with the situation of earlier Eliot characters such as J. Alfred Prufrock, as well as with an eye toward Eliot's own personal history. "The Cocktail Party" represents Eliot's reworking of themes and preoccupations that had long been central to his art and life.

Matthew J. Bolton, Ph.D.

Works Cited

Ackroyd, Peter. *T. S. Eliot: A Life*. New York: Simon & Schuster, 1984.

Eliot, T. S. "Selected Essays." *Selected Essays: 1917–1932*. New York: Harcourt, Brace and Company, 1932.

_____. *The Complete Poems and Plays: 1909–1950*. New York: Harcourt, Brace & World, 1962.

_____. *Inventions of the March Hare*. Ed. Christopher Ricks. New York: Harcourt Brace, 1996.

Discussion Questions

1. In your opinion, what is at the root of Edward and Lavinia's marital problems in Acts I and II? How do you account for the seeming harmony between them in Act III? How do you imagine each has changed over the two years that divide Act II from Act III?

2. Eliot has a penchant for coining peculiar and suggestive names. How do the names of some of "The Cocktail Party's" characters reflect their personalities or the roles they play in life? Consider, in particular, the surnames Shuttlethwaite, Chamberlayne, Coplestone, and Quilpe.

3. Does "One-Eyed Reilly," the song that Harcourt-Reilly sings as the Unidentified Guest, have any symbolic resonance? How might its lyrics inform the character of Harcourt-Reilly and illuminate some of the larger themes of the play? Refer both to the song as Harcourt-Reilly sings it (311-12) and as it appears as appended to the play (388).

4. Alex notes that the indigenous people who Celia died defending "died anyway" (381). Does the death of her charges render her own death meaningless? What does her death represent?

5. By the end of Act II, Alex, Julia Shuttlethwaite, and Reilly are all revealed to be guardians of the play's other characters. To what extent are their public personae—that of the socialite, the busybody, and the savant, respectively—masks?

6. On the subject of the guardians, does there seem to be a hierarchy among Alex, Julia, and Reilly? If so, how does this hierarchy replicate or invert our initial assessments of these three characters?

7. What are the elements of this play that most clearly function as comic devices? How does Eliot subvert the conventions of comedy in order to make a point about religious vocation and the spiritual life?

8. By the play's conclusion, Edward and Lavinia Chamberlayne are reconciled, Celia has followed her religious vocation through to its logical end of martyrdom, and Alex, Julia, and Reilly are revealed to be in league. There is only one character whose fate is left undecided: Peter Quilpe. What do you imagine the future holds for Peter? What path will he follow having learned of Celia's fate?

9. Does Eliot's sense that modern life and society distracts one from one's spiritual calling still hold true today? How have specific historical, social, and technological developments of the last fifty years either added or cleared away some of these distractions?

10. "The Cocktail Party" was filmed and broadcast on television by the BBC in 1952. If you were casting and directing a television or film version of the play today, who would you cast in its major roles? What sorts of choices would you make in terms of the film's setting, tone, music, costumes, and direction?

Essay Ideas

1. Read a few of Eliot's early poems, including "The Love Song of J. Alfred Prufrock," "Portrait of a Lady," and "Journey of the Magi." Compare one of the characters from "The Cocktail Party" to one of these early Eliot characters. Contrasting Celia Coplestone with J. Alfred Prufrock (note the "formation" in each one's surname) might make for a particularly good essay.

2. Read one of Eliot's essays on drama, such as "The Possibility of a Poetic Drama," "Four Elizabethan Dramatists," or "Poetry and Drama." What is Eliot's dramatic theory as evinced by the essays you have read and how does he put this theory into practice in "The Cocktail Party?"

3. Excerpt a passage from the play that you find particularly beautiful, strange, or haunting. Explicate and analyze the passage as you would a poem of comparable length. How can this passage serve as a key to open up some of the larger themes of the play? What insight does your analysis give you into Eliot's poetic voice in "The Cocktail Party?"

4. How does "The Cocktail Party" function as a social critique? What aspects of modern society does Eliot single out as being particularly troubling? What are some of the institutions or practices which he satirizes or parodies?

5. In the comic plays of Ben Jonson, a contemporary of Shakespeare whom Eliot much admired, each character was meant to represent one particular emotion, foible, or humor. How might the characters in "The Cocktail Party" be read, in a similar fashion, as each embodying one particular human characteristic?

6. Trace one particular image across the course of the play. How does the desert, for example, reappear in various forms from the first through the final act?

7. Read Eliot's previous play, "The Family Reunion." How does "The Cocktail Party" differ from its predecessor? Pay particular attention to changes in genre and in Eliot's use of various theatrical conventions. What themes carry across from one play to the next?

8. Edward, Celia, and Reilly all offer descriptions of Hell. Edward argues, "Hell is oneself, / Hell is alone, the other figures in it / Merely projections" (342). Celia and Lavinia describe Reilly as "the Devil" and "a devil" (321; 351). Discuss the contrasting visions of the infernal as offered by these characters. Does one seem to speak for the author?

The Crucible

by Arthur Miller

Content Synopsis

The play is set during the Salem witchcraft trials in Massachusetts in the spring of 1692. Act I opens in the house of Reverend Samuel Parris, where Parris's ten-year-old daughter Betty, is ill and unresponsive. A woman from the village delivers the message that the doctor cannot find any illness and that Parris should "look to unnatural things" for the cause of Betty's condition (9). Parris is unwilling to acknowledge this as a possibility. His position in the town is uncertain because of factions that oppose him and having a child possessed by the devil would seriously harm his reputation. He then has a discussion with his seventeen-year-old niece, Abigail Williams, which reveals that he has happened upon the girls dancing in the forest the night before with Tituba, their slave from Barbados. Parris then turns his interrogation to the subject of her dismissal as a servant to the Proctors." He says that he has heard that Elizabeth will not come to church because she "will not sit so close to something soiled" (12). Abigail responds that Elizabeth Proctor is a "lying, cold, sniveling woman" (12). She maintains that her name is "white," meaning that her reputation is untarnished (12). In the house, below, a crowd of people awaits news of Betty.

The Putnams come in and Ann Putnam tells Parris that her daughter Ruth is also sick and that Betty had been seen flying over the village. They are both convinced the children are victims of witchcraft. Parris cautions them against jumping to conclusions but also tells them he's summoned Reverend John Hale, who "has much experience in all demonic arts" (14). Mrs. Putnam admits that she's sent her daughter Ruth to ask Tituba to speak to the dead in order to find out why her seven other children died. When asked, Abigail admits that Ruth and Tituba were indeed "conjuring spirits" (16). When the adults leave, Abigail is left in the room with Betty as well as two servant girls, Mary Warren and Mercy Lewis. Mary Warren, who is the Proctors' servant, pleads with Abigail that they must tell "the truth"; that they had just been dancing in the woods. If convicted of witchcraft, they'll be hung, she fears (18). Betty wakes up and tries to "fly" out the window. She accuses Abigail of drinking blood in order to kill Elizabeth Proctor. Abigail threatens the girls with murder if they tell the truth and screams at Betty to stop her act. Betty falls still again.

In the midst of all this, John Proctor, a farmer in his thirties, arrives. He orders Mary Warren, his servant, to go back home. Warren and Mercy Lewis leave. Proctor rebuffs Abigail's advances on him, revealing in their dialogue that they've had an affair. Proctor insists, "I will cut off my hand before I'll ever reach for you again" (23). Abigail accuses Elizabeth of gossiping about her. The sound of voices singing a psalm causes Betty to wail, which brings back Reverend Parris. He sends for the doctor. Rebecca Nurse, an elderly, respected woman in the village, comes in and gently proclaims Betty's "sickness" a childish act. Proctor questions Parris's arrogance in calling on Reverend Hale without consulting members of the church. Putnam, who obviously disagrees with Proctor, points out that Proctor rarely comes to church. Proctor reveals his true feelings about Parris, that he stays away because he "hardly ever mention[s] God any more" since he is always preaching "hell-fire and bloody damnation" (29, 28). Proctor and Parris argue about the minister's salary and his firewood until Rebecca urges them to make peace. Proctor moves to leave, but not before getting into a friendly quarrel with Giles Corey. Giles Corey is a man in his eighties who makes liberal use of the justice system, having already been to court six times that year for perceived assaults on himself and his property. Proctor asks Corey to help him bring his lumber home. Putnam then demands to know where he's gotten it from; revealing another source of friction in the village: a dispute between Putnam and Proctor over land rights.

Reverend John Hale arrives laden with books. He hears out the concerns of the villagers, but insists they must be objective. He examines Betty, then questions Abigail about the dancing. Tituba is brought in and instantly Abigail "confesses" that Tituba had made her and Betty drink blood. Tituba insists that it is chicken blood, that she has not conjured the devil and that she loves Betty. Abigail accuses Tituba of making her laugh in church and of bringing her nightmares. The men threaten Tituba into "confessing" that she'd seen two women, Sarah Good and Sarah Osburn, with the devil. Abigail makes a show of confession, too, and asserts that she's seen others with the devil. Betty joins in with more accusations as the act closes.

The setting for Act II is the Proctor house, eight days later. Elizabeth Proctor urges her husband to go tell the sheriff, Cheever, about his adulterous affair in order to expose Abigail as a fraud.

Court proceedings against the accused witches are well under way. While Proctor is mulling this over, Mary Warren returns from court, where she is one of the group of "victims." She gives Elizabeth a poppet—a doll—she's made while she was in court as a witness. Mr. Hale arrives and questions them about their religious faith. When asked to recite the Ten Commandments, Proctor forgets the commandment prohibiting adultery. Proctor then tells Hale that Abigail had told him they'd been surprised in the woods by Parris. Hale is not completely convinced she is a fraud since Tituba, Sarah Good and Sarah Osburn have all confessed to witchcraft. Giles Corey and Francis Nurse arrive to announce that their wives have been arrested for witchcraft. Cheever arrives and finds the poppet from Mary. When he finds a needle stuck in the poppet in the same place where a needle had been drawn out of Abigail earlier that night, he charges Elizabeth with witchcraft. Despite Mary's testimony that she'd made the poppet and put the needle there herself, Elizabeth is taken away. Proctor is defiant and enraged. After everyone leaves, Proctor convinces Mary to testify in court.

An additional scene in Act II was added in a later production of the play. In this scene, Proctor and Abigail meet in the woods at night. It is thirty-six days since Elizabeth has been arrested. Proctor warns Abigail that if she will not withdraw her accusations against his wife, he will expose their affair. Abigail persists in the deluded belief that Proctor will marry her when Elizabeth is dead and refuses.

Act III takes place in the Salem meeting house, in the vestry outside of the court room. Martha Corey is on trial. Giles Corey, Francis Nurse, John Proctor, and Mary Warren interrupt the proceedings. They assemble in the vestry with Deputy Governor Danforth, Sheriff Cheever, Reverend Parris, and Reverend Hale. Proctor pushes Mary Warren to confess that her fits have all been an act, and that all the girls who are supposed witchcraft victims are acting. Danforth is suspicious, having not doubted the girls at all up until now. Instead he accuses Proctor of witchcraft and of trying to undermine his court. They then receive news that Elizabeth is pregnant, which means that, if found guilty, she will not be hanged until after the baby is born. Danforth asks Proctor if he will now drop the charge that the girls are frauds. Proctor refuses. He, with Giles Corey and Francis Nurse, then presents a petition attesting to their wives' innocence. They are shocked when Danforth demands that the signatories be called in for questioning.

Danforth calls for a recess and summons the girls. He questions Abigail about Mary Warren's accusations. Abigail maintains her innocence. Proctor then tells Danforth about the dancing in the woods. Parris admits to seeing them. Danforth then demands that Mary pretend she is being attacked by a witch, but she cannot do it. When Danforth turns back to questioning Abigail, she goes into one of her fits, claiming to feel a cold wind blowing through her. The other girls follow her lead. Proctor cries out that Abigail is a "whore" (110). He confesses that he has committed adultery with her. Abigail denies it. Elizabeth is then summoned to back up Proctor's confession. When questioned, however, she is evasive and says she had thought Proctor "fancied" Abigail and therefore she fired her, but attests that he did not commit adultery (113). Proctor cries out that he has confessed, and pleads with Danforth to see that she is trying to protect him. Hale speaks up on Proctor's behalf, saying that he's always been suspicious of Abigail.

At this point, Abigail starts in on one of her fits, followed by the other girls. They claim to see Mary Warren's spirit in the form of a bird trying to attack them. Then they start mimicking everything Mary says, until Mary breaks down and accuses Proctor of bewitching her. Danforth calls for John Proctor to be arrested. Giles Corey is also arrested, for contempt. Reverend Hale announces he's quitting the court and storms out.

Act IV takes place in the fall in a jail cell, just before dawn. Danforth, Hathorne and Parris meet to discuss the status of the people who have been found guilty of witchcraft. John Proctor, Rebecca Nurse, and Martha Corey are about to be hanged. When Parris tells them that Abigail and Mercy have run off with money stolen from him, they become very worried. They talk of the town turning against the court now that so many have been accused and arrested. Reverend Hale enters. He has been working among the accused, pleading with them to confess so that they will live. Danforth refuses to hear any pleas for pardon or postponement; twelve have already been executed and seven are set to hang that day. They decide to talk to Proctor in hopes he will confess and set an example for others. Elizabeth is brought to them, too, in order to help convince him. Elizabeth, however, will not tell Proctor what to do. Proctor desperately wants her approval. He decides that he will confess, saying he is not a saint. When they ask him to write and sign the confession, he is again distraught and falters. He doubts himself even more when Rebecca Nurse is brought forth to see his confession. He proceeds with the confession, but refuses to name any accomplices. Hale and Parris urge Danforth to accept the confession. Danforth gives him the statement to sign. He signs it, then rips it up. He protests that Danforth's word that he has confessed should be enough. Proctor cries out that he cannot sign away his good name; Danforth then refuses to accept the confession. Proctor accepts that he will hang, but he is now at peace that he has done the right thing. He and Rebecca Nurse are taken away to be hanged and the play ends.

In the epilogue, "Echoes down the Corridor," Miller writes that Parris was voted out of office shortly after the trials; Abigail was rumored to be a prostitute in Boston; and twenty years later, the government awarded compensation to the families of the wrongfully convicted. The congregation also rescinded their excommunications. Elizabeth

Proctor remarried four years later. "To all intents and purposes," he finishes, "the power of theocracy in Massachusetts was broken" (146).

Historical Context

There are two different historical time periods that are relevant to readings of "The Crucible." The first is the actual setting of the play, Salem, Massachusetts, in 1692. The second is the time when the play was written and first performed, in the early 1950s in the United States.

The community of Salem, Massachusetts in 1692 was composed mainly of Puritans. Puritanism was founded as a reform movement in response to the Elizabethan church in England, around 1560. The Puritans believed "that the Scriptures did not sanction the setting up of bishops and churches by the state. The aim of the early Puritans such as Thomas Cartwright was to purify the church (hence their name), not to separate from it" (McCarthy). However, by 1567 the Puritans were worshiping secretly in their own church. Political failure led to their persecution in the early 1600s, and many Puritans fled to Europe and America. Those who remained eventually rose to power after the English civil war in the mid-1600s. In 1661, during the Restoration, Puritans were cast out of the Church of England.

In New England, the Puritans held great influence in the latter part of the seventeenth century. Gradually their power was worn away by the opening up of frontier settlements in and beyond New England. As a colony of England, Massachusetts was governed by a charter negotiated with the English government. A new charter enacted in 1692 changed its governing system from a theocracy to a political, secular state, and dropped religious requirements for voting rights.

For centuries Christians in Europe and New England believed they were at war with witches, who they defined as servants of Satan. The belief "reached epic proportions in Europe during the fifteenth, sixteenth, and seventeenth centuries" (Richardson 4). Laws attempted to deter threats to Christianity by witchcraft and condoned the persecution of witches in France, England, and Germany. In Germany especially, "many thousands lost their lives between 1550 and 1650"; thus, "the subject of witchcraft was a universal topic in the 1600s, and Puritan New England and Salem shared these deeply felt moral and religious concerns" (Richardson 5).

While there were several isolated witchcraft cases tried prior to 1692 in New England, only the Salem trials boasted such a large number of accused and condemned witches. Nineteen of the thirty-six witch executions in America under the early colonial laws occurred in Salem in 1692. The accusers were mostly young girls who were seized with strange fits and complaints of biting and pricking by invisible spirits. Some scholars believe these girls were dabbling in "black magic" experiments, perhaps with the guidance of Tituba, a slave from Barbados. Others have attributed their symptoms to physical causes, including ergot poisoning (a fungus in the wheat used to make bread) and an encephalitis outbreak (see Laurie Winn Carlson, "A Fever in Salem" [Chicago, 1999]). Richardson also notes that episodes of witchcraft on both continents coincide with periods of social and political unrest. Recently, a connection has been made between the witchcraft "hysteria" and the French-Indian wars occurring just north of Massachusetts in Maine, as some of the victims (also the accusers), were refugees from these wars, and some of the accused were suspected traitors (see Norton, "In the Devil's Snare"). Whatever the cause, it is almost certain that some witchcraft accusations were the result of economic and social strife that already existed in Salem Village, a less prosperous, agrarian community just outside of the prosperous shipping community of Salem Town. For example, Rebecca Nurse, one of the convicted who refused to confess, was accused by Ann Putnam, Sr., whose family had boundary disputes with the Nurse family, of causing the death of fourteen of Putnam's family and friends.

Betty Parris, the nine-year-old daughter of the new Village minister, and his niece, eleven-year-old Abigail Williams were the first accusers. Tituba has been brought to Salem by Parris, who formerly lived in Barbados. Unable to find a physical cause for their fits of hysteria, the doctor suggests Satanic influence. At the time this was not unheard of; "[u]nexplainable behavior, diseases, and misfortunes; commonly believed to be the result of spiritual forces at work in the world" (Richardson 7). Reverend Parris called for help from other local ministers, and the community had a public day of fasting and prayer. In addition to Betty and Abigail, eleven other women and girls were stricken with symptoms of hysteria, including loss of speech, sight, and hearing; muscle spasms; trancelike states; choking; and visions which they claimed pinched, pricked, and otherwise injured them. Encouraged to identify the spirits who supposedly attacked them, they named Tituba, Sarah Good, a poor woman with the reputation of "a nagging shrew," and Sarah Osborne (or Osburn, or Osburne), a prosperous widow who was the subject of gossip (Richardson 8). The three women were arrested on February 29, 1692 and sent to a Boston jail to await trial. Shortly thereafter, Martha Corey, Rebecca Nurse, Bridget Bishop, and the five-year-old daughter of Sarah Good, Dorcas, were accused and arrested.

The first court of Oyer and Terminer ("to hear and determine") convened for the first time on June 2. The delay in trial was the result of the loss of the Massachusetts charter as an independent commonwealth in 1684. The new charter was finally granted in May 1692. During the time without a charter, no legislative actions could proceed. Meanwhile, the jails had rapidly filled with accused witches while the Governor awaited the charter. The first interrogation resulted in the first execution by hanging,

of Bridget Bishop. Twenty-seven more convictions followed between June and September. Nineteen of the convicted were hanged, including John Proctor, Rebecca Nurse, and Martha Corey, all real historical people who also appear in Miller's play. Giles Corey refused to stand trial and was pressed to death by stones. Three others died in prison. The others escaped, confessed and were released, or were released due to pregnancy. One of these last was Elizabeth Proctor.

In his introduction to his "Collected Plays" (1957), Miller explains that the play came out of the question that arose for him when he discovered, upon looking at the records of the trials, that Abigail Williams had been a servant for the Proctors for a short time and that she resisted accusing John Proctor but not Elizabeth. In order to explain this, he invented their affair and accordingly changed their ages, making Abigail older and John Proctor younger.

In October 1692 Reverend Increase Mather, the president of Harvard College and the colony's ambassador to England who negotiated their new charter, led a group of ministers in urging the Massachusetts legislature to no longer consider "spectral evidence" in cases of witchcraft. "Spectral evidence" was "either an 'apparition' of the accused person attempting to cause some injury to the victim or the 'specter' of a dead person who appeared in a vision and attributed his or her death to the accused." (Richardson 11). Mather also recommended the use of credible witnesses and the rejection of public tests where the afflicted went into fits when the accused were brought before the court. He questioned the testimony of fights between two parties and of "mischief" such as damage to crops and livestock attributed to the accused. In January 1693, forty-nine of the accused were released from prison on the basis of insufficient evidence; the three remaining accused were freed and later pardoned by Governor Phips. In January 1696, twelve of the previously "afflicted" repented of their participation in the trials, signing a statement of contrition. In 1697 Judge Samuel Sewall publicly repented his role in the trials. Reverend Parris resigned from his ministry, which had been challenged for most of the time he was in Salem, in 1697. In 1711, twenty-one of the survivors and families of the accused were granted a reversal of their attainders, which was the legal loss of their civil rights, and received financial compensation for debts incurred from the trials. As recently as 1957, the General Court passed a Resolve which cleared the names of all the accused.

Joseph McCarthy , a United States Republican senator from Wisconsin from 1947 to 1957, was "undistinguished and obscure" until 1950, when he made a speech at Wheeling, West Virginia, in which he claimed to know the names of Communists in the State Department ("McCarthy"). After Republicans won control of the Senate in 1953, McCarthy became chairman of the Senate permanent investigations subcommittee and "used his position to exploit the public's fear of Communism," represented by what was seen as the U.S.'s chief enemy throughout the Cold War, the Soviet Union ("McCarthy"). In public hearings, McCarthy led the committee through numerous attacks on supposed Communists, at times using unidentified informants, and encouraged those accused to list names of others involved in communist activities. The left-leaning entertainment industry was especially vulnerable, and scores of careers were destroyed through "blacklisting." Miller himself came before the Congressional committee in 1957.

McCarthy's power began to wane when, in 1954, the army responded to charges made on their own personnel by accusing McCarthy "of seeking by improper means to obtain preferential treatment for a former consultant to the subcommittee" ("McCarthy"). Though McCarthy, his Chief counsel, and an aide were cleared of the charges, the Senate censured McCarthy for unethical and insulting activities conducted during the course of his trial. His influence continued to diminish after the Democrats again took control in 1955. McCarthy's legacy of unbridled accusations gave rise to the term "McCarthyism," "which denotes similar assaults characterized by sensationalists tactics and unsubstantiated accusations" ("McCarthy").

The parallels between the Salem witchcraft trials and the McCarthy hearings have been discussed and questioned by various critics at length. Some early critics saw the play as a "false analogy" because "there were no witches but there were communists" (Bigsby 172). Miller has countered that to say that there were no witches is "dangerous"; but, "beyond that, it was the procedures practiced in both 1692 and the 1950s which interested him, the coercive power of the state, its rallying of a popular support based on fear" (Bigsby 172). Christopher Bigsby further notes that "The Crucible" has gone on to be Miller's most produced play and has struck a chord with audiences all over the world, thus addressing "the particularities of new injustices" and therefore transcending that particular period in history (172).

Societal Context

Gender and class played important roles in the Salem witchcraft trials. The Puritan community of Salem placed heavy restrictions on women's roles and freedoms in the seventeenth century. As elsewhere, women were seen as men's property and were not entitled to voting and other rights. Historically, eighty percent of the accused witches in colonial America were women. The percentages are even higher for the persecution of witches in Europe, where women accounted for over ninety percent of "witches" who were executed. That women were historically accused more often than men was directly related to the belief that women were more vulnerable to temptation and sin than men. (See Religious Context).

Economic inequality also clearly played a role. In "Devil in the Shape of a Woman," an analysis of witchcraft in colonial New England, Carol Karlsen makes a connection between the inheritance system and the numbers of accused and convicted witches. Often, those accused challenged the status quo where women could not generally own or inherit property. The exceptions to these restrictions were when she was widowed and no other male relative could inherit. Many of those convicted had no male relative and, additionally, no legitimate intermediary in the eyes of the court to help them with their case. Miller implicitly makes the observation in "The Crucible" that at least some accusations were based on land rights, as he explains feuds among the Proctors, Coreys, Nurses, and Putnams, however he falls short of making any connection between these feuds and gender.

Abigail, who begins the play strenuously objecting to the charges of witchcraft, unwittingly stumbles upon a strategy for revenge as well as power. Abigail tries to destroy the marriage between the Proctors by accusing Elizabeth of witchcraft. Though undoubtedly she wants John Proctor for herself, she also seeks revenge for being fired from her job. She implies that Elizabeth has gossiped about her and because of that she is unable to find work elsewhere. As a young woman servant in colonial New England, whose own immediate family was killed by Indians, Abigail had few avenues of power open to her. The depiction of the women in the play seems to mimic the enduring representations of women as either angel or whore; in this construct, Elizabeth is the angel and Abigail, the whore. Neither character is developed much beyond this polarity, since the focus of the play is on John Proctor.

According to Terry Otten, feminist critic Wendy Schissel sees Miller's unsympathetic portrayal of Abigail as a temptress as proof of misogyny. Furthermore, Schissel accuses Miller of "'blaming the victim'" since Abigail's youth technically makes her a victim of rape (Otten 70). However, Otten argues the heart of the play is John Proctor's struggle over his own guilt in the adulterous affair; Miller "in fact uses Abigail to expose, not conceal or excuse Proctor's guilt, and he uses Elizabeth to reinforce rather than exonerate Proctor's culpability" (70–71). In the play, Proctor falls from grace because of his sin of adultery. While certainly Proctor's sin is his own weakness in entering into an affair with Abigail, he does take full responsibility for it. It is only when Abigail becomes a ringleader of accusers that Proctor begins to see her as loathsome.

Religious Context

Puritans based their theology on Calvinism, stressing predestination and public worship based in Scripture. This meant that they also believed that the state should not be responsible for setting up bishops and churches. New England Puritans "maintained the Calvinist distinction between the elect and the damned in their theory of the church, in which membership consisted only of the regenerate minority who publicly confessed their experience of conversion" ("Puritanism"). They believed ardently in original sin, which could only be expiated through hard work, self-discipline, and self-examination. Sins ranging from blasphemy to gambling to adultery were all penal offenses. Women's roles were severely circumscribed and "any wife who refused obedience to her husband was likely to be punished" (Barstow 79).

While the belief in witchcraft as understood to be consisting of the worship in pagan gods and of magical spells prefigures Christianity, it is Christianity that came to see witches as representing an evil force in the world, to be exterminated at all costs. Feminist scholars see the large-scale persecution of witches, who were mostly women, as symptomatic of the misogyny inherent in medieval Christian beliefs. Because women menstruate and bear children, and were seen to be incapable of higher intellectual thought, they were thought to be more vulnerable to temptation by the devil. According to the medieval Christian worldview, a witch "was considered to be one who had agreed to serve the devil by performing evil acts in the world. Supposedly, witches would make a contract with Satan by signing in his book, and would thereafter have amazing powers to fly through the air, perform great feats of strength, change appearance, and cause misfortune or death to their victims" (Richardson 4–5). They were thought to work alone or with animal companions, called familiars, and often held witches' Sabbaths, "depraved festival[s] of devil-worshipping ceremonies, feasting, and sorcery," at night in groups or covens (Richardson 5). Witches were believed to be the intermediaries through which the devil exerted his power. The Puritans of New England in the late 1600s believed that witches could assume the form of someone known to the afflicted and appear to them in visions or dreams, in which they could do harm. It was also believed that the devil could not assume the form of an innocent person and therefore anyone who appeared in such visions were assumed to have contracted with the devil; however this is one belief that came into question in the course of the Salem trials. Furthermore, any unexplained diseases or behavior was often attributed to witchcraft.

While later scholars would dismiss the Salem witchcraft trials and the overall phenomenon that one scholar has termed the "witchcraze" as hysteria based on the erroneous belief in non-existent witches, others claim "witch" as a term connecting one to a pagan belief system that predates Christianity. Contemporary witches, or pagans, define their religion as one based on a pantheistic belief in gods and goddesses intimately connected to nature. While Christians might see their worship as service to the devil, contemporary pagans reject the construction of the devil altogether, putting their beliefs into a wholly separate system that rejects duality. Journalist Margot Adler, in her history of paganism [?], notes that "pagan" comes from the Latin word for country dweller, and that the stigma attached to the word is "the end result of centuries of political struggles during which the major prophetic religions, notably Christianity, won a victory over the older polytheistic religions" (Adler 9). Adler further observes that "the old Witches were often the wise people of the village, skilled in healing and the practical arts" (11). Contemporary scholars, recognizing this enduring tradition, now suggest that at least some of the persecuted in Europe and America during the fifteenth through seventeenth centuries were "real" witches, or at least practiced simple forms of "witchcraft" including the preparation of herbal remedies and attending women in childbirth.

Scientific & Technological Context
Reverend Hale, the "expert" that Reverend Parris brings in, exhibits a rhetoric and manner that speaks of "scientific" objectivity; he insists that "[w]e cannot look to superstition in this. The Devil is precise" (38). The irony for a contemporary audience is, of course, that the belief that someone can be possessed by a devil or a witch is precisely, to most in the twentieth century, preposterous and superstitious in itself.

The medical doctor represents science as we now understand it today. However, in deference to his own limitations, the doctor's failure to diagnose a physical cause for Betty's illness leads Parris and others to accusations of witchcraft. Indeed, the doctor himself suggests this. At this time in history, doctors attributed any physical or psychological symptoms they could not otherwise explain to the work of the devil.

It should also be noted that some scholars connect the persecution of witches to the practice of midwifery. Midwives were women healers who helped at births as well as performed the role of general healer. Indeed, doctors saw the attendance on women in childbirth as beneath them and it was only later in history that they began to take over this work. As doctors began to specialize and develop technology such as forceps, they also claimed childbirth as within their sphere and consequently drove most midwives out of business. While this phenomenon would not be seen until the nineteenth century, the seeds for this movement were being planted at this time. Certainly midwives were especially vulnerable to accusations of witchcraft; on one hand they held special knowledge of women's bodies and the mysteries of pregnancy, including preventing it; on the other, their work naturally put them into contact with miscarriages and infant deaths that some may have hoped to find explained through charges of witchcraft. The connection of witchcraft to midwifery can be seen in "The Crucible." Ann Putnam, who has lost seven babies, is one of the few adults to make charges of witchcraft. Her daughter Ruth, one of the young accusers, is her only surviving child. The person they charge, Rebecca Nurse, has been Ann Putnam's midwife.

Biographical Context

Arthur Miller was born in 1915 in New York City, the son of Jewish parents. Miller was never particularly religious, but he did "declare his commitment to a Jewish culture" (Bigsby 3). His first play was produced at the University of Michigan in 1936. Miller gathered material for a book of reportage in Army camps during World War II. He won the New York Drama Critics' Circle Award for All My Sons, produced and published in 1947. His most famous play, "Death of a Salesman," was produced and published in 1949, and won the Pulitzer Prize. "The Crucible" was first performed in 1953. While its initial reception was not wholly enthusiastic, it has been one of Miller's most widely produced plays.

Three years after the first performance of "The Crucible," Miller appeared before the House Un-American Activities Committee, but refused to name other so-called communists. He was prosecuted and convicted in 1957 for contempt of Congress; the conviction was reversed the following year. According to Terry Otten, Miller had "briefly flirted with communist ideology" before writing his play; more importantly, he saw "The Crucible" as a response to "the growing anticommunist sentiment in the United States" (64). Otten rejects any description of the play as "quasi-Marxist," however, observing that Miller did not embrace Marxism "to any significant degree" and as having crafted a play about an "individual caught in the historical moment" (64–5).

Miller wrote in his autobiography that the inspiration for "The Crucible" had roots in an interest in the Salem trials that emerged while he was in college. Then, by chance, he read Marion Starkey's "The Devil in Massachusetts." He was interested in the subject not only for its parallel to the McCarthy hearings, but also to "something deeper—that same strain of American Puritanism that runs across American literature" (Otten 62). Miller felt "strangely at home" with the people of Salem, connecting "'the same fierce idealism, devotion to God, tendency to legislate reductiveness' and 'longings for the pure and intellectually elegant argument' he found in Jewish heritage" (Otten 62).

"The Crucible" was made into a successful film in 1996 and has been performed all over the world. Miller died in 2005 at the age of eighty-nine and is regarded as one of America's greatest playwrights.

Alyssa Colton, Ph.D.

Works Cited

Adler, Margot. *Drawing Down the Moon: Witches, Druids, Goddess-Worshippers, and Other Pagans in America Today*. Boston: Beacon, 1979.

Barstow, Anne Llewellyn. *Witchcraze: A New History of the European Witch Hunts*. San Francisco and London: Pandora, 1994.

Bigsby, Christopher. *Arthur Miller: A Critical Study*. Cambridge: Cambridge U P, 2005.

Gussow, Mel. *Conversations with Miller*. New York: Applause, 2002.

Karlsen, Carol. "The Devil in the Shape of a Woman: Witchcraft in Colonial New England." New York: W. W. Norton, 1987.

McCarthy, Joseph Raymond. *The Columbia Encyclopedia*. 6th ed. 2005. 4 February 2006. <http://www.encyclopedia.com>.

Miller, Arthur. "The Crucible: Text and Criticism." Ed. Gerald Weales. New York: Viking, 1971.

—————. "Introduction." Collected Plays. New York: Viking, 1957. Excerpt rpt. in Miller, The Crucible: Text and Criticism. 161-169.

Norton, Mary Beth. *In the Devil's Snare: The Salem Witchcraft Crisis of 1692*. New York: Knopf, 2002.

Otten, Terry. *The Temptation of Innocence in the Dramas of Arthur Miller*. Columbia and London: University of Missouri P, 2002.

Puritanism. *The Columbia Encyclopedia*. 6th ed. 2005. 4 February 2006. <http://www.encyclopedia.com>.

Richardson, Katherine W. *The Salem Witchcraft Trials*. Salem, MA: Essex Institute, 1983.

Discussion Questions

1. Discuss the background details about the history of Salem and the characters in his play that Miller gives in the text. How important is this information for someone who is watching the play, who may not have read the text?

2. What knowledge, stories, and impressions did you initially have of the Salem trials before reading the play? In what contexts have the witch trials been portrayed or alluded to in language and popular culture? How much of this has been influenced by "The Crucible?"

3. What factors contribute to Reverend Parris's change in attitude from denying bewitchment to embracing the accusation of witches?

4. What information is given about Abigail? How does this information serve to characterize her? Do you find her a sympathetic character?

5. Who is Tituba? How is she characterized? What is her place in the social fabric of Salem? How does this affect her confession?

6. Describe the characters of Elizabeth and John Proctor. What is the conflict between them? How is it expressed, and how does it play a role in the story?

7. Why does John Proctor hesitate to expose Abigail? Do you think his anger toward Elizabeth is warranted?

8. Do you think John Proctor is a hero in the play? In what ways does he fit (or not fit) the classical definition of a tragic hero?

9. Discuss the depiction of Danforth. Miller contends that he represents the evil who persecuted the witches in Salem. Is he evil? If so, what kind of evil does he represent?

10. Do you think John Proctor made the right decision in refusing to confess?

Essay Ideas

1. In what ways would "The Crucible" be considered a tragedy?

2. Drawing on classical definitions of tragedy and tragic character, find specific examples to support your answer.

3. Discuss how gender, race, and/or class are elements integral to the plot and outcome of "The Crucible." Which of these play the most significant role?

4. Compare the play to the historical documents of the Salem witchcraft trials. Identify what was used and what Miller made up. Why were these changes made? What is the ultimate effect of these changes?

5. How does the play represent a period in history, and is it accurate?

6. At the end of the play John Proctor refuses to sign away his good name. What do names and naming represent in the text? Why is his name so important?

7. Examine how the institutions of law, church, and medicine fail to prevent the execution of innocent victims. What, ultimately, is being said about individuals and institutional authority?

French playwright Edmond Rostand. He wrote "Cyrano de Begerac" in 1897, which is featured opposite.
Photo: Library of Congress, Prints & Photographs Division, LC-DIG-ggbain-02730

Cyrano de Bergerac

by Edmond Rostand

Content Synopsis

Act I

The play opens inside a theatre. Various people are gathering to watch a play—a cavalryman and a Musketeer, two flunkies who play cards in the gloom, an upright citizen and his son, two pages who are up to mischief, a pickpocket and his apprentices and a group of gentlemen included a baron called Christian de Neuvillete. Christian is here in hopes of seeing a beautiful girl he has previously seen in the theatre. A group of fashionable ladies enter, but none of them is the right one. The orchestra starts to play, heralding that the play for which everyone has gathered is soon to begin. A pastry cook and friend to poets and artists, Ragueneau, enters looking for Cyrano de Bergerac and calls over Cyrano's friend, captain of the guards, Le Bret. Cyrano is described to the assembled gentlemen as a poet, fighter, physician and musician. Ragueneau also describes de Bergerac's excessively large nose.

Finally, Roxanne enters and Christian recognizes her as the woman he has fallen in love with. A nobleman walks in and is seen to be looking at Roxanne. This is the Comte de Guiche, nephew-in-law of Cardinal Richelieu and so unable to wed this woman that he desires. As a result he plans to have her married to his protégé, a Viscount called Valvert. Christian moves to talk to her but his friend Ligniere warns him away. Le Bret and Ragueneau

comment that Cyrano has not arrived and express hope that he has not seen the playbill. Cyrano has promised to kill the actor Montfleury if he does not avoid the stage for a month, yet he is planning to appear in that night's performance.

Christian then finds a pickpocket's hand in his pocket and, in apology, the pickpocket volunteers the information that Christian's friend Ligniere is to be attacked by one hundred men that night as he has insulted a gentleman in a poem. The pickpocket also tells him where the attack is to occur. Cardinal Richelieu is noticed as being present in the playhouse and the play starts. Montfleury mounts the stage and Le Bret comments once more on the absence of Cyrano. Montfleury starts to speak but is interrupted by a voice calling insults. The actor tries to continue and the owner of the voice enters, revealing himself as Cyrano de Bergerac. He continues to tell Montfleury to leave the stage and not return for a month. The crowd calls for the play but Cyrano blocks it, challenging the whole audience to try and stop him. Finally, Montfleury flees the stage.

The crowd asks why Cyrano took such action and he tells them it is because of the man's poor acting and another, secret answer. There are protests from the theatre owner at having to return the audience's money, so Cyrano takes out a bag of coins and gives it to him. As the crowd disperses, a Citizen warns Cyrano that the actor's patron is the Duke who will seek out Cyrano and have him killed. In response, Cyrano asks why the citizen is looking at his nose. Is it, he asks, because it is too big? The citizen protests that it is small and Cyrano replies with a speech about just how big his nose is. He attacks the citizen, who leaves.

The gentlemen discuss among themselves who is to deal with Cyrano and Valvert decides to do it. He approaches and tells Cyrano his nose is big. Cyrano scoffs that he could not think of a better insult and proceeds to list dozens of possible insults the man could have used. Valvert gets angry and the two argue, Cyrano using his words to baffle and humiliate the other man. A challenge is made and Cyrano declares he will invent a ballade while they duel and will kill the other man on the last word. He then does exactly that.

People leave the scene and Le Bret offers to go to dinner with Cyrano, but the latter has given all his money for the month to the theatre owner. The food seller offers him free food and he takes a meager amount and makes it into a banquet. While he eats, Le Bret enumerates Cyrano's many enemies. He finally asks for the real reason for Cyrano's dislike of Montfleury. Cyrano reveals it is because the fat actor had made a pass at the woman Cyrano loves. Le Bret enquires further and Cyrano composes a sonnet to reveal that he loves his cousin, Roxanne. When Le Bret asks what he intends to do, Cyrano replies that he cannot tell her how he feels because of his ridiculously large nose. Le Bret protests and Cyrano argues. They are finally interrupted by Roxanne's chaperone who requests a meeting between Cyrano and her mistress.

As Cyrano leaves to meet with Roxanne he meets Ligniere, drunk, being carried in by two friends. Ligniere has received warning about the attack that is planned for him. Cyrano tells Ligniere that he will lie in his own bed tonight, unmolested, because he, Cyrano, will take care of the one hundred men. He sets off with a retinue of friends and onlookers to take care of the matter.

Act II

Ragueneau is in his shop, surrounded by chefs making food. Ragueneau describes the food in terms of poetry. His wife, Lise, comes in and attacks him for allowing poets to eat the food in return for their writings. Cyrano enters and finds from Ragueneau that it is six o'clock in the morning. The chef says that he saw the events of the previous night. Cyrano asks which ones and Ragueneau mentions the duel/ballade with Valvert. Lise notices a cut on Cyrano's hand but he dismisses it. He takes paper and a quill from Ragueneau and hesitantly starts to write a letter to Roxanne. As he writes, a group of poets enter for their free food and Lise is courted by a Musketeer. Finishing his letter, Cyrano notices this and warns off both Lise and the Musketeer.

Returning to his table, Cyrano signals Ragueneau who takes the poets away leaving Cyrano alone as Roxanne enters. They talk and Roxanne reminds Cyrano of happy childhood memories. She then notices the mark on his hand and enquires as to how he got it. He reveals it was while fighting with one hundred men. She asks for more but he presses her for her story instead. She reveals that she is in love. She describes the man in vague enough terms that Cyrano believes that she means him until she uses the word 'beautiful' then he pulls away from her, saddened. She tells Cyrano that she is in love with Christian and Christian will shortly be in the same Guards' company as Cyrano. She is worried that he will be ill-treated upon joining the company and so has come to ask Cyrano to take care of him. Cyrano promises and she leaves.

Cyrano's company of men arrives, including Le Bret. They are followed by people who have heard of his fight with the hundred men. Cyrano is in no mood to entertain them following his discussion with Roxanne and is rude to them in poetic form. The Comte de Guiche comes in and Cyrano argues with him and refuses to join his retinue. It is revealed that he was the man who set the hundred men on the poet. Cyrano insults him again and he leaves. Le Bret argues with Cyrano about his stubbornness and Cyrano replies in typically verbose fashion.

Finally, Le Bret mentions Roxanne and Cyrano shies away from the conversation. It is then revealed that Christian has entered the group. Some of the cadets try to tease the young man. They tell him not to mention Cyrano's nose for fear of what will happen. Cyrano then starts to tell the story of his fight with the hundred men. Christian keeps interrupting with references to his nose, but Cyrano does not rise to the bait because of his promise to Roxanne. The cadets are baffled at Cyrano's restraint until finally he snaps and orders all from the room except Christian. He then embraces the younger man, supposedly for his courage, and tells him that he is Roxanne's cousin and that Roxanne has told him that she loves Christian. Christian admits to fear of speaking to Roxanne because he will not know what to say. Cyrano volunteers to put his words into Christian's mouth like a dramatist writing for an actor.

They end their conversation with an embrace and the cadets look in wonder at the lack of any response to Christian's comments on Cyrano's nose. The Musketeer overhears this exchange and believing that the topic is now open for abuse makes comments on the nose. Cyrano knocks him to the floor, the cadets cheer and they all leave, Christian at the rear calling that Cyrano has not given him Roxanne's address.

Act III

Ragueneau is outside Roxanne's house, complaining to her chaperone that his wife has left him for the Musketeer and, having been ruined, he has had to become Roxanne's steward. Cyrano approaches, singing. Roxanne comes out to speak with him and tells him of the wondrous nature of Christian's words. As she talks, he is by turns jealous and proud of his work. The Comte de Guiche, who still loves Roxanne, comes in and tells her that he must

leave to go and fight at Arras. He also tells her that he is now colonel of the Guards and so they are going to have to go with him, including Cyrano and Christian. She tells de Guiche that the best way to punish Cyrano for his past rudeness would be to leave him and his cadets behind, away from the fight. In doing so, she lets the Count believe that she loves him. He promises to return, masked, to consummate that love.

The Count leaves and Roxanne calls for Cyrano. She tells him that Christian is coming and she expects him to talk to her about love. She goes indoors. Cyrano finds Christian and informs him of the topic of conversation. Cyrano tells him to leave so that they can work on what he will say, but Christian refuses, saying that he will use his own words. However, when Roxanne emerges, Christian loses his confidence. He talks with Roxanne but cannot find the words to say anything other than that he loves her. She grows angry and leaves. Cyrano emerges and scoffs at him for his efforts. Then Roxanne appears at her bedroom window and, as the night is dark and cloudy, Cyrano proposes that he whisper words for Christian to say. He does this, line by line, and Roxanne is soothed and enchanted by the words. When she questions the halting nature of Christian's words, Cyrano takes over and speaks in an approximation of Christian's voice. She is completely under his spell and in the guise of another he is able to truly open his heart to her. As the conversation reaches its peak, Christian interrupts to request a kiss.

Cyrano tries to deny the kiss but further discussion is interrupted by the arrival of a Capuchin monk. Roxanne goes into the house. Cyrano sends the monk on his way and when Roxanne once more emerges he tries to prevent the kiss by excessive verbosity. It is not enough and Christian climbs up to kiss Roxanne.

The monk returns with a letter for Roxanne. It is from de Guiche who is waiting in a nearby convent for her to come to him. Instead of doing what it says, she informs the monk that the letter contains instructions for him to marry her and Christian immediately. She pretends it is against her wishes and the monk believes her but feels he must do his duty. The couple goes into the house with the monk to be married and de Guiche enters, masked. Cyrano accosts him and plays word games with him to confuse and delay him, pretending to have fallen from the moon.

Finally, the delay has been sufficient. Cyrano stops his act and tells de Guiche of the wedding. Roxanne and Christian emerge as part of a wedding procession. In retaliation, and in order to defer the wedding night, de Guiche confirms the order for Christian and Cyrano and their regiment to go to the battle at Arras, leaving immediately. As they leave, Roxanne makes Cyrano promise to ensure that Christian writes to her every day. He promises.

Act IV

At the siege of Arras, the Guards are asleep while Le Bret and Carbon keep watch talking about the lack of food. There is the sound of gunfire as the enemy try to shoot a returning Cyrano. He has passed through enemy lines in the night to post a letter to Roxanne, something he does every night. Those on guard curse him for not bringing back any food but he protests that he has to travel light. They are besieging Arras while they themselves are under siege and so they are starving. The guards start to wake and they all talk about the lack of food and what they would wish to have. Cyrano chides them and then talks to them about living a good life as a Gascon, which they all are, causing them to cry. When Carbon protests he answers that homesickness is a better reason for crying than hunger.

Cyrano sees de Guiche approaching and encourages the cadets to act as if nothing was wrong in order to deny the man the satisfaction of

seeing them in poor spirits. De Guiche takes issue with Cyrano's dress but Cyrano counters with the fact that de Guiche left his white officer's scarf behind during a battle. De Guiche explains the circumstances and how he had pretended to be an ordinary enlisted man in order to escape and lead his troops. Cyrano tells him he should not have resigned his status so easily and asks for the scarf so that he can wear it fearlessly in battle. De Guiche protests that the scarf is lost behind enemy lines. In response, Cyrano pulls the scarf from his pocket.

De Guiche takes back his scarf and uses it to signal to a Spanish spy in his pay. The spy will now inform the enemy that half the army is absent and so the company of Guards will be attacked. The aim, apparently, is to gain time, but de Guiche will gain the bonus of the Guards being killed in the process. As it seems inevitable that they will be killed, Christian asks Cyrano for a last letter to Roxanne. Cyrano has already written one for such an occasion and he lets Christian read it. Christian spies tear stains on the letter, which Cyrano admits to only out of poetic zeal.

Further conversation is interrupted by the approach of a coach and horses. When it arrives, the cadets discover that it contains Roxanne. She has come to see her husband. Cyrano warns her of the impeding attack but she resolves to stay. De Guiche also tries to get her to leave, but she will not. De Guiche leaves to check his cannons and to get himself out of the center of the attack. Le Bret takes Roxanne's handkerchief to use in place of their lost flag, and one of the cadets comments that they are happy to see her but would wish for some food as well. Roxanne replies by listing all the foodstuffs she plans to have for breakfast. When the cadets are confused she directs them to her coach which is packed with hidden food. The coachman reveals himself to be Ragueneau. He climbs down and helps the cadets to unload the food. They all eat. They determine to keep the food from de Guiche if he returns, which he promptly does. They hide all the food. De Guiche comments that they look too well. He asks Roxanne again if she will leave. When she says no, he determines to stay and fight. This encourages the cadets to offer him some food, but he declines. Still, this is enough for them to finally accept him.

Just before the attack Cyrano takes Christian aside to explain that where the young man thought Cyrano had sent one letter, he had sent many. Christian asks how many times he is supposed to have written and Cyrano admits that it was twice a day, every day. This fact makes Christian realize that Cyrano loves Roxanne too. Before he can say anything, Roxanne approaches and admits that she made the perilous journey because of the many wondrous letters. However, she now believes him too beautiful to love. The true soul revealed in the letters is smothered by his good looks and she wishes he was ugly. In response, he asks her to leave him alone. He speaks with Cyrano, who has heard the conversation, and tells him to reveal all to Roxanne and let her choose between the words and the looks. He tells Roxanne that Cyrano has an important message for her and, taking his musket, he heads for the battle. Roxanne approaches Cyrano and after confirming that she loves the writer of the words no matter how ugly, he starts to tell her the truth. At that moment, Le Bret rushes to Cyrano and whispers to him. Cyrano stops what he was saying and tells Roxanne that he can never say it now as Christian has been shot.

The cadets carry Christian in and, while battle rages, Cyrano kneels over him and tells him that Roxanne chose him. Christian shouts her name and dies. She approaches and finds Cyrano's last letter in his dead hand. Knowing that Roxanne will read the letter and be mourning the wrong man, Cyrano gets de Guiche to take Roxanne to safety while he leads the charge in the battle, hoping to die.

Act V

Fifteen years later, in a convent garden, nuns sing an autumn carol. Two nuns relate each other's sins to the Mother Superior. Mother Marguerite replies that Monsieur de Bergerac will be upset with them when he visits later. They speak fondly of him and talk about the fact that he has visited on each Saturday for fifteen years ever since his cousin came to live in the convent.

Roxanne enters with an older de Guiche and the nuns retire. De Guiche is questioning her about the future but she replies that she will stay in the convent forever faithful to Christian's memory and still wearing his last letter next to her heart. He then asks about Cyrano and she says that he visits every week at four o'clock exactly. As she finishes saying this, Le Bret comes in, looking unhappy. She asks after Cyrano and he replies despairingly that his friend's condition is not good. He owns nothing and loses weight constantly. De Guiche admits that he envies Cyrano for his independence and free spirit. He then warns Le Bret that Cyrano's enemies might be looking for ways to kill him in a seeming accident.

Ragueneau enters, agitated. Roxanne instructs him to tell his problems to Le Bret while she escorts de Guiche from the convent. Ragueneau tells Le Bret that Cyrano has been hit on the head by a large log dropped from a window and is only just alive. Ragueneau fetched a doctor who bandaged him but Ragueneau is still worried that Cyrano might try to get up and visit Roxanne. Le Bret and Ragueneau leave to try and prevent this. Roxanne re-enters and sits to wait for Cyrano. The clock strikes four but there is no sign of Cyrano. Late for the first time in fifteen years, Cyrano arrives a few moments later.

Roxanne chides him for his lateness and he replies that a visitor held him up. The way he talks lets us know that he is describing Death as his visitor. Cyrano says he has sent him away for the time being. Roxanne encourages him to his usual banter with the nuns and though he manages, it is obvious that something is wrong. He tries to give her all the court gossip, as usual, but then he stops speaking, seemingly having passed out. Roxanne goes over to him and wakes him. He claims the cause as being his wound from Arras and she mentions her wound as being shown by the letter she carries. He asks to finally be allowed to read it. She gives it to him and he reads it aloud. As he reads the words of love, she recognizes his voice as being the voice from the darkness when Cyrano wooed her in Christian's name. She tells him so and he tries to deny it. She presses the matter and he continues to deny it, but finally he has to admit it. He is about to explain why he never said anything when Ragueneau and Le Bret run in, scalding him for leaving his sick bed. They tell Roxanne that Cyrano has killed himself to visit her. Cyrano takes off his hat to show the wound and the bandages.

Roxanne tells Cyrano that she loves him, but he deflects it. She expresses feelings of guilt, but he absolves her of blame. The moon comes out and he starts to talk in poetical form but this soon becomes delirium. He emerges from this state and asks Roxanne to never stop grieving for Christian, but to spare some small measure of grief for him too. He then stands and draws his sword, facing Death on his feet. He tries to duel with the image of Death in his mind, but fails and falls back into Le Bret's arms. Roxanne kisses his forehead, he opens his eyes, recognizes her, smiles, and the play ends.

Historical Context

Cyrano de Bergerac was written by Edmond Rostand in 1897. In the late nineteenth century, the fashion in French theatre was for realist plays, such as the didactic and moralistic plays of Eugene Brieux. In the rest of Europe, playwrights such as Ibsen, Strindberg, Hauptmann, and Giacosa were also writing realistic, and sometimes quite grim,

plays. Rostand's "Cyrano de Bergerac" came in stark contrast to these plays. As an historical romance it was out of convention, but as such it was immensely popular with audiences. The play itself is set in the mid-seventeenth century with the first four acts occurring in 1640 and the last act in 1655. This was during the reign of King Louis XIII of France, a period that, by the nineteenth century, was seen as France's golden age. As such, it was a time ripe for romanticizing in literature. Thus, Alexandre Dumas popularized the historical period with his famous book "The Three Musketeers" (1844), and it can be argued that Rostand's play is both a parody of and homage to this earlier book. In fact, the Musketeer character in Rostand's play is at one point identified as Dumas's d'Artagnan who, like the character of de Bergerac, was from Gascony.

Just as Dumas's book was later discovered to be based on the memoirs of the real Monsieur d'Artagnan, who was Lieutenant Captain of the first company of the King's Musketeers, so Rostand's main character was a real historical figure. Hector Savinien de Cyrano de Bergerac was born Savinien Cyrano in Sens, southeast of Paris, in 1619. The 'de Bergerac' came from the name of some land owned by his family near to Chartres rather than from the town of Bergerac. Although he was a playwright, poet, duelist and soldier as described by Rostand, he was also much different from his fictional counterpart. He wrote a play, "La Mort d'Agrippine," as well as two works of science fiction. He had no great Roxanne in his life and may even have been homosexual. Additionally, as a free-thinker in a more censorious time, his writing was often turned more towards mocking the establishment, especially the Church (Keates). Despite the perhaps larger than life character of the real man, it is still easy to see why Rostand saw this fascinating man as a fit subject for a romantic comedy.

Societal Context

The scenes within the play which represent aspects of society can be seen as more a reflection of Rostand's own time than of the period in which the play is set. The various characters in the opening scene, each in their own way corrupt or corrupting, would seem to be a commentary by Rostand on loose morals and lack of honor in the contemporary French nation. This is added to with the scenes between the Musketeer and Ragueneau's wife, her infidelity, and finally, her leaving him altogether. In addition, characters such as de Guiche would seem to be a commentary on the people with power and the ways in which they choose to use, and abuse it.

More centrally to the plot is a criticism of the esteem in which society holds the notion of 'beauty' and beautiful people as opposed to its respect for wit, creativity, and intellect. Thus, Cyrano lives with a constant battle between his lack of self-regard and his awareness of his capabilities as both a wordsmith and a swordsman. It would seem that he feels it is sufficient for an ugly man to demonstrate the latter two qualities in public, but not to show signs of love. The fear that society, embodied in Roxanne herself, would question his ability to feel love because of his looks, causes this man who constantly expresses himself to be either silent or to use Christian as the cipher for his declarations of devotion.

Religious Context

The role of religion in the play is more representative of the time at which Rostand was writing rather than the period on which the play is set. In the mid-seventeenth century religion would have been a large part of everyday life, especially with respect for the clergy at a high level. This is not reflected in the play, but rather religion is used as a dramatic conceit and not otherwise referred to. The real Cyrano de Bergerac was a man before his time, who insisted on reason as opposed to superstition. This would be a view more popular during the Enlightenment of the subsequent century. It is this change in thinking which occurred in the eighteenth and nineteenth centuries that Rostand reflects in his play.

Religion only features overtly twice in the play. The first instance is the character of Cardinal Richelieu who is referred to in the opening act as being present in the theatre. After Cyrano drives away Montfleury and kills Valvert, Le Bret informs his friend that the Cardinal was present and would have seen what happened. This represents some kind of warning, but Cyrano's reaction is flippant and carefree. He merely comments that the Cardinal is also a writer and would not object to someone else's work being driven from the stage.

The second instance of religion is the role of the monk during the balcony/wooing scene. In this case the monk, and therefore his religion, are shown as being nothing more than a tool for the other characters. Initially de Guiche has simply used the monk, sending him from the convent to fetch Roxanne for an illicit liaison. However, Roxanne turns this around and once again makes use of the monk, this time for her own ends, by tricking him into marrying her and Christian. Once again this shows a post-Enlightenment lack of respect for the authority of the church.

Scientific & Technological Context

Rostand's play concentrates on aspects of love and honor and thus contains little of a scientific or technological theme despite the real Cyrano de Bergerac's interest in the subject. He wrote two books which can be seen as forerunners of modern science fiction: "The Other World: The Comical History of the States and Empires of the Moon," (1657) and "The Comical History of the States and the Empires of the Sun" which he died without finishing. However, although these books used some of the current scientific knowledge to describe voyages to the Moon and the Sun, they were mostly conceived as satire.

Biographical Context

Edmond Rostand was born in 1868 in Marseilles, France to a wealthy family. His father was an economist, journalist and a poet. While studying for his law degree, Rostand became enamored with literature and the theatre. Despite achieving his law degree, he became a playwright. In 1890, he published a book of poetry entitled "La Musardieses," which emerged largely unnoticed. This was followed by other smaller works and two full plays, "Les Romanesques" (1894) and "La Princesse Iointaine" (1895), before he produced what was to be his most popular and most enduring play, "Cyrano de Bergerac" (1897). The role of Cyrano was reputedly written especially for celebrated French actor, Constant Coquelin, and owed much to the actor's input.

Rostand continued his writing career with an historical drama, "L'Aiglon" (1900), which is considered his second greatest play (Bird, viii) and in which the central role was first acted by Sarah Bernhardt.

After the production of "L'Aiglon," Rostand underwent a serious operation. Complications from this led to pleurisy from which he never really recovered. In a move to a kinder climate, Rostand went to live at the Villa Arnaga in Cambo-les-Bains in the French Basque Country until his death.

His health did improve from his new location and in 1910, he produced his next play, a dramatic fable entitled "Chantecler." This was his last major play. He died in 1918 from pneumonia.

Calum A. Kerr, Ph.D.

Works Cited

Bird, Edward A. "Introduction." *Cyrano de Bergerac*. Toronto: Methuen, 1968.

Butler, Mildred Allen. "The Historical Cyrano de Bergerac as a Basis for Rostand's Play." *Educational Theatre Journal* 6.3 (1954): 231–240. The Johns Hopkins University Press.

Fort, Alice B. and Kates, Herbert S., "Gerhart Hauptmann." *TheatreHistory.com*. 21 Aug 2008. <http://www.theatrehistory.com/german/hauptmann001.html>

Keates, Jonathan, "The Paladin of Panache." *Literary Review*. 22 Aug 2008. http://www.literaryreview.co.uk/keates_02_08.html

Rostand, Edmond. "Cyrano de Bergerac." Trans. Anthony Burgess. London: Nick Hern Books, 2002.

Rostand, Edmond. "Cyrano de Bergerac." Toronto: Methuen, 1968.

Discussion Questions

1. Examine the representations of honor in "Cyrano de Bergerac."
2. What is the purpose of Cyrano's speech listing nose insults?
3. Discuss the various examinations of beauty in the play.
4. Examine the way different characters use deception.
5. Cyrano is both poet and soldier. Discuss the contradictions in this.
6. What is the role of de Guiche in the play?
7. Discuss the idea of 'Platonic love' in relation to Roxanne and Cyrano's regard for her.
8. What is the relevance of the blood and the tears on the final letter to Roxanne?
9. The style of writing changes over the course of the play. Discuss the effect this has on the action.
10. Discuss the way the play deals with the differences between the written and the spoken word.

Essay Ideas

1. Compare Rostand's character with historical accounts of the real Cyrano de Bergerac.
2. In what way is this play out of its time?
3. Compare and contrast the characters of Cyrano and Christian.
4. Discuss the symbolic nature of Cyrano's nose in the play.
5. The play ends with Cyrano's death, a traditional ending for a tragedy. Discuss the ways in which the play is both typical and atypical of this genre.

Playbill for Lewis Morrison's 1888 production of Johann Wolfgang von Goethe's "Faust." Written in 1808, "Faust" is featured on page 85. Photo: Library of Congress, Prints & Photographs Division

Death of a Salesman

by Arthur Miller

Content Synopsis

"Death of a Salesman," Arthur Miller's most celebrated play, features Willy Loman, a failed salesman in his early sixties living in 1940s Brooklyn. There is also his devoted wife, Linda, and his two sons. Biff is thirty-four and Harold "Happy" is thirty-two. The action takes place, for the most part, in and around the Loman's apartment, in the last twenty-four hours of Willy's life.

Act I

It is late on a Monday evening. Willy has just returned from a business trip in the car and appears worn out. Linda has been waiting for him. He confesses to her that he was unable to concentrate on driving and nearly ran someone down, and that at one point he thought he was driving a car he had twenty years previously. He is fretting over his struggle to make money through his sales and we also learn that he is at odds with his son Biff who has failed to establish himself in business or indeed to make any kind of proper living for himself at all. Linda, as is her wont, endeavors to soothe Willy, but Biff and Happy, who are upstairs in bed, are roused by Willy's complaining. Happy informs Biff, who has just returned from a spell working on a ranch out West, about Willy's worrying state of mind. Biff in his turn reveals his profound dissatisfaction with his life; he doesn't know what to make of himself: "I don't know what the future is. I don't know what I'm supposed to want" (Miller 16). Happy has a steady job as a buyer at a store, and his own car and apartment, but chafes at the essential inferiority of his position; he is making nowhere near as much money as he would like. Biff suggests they get together to build up a family business in the West. Happy is enthusiastic but reserved about the amount of money that they could actually make from this. Biff finally decides that he will ask an old business acquaintance, Bill Oliver, for a loan with which to make a fresh start. They return to bed. Alone in the kitchen, Willy reverts to happier memories of the past during the boys' high-school days, when he and Biff were comrades. The boys and Linda all appear as their younger selves. They talk excitedly about a forthcoming football game in which Biff is due to take part. Bernard, one of their classmates who lives next door, comes to remind Biff that he ought to be studying for his final examinations, but the Lomans all scoff at his conscientiousness. In front of the boys, Willy boasts about all the great sales he's just made but when left alone with Linda is forced to admit that he's actually made very little money. He also reveals to Linda his fear that people make fun of his appearance. Linda, as ever, comforts him but Willy is racked with guilt as he recalls the memory of his mistress, known only as The Woman. With an effort, he turns his attention back to Linda, but is further agitated when he notices her mending stockings, as he has given stockings to his mistress as a present. He demands that Linda throw them out.

Willy is recalled to the present only when Happy comes down out of bed to talk to him. Charley, Bernard's father, appears, complaining about the noise that Willy has been making. Happy returns to bed while Willy and Charley play cards. Charley knows all about Willy's financial problems as Willy habitually borrows money from him. Charley, a taciturn but kindly man, offers him a job, but Willy, affronted, declines. Willy is again distracted by his memories; this time he recalls his elder brother Ben (now dead) who years before made a fortune abroad. Willy turned down the chance to go with him and has seemingly regretted this as a missed opportunity ever since. Ben appears onstage and Willy addresses him directly, much to the bewilderment of Charley, who goes back next door. Willy continues talking with Ben, eagerly questioning him about their father, a travelling salesman who left when Willy was just a baby. Ben then leaves, although Willy entreats him to stay. Then Willy returns to the present as Linda comes down to ask him to come up to bed. He refuses and goes for a walk, still wearing his slippers. Biff and Happy take advantage of his absence to discuss his increasingly erratic behavior with Linda. Linda reveals that he is no longer even receiving a salary and is working on commission, and fears he has become suicidal. It seems he has tried to deliberately crash the car and also to inhale gas. Linda also taxes Biff about the unceasing tension between him and his father. Biff reveals his confusion and frustration at not being able to live up to Willy's expectations. When Willy returns, he and Biff as usual fall to arguing, but Happy quickly intervenes with an idea for him and Biff to go into business together selling sporting goods, with the loan that Biff hopes to get from Bill Oliver. Willy is instantly thrilled and Biff also is enthusiastic. On this happier note, the family finally retires to bed.

Act II

It is the following morning. Willy and Linda talk brightly about Biff, who has already left for his meeting with Oliver. Linda declares that Biff's attitude has changed; he has become more hopeful. Willy is further elated when Linda tells him that the boys are going to treat him to dinner at a restaurant that evening. With new-found confidence, he determines to ask for promotion at work that day. However his meeting with Howard, his employer, is disastrous. Far from giving Biff a better deal, Howard dismisses him altogether, tactfully suggesting that he come back when he is feeling better. Willy, in despair, tries to remind Howard how he spent his life building up the firm. Howard is unmoved and goes out. Left alone, Willy again recalls the opportunity he had to go with Ben to Alaska.

The next scene takes place in Charley's office. Bernard, now a lawyer, has dropped in to see his father. Willy enters and they greet each other warmly, but the contrast between Bernard's obvious success and his own sons' particularly Biff's failures is painful for Willy. Willy asks Bernard why Biff never managed to make anything of himself. Bernard does not have the answer but recalls that during their final high school examinations Biff failed math, and although initially prepared to make up the subject at summer school, seemed to lose all motivation following a visit to Willy in Boston. Willy appears shaken by this. Charley arrives and Bernard leaves for a case in the Supreme Court. Willy has come to borrow money once more, but again turns down Charley's job offer and takes an almost tearful farewell of him.

Later that day, Happy is waiting for Biff and Willy at the restaurant. He talks light-heartedly with Stanley, a waiter, and chats up a glamorous customer, Miss Forsythe. Biff arrives but is extremely perturbed. He reveals that Bill Oliver wouldn't even see him and that in a fit of pique he stole a fountain pen from his office. When Willy comes, he immediately starts questioning Biff about his meeting and also reveals that he himself has been fired. This increases the pressure on Biff to provide some 'good news,' but he finally tells the truth. Willy immediately recalls the day when news came that Biff had failed his high school examination. Biff leaves in distress and Happy follows, along with Miss Forsythe and Letta, one of Miss Forsythe's friends. Willy, left behind, remembers the traumatic day when Biff came to see him in Boston after failing his exam and accidentally discovered his infidelity with his mistress. Stanley comes to him, abruptly rousing him out of his memories. He declares he has to get some seeds planted and hurries off leaving Stanley mystified.

Biff and Happy arrive home. Linda is furious with them for abandoning Willy in the restaurant and orders them both to leave. Meanwhile, Willy is out in the garden planting the seeds he has bought. Once more, he imagines Ben is with him, and they discuss his plan to raise money for the family through the insurance that will be paid out in the event of his death. Then Biff comes to him to inform him that he is leaving for good. Biff hopes to go without any more fighting, but Willy accuses him again of wasting his life, provoking a final violent confrontation. Biff makes it clear that he cannot be what Willy wants him to be and that for too long, Willy has been feeding off lies and delusions about his own and his sons' importance in the world and forcing his family to do the same. Willy still attempts to deflect away such recriminations by accusing Biff of spite. Biff is finally spent by his emotions, breaks down in sobs and goes upstairs. Seeing his tears, Willy swings from anger to overwhelming affection. While the rest of the family retreat upstairs he remains in the kitchen, intent on his final grand plan of suicide, and puts it into action by driving away in the car at top speed.

Reqiuem

It is just after the funeral. Linda, Biff, and Happy are at the graveside, along with Charley but (contrary to Willy's own expectations) no one else has come at all. Biff remarks that Willy never knew who he was, but Happy clings stubbornly onto Willy's old dream of making it big and insists he is going to make it come true. Linda takes a moment to say a final goodbye to Willy before leaving the graveyard.

"Death of a Salesman," with its searing portrayal of social and family issues, and unusual mode of presentation, has a sound reputation as one of the greatest of all American plays. It won the Pulitzer Prize in 1949. Willy Loman is an Everyman for his time, ensnared by the American consumer dream, struggling to provide for his family and to leave his mark on society, yet too proud to admit defeat, at least to the outside world. Miller dispenses with conventional structures and periods to take us deep into Willy's mind where past and present fuse together as he endeavors to make meaning out of his life and to understand where things went wrong. This technique makes it easier for the audience to identify with him and to understand the nature of his problems and delusions. Critics debate whether his story is finally tragic or merely pathetic. He is not a grand figure, he achieves no self-realization, his final act of self-sacrifice appears more misguided than heroic and does not have the desired results: there is no large crowd of mourners, as he had fondly imagined, and we do not even know if the insurance money has been paid out upon his death. In any case, Biff, whom he has intended as the prime recipient, does not want the money as he has repudiated all of Willy's ideas. In the end, however, it is precisely the fact of Willy's littleness in the scheme of things, his desperate attempt to maintain a living in the anonymity of the urban jungle, that has such resonance with modern audiences; his struggles are all too common, his hopes and failures all too recognizable.

Historical Context

"Death of a Salesman" appeared in the years immediately following the Second World War, ostensibly a time of new hope and prosperity for the country. But the awed reaction to the Broadway premiere in 1949 showed that the play articulated concerns that were already beginning to emerge about this new age of consumerism and wealth, exposing cracks in its supposedly idyllic social façade. It was seen as the first major play to challenge the long-standing American dream of seizing the opportunity to earn one's own personal success and fortune. This great dream appears distinctly tarnished in the play as it appears to have degenerated into a pursuit of material wealth for its own sake, as underlined by the frequent references to payments on house, car and all manner of gadgets. Willy finds it increasingly difficult to keep up appearances of material wealth but cherishes the dream to the last: even his final act of suicide has a mercenary motive. Willy is also seen to make things even harder for himself by buttressing his pursuit of material and social success with what appear to be archaic values in the world of the play: notions of loyalty, friendship and respect. However, he is forced to admit sorrowfully to Howard that such things do not seem to matter anymore. He clings to his idea that 'the man who creates personal interest is the man who gets ahead' (Miller 25). The truth is that the America of the mid twentieth century is seen to operate on hard-headed business principles rather than on the kind of chivalric values that Willy espouses. (See also Societal Contexts.)

Societal Context

Societal expectations put a great strain on Willy. His main problem is that he surrenders entirely to the lure of the American capitalist dream and when he fails to realize it, he feels he has no other resources to fall back on. Ben, who symbolizes the fulfillment of this dream to Willy, is a pervasive, somewhat mocking, presence in the play. Mention should also be made of Dave Singleman, the salesman still working at the time of his death at the age of eighty-four, whose apparently

resounding success (as reflected by the huge turnout at his funeral) fatally influenced Willy's choice of career. Willy is not entirely condemned for his vain dreaming, however: in a much-quoted passage at the scene of Willy's funeral, Charley points out that 'a salesman is got to dream, boy. It comes with the territory' (Miller 111). Charley thus recognizes that a salesman has got to think big, to live on the hope and dream of making good sales. Willy however is so enslaved by the lure of social and material success that he appears unable to envisage any other kind of life. With his natural talent for manual work and the whole family's love of the countryside, 'those grand outdoors' (Miller 66) the Lomans could have led a very different existence. Instead, they continue to stifle in an unsympathetic urban environment. Willy's story illustrates the dire consequences of making the wrong career choice and sticking to it; this condemns him to a lifetime of social struggle and personal and psychological turmoil. However, to the end of his life, he dreams of raising a proper garden, and just hours before his suicide is planting seeds which reflects his natural inclinations as well as being symbolic of his doomed attempts to make something grow and flourish.

Willy also suffers because he feels unable to live up to the socially-constructed and masculine image of himself as provider for the family. This prevents him from revealing the true state of his affairs to his sons and asking for their, or anyone else's, help. Instead, he prefers to mull over things in his mind and to try to find his own way, which in the end drives him to suicide. The real tragedy is that in his struggle to live up to society's expectations he is unable to accept the natural healing love of his family. Linda is utterly devoted to him, yet he cheats on her and the discovery of this liaison is what first drives a wedge between him and Biff. He also fails to see that Biff, in spite of all their quarrels, cares deeply about him. And his pursuit of a futile social dream proves damaging to the family as he endeavors to instill his ideas into his sons' minds, thus transmitting the flaws of one generation to the next. Moreover, in his over-emphasis on creating the right impression in society, of being 'well-liked', he appears to neglect to teach his sons basic moral values. He does not discourage Biff from stealing at an early age or from cheating in his final exams; and Biff grows up to be a habitual thief. Happy, too, becomes an inveterate womanizer and bribe-taker. Moreover, while Willy's grand plans for Biff and Happy fail to materialize, their neighbor Bernard, quietly, without fuss, attains the social success that Willy is so desperate for, by dint of his own hard work.

Scientific & Technological Context
The fruits of technological progress are clearly to be seen in the play; ordinary households now have more gadgets than ever before, and when Willy goes to see Howard, he finds him preoccupied with his new wire recorder, insisting on demonstrating its capabilities before he will even let Willy get a word in. However, these household improvements bring their own troubles; they have to be paid for in installments (at least in the Loman household) and are forever incurring extra expenses; the shower drips, the refrigerator uses up one belt after another, the car keeps on breaking down. Willy is finally driven to exclaim 'I'm always in a race with the junkyard! They time those things. They time them so when you finally paid for them, they're used up' (Miller 57). (Incidentally, as Willy acrimoniously remarks, Charley's refrigerator has never given any trouble. This is another way his neighbor has upstaged Willy). Furthermore, two notable modern inventions; domestic gas heating and the automobile, take on distinctly sinister overtones as they become the means by which Willy tries to end his life and finally succeeds. Technological advancements, as seen in the play, have contributed little to human happiness.

On a different note, Miller draws on psychology, a burgeoning science throughout the first half of the twentieth century to adopt a stream-of-consciousness approach to the play. What we see happening onstage are reflections of what is passing through Willy's mind where past and present co-exist, resulting in an unconventional non-linear narrative style. Miller, like Eugene O'Neill, also utilizes psychological concepts popularized by the likes of Sigmund Freud regarding the importance of the family, and particularly parental influence, in shaping individual development. Biff and Happy are dominated, obviously, by their father's hopes and expectations; Biff finally rebels against this.

Religious Context
There appears to be no sense of any divine agency in "Death of a Salesman." None of the Lomans, or anyone else, appeal to any kind of religious belief. The post-world-war society appears to have pinned all its faith in tangible and visible signs of social and material success.

Biographical Context
For many observers, Willy Loman is an Everyman figure for modern times, but the character had an intensely personal application for Miller. The model for Willy was his travelling salesman uncle Manny Newman, a braggart with a well-developed sense of competition who was always comparing Miller to his own sons, Buddy and Abby (Buddy, like Biff in the play, never lived up to the promise of his high school days). Miller revealed in later days that Manny was always full of big plans for himself and his family, which never came to fruition. A chance meeting with Manny outside a performance of his earlier play "All My Sons," in 1947 was Miller's immediate inspiration for "Death of a Salesman," although he had already written a short story about an unsuccessful salesman before this. Miller also drew on the character of his own father for the play. The family theme is

central to Miller's plays as a whole, as to twentieth-century American drama more generally from Eugene O'Neill onwards. "All My Sons," his first important work, like "Salesman" features the head of a household who is eventually driven to suicide. After "Salesman," he wrote several more plays that gained critical and popular acclaim, notably "The Crucible," an account of the Salem Witchcraft trials of 1692, arising from his own persecution in the anti-Communist McCarthy era. Miller was still writing at the time of his death on February 10, 2005, fifty-six years to the day that "Salesman" premiered on Broadway in 2013. None other of his characters ever captured the public imagination in quite the same way as the well-meaning and hapless Willy Loman.

Gurdip Panesar, Ph.D.

Works Cited

Bloom, Harold, ed. *Arthur Miller's Death of a Salesman: Contemporary Literary Views.* New York: Chelsea House Publishing, 1995.

Miller, Arthur. "Death of a Salesman," Harmondsworth, England: Penguin. 1998.

Siebold, Thomas, ed. *Readings on "Death of a Salesman,"* San Diego: Greenhaven Press, 1998.

Discussion Questions

1. What is the effect of combining past and present events as Miller does in the play? Do you find it distracting? Why or why not?
2. Do you think that Linda is over-protective of Willy? Why or why not?
3. Discuss Miller's portrayal of female characters in the play.
4. Do you think that Willy's good points ultimately outweigh the bad? Explain.
5. Do you find the Lomans too self-pitying? Why or why not?
6. Is the dialogue of the play altogether naturalistic? Answer with reference to specific examples.
7. What is the effect of the play's title? Do you think it is a good choice? Explain.
8. Do you think that Biff makes Willy a convenient scapegoat for all of his problems? Why or why not?
9. Compare and contrast the characters of Willy and Charley.
10. In what way (if any) can Willy be accounted heroic?

Essay Ideas

1. Analyze Miller's use of symbolism in "Death of a Salesman."
2. Examine the role of parental influence in "Salesman."
3. Analyze the role of money in "Salesman."
4. Examine the theme of conflict in "Salesman."
5. Analyze Miller's narrative and stage techniques in "Salesman."

Norwegian playwright Henrik Ibsen. His "An Enemy of the People," written in 1882, is featured opposite. Another Isben play featured in this work is "The Wild Duck," on page 229. Photo: by Gustav Borgen NFB-1977B restored

An Enemy of the People

by Henrik Ibsen

Content Synopsis

When good-natured and generous Dr. Stockmann's hunch that the water flowing into the town's health spa is contaminated by the nearby tannery is scientifically confirmed, he expects to be congratulated for his discovery. Instead, his neighbors vilify him and the town is polarized. His proud and puritanical brother, Peter, who has never liked or approved of him, contests his findings. He claims Dr. Stockmann does not have the good of the town at heart, does not appreciate how essential the baths are for the town's financial prosperity, or realize how costly the changes he says are necessary to restore the purity of the baths would be. Peter is also the town's mayor.

Morten Kiil, owner of the tannery and Dr. Stockmann's father-in-law, does not believe the baths are polluted. He thinks Stockmann is playing a trick on his brother and other leading citizens in order to get revenge for being removed from the town council. The men who run the newspaper declare their support for Dr. Stockmann at first, hoping to use the problems with the spa, under the guise of concern for democracy and the common people, to generate a scandal that will shake up the town politics and put their party in power. They speak of the need to have the support of the majority behind them and they plan to organize demonstrations. Hovstad, the editor, promises to print Dr. Stockmann's editorial concerning the dangers of the baths.

However, Peter shows them how their interests will not be served if they allow Dr. Stockmann's critique of the baths to be accepted. He argues that the doctor is exaggerating the problem, that he is giving neighboring towns an advantage in the competition for visitors coming to use the baths, and that the people—the small homeowners and merchants—will be taxed to finance the reconstruction. The newspapermen withdraw their support.

Dr. Stockmann argues that Peter is upset because he is responsible for where the conduits for the baths were laid, against Stockmann's warnings. Peter agrees that is partly true, but argues that preserving the appearance of his authority as mayor is necessary for the good of the town, as is the immediate opening the spa. He says Stockmann is not motivated by a pursuit of truth but by a warped personality; that he is unable to respect authority and he is rebellious by nature. He insists that if Stockmann challenges the baths, he will bring harm to his wife and children, he will be taken off the board of directors of the baths, and his professional reputation will be tarnished.

Peter orders Stockmann to write another report for the newspaper saying that after further investigation, he has concluded that his earlier report was wrong and that he has confidence the board of directors of the baths will take any steps necessary to deal with whatever minor problems might exist. Stockmann refuses. Peter's pressure only serves to strengthen Dr. Stockmann's conviction to defend the truth.

Dr. Stockmann's daughter, Petra, a schoolteacher, supports her father entirely. His wife is frightened by Peter's threats. Her husband is right, she agrees, but the world is full of injustice, and they will be forced to live in poverty. Stockmann says he will not back down, for the sake of his integrity and as an example for his children.

When the newspapermen refuse to print his essay explaining why the baths must be shut down and rebuilt, Stockmann vows to issue his report as a pamphlet, or rent a hall and read it publicly. Horster, a ship's captain and one of Dr. Stockmann's few supporters, offers his house. The reading is a big event. The townspeople gather and reporters come to cover it for the newspaper. Stockmann's enemies, led by his brother, take over the meeting, condemn his motives, and attack his report. They do not let him read his report or speak about the baths when they finally give him the floor.

When Stockmann speaks, he is angry that the meeting has been stolen and that the people have allowed it and will not listen to facts. He asserts that he considers that the majority is never right, and is in fact the enemy of truth and freedom. The minority, who can see further than the majority, are the bearers of truth. Stockmann says that public opinion is a coercive, ignorant, and destructive force. People must be educated to cultivate their reason and intelligence in order for authentic democracy to function correctly. He excoriates the people for maintaining that the baths are safe just to further their own economic interest. The crowd is angry and Stockmann is censured as an enemy of the people.

The next morning, Stockmann picks up stones which mobs of angry townspeople lobbed into his house after the meeting. He tells his wife he will keep them to give to his sons as a legacy. His family is evicted from their house; his daughter is fired from her teaching job. Horster's support

for Stockmann has cost him his position as ship's captain. His brother informs him he has been fired from the board of directors at the baths, that no one will seek his services as a physician, and that he ought to leave town and come back after some time has passed to apologize. Stockmann refuses to submit.

But more pressure to reverse his position comes from his father-in-law, Morton Kiil, who is the owner of the tannery responsible for contaminating the baths. Kiil wants his reputation restored, which can only happen if Stockmann recants. To force him to do so, Kiil buys up all the shares in the baths with the money he had intended to leave to his daughter (Stockmann's wife). If Stockmann capitulates, the shares will gain in value and his family's financial future will be assured. If he refuses, the shares will be worth nothing.

The newspapermen now think that Stockmann's report on the baths was part of a plan with Morten Kiil to make a profit by lowering the value of shares in the bath so he could purchase them. They promise to turn public opinion in his favor when he reverses his position if he will give them a cut of the profits when the stocks go up. Stockmann brandishes his umbrella at them and they flee.

Stockmann refuses to back down or submit to Kiil's blackmail. He will remain in the town and write against the corruption he has uncovered. Horster offers the Stockmanns his house to live in. Stockmann will doctor to the poor who cannot pay and most need care. When his sons are sent home from school because other boys fought with them, Stockmann determines that he will teach them himself and make them decent and independent. He will open a school with Petra in Horster's dining room and teach other poor children. His wife supports him but is nervous about the future. Petra admires him. He feels unbeatable because he is standing alone, true to right principles, unmoved by corrupt self-interest or public pressure.

Symbols & Motifs

Pollution is a recurring motif in "An Enemy of the People." It occurs in the play at first as the actual pollution of water but soon pollution becomes a symbol of the characteristic way the town is governed. The characters' integrity, their minds, and their social behavior are shown to have been polluted by self-interest, lust for power, conformity, and political corruption.

The apparent conflict between the individual and society is also a recurring motif. Unbridled self-interest is shown to be one of the chief contaminants of the social good. Stockmann, his daughter Petra, and Captain Horster are individuals who adhere to their values and beliefs despite the social pressure brought against them to capitulate and they remain "pure." Characters like Peter, who proclaim the importance of conforming one's own interests to the interests of society, are hypocrites who manipulate the social agenda to benefit themselves.

Hypocrisy as a motif also pervades the play. The newspaper men, the school board, and many of the townspeople are shown as hypocritical, espousing values that they willingly sacrifice for the sake of their financial interests or because of their social cowardice.

Historical Context

Ibsen wrote "An Enemy of the People" in response to the way his previous play, "Ghosts," (1881), was condemned and vilified. Ibsen was personally attacked by the public and by the critics. With such themes as sexual vice, moral corruption, and syphilis, "Ghosts" turned Ibsen into a public enemy. In Norway, the published edition of the play hardly sold and no theater would produce it. Dr. Stockmann, by revealing the pollution of the baths, represents a version of Ibsen himself, the playwright who brought social disease and corruption into the light, and, although defamed, kept to his calling.

"An Enemy of the People," however, was a popular and a critical success. Despite its obvious resemblance to Ibsen's own situation, he drew the story of "An Enemy of the People" from several actual, historical events. The Medical Officer at a health spa in Bohemia in the 1830s issued a public warning after a cholera epidemic broke out, and the guests all left. Rather than being praised, he was condemned by the townspeople, who threw stones at his house. The Officer left the town. In 1880, a chemist in Oslo caused a public uproar after he questioned the sanitary conditions of a steam kitchen.

The themes of the tyranny of the majority and the importance of the individual explored in the play are rooted in the historical context of the nineteenth century. The great social upheavals of the final decades of the eighteenth century reshaped the way people thought and how governments were formed in the nineteenth century. The movement for democracy based on the will of the people spread throughout countries as apparently different from each other as Russia, the United States, England, France, and Ibsen's own Norway. Jacksonian democracy in America, the freeing of the serfs and the rise of anti-tsarist movements in Russia, the constitutionalizing of the British monarchy, and the instability of the French royal and popular governments all showed how powerful an influence the majority could have on shaping society.

Societal Context

As a man who asserts his individual values within a social framework and who grounds those values on his own independent and tested judgment rather than on conformity to mob pressure, Dr. Stockmann embodies the virtues of civic responsibility and social integrity. His detractors, because they ground their actions on self-interest but do not assert the strength of individualism or challenge their own prejudices, are devious and motivated by the vices of selfishness and hypocrisy. Like Morton

Kiil, they care about their reputations but not about the consequences of their actions.

Dr. Stockmann's opponents have no qualms about besmirching his reputation rather than engaging in a true social discourse in which they mobilize facts and arguments in order to fashion a respectable rebuttal. Their lack of honor is a social as well as an individual failure. They represent a social system that favors a majority, and an uneducated majority at that.

The theme of education runs through the play in order to assert the principle that a society not grounded on an educated majority remains a tyranny, especially when the majority rules.

Religious Context

There is no overt religious context in "An Enemy of the People." Stockmann does not voice any religious principles; his realm is the social realm. But a reader may see Stockmann as embodying some of the principal religious values and actions that are ennobling, like sacrificing earthly interests in the name of a high and good idea, or living with faith in the honor of good works despite opposition from evil or cynical forces.

Scientific & Technological Context

Dr. Stockmann is a scientist—a man who puts the objective truths that scientific technology can establish, in this case the laboratory analysis of a sample of the waters at the baths, over his own self-interest. He is also a teacher who attempts to instruct his fellow townspeople in the importance of adhering to facts, to the truth and to honorable behavior. He demonstrates that some things that cannot be seen with the naked eye, like bacteria, do exist and there are techniques and mechanisms for discovering them.

The town's corruption represents an anti-scientific attitude, one based on keeping knowledge hidden if that knowledge may force people to act in ways they would rather not. The scientific attitude is shown to transcend individual self-interest and to point the way to an objective reality whose demands must be respected for the general good.

Great advances in science were being made at the time Ibsen was writing, and they were not always appreciated. In 1880, the technology of microscopy lead to the discovery of the bacillus that is responsible for typhoid and of the parasite responsible for malaria. The scientist Charles-Louis-Alphonse Laveran met skepticism when he presented his findings on malaria to the Academy of Medicine at Paris.

The power of technology is also clear in the play. The very problem of pollution from the tannery would not have existed if the course the water followed had been laid out as Dr. Stockmann advised rather than as his brother demanded. Thus the value of science in determining the application of technology is also a concern of the play.

Biographical Context

Ibsen was born in Skien, a small port town in Norway on March 20, 1828. His father was a prosperous merchant until Ibsen was eight, when he lost his fortune. His mother was a painter. Ibsen's childhood was defined by their poverty and the social ostracism they faced. At fifteen, Ibsen was apprenticed to a pharmacist and also began writing plays. At eighteen, he fathered a child but abandoned both the woman, ten years his senior, and the child and moved to Oslo, intending to enter the university. Instead he began writing plays. His first play, "Catalina" (1850), was published under the pseudonym Brynjulf Bjarme, but not performed. "The Burial Mound," (also 1850) was staged unsuccessfully. Between 1851 and 1863, Ibsen was employed as a stage manager at several Norwegian theaters. In 1866, with "Brandt," he achieved popular success.

Ibsen married Suzannah Thoresen in 1858. Their son, Sigurd, was born in 1859. In 1864, Ibsen received a grant from the Norwegian government to travel and with additional aid from the Norwegian writer, editor, and theater director Bjornstjerne Bjornson (1832–1910), Ibsen left for Italy and remained abroad, living in Rome, Munich, and Dresden over the next twenty-seven years, returning to Norway infrequently.

In 1877, Ibsen stopped writing mythological or historical dramas in verse. With "Pillars of Society," he began to use contemporary social issues, gender, political and psychological conflicts as the material for his plays. One of Ibsen's most well-known plays, "A Doll's House," concerning the birth of a woman's awareness of the demands for self-abnegation that women faced in marriage, appeared in 1879. In 1882, he wrote "An Enemy of the People." In it he argued against the wisdom of the majority, analyzed the power and the methods of political manipulation, and presented a drama in which one person, guided by his integrity and by his dedication to truth and personal honor rather than self-interest and financial security, challenges a corrupt status quo and emerges a hero because

of his resolve, although vilified by his townsman and defeated in his original mission. In 1884, Ibsen wrote "The Wild Duck," a counter-companion play to "An Enemy of the People." In it, he probed the problem of a heartless exploitation of truth and honesty. Ibsen's subsequent plays include "The Master Builder" (1892), "John Gabriel Borkman" (1896), and a classic of modern psychological drama, "Hedda Gabler" (1890). In 1899, Ibsen suffered several strokes. The first impaired his ability to walk. The second, a year later, affected his ability to remember words. Ibsen died in Christiania (Oslo), Norway on May 23, 1906.

Neil Heims, Ph.D.

Works Cited

Beyer, Edvard. "Ibsen: The Man and His Work." Translated by Marie Wells, A Condor Book/ Souvenir Press (E & A) LTD, 1978. Print.

Ibsen, Henrik. "An Enemy of the People." Chicago: Ivan R. Dee, 2007. Print.

Discussion Questions

1. Do you think that Dr. Stockmann ought to have told his brother and the board of directors about his suspicion regarding the baths and that he was going to have them tested before he did anything? Why or why not? Consider his reasons. Do you think they are valid?

2. What role does hypocrisy play in the way several important characters in "An Enemy of the People" are drawn?

3. What is Ibsen's view of democracy in "An Enemy of the People"? Do you agree with it?

4. According to "An Enemy of the People," what does an individual owe to society and what does society owe to the individual? Do you agree? Why or why not?

5. Is Dr. Stockmann noble, admirable, and heroic, or stubborn and foolishly unrealistic? Defend your position.

6. According to Ibsen in "An Enemy of the People," what role does money play in the formulation of public policy?

7. Discuss the roles that Mrs. Stockmann and Petra play in "An Enemy of the People." How do their actions and attitudes affect the way the audience feels about Dr. Stockmann and his actions?

8. Discuss some present-day events or circumstances that remind you of the events and circumstances depicted in "An Enemy of the People." Show how and why you find a resemblance.

9. At the end of "An Enemy of the People," the audience knows what Stockmann, his family, and Captain Horster will do, but knows nothing about how any of the other characters will do, or what will happen with regard to the baths. Is this a weakness or strength in the play? Why or why not? If you were to write a sequel to "An Enemy of the People," how would you resolve these issues? Why?

10. What is a "well-made play?" How is "An Enemy of the People" an example of the well-made play? What does it derive dramatically from being a well-made play?

Essay Ideas

1. Analyze the characters of Dr. Stockmann and Peter and compare and contrast them.

2. Discuss Ibsen's use of irony in "An Enemy of the People."

3. Examine the way Ibsen uses the technique of foreshadowing in "An Enemy of the People."

4. Contrast Captain Horster's character with Editor Hovstad's character.

5. Discuss the importance assigned to education in "An Enemy of the People."

The Family Reunion

by T. S. Eliot

Content Synopsis

A play in verse, Eliot's "The Family Reunion," reworks Aeschylus's "Oresteia," setting the classical Greek tragedy in an English country house and wedding it to a Christian ethos. Harry, Lord Monchensey, a recent widower, returns after a seven-year absence to his family's estate, Wishwood. Harry's mother, Amy, has taken pains to hold time in abeyance at Wishwood, hoping that Harry will find it as he left it and be ready to assume lordship of the manor. His room is as it was and his uncles and aunts have gathered to greet him. Yet Harry arrives a haunted man who, try as he might, cannot find solace in his boyhood home. Harry may or may not have pushed his wife overboard during an ocean cruise—he himself seems unsure as to what exactly happened on the night of her death. He muses, midway through the play, "Perhaps / I only dreamt I pushed her" (275). Because of his wife's death and of his having desired her death, he is plagued both by a guilty conscience and by a force that is at least partly external to himself: the Eumenides, or avenging furies that dogged Orestes.

Over the course of his visit, Harry will unfold his own guilt to both his boyhood love, Mary, and his wise aunt Agatha. At key points in the play, the Furies appear to Harry, reminding him of his crime. They are at first invisible to all but Harry, a fact which serves to enrage him. He asks Mary, "Are you so imperceptive, have you such dull senses / That you could not see them?" (253). Eventually, however, both Mary and Agatha will see the Furies. Harry's manservant, Downing, reveals that he has long been able to see Harry's "ghosts," as he calls them, but that "I knew they was to do with his Lordship , / And not with me, so I could see them cheerful-like, / In a manner of speaking. There's no harm in them" (289). The Furies become a sort of spiritual litmus test, for only the most enlightened characters are able to perceive them. Indeed, the more enlightened one is, the less the Furies seem like spirits of vengeance. By the play's conclusion, Harry has undergone a spiritual transformation. He therefore sees the furies not merely as avenging punishers, but as "bright angels" whom he must follow to a new life of purgation and religious worship. He leaves Wishwood no longer the pursued, but the pursuer.

Just as Harry unburdens himself of the secrets of his grim marriage, so does he learn of family secrets which have long been hidden from him and which will help to determine his own fate. Agatha tells him that she had an affair with his father, and that his father nearly killed his pregnant mother out of his desire to begin a new life with Agatha. Harry, therefore, bears and must atone for not only his own sins, but the sins of his father. The Furies call on Harry to recognize not only sins he has committed, but the original sin with which he was born. Agatha's revelation makes Wishwood a second Eden and Harry a Christ figure.

Incidents and dialogue involving spiritually unenlightened stock characters drawn from parlor comedies and detective stories counterpoint the narrative arc of Harry's spiritual transformation. Harry's two brothers, for example, stand in sharp contrast to him. While both John and Arthur are expected at the reunion, each is delayed by a car accident. The distractions of the outside world therefore prevent them from returning to their family roots and to the spiritual enlightenment that Harry finds at Wishwood. The brother's lives seem to be full of incident, but empty of meaning. Harry's uncles and aunts—with the exception of Agatha, of course—likewise seem spiritually dead. Like characters from Eliot's earlier poetry, there is no substance beneath their parlor talk. When they join to become a Greek chorus, they voice a collective need for illusion and blind reassurance: "Hold tight, hold tight, we must insist that the world is what we have always taken it to be" (243). Finally, Dr. Warburton and Sergeant Winchell, representatives of medicine and the law, gain no access to the nature of Harry's crime and punishment. They therefore serve as foils to Agatha, Harry, and Mary, who, by approaching the question of guilt from a religious—rather than a psychological or criminological—point of view, ascertain its true nature.

Eliot loosely based his play on Aeschylus's "Oresteia—Agamemnon," "The Libation Bearers," and "The Eumenides"—three plays that follow the history of Orestes, a young man whose mother, Clytemnestra, kills his father, Agamemnon. Seeking vengeance, Orestes in turn kills his mother. As a punishment for his deeds the Eumenides, or furies, hound Orestes. At the conclusion of "The Eumenides," he atones for his crime and is released. The Eumenides are not the only feature of Aeschylus's play that Eliot has incorporated into "The Family Reunion." The play features a cho-

rus, a convention of ancient Greek tragedy. Yet the play modulates from a classical Greek to a Christian worldview, as Harry finds that the furies do not seek revenge, but rather offer the opportunity for atonement and the expiation of sins. The play ends, moreover, with Agatha and Mary speaking in the ritualized cadences of a liturgy. Eliot's method throughout "The Family Reunion" lies in juxtaposing what he termed "the natural surface appearance" of everyday life with non-naturalistic passages which "remove the surface of things" (9). Beneath its murder-mystery surface, "The Family Reunion" is a play about redemption. As Aunt Agatha puts it, "What we have written is not a story of detection, / Of crime and punishment, but of sin and expiation" (275).

Historical Context

"The Family Reunion" was produced at the Westminster Theater in 1939, where it ran for only five weeks. The play's commercial failure may in part be due to problems with Eliot's script and with the production itself, but timing was also a factor. Rapidly-escalating events in Europe would have held the attention of every Londoner, and it was not the Westminster Theater, but the theater of war on which their eyes were fixed. Later the same year, of course, England went to war with Germany. Eliot's budding second career as a playwright was put on hold, for the theaters were out of commission. He returned to writing poetry, producing the patriotic "Defense of the Islands" and the third of the "Four Quartets," "The Dry Salvages," which deals obliquely with the Luftwaffe's nightly bombing raids of London. Eliot also served as a fire warden, sitting up all night twice a week to watch the night skies.

There are several layers of irony, then, in "The Family Reunion's" 1939 vision of a permanent, settled order at the ancestral home of Wishwood. "Nothing is changed, Agatha, at Wishwood," Amy rebukes her sister. "You'll find you know the country as well as ever," Gerald similarly assures Harry. Of course, Eliot means such assurances to ring hollow, for while Wishwood may have remained the same, Harry himself has changed during his eight years abroad. Agatha apprehends a deeper truth than do Amy and Gerald when she argues, "At Wishwood he will find another Harry. / The man who returns will have to meet / The boy who left" (229). The play returns, repeatedly, to this notion that the transformation of the inner man means a transformation of his relationship to the outer world, such that, as Eliot writes elsewhere, "all time is unredeemable" ("Burnt Norton," line 5).

Yet there is a further irony to Amy's vain efforts to keep Wishwood from changing. Within a few months of "The Family Reunion's" closing, the nightly bombing runs on London would prove that the spirit of place and permanency that the play evokes is an illusory one. The city was decimated by bombs and incendiary devices, and while a country house such as Wishwood would likely have been spared, similarly historic structures within the city were reduced to rubble. Family life, too, was disrupted by the war, and Harry and his brothers would have been far from Wishwood by 1940, serving in some capacity in the European theater. There is, then, a sepia-toned nostalgia to Eliot's depiction of the settled, comfortable life of the country gentry. In the years after the war, both economic hardships and the death of so many of England's young men would have made Wishwood quite a different place. It is important to remember, too, that this is an American's vision of English life, and Eliot's foreignness may add one more layer of romanticism to his depiction of Wishwood's timeless, fixed social order.

When "The Family Reunion" was revived in 1946, it was a popular and critical success. Yet the initial failure of the play continued to bother Eliot, and he wrote his subsequent plays with an eye to courting a popular audience. Eliot's next play, "The Cocktail Party," was well received, having a long run on Broadway and being adapted for television.

Societal Context

The English manor house is frequently invoked as a microcosm for English society as a whole. Wishwood reflects, in its lords and ladies, guests, poor relations, and servants, the class division of the larger society of which it is a part. The denizens of Eliot's country house are familiar English types: the aristocratic Amy and Agatha, the ne'er do well younger son, the befuddled old ex-colonial uncles and dowager aunts, the melancholy provincial doctor, the officious constable, the faithful Cockney manservant. There are a few reversals which seem to challenge the settled order of things. The servant Downing, for example, will reveal himself to possess deep insight into the spiritual nature of Harry's calling. Yet on the whole, the social order at Wishwood seems to be fixed. Again, much of what seemed fixed in 1939 would be radically transformed by 1945, and it is only in one of Eliot's post-war plays, "The Confidential Clerk," that social class becomes mutable and characters have the ability to move from servant to master.

Eliot was deeply invested in what he termed, to borrow the title of one of his essays, "the possibility of a poetic drama." Through his criticism and through his completed plays and unfinished dramatic experiments, he tried to revive the practice of publicly-spoken verse that had animated the Elizabethan and Jacobean theater. After his conversion, he became particularly interested in the public role of the poet, and in the notion that poetry must have some degree of social utility. His interest in the stage seems to grow out of this ideal of creating a culture of spoken poetry which would reveal the religious pattern underlying daily life. In this respect, "The Family Reunion," like all of Eliot's plays, positions itself against the realism that held sway on the contemporary stage and, in a different sense, in the cinema.

Religious Context

"The Family Reunion" is an explicitly religious play, for the classical furies that pursue Harry, become, by its conclusion, "bright angels" whom he must follow to a new life of purgation, worship, and service. Over the course of the play, Harry comes to acknowledge his own sinfulness and his readiness to expiate his sins. He fled to Wishwood seeking refuge from the guilt he feels over his role in his wife's death. Yet he learns from his Aunt Agatha that it is not just his own personal sin that weighs on him, but an inherited, original sin. Harry's father intended to kill his pregnant wife so that he could be united with his wife's sister, Agatha. Yet Agatha stopped him, largely for the sake of the unborn child. She tells Harry: "You would not have been born in that event: I stopped him" (274). Harry bears the curse of this intended murder, and it is not only for his own sins, but for the sins of his father that he must endure purgation. Indeed, Agatha muses: "It is possible / You are the consciousness of your unhappy family, / Its bird sent flying through the purgatorial flame." Wishwood, in this reading, becomes a second Eden, and Harry's father a second Adam who sins and passes on his original sin to his descendants. By recognizing his own fallen nature, Harry may begin to atone for himself and for his people. One might therefore read him as a Christ figure, who sacrifices himself for the sins of his fathers.

It is fitting that Eliot would take as the theme of his play the conversion of a sinner. Eliot himself had converted to Anglicanism a decade before writing "The Family Reunion." Although raised a Unitarian, he had drifted away from Christianity as a young man. When he adopted a new faith in middle age, it was one that stands at odds with the liberal-humanistic bent of Unitarianism. The rituals and orthodoxy of the Church of England seemed to offer Eliot structure, form, and aesthetics which he could not find in the church of his youth. Harry likewise adopts a strict faith which his gentrified family cannot comprehend. In leaving Wishwood, he declares that he will seek out:

> The worship in the desert, the thirst and deprivation,
> A stormy sanctuary and a primitive altar,
> The heat of the sun and the icy vigil,
> A care over lives of humble people (281).

His family misconstrues Harry's purpose. His mother announces, "Harry is going away—to become a missionary" (286). The rest of the family immediately begins to talk of the practical preparations he ought to make for such a "profession," as Gerald terms it: learning languages and medical procedures, being inoculated, earning some "religious qualifications" (286). They see Harry's conversion in terms of its social utility. But while Harry certainly has a mission, he is no missionary. His calling is not to be an evangelist or a charity worker, but through inner and outer suffering to test himself. The play leaves Harry just over the threshold of conversion, working out for himself the mandates of his new faith.

Scientific & Technological Context

Although Eliot commented in the months leading up to his composing "The Family Reunion" that he was making a study of Ibsen's plays, his own play departs from the sort of realism that animates works such as "Hedda Gabler" or "A Doll's House." Drama during the first half of the twentieth century, too, often creates the illusion that the audience is looking through a "fourth wall" onto a scene from "real life" which is unfolding in front of them. This emphasis on verisimilitude may in part spring from advances in the arts of stagecraft, lighting, and other theatrical effects. The Victorians and their inheritors simply had the technology to create in their darkened theaters the illusion of the real. Greek and Elizabethan playwrights, on the other hand, created no such illusions; they embraced the artifice of the stage. It is this Greek and the Elizabethan mode of drama that Eliot takes for his model in "The Family Reunion" and in his subsequent plays. He invokes realism—the studied banalities of Ivy, Violet, and Gerard—only as a foil for setting off non-naturalistic dramatic elements such as the chorus or the appearance of the Eumenides. By so doing, Eliot means to get at a truth which lies deeper than everyday conversation and the surface appearances of the world. By contrasting the artificiality of parlor talk with the artifice of the chorus, he seems to suggest that poetry and religion have access to a truth which is obscured by real life.

It is not surprising, then, that Eliot was unimpressed by the BBC's television version of Eliot's next play, "The Cocktail Party." He declared television an insufficient medium for the play (Ackroyd 308). He also turned down an offer for his play to be made into a film.

It may be worth saying something about the role that science and technology play in the lives of Wishwood's inhabitants. Although no Luddite, Eliot had a complex relationship with technology, one which is reflected in his poems and plays. He hated the telephone, for example, using it only when absolutely necessary. He seems, on the other hand, to have gotten some satisfaction out of his daily commute on the London Underground, and tube trains and stations appear at several places in his poetry as a zone of meditation and contemplation. His litmus test for the merit of any given technological advance seemed to be whether it frustrates or encourages contemplation. Perhaps the most resonant symbol of modern technology in "The Family Reunion" is the automobile. Each of Harry's younger brothers, John and Arthur, gets into separate car accidents that prevent them from returning to Wishwood. The car therefore fails to deliver on its promise of providing reliable transportation; instead, it is the means of frustrating their return to the ancestral home. Ironically, Winchell, the local constable, arrives with news of John's accident having traveled not by automobile, but by bicycle and foot. The play would suggest that modern technology is nothing in which to put one's faith.

Biographical Context

Born into a prominent St. Louis family in 1888, T.S. Eliot was raised a Unitarian. He attended Harvard and in 1914 moved to England, where he studied philosophy at Oxford University. The next year he married an Englishwoman, Vivienne Haigh-Wood, and began pursuing a rigorous program of writing criticism and book reviews. He worked as a middle school teacher, as an extension lecturer at University College, and as a clerk at Lloyd's Bank before eventually moving into editing and publishing. In 1922, he became editor of "The Criterion," while in 1925 he left the bank to take a position with the publishing House Faber & Gwyer.

Eliot published "The Love Song of J. Alfred Prufrock" in 1915, followed by the collection "Prufrock and Other Observations" in 1917. This was followed by "Poems" (1920) and his first book of criticism, "The Sacred Wood" (1920), which gathered excerpts from some of the dozens of book reviews and critical pieces Eliot had written over the previous five years. In 1922, he published "The Waste Land." The poem was received with great acclaim. Conventional wisdom would break Eliot's life and career into two parts. In the first phase, Eliot creates through his essays and poetry—particularly with the 1922 publication of "The Waste Land"—the movement that would come to be called Modernism. The second phase begins in 1927 with his conversion to the Anglican faith, after which he writes poems and plays which are of a more explicitly religious nature and which in some ways fly in the face of his Modernist contemporaries. "Ash Wednesday," "Four Quartets," and Eliot's plays are all the products of the post-conversion.

In 1927, Eliot was baptized into the Church of England. Later that same year, he became a British citizen. Much of his poetry after his conversion dealt with religious themes. "Journey of the Magi"

(1927) and "Ash Wednesday" (1930) are two such overtly Christian poems. In the 1930's Eliot turned his attention to drama, writing "Choruses from the Rock" and "Murder in the Cathedral," both for the stage.

It is difficult, if one knows something of Eliot's life, not to read the guilt-ridden widower Harry Monchensey as a stand-in for Eliot himself. The Eliots' marriage had been fraught from the start. Vivienne suffered from a variety of psychological and physiological conditions, and her various medications only exacerbated her unpredictable behavior. Only a few months before Eliot started writing his play, Vivienne was committed to a mental asylum, where she would live for the rest of her life. Eliot had not seen her for some years before the committal, and he never visited her in the sanitarium. Harry muses, "You would never imagine anyone could sink so quickly" (235); it is a sentiment Eliot might well have voiced himself. Other characters' descriptions of the dead wife sound reminiscent of Vivienne. Amy complains "She never wanted / Harry's relations or Harry's old friends; / She never wanted to fit herself to Harry, / But only to bring Harry down to her own level" (230). A recent biography of Vivienne takes its title from a line of Amy's, in which she terms Harry's wife "A restless shivering painted shadow" (230).

If Harry's dead wife represents Vivienne, than the patient Mary represents Emily Hale, the woman with whom Eliot had been in love before coming to England. Eliot had resumed a platonic relationship with her in 1931 when he was lecturing at Harvard, and Hale visited England every summer throughout the 1930's. Yet Eliot, like Harry, seemed to think that by having made a precipitous marriage as a young man he had irrevocably cut himself off from a future with Emily Hale. While she apparently understood herself to be informally engaged to Eliot, he never did resume a romantic relationship with her. Like Harry, Eliot embraced in the wake of his marriage a new life of religious discipline which he saw as shutting off the possibility of a second marriage. Although he would marry again sometime later, after Vivienne's death, it would not be to Emily Hale.

Finally, it is worth noting that Eliot, again like Harry, exiled himself from his large family when he left America in 1913. Eliot felt certain guilt about this, a guilt which centered particularly on his abandoning his mother. Harry's decision to leave Wishwood has profoundly affected his mother Amy, and his conversion at the play's end will kill her. Eliot's relationship to Charlotte Eliot was a similarly fraught one. Her 1921 visit to England, for example, led Eliot to a nervous breakdown. Note, too, that Eliot takes as the source of his play the Oresteian trilogy, three plays about a son who kills his mother.

In many respects, "The Family Reunion" sets the pattern for the remainder of Eliot's career. His two subsequent plays, "The Cocktail Party" and "The Confidential Clerk," find Eliot experimenting with his verse and moving toward a more conversational tone. The chorus and other features of the Greek tragedy do not appear in either. Yet the theme remains much the same: the mandates of a religious calling and the tension between the surface truths of the everyday world and the deeper truths of the spiritual life.

Matthew J. Bolton, Ph.D.

Works Cited

Ackroyd, Peter. "T. S. Eliot: A Life." New York: Simon & Schuster, 1984.

Eliot, T. S. "Selected Essays: 1917–1932." New York: Harcourt, Brace and Company, 1932.

_____. "Introduction to Shakespeare and the Popular Dramatic Tradition by S. L. Bethell." London: P.S. King and Staples, 1944.

_____. "The Complete Poems and Plays: 1909–1950." New York: Harcourt, Brace & World, 1962.

Seymour-Jones, Carol. "Painted Shadow: The Life of Vivienne Eliot." London: Constable, 2001.

Discussion Questions

1. What is the mode of Christianity that "The Family Reunion" seems to endorse? Does Christianity mean something different to Harry than to the various members of his family?

2. In this play, as in Eliot's famous poem "The Waste Land," the desert and the sea are both invoked as symbols. Trace the deployment of desert and sea imagery across the play.

3. "The Family Reunion" follows Harry's spiritual transformation. Do other characters undergo a similar, if less dramatic, transformation? Is Mary, for example, radically different at the end of the play than she was in the beginning?

4. One criticism that was frequently leveled against "The Family Reunion" when it was first staged, centered on the unspecified nature of Harry's religious mission. Is Harry's resolution to "follow the bright angels" specific enough to be satisfying? In your own mind, what will Harry's future hold for him?

5. Rank the characters in terms of their degree of spiritual enlightenment. You might want to make two lists: one for how they stand spiritually at the beginning of the play, and a second for how they stand by its conclusion.

6. Ivy, Violet, Gerard, and Charles might be considered "flat" characters: each is a type rather than a rounded person. What distinctions can you make among these uncles and aunts? Do they represent different sorts of spiritual blindness?

7. What is the effect of having the least aware of the play's characters—Ivy, Violet, Gerard, and Charles—double as the play's chorus? What is the relationship between their individual consciousness and the "collective consciousness" of the chorus? (8). Play detective and psychologist for a moment: what really happened on the cruise ship the night that Harry's wife drowned?

8. What is Dr. Warburton's role in the play? Is he a "flat" or "round" character? What ideas come into conflict during his interview with Harry?

9. Eliot insisted that the furies must be shown on stage, and vehemently disagreed with a director who suggested that the audience sense their presence from Harry's reactions. Are the furies a psychological projection on Harry's part, or do they have an independent existence? What conclusions can we draw from the fact that Agatha, too, can see the furies?

Essay Ideas

1. Read Aeschylus's play "The Eumenides." How does Eliot appropriate, subvert, or transform this source in "The Family Reunion"?

2. Although the chorus is a convention found in all ancient Greek tragedies, different tragedians used the chorus in different ways. How does Eliot use his chorus? What is its relationship to the play's characters? How does it advance or comment on the plot? For whom does the chorus speak?

3. During the second half of the 1930's, Eliot was writing not only "The Family Reunion," but also a series of poems that would become "Four Quartets." Read one or all of these three poems and contrast their language and themes with those of "The Family Reunion."

4. Locate several points in the play where characters make references to the theater or use the stage play as a metaphor. How do such references comment on the difference between artifice, artificiality, and reality? What do these theater metaphors and references suggest about Eliot's dramatic theory and practice?

5. How does "The Family Reunion" subvert genre by raising expectations that it will fail to deliver on, or which it will deliver on in a way that renders the expectation unrecognizable? Early on, for example, the play promises to be both a murder mystery and a romance. How does the evolving action of the play invoke and transform such genres?

6. Identify a passage which you find particularly moving, evocative, beautiful, or strange. Analyze it as you would a poem of comparable length.

7. Like so many of Eliot's poems, "The Family Reunion" is a meditation on the nature of time. Contrast the different attitude towards time that Amy, Agatha, Harry, and other characters hold. Pay particular attention to "the loop in time" to which Agatha refers: "When the loop in time comes—and it does not come for everybody— / The hidden is revealed, and the specters show themselves" (229).

Faust, Part One

by Johann Wolfgang von Goethe

Content Synopsis

"Faust, Part One" begins with a Dedication. The poet/dramatist addresses the shadows to which he is going to give substance through art, summoning them to him and asserting his trembling power as a creator over the natural world, from which he draws the content of his work.

Following the Dedication, the Prelude presents a conversation about the nature of dramatic art and the demands it places upon the theater—whether from the perspective of an audience wanting entertainment, of an artist wanting to compose a work with depth and a chance at immortality, of a director who must consider the imperatives of the box office, and of an actor who cares about shining on the stage.

The Prelude concludes with an overview of the landscape of the play about to begin as the director instructs the playwright to use all the resources of the stage to tell a grand story.

The Prologue takes the reader to Heaven. A chorus of angels sings God's praises and God and Mephistopheles wager over the fate of Faust's soul. God instructs the devil to tempt Faust away from his salvation by offering him the powers of Hell, thus giving Faust the opportunity to achieve his salvation by freeing himself from the diabolical snares set for him.

Faust is troubled: Despite his learning, life has no meaning, joy, or savor for him. Attempting necromancy, he conjures an earth spirit. The spirit chides Faust, telling him that he has become a terrified and empty man, only a worm, not a living version of the godlike and creative force he might be.

Faust turns the scorn he has for himself on scholars in general, particularly on his unimaginative student Wagner, who confines himself to dry and laborious study. Wagner cannot tap the spirit of knowledge that Faust believes to be indwelling in the human breast, the spirit he is seeking in himself to liberate.

Easter Sunday, Faust and Wagner go out walking among the townsfolk celebrating the holiday, and Faust speaks of the glories of spring, of the risen Savior, and of how the display of civic peace around them and the contented humanity they see constitute the "true heaven." Nevertheless, Faust also tells Wagner, two souls inhabit his breast: one, content with earthly pleasures; another that longs to soar above the terrestrial sphere. Faust notices a little black dog making wide circles around them, and senses that it is some kind of spirit.

The dog is, in fact, the devil. He follows Faust home and growls as Faust pores over the Bible. As Faust finds nothing in the Bible to satisfy his longing and when he begins again to conjure, the dog metamorphoses into Mephistopheles, the devil, taking the guise of a wandering scholar. Faust recognizes the devil, the great power of negation, and tells him to leave, but the devil stays and offers to show Faust his power. Faust falls asleep, and the devil vanishes. Faust wakes wondering if he has only dreamed or if he really has the power to summon spirits to his aid.

The devil returns dressed like a young nobleman and invites Faust to "experience Life" with him. Faust complains his life is frustrating and full of pain and that he would prefer death. He curses all the temptations towards pleasure that simply ensnare and betray desire, although he admits he desires to experience sexual love. Mephistopheles advises Faust to enjoy himself. He offers himself as Faust's slave on condition that Faust become his after death. Faust is cavalier about the afterlife but doubts what joys the devil can give him. The devil assures him nothing is out of his reach. Faust agrees, with the caveat that he will belong to the devil only "When, to the Moment I say: 'Ah, stay a while! You are so lovely!'" (1700). Faust signs his bargain with the devil in blood.

Borne aloft on the devil's cloak, from on high, Faust sees friends drinking, carousing, and teasing each other about their sexual conquests and failures in Auerbach's wine cellar, and then, with the devil, he enters the tavern and joins the merry-making. Mephistopheles complains how bad the wine is and bores holes in the table from which wines flow and then turn into flames. When the astounded company attacks him for evil magic, the devil puts a spell on them. They see themselves in enchanted lands, and then brawl with each other. Mephistopheles vanishes with Faust, and the patrons are left in amazement.

Mephistopheles brings Faust to a witch's kitchen. After drinking a flaming brew, Faust's ennui is replaced by lust.

Faust first sees Gretchen when she is out for a walk. He takes her arm but she frees herself and flees, but she remembers him and longs to see him again. He orders Mephistopheles to win the girl for him, but the devil is unsure he can because of her innocence and purity. Faust threatens to break off the bargain and the devil capitulates.

Faust and the devil appear in Gretchen's room just after she has gone out. The devil leaves a box full of jewels to tempt her. She finds them, tries them on, and is enraptured by her own appearance. To the devil's chagrin, when Gretchen's mother sees the jewels, she senses something unholy and gives them to the church. Nevertheless, Gretchen continues to think of the jewels and of her unknown admirer.

When Gretchen receives a new casket of jewels, excited and mystified, she shows them to her neighbor, Martha. She hides the jewels from her mother and looks at herself in the mirror wearing them when she visits Martha.

Mephistopheles arranges through a ruse for Gretchen to meet Faust in Martha's garden. With proclamations of transcendental love, Faust wins Gretchen. He tries to sublimate his desire into romantic nature worship. Mephistopheles, however, goads him on and Faust succumbs to lust, and Gretchen yields believing his holy vows of fidelity although she tells him she feels stifled by his friend (whom she does not know is the devil, but senses "that there's no spirit of love" in him). Faust gives her a vial filled with a sleeping potion to give to her mother so that they may meet in her room. Faust believes, and assures Gretchen, that the potion is harmless. It is not. By administering it, although without murderous intention, Gretchen becomes guilty of the death of her mother.

News of Gretchen's dishonor spreads, and her brother, Valentine, challenges Faust to a duel, but with the devil empowering him, Faust kills Valentine, who berates Gretchen to her face as a whore as he dies. Gretchen, fallen, overcome by guilt and remorse, painfully feels the loss of her innocence and purity.

Mephistopheles leads Faust away from the visible world of lust and desire and takes him to the hidden world where the powers that command and control the visible world gather. They join the witches' celebration, Walpurgisnacht, and Faust sees the forces that are hidden to mankind. Faust also sees the phantom of his Gretchen with her throat slit. However, this vision is obscured by a phantasmal spectacle: a pageant of spirits and ideas that appear, present themselves, and recede into oblivion.

Once they have all vanished, Faust awakens to the realization that as his sensorium was being overloaded with supernatural visions, Gretchen, in torment, was being taken to prison for poisoning her mother and drowning her baby. Faust insists that Mephistopheles help him to save her. The devil agrees and, after befogging her jailers' senses, brings Faust to Gretchen's prison. Although she recognizes him and loves him, Gretchen refuses to flee with him: she senses the devil's presence in him. She dies in prison, a voice from above declaring her eternal salvation. She calls out to Faust, exhorting him to follow her in death and leave his life of damnation. He does not but flees with the devil to more life.

Symbols & Motifs

The subversive power of longing and of desire and the limitations of mankind's power to accomplish its desires and to satisfy its longings serve as the central motifs of "Faust." Faust is a discontented scholar, a man who has studied nature using reason and science but has been unable to find something that makes him care to be alive. What he has overlooked is the root cause of his study, his own desire not for knowledge of the world but for control of the world by means of his knowledge. The devil appears in the play as the symbol of self-centered and unconstrained desire when it is empowered and allowed to rule. The devil does not give Faust the power to know but the power to control. The devil's intelligence is in knowing how to subvert mankind by tempting them to follow appetites that subvert their goodness and purity. These are the things that fall away when the purity of reason or temperance is disturbed.

Faust's desire for Gretchen is a desire to control her desire. The power to dominate and determine not only the actions but also the feelings of others and to control them is equated in the play with lust. Gretchen, a type of the fallen woman, is made to symbolize nature itself. By using the case of Gretchen, the play argues that when mankind controls nature, mankind corrupts nature, just as Faust corrupts Gretchen by turning her head with the devil's gifts away from her own modesty.

The devil's ability to subvert is set against the motif of innocence, which is symbolized and personified by childhood, the time believed to come before the onset of sexual desire. Gretchen's little sister, who died in childhood represents the purity of childhood and the power of that purity, demonstrated by how Gretchen cared for her sister.

The witches and their ceremonies symbolize our dark desires and riotous binges. Gretchen at her spinning wheel represents the way we weave our own fate when we succumb to our own unbridled desires, and when we lose control of our desires, our appetites, and ourselves.

Historical Context

Goethe worked on the first part of "Faust" during the last decades of the eighteenth century and first published it in 1808. It was a time of enormous social upheaval, and the revolutionary time caused revolutionary changes in the consciousness of mankind as a whole and in that of the writers and musicians of the time, and in the form and content of their work.

In the American colonies, the causes of individual liberty and representative government, of government constitutionally grounded on reason and common sense rather than on compelled obedience to traditional power, were at the root of the rebellion against England. In France, Jean Jacques Rousseau's philosophical writings of regarding the rights of individuals to live in accord with the freedom into which they had been born and nurtured by an education designed to nurture the person and the citizen rather than to chain up the subject, provided a foundation for the ideas that led to the French Revolution of 1789.

In Germany, an artistic movement that emphasized the liberation of emotion, called "Sturm und Drang," Storm and Stress, took hold in the 1770s, represented in great measure by Goethe's novel, "The Sorrows of Young Werther," and exerted its power at least until the end of the century. The turbulence of Beethoven's symphonies represented the explosion of the human spirit. The explosion of the human spirit not only resulted in the vision of human liberty, as portrayed in Beethoven's opera, "Fidelio," but in savage individualism, as in Napoleon's seizure of power, an act that made Beethoven tear up the dedication to Napoleon that he had originally attached to his heroic Third Symphony. Mankind had diabolical as well as divine energies.

In "Faust," Goethe composed a complex drama of the conflict between the diabolic and the divine, between the explosive desire for emotional liberty and for mystical commerce with nature. "Faust" told of a force that was moving the English Romantic poets like Blake, Wordsworth, Coleridge, Keats, and Shelley, and the brutal and diabolical self-aggrandizement and grabbing for grandeur that warlords like Napoleon represented.

Societal Context

"Faust" is set in a world of traditional conventions and well-defined roles and expectations. Faust's early relationship with Gretchen reflects conventional gender roles. Men are active; women are passive. Young men may experience, although they are expected to control, their lust. Young woman are thought not even to recognize that there is a sexual component to their nature, and when they do, it is because it has been awakened by a man.

Faust is a man of rank, a scholar-teacher, a man who can exercise influence on the formation of young men. He is shown with Wagner, an advanced student and Goethe includes an encounter between a young man seeking a teacher who converses with Mephistopheles, thinking he is Faust, about learning. The students are males. Education was not available to young women.

Despite the class ranking, the scene in the tavern shows that men of lower rank were not particularly intimidated by gentleman. Nor is Gretchen's brother the soldier when he challenges Faust in defense of his sister's honor.

Religious Context

Although many of the devices of religion are present in "Faust," the work is a psychological rather than a theological drama. The devil is a principal character, but he represents the force of unleashed psychological energy rather than the external marplot of "Genesis." There is a Prologue in Heaven in which God and Angels are presented. There are choruses of blessed and damned spirits. The very action of the drama centers on a man's eternal soul and its eternal salvation or damnation.

Nevertheless, Faust is not really concerned with theology or religion but with human ambition, human passion, human psychology, and with anatomizing them and the forces and conditions by which they are generated and the effects they have. The play is not about how Man copes with God or exists in relation to God but how Man copes with being himself, with being in relation to other people and to nature: how Man exists given the circumstances of being Man.

Scientific & Technological Context

Magic is the primary technology of "Faust, Part One." Learned as he is, Faust's knowledge leads him to the mystical science of conjuring spirits. The power that can be derived through the technological application of scientific knowledge, the power achieve by designing mechanisms and machinery for negotiating the limitations of the world, is not the kind of power that Faust seeks. He pursues the supernatural, and, consequently, the devil is the purveyor of the technology Faust uses to achieve his desires. Unlike Leonardo, for example, Faust has no interest in a flying machine. He has the devil's cloak to transport him through the airways above the earth. The devil is a vintner, too, who can make wine flow from bung holes in a table. In the second part of Faust, Goethe will explore Man as a re-fashioner of the earth by means of scientific knowledge and the application of the technologies it can generate. But in the first part, science gives way to magic and the complexity of work to the vicissitudes of wishes.

Biographical Context

Goethe was a man who stood at the center of the world when he lived. He represented the apotheosis not only of German literature but of German thought and German culture. A century after his death, when the German temperament had become marked with and defiled by the invidious brand of the Third Reich, Goethe remained as a reminder of its humane possibility. During his lifetime and throughout the nineteenth century, his influence extended to philosophy, science, psychology, and statecraft. His work is an encyclopedia of wisdom, and his verse has served as the text for innumerable "Lieder," songs, by the greatest of the great German composers from Franz Schubert at the end of the eighteenth century, through Johannes Brahms, to Gustav Mahler during the first decade of the twentieth. In his poetry, novels, drama, and non-fiction writings he explored the vicissitudes of the romantic temperament and the discipline of the classical ideal. "The Sorrows of Young Werther" (1774) permeated European consciousness, drove young men to suicide in imitation of its lovesick

hero, and was treasured by Napoleon. In "Faust," he explores the workings of consciousness and the power of the unconscious. In all his work, Goethe contemplated the conflict between the longings of the spirit and the constraints of civilization.

Goethe was born in Frankfurt, Germany, on August 28, 1749. His parents were scions of the nobility and of the governing classes. Goethe was richly educated by private teachers, and learned Latin, Greek, French, and English as well as German. He was also taught to exercise the graces of the body as well as of the mind by lessons in horseback riding, fencing, and dancing. His interests were broad and they remained so throughout his life as indicated by his scientific analysis of color, his study of species, and his serving as chief counselor to Carl August, the Grand Duke of Weimar, where Goethe lived most of his life.

Goethe and Christiane Vulpius lived together as man and wife from 1788 until her death in 1816. In 1806, after surviving an attack by French soldiers occupying their house in Weimar, she consented to marry Goethe. They had one child, Karl August von Goethe, who died two years before his father. His wife, Ottilie von Pogwisch, took care of Goethe in his old age.

Goethe's other significant relationship involved an apparently platonic passion he shared with Charlotte von Stein, beginning in 1774, which Goethe broke off without explanation twelve years later. Goethe died on March 22, 1832 in Weimar.

Neil Heims, Ph.D.

Work Cited

Goethe, Johann Wolfgang von. Faust, Part One. Trans. A.S. Kline. "Poetry in Translation." A.S. Kline. Web. 25 May 2010. <http://tkline.pgcc.net/PITBR/German/Fausthome.htm>.

Discussion Questions

1. Discuss the purpose of the three introductory scenes in "Faust, Part One." Are they necessary? In what way, if so? If not, what are they there for? Do they enrich the play or do they detract from it? Explain how.
2. Is Faust a villain or a hero?
3. Although the devil is commonly known as "the father of lies," show how you can argue that, in "Faust, Part One," Mephistopheles is a continuing source of truth.
4. Considering some of the major themes of the play, discuss how relevant "Faust" is to your own life and to the contemporary world.
5. Discuss the conflict between what is actually possible and what can be wished for and how that conflict can be resolved.
6. Is "Faust" an immoral play?
7. How responsible is Gretchen for her "fall?"

8. Is there something incongruous in the play considering that its main action—after the opening scenes that show Faust in search of ultimate knowledge and power through the command of arcane knowledge—is a tawdry seduction by an older, apparently respectable and cloistered scholar of a young and, until he meets, her sexually virtuous maiden?
9. Describe the relationship that Faust has with the devil. Rather than an amiable partnership or collaboration, it seems to be full of tension and hostility. What constitutes the tension and what seems to be at the root of Faust's discontent since the devil does whatever Faust requires of him?
10. Discuss the extent and the significance of the role that animals play in "Faust."

Essay Ideas

1. Analyze Faust. What kind of person is he? What bothers him at the beginning of the play? What, if anything, has he learned at the end of the play? Has he changed? Is he admirable or contemptible?
2. Describe Gretchen. Is she a drawn with depth or is she introduced as a dramatic device for the presentation and exploration of Faust's character?

3. Discuss the devil as a character? How does Goethe portray him? What are his characteristics? How do you account for them?
4. In what way can "Faust, Part One" be considered an encyclopedia?
5. What is the role of comedy in "Faust, Part One"?

The Frozen Deep

by Wilkie Collins

Content Synopsis

"The Frozen Deep" began as a play meant for amateur production at Charles Dickens's Tavistock House. In its novel form, first published in 1874, it retains some of its theatrical aspects: short, dialogue-driven scenes involving a small number of characters, a rapidly paced plot, and sparse descriptive details. The novel opens on the eve of a two-vessel Arctic expedition around 1845 ("between twenty and thirty years ago," says the narrator) at a ball given in celebration of the upcoming voyage (3). Mrs. Lucy Crayford, one of the novel's five principal characters, is dancing with Captain Helding, who questions her about the other female lead, Clara Burnham. Over the course of the conversation, we learn that Clara is an orphan living under the Crayford's care. She is of delicate health, partly owing to some secret that has been oppressing her, and partly owing to her unusual education in the Scottish Highlands. There, Mrs. Crayford informs the captain that Clara's head was filled with all sorts of superstitious notions, chief among them the belief that she possesses the "Second Sight"—the ability to see into the future. Captain Helding is shocked by this revelation, particularly, as he says, "in these enlightened times" (5). He urges Mrs. Crayford to help her friend by becoming Clara's confidante and allowing her to unburden herself.

Mrs. Crayford takes the captain's advice and encourages Clara (who has just reacted with barely suppressed agitation to the news that a ship from Africa is due soon) to discuss the secret that is troubling her. During Mrs. Crayford's discussion with Clara, we learn of Clara's history prior to her father's death. While she was living with her invalid father in Kent, a gentleman named Richard Wardour met and fell in love with her. By Clara's account, Wardour was too bold while she was too passive, and Wardour left for Africa presuming he and Clara were engaged. Clara, who had been unable to disillusion him in person, sent him a letter explaining his erroneous belief and her intention not to marry him. Mrs. Crayford asks Clara why she is still troubled, to which Clara replies, "What I wrote required an answer, Lucy-asked for an answer. The answer has never come. What is the plain conclusion? My letter never reached him" (14).

To complicate matters further, Clara has fallen in love with young Frank Aldersley, and though Mrs. Crayford warns Clara not to engage herself to him until she has definitively broken things off with Richard Wardour, Clara cannot help but admit her love when Frank confronts her. Clara immediately realizes her error, but we are told, "It is Clara who says, 'Oh! What have I done?' —as usual, when it is too late" (18). Between Clara's inability to assert herself with Wardour and her similar inability to withhold her affection from Frank, the issue of whether Clara's weakness is to blame for subsequent events is raised. Clara, who embodies the feminine passivity idealized during the Victorian period, may represent Collins's subtle critique of this gender role.

Richard Wardour turns up in the very next scene-his ship has arrived and he has come straight to the ball-and he is ready to marry Clara as he promised before he left. She informs him of his mistake, but when questioned about whether she has engaged herself to another, Clara equivocates. Wardour believes himself betrayed and leaves Clara with an ominous warning: "the man who has robbed me of you shall rue the day when you and he first met" (23).

Clara is filled with foreboding and she convinces Mrs. Crayford to go with her to see the ships off the next day. Frank, it turns out, has safely made it aboard, but the two women also discover that a new recruit has been added to the roster-none other than Richard Wardour. He and Frank are traveling to the Arctic on separate ships; however, Clara is still convinced a deadly meeting will take place between them.

The story here moves forward two years and relocates the narrative focus to the Arctic Expedition. The expedition is a complete failure: the ships have become locked in the ice, many of the men are ill, and slowly, all of the men are starving. The dark mood of the scene is only slightly alleviated by his introduction of John Want, a member of the expedition whose constant grumblings during his preparation of "bone soup" provide some comic relief. It is decided that a group of the men will form an exploring party in search of aid while the others stay to care for those too weak or ill for traveling. Frank asks to be one of the party, but is told by Crayford that the men will throw dice for spots. "Chance shall decide among us who goes with the expedition and who stays behind in the huts" (37). The conversation next turns to Wardour, whom Frank calls the "Bear of the Expedition" because of his surliness. The conversation makes clear that

although Frank has no liking for Wardour, the two men have yet to discover the woman they have in common.

The men all gather together to cast dice—a roll over six to go, under six to stay—and significantly, Wardour throws a six. The scene is the first in the novel where we see fate and chance so obviously collide. If Wardour is fated to confront Frank, as Clara believes, it will not matter what he rolls. Indeed, the indecisive cast of the die may be chance's way of bowing out of the situation altogether. Ultimately, Wardour ends up with a two (cast by Frank at his request), while Frank rolls an eight for himself. It seems as if the two men will be separated.

Wardour professes that he does not care whether he stays or goes, and Crayford questions him about his lack of spirit. In a scene that mirrors Clara's confession to Mrs. Crayford, Wardour relates his history with Clara (although without mentioning her name), and his desire for revenge upon the unknown man who stole her heart. Like Clara with her ominous premonition, Wardour is convinced that he shall one day meet this man: "it is no matter whether I stay here with the sick, or go hence with the strong. I shall live till I have met that man! There is a day of reckoning appointed between us" (47). Wardour's belief in fate has left him a passive participant in his own life. Crayford voices his disappointment with his friend's vengeful mindset, but offers to let Wardour chop up Frank's berth (for firewood) as a way to help Wardour get his mind off his troubles.

By this point in the novel, the reader has most likely noticed the appropriateness of Wardour's name. He has a war-like spirit, he will later be at war with himself, and he has more than his fair share of Wardour, particularly for Clara's tastes. While Wardour is chopping up Frank's berth, we learn that this young man, too, is aptly named. His open, earnest love for Clara prompted him to carve their initials in one of the wooden beams of his berth, thus proving Frank far too frank for his own good. Wardour, seeing the initials, immediately suspects that he has discovered in Frank Aldersley the enemy he has sworn vengeance on. He confirms Frank's connection to Clara in a subsequent conversation with Frank and Crayford. Crayford also catches on that the girl Wardour loved is none other than Clara. Before Crayford has a chance to reflect on this, Captain Helding enters the cabin to inform them that a member of the exploring party has been injured and that Wardour is needed to fill his place. Thus, whether by fate or chance, Frank and Wardour will be thrown together after all.

This turn of events fills Crayford with dread and he tries to convince first Wardour and then Frank to forego the exploring party. Neither complies. Crayford is torn—he does not feel it is proper to say something to Frank about Wardour since Wardour has not actually committed any crime. However, he is worried about Frank's safety. In the end, he compromises, begging Frank "While you can stand, keep with the main body" (61).

Unfortunately, the very next scene finds Wardour and Frank alone-"alone on the Frozen Deep!" the narrator proclaim-and while a weakened Frank sleeps, Wardour struggles within himself, tempted to leave Frank to certain death and have his revenge (62). The scene cuts away before Wardour makes his decision, and the reader is returned to England where Clara and Mrs. Crayford patiently await news of the men in the Arctic. Clara slips into a trance and Mrs. Crayford watches in alarm as she cries out the same warning Crayford had given to Frank. Clara has a vision of Frank asleep and at Wardour's mercy—as we know he is from the previous scene. Clara comes out of her trance fatigued and weak, and Mrs. Crayford is left to wonder if Clara really does have the Second Sight.

The next day, news arrives that a whaling vessel has come across survivors of the Arctic expedition. Crayford's name is on the list of survivors while Frank and Wardour are listed as "Dead or Missing." Clara sees this as confirmation that her vision was correct, while Mrs. Crayford argues that it is unchristian to give up hope. A doctor is called to treat the rapidly failing Clara, and he advises both women to journey out to meet the survivors and discover whether Frank and Wardour are really dead.

The two women sail for Newfoundland aboard, appropriately enough, the Amazon. The Crayfords are reunited, but there is still no news of Frank or Wardour. In fact, Crayford will give Clara none of the circumstances surrounding their disappearance. His wife has urged him to keep quiet on the subject because "she will accept it as positive confirmation of the faith, the miserable superstitious faith that is in her" (86). Clara, frustrated at Crayford's guarded answers to her questions, decides to interview one of his men, Steventon, and thus learns of the events that led to the two men's disappearance. Frank, it seems, fell ill after the exploring party set out, and Wardour volunteered to remain with him while the rest went on. That was the last time they were seen.

Clara has another premonition that something "dreadful" is coming nearer, and Crayford takes her into the garden for some air. The moment after they leave, a "sinister and terrible" looking man appears at the door, begging for food. He is given some which he divides into two portions, one of which he stows in his satchel. Steventon and Mrs. Crayford question him and learn that he has been shipwrecked on the Newfoundland shore. He refuses to tell them why he saves half his food, but raves wildly about the young woman he is searching for.

At that moment, Crayford returns from the garden and immediately recognizes Wardour. He seizes his former friend and demands to know what has become of Frank. Hearing the two men's names, Clara also enters the cabin and Wardour, seeing her, rushes back onto the beach. He returns carrying Frank in his arms. The very weak Frank and Clara are reunited, while Wardour, his strength now used up, collapses in Crayford's arms, and relates the tale of his redemption. Clara, Frank, and Crayford gather around him as he says his final goodbyes, and with Wardour's death, the novel ends.

Historical Context

In 1856, Charles Dickens wrote from Paris to the sub-editor at his Household Words magazine, "Collins and I have a mighty original notion (mine in the beginning) for another Play at Tavistock House" (Ackroyd, 761). Dickens was referring to the theatrical version of "The Frozen Deep," which Collins wrote expressly for Dickens's annual "Twelfth Night" production. Both the play (which directly references it) and the subsequent novel are based on Sir John Franklin's ill-fated search for the Northwest Passage. Franklin, a popular public figure, had led two previous expeditions to the northern regions, but his 1845 voyage, consisting of two ships and over a hundred men, was to be his greatest undertaking. Search parties were sent after the expedition beginning in 1848, when the food supply would have run out, but it was not until Dr. John Rae's 1854 report that anything conclusive was known about Franklin and his men. Basing his report on interviews with Inuits in possession of artifacts from the expedition, Rae concluded that Franklin and his crew resorted to cannibalism, a charge that was hotly debated in the media. Dickens was one of Franklin's staunchest defenders, printing numerous articles in "Household Words" on the subject. Characteristic of the controversy, "an editorial writer [for the Times] argued that if Eskimos could live through 'starving times,' it would be 'strange indeed that the white men should not have been able to accomplish the same feat'" (Brannen 14). The implicit racism points to the larger issue in the debate—England's imperial ideology. Instead of spreading civilization's softening influence, if Franklin and his men had turned

to cannibalism, they had become more savage that the native "savages." Lillian Naydor writes, "Because cannibalism was associated with the most primitive of cultures, Rae's allegations called into question the moral justification of Empire; it blurred the boundary between the savage and the civilized" (2).

Any reading of "The Frozen Deep" must consider this controversy. The complete order among the men of the Sea-Mew and the Wanderer directly refutes the vision of chaos painted by Rae. The lengthy preparation of the "bone soup" would have called to the Victorian reader's mind Franklin and the charges brought against him and his men.

Societal Context

"The Frozen Deep" presents us with a typical view of Victorian society. The men in the novel go off on adventures while the women wait patiently at home. This separation of the sexes was idealized during the period (and by Wardour in his "No women!" proclamation). Women were thought to belong in the domestic sphere while men dominated the public sphere. When Clara and Mrs. Crayford step outside their domestic roles, Collins ironizes the situation, having them sail aboard the Amazon as if their boldness puts them on a par with the fabled warrior women.

While it is not given much explicit attention, the novel is set against the backdrop of British imperialism—thus the mention of ships going to and from Africa, and the purpose of the Arctic expedition: to find the Northwest Passage, thought to be a potentially important trade route. Clara's dread of the returning African vessel and the failure of the Arctic expedition may be a subtle critique of the imperialist enterprise, against which Collins takes a stronger stance in "The Moonstone."

Religious Context

Collins' novel is both about a physical journey to the ends of the earth and about Richard Wardour's spiritual journey to the brink of temptation and back. In her essay on religion in "The Frozen Deep," Carolyn Oulton writes, "For Collins, the influence of religion is felt through a personal response to temptation" (158). In sending his hero to "the frozen deep" with his greatest temptation, the helpless, unconscious Frank Aldersley, Collins shows us a man stripped of all civilizing influences, with only his moral sense to guide him. Wardour's triumph over the fate both he and Clara believe in demonstrates the power of both faith and human agency.

Scientific & Technological Context

Early in "The Frozen Deep," Captain Helding refers to the novel's mid-Victorian setting as "these enlightened times," a characterization which is called into question almost immediately. It is true that this was the period when railroads first criss-crossed the country, photography was invented, and major discoveries in geology and medicine began to shape our modern-day view of the world. It was also, as Mrs. Crayford says, a time when many "believe[d] in dancing tables and in messages sent from the other world by spirits who can't spell" (5). Pseudo-sciences such as phrenology (the science of determining characteristics of personality based on the shape of the head) and physiognomy (the science of determining personality based on facial features), along with the spirit-rapping to which Mrs. Crayford refers, were held up alongside legitimate science, and it was a long time before the chaff was separated from the grain. Furthermore, scientific discoveries such as the extinction of species seemed too many to be a threat to firmly held religious beliefs and the teachings of the Bible.

Collins seems skeptical of scientific pursuits throughout the novel. The doctor who treats Clara refers to her as his "interesting patient"—a specimen of sorts—and in his strict adherence to scientific knowledge, he is entirely dismissive of

Clara's prophetic visions. Additionally, as Lillian Nayder notes, "Victorians conceived of Arctic exploration as a scientific rather than an economic undertaking" (2). In both repeating through fiction the historical failure of the expedition and in foregrounding Wardour's spiritual journey rather than his physical one, Collins leaves space in his novel for both the truths of science and the truths of spirituality to exist.

Biographical Context

Wilkie Collins (1824–1889) began his literary career with the publication of his father, the painter William Collins's biography, a work William had requested of his son shortly before his death in 1847. At the time of the biography's publication, Collins was unsure of what career path to follow. He enjoyed writing, and had already written one novel that failed to interest publishers, but he was also contemplating painting, the profession of his father and younger brother. At the same time, Collins was studying law at Lincoln's Inn, and in 1851, he became a barrister. Literature won out however, and after the 1850 publication of "Antonina," Collins dedicated himself to his literary career. His creative output marked him as one of the most prolific writers of the period. In less than forty years, he wrote twenty-three novels, fifteen plays, over fifty short stories, and more than one hundred nonfiction pieces. As Paul Lewis notes, scholars are still identifying all of his work. Chief among his novels are "The Woman in White" and "The Moonstone," works which solidified Collins's reputation as one of the founders of the detective fiction genre.

Collins owed some of his success to the encouragement and influence of his close friend, Charles Dickens. Dickens contributed ideas to the theatrical version of "The Frozen Deep," and in the Tavistock House production of the play, Dickens filled the role of Richard Wardour while Collins played Frank Aldersley. The production was a huge success, and in July of 1856, Collins and Dickens reprised their roles in a performance for Queen Victoria.

Although Collins never married, he had two long-term relationships, one with Caroline Graves (thought to be one of the sources for "The Woman in White"), and the other with Martha Rudd, with whom he had three children. Poor health due to gout and a dependency on opium led to Collins's death in September of 1889.

Jen Cadwallader

Works Cited

Ackroyd, Peter. Dickens. New York: Harper Collins, 1990.

Brannan, Robert Louis, ed. *Under the Management of Mr. Charles Dickens: His Production of "The Frozen Deep."* Ithaca: Cornell UP, 1966.

Collins, Wilkie. "The Frozen Deep". London: Hesperus, 2004.

Lewis, Paul. The Wilkie Collins Pages. 18 April 2006. http://www.wilkiecollins.com.

Oulton, Carolyn. "A Vindication of Religion: Wilkie Collins, Charles Dickens, and "The Frozen Deep." *Dickensian* 97(2): 154–158, 2001.

Naydor, Lillian. "The Cannibal, The Nurse, and The Cook in Dickens's The Frozen Deep." *Victorian Literature and Culture* 19: 1–24, 1991.

Robinson, Kenneth. *Wilkie Collins, A Biography.* New York: MacMillan, 1952.

Discussion Questions

1. The narrative of "The Frozen Deep" shifts in and out of present tense. Is there any significance to Collins's use of the present tense? How does it affect your reading of the novel?

2. We learn of Clara first through Mrs. Crayford's opinion of her. How does this color your perception of Clara? Do you ever disagree with Mrs. Crayford's assessment of her friend?

3. Collins employs heavy foreshadowing through Wardour's threat and Clara's premonition. Is this foreshadowing ever ironic? How does it relate to the theme of fate versus chance that is so pervasive in the text?

4. Do you believe that Clara has the Second Sight, or do you agree with Mrs. Crayford's notion that her reading material has influenced Clara?

5. Analyze John Want's character. Why does he have a prominent role in some scenes of the novel?

6. Wardour proclaims that he likes the Arctic "because there are no women here" (40). What is the significance of the separation of the sexes in the novel?

7. Compare Wardour's account of his relationship with Clara to her account of it. Are there any significant differences? If so, what do these differences reveal about the two characters?

8. Is Crayford wrong not to warn Frank about Wardour's possible intentions toward him?

9. Has Wardour redeemed himself by the end of the novel?

10. What is the significance of Wardour's death?

Essay Ideas

1. Clara says, "[Wardour and Frank] will meet—there will be a mortal quarrel between them—and I shall be to blame" (24). Is she to blame for the conflict between the two men? Support or refute her claim using evidence from the text.

2. Analyze the way in which this novel complicates traditional notions of the literary hero.

3. Analyze the role of friendship in the novel.

4. Analyze the interplay of fate, chance, and free agency in the novel.

5. Analyze the symbolism of the Arctic in the novel.

Music sheet cover for the play "She Stoops to Conquer." Written by Oliver Goldsmith, the play is featured on page 165. Photo: Library of Congress, Prints & Photographs Division, LC-USZ62-2308

The Glass Menagerie

by Tennessee Williams

Content Synopsis

Tennessee Williams' semi-autobiographical play "The Glass Menagerie" features the Wingfields, a family living on the edge of poverty in late 1930s St Louis. Amanda, the mother, is a small vivacious woman who clings to rosy memories of her past as a Southern Belle. Laura, her daughter, who is in her early twenties, is slightly crippled and almost pathologically shy. Tom, her son, described as "a poet with a job in a warehouse" (Williams ix), is also the narrator of the play. There is also Jim O'Connor, a friend and co-worker of Tom's, who appears in the final two acts.

The play opens with Tom, as narrator, directly addressing the audience. He explains that the play is based on his recollection of his earlier family life, and that it is therefore a memory play and not realistic. He also sketches in the social and political background of the play: the Depression in America and the brutalities of the Spanish Civil War in Europe. He briefly introduces all the characters, including one who appears only as a photograph: his father, who had deserted the family long since.

Scene I

The family is having supper in their apartment. Conversation is dominated by Amanda, who first irks Tom by nagging at him to eat in a refined manner, and then falls to recalling her genteel girlhood in the South and her apparently endless list of suitors at that time. She blithely remarks that Laura should also stay 'fresh and pretty' (Williams 5) for gentleman callers, willfully ignoring the fact that Laura neither expects nor desires any. Laura observes, regretfully, that her mother is afraid of her turning into an old maid.

Scene II

Laura is alone, polishing a small collection of glass figurines that she treasures. On hearing her mother come in, she starts guiltily, puts the collection away and pretends to be absorbed in studying a typewriter chart. Amanda appears shell-shocked by something, increasing Laura's nervousness. Amanda—who clearly is given to theatrical gestures—slowly builds up to the revelation that she has found out Laura's 'deception' (Williams 9): Laura has long since dropped out of the secretarial course her mother had enrolled her for, and has gone on pretending that she was still attending. Laura explains that the classes made her so nervous that she was physically sick and felt she could not go back and so has spent her days walking and going to such places as the zoo. Amanda, understandably, is chagrined by Laura's evident inability to forge some sort of career and asks despairingly, "What is there left but dependency all our lives?" (Williams 12). She points out that some girls marry, at which Laura unexpectedly reveals that she did have a crush on a boy once, in high school. Amanda, with rising optimism, declares that Laura will make a good marriage in the end, but Laura is more dubious.

Scene III

Tom, as narrator, explains that after the business college debacle, Amanda has become more determined than ever to find a suitable gentleman caller for Laura. To this end, she begins a telephone subscription campaign in order to make extra money, but we are shown one less-than successful instance of this, when a prospective client abruptly hangs up the phone. In the next part of the scene, Amanda and Tom are engaged in a violent quarrel while Laura looks on desperately. Amanda berates Tom for drinking, staying out late at night, and reading immoral books like those of D. H. Lawrence, while Tom reveals the extent of his frustration with his constricted home life and dreary low-paid job. He is about to leave, when Amanda once more asks where he is going. Irritated beyond measure, he responds with a catalogue of lurid and imaginary adventures and finishes by labeling his mother as a witch. Amanda is stunned into silence by this prodigious insult. As Tom barges out, he accidentally knocks over and shatters one of Laura's glass pieces. Laura cries out in dismay. Amanda storms out while Tom contritely gathers up the broken glass.

Scene IV

Having left the apartment after the quarrel, Tom returns in the early hours. He has been drinking. Laura is waiting up for him. Tom explains he spent the night at the cinema which also featured a stage show with a magician. He gives Laura a magic scarf and opines that the best trick of the night was when the magician got himself out of a nailed-down coffin without removing a single nail. He observes that "that is a trick that would come in handy for me: get me out of this two-by-four situation!" (Williams 21). Laura implores him to make up his quarrel with Amanda. Later on at breakfast-time, Laura leaves to do some shopping;

she slips and falls on the way out, prompting both her mother and brother to come to her aid; however she is not hurt. Left together, Amanda and Tom maintain a frosty silence for a time, but eventually Tom apologizes over his behavior the night before. Amanda becomes tearful, saying that she only wants the best for her children. Tom gently acknowledges this, but before long, both revert to their usual attitudes when she again begins interrogating him about where he goes at night. She is unable to accept his simple explanation that he goes to the cinema in order to find the adventure that is lacking in his everyday life. However, she does not want another confrontation with him; instead, she wants to talk to him about Laura. She confides to him her fears for Laura's future and asks him to arrange a date for Laura by bringing home some nice young gentleman from the warehouse. When she finally extracts a promise from him that he will do so, she goes back to vigorously conducting her telephone subscription campaign.

Scene V

It is early evening; the family has just finished supper. Amanda as usual, is going on at Tom to improve his ways; she wants him to smarten up his appearance and also to stop smoking. Tom nevertheless goes on smoking, stepping out onto the fire-escape to do so. Here, he pauses to address the audience, commenting on the nearby dance-hall where couples dance against an ominous background of the build-up to war. Amanda then comes to join him. He has a surprise for her; they are going to have a gentleman caller as he has actually invited Jim O'Connor, one of his work colleagues, over to dinner the next day. She is instantly thrilled and fervently starts planning for the visit. She also questions Tom thoroughly as to Jim's character and prospects. Tom warns her not to expect too much of Laura, as Laura is 'terribly shy' and indeed 'peculiar' (Williams 36). He then goes out to the movies, leaving Amanda momentarily disconcerted. However she soon brightens up again as she calls Laura, who has been washing the dishes, into the room.

Scene VI

This scene opens with Tom, as narrator, outlining Jim O' Connor's background. Tom has known him since high school, when he was extremely popular and successful. However, he does not appear to have fulfilled the promise of his early days and is now, like Tom, stuck in a warehouse job. Amanda, meanwhile, has decorated the apartment in readiness for the visit and has also lavished attention on Laura, transforming her appearance. Amanda herself dresses up for the great occasion, wearing one of her old frocks which once more revives memories of the dances and drives and good times of her girlhood. Laura is plainly agitated by all the fuss and becomes even more so when Amanda reveals the full name of the expected caller. Laura realizes that this is the same boy she had a crush on in high school. Tom and Jim arrive and talk a while together as they wait to be let into the apartment (Tom has forgotten his key). Jim admonishes Tom that he is in danger of losing his job, as he does not keep his mind to it. Tom is not unduly concerned as he divulges that he has already applied to join the Merchant Marines. Laura, having been ordered by Amanda to open the door, meets with Jim only long enough to shake hands. Amanda, by contrast, almost overwhelms him with her display of sociability and coquettish charm. Laura does not even come to the dinner table.

Scene VII

Amanda, Tom, and Jim have just finished dinner when the lights suddenly go out, owing to Tom's failure to pay the electricity bill. Amanda demands that Tom help her with the dishes, deliberately leaving Jim with Laura in the soft romantic glow of candlelight. Jim's friendly and relaxed manner wins Laura's confidence. She even confesses her former admiration for him in high school and recalls his former nickname for her, 'Blue Roses,'

which arose from his misapprehension of the word "pleurosis," an illness that once kept her out of school. He gently chides her for having been so self-conscious about her disability which she felt created a barrier between herself and her classmates and judges her to have an inferiority complex. He also appears nostalgic for his own past glories. However, he is still determined to get on in the world and is taking night-school classes. His relationship with Laura blossoms rapidly to the point when she shows him her treasured glass collection and they waltz to the music that can be heard from the neighboring dance-hall. As they dance, he clumsily knocks over one of the glass figurines, a unicorn, so that the horn breaks off. Laura takes this quite calmly, pointing out that the unicorn is now just like an ordinary horse. Jim by now appears quite taken with her and kisses her, but immediately afterwards becomes perturbed and reveals he already has a girlfriend. Laura is devastated but keeps up a brave front and gives the unicorn to him as a souvenir. Amanda comes in, only to be informed by Jim that he is leaving to pick up his girlfriend Betty from the train station. Amanda is utterly taken aback and, after Jim goes, vents her frustrations on Tom. Tom is equally surprised, having had no inkling of Betty. Stung by his mother's accusations, he rushes out of the apartment leaving Amanda to comfort Laura. He ends the play with a final address to the audience, explaining that not long after that he was fired from his job and left the family home for good. He has been wandering around the country ever since, but he has not been able to forget Laura, as he tried to do.

"The Glass Menagerie" has enjoyed phenomenal success since it first opened in 1945. Its mix of lyricism and wry humor, its memorably contrasting characters, its use of unusual stage devices and striking symbolism have found favor with audiences and critics alike. The stage devices written into the original script include not only Tom as narrator but also music, in particular a sad sweet theme called the Glass Menagerie which principally represents Laura, and the use of a screen with captions and pictures to comment on the action. For instance, the scene in which Tom reveals he has invited Jim to dinner opens with the screen bearing the word 'Annunciation.' The play's use of lighting is also notable. Although the playwright directs that the stage should be generally dimly lit as befitting a 'memory play' (Williams xx), a stronger light is often used to highlight different characters at certain times (including the absent father's photograph). It often falls upon Laura, illustrating the fact that although she is so often a silent spectator she has a central role in the play; she keeps the family bound emotionally as both her mother and brother strive to protect her. The use of such innovative devices was introduced by Williams to heighten the play's deliberately non-realistic style and to strengthen its emotional appeal. They may not always work as he originally intended—in particular, the screen device lends a flavor of irony which he seemingly was unaware of—but they are in keeping with his general approach to what was for him a very difficult and sensitive subject.

Symbolism is also important in this play, as in so many of William's works. The most obvious is that of Laura's glass menagerie, which denote her beauty and fragility, particularly the unicorn which like herself may be perceived as being singular and 'freakish' (Williams 66) and —significantly—broken by Jim. Another example is that of the fire-escape. Tom frequently passes over it, signifying his ability to ultimately escape from the apartment; but when Laura is shown crossing it, she falls.

Historical Context

As well as being a very personal play, "The Glass Menagerie" consciously functions as a document of its times. This is due to Tom, as narrator, providing the social and political background to the action and commenting on the sickness of the age with the build-up to world war in Europe and the lingering effects of the Great Depression in America. Tom is able to view this clearly, with hindsight, from the standpoint of several years later. In this way, the audience is also made well aware of the larger context of the play. It is an important dimension as it shows that the characters' attempts to live through various forms of illusion are not unique; this also pertains to society. Although threatened by economic deprivation, social breakdown, and the onset of war, people take refuge in immediate pleasures with no thought to the future: 'here there was only hot swing music and liquor, dance halls, bars, and movies, and sex that hung in the gloom like a chandelier and flooded the world with brief, deceptive rainbows' (Williams 30).

Societal Context

Like many families in the Depression-hit era, the Wingfields struggle to make ends meet; and their situation is exacerbated further by the gradual breakdown of the family unit. At the beginning of the play, the father has long since deserted them; at the end Tom does the same. This is an economic as well as an emotional blow for Amanda and Laura as they are dependent on the men as breadwinners and so are left facing a precarious future. As women, they do not appear to have as much earning power; although it is true that Laura, at least, is given the chance to make a career for herself, but is unable to take it. This makes Amanda even more anxious to find a good husband for her, so that she can finally attain a place in society. However, although Amanda has the right intentions, she goes about things the wrong way as she tries to mold Laura in her own image as the girl who led a privileged existence as a Southern Belle. She clearly has found it hard to make a mental adjustment to the altered social conditions that she finds herself in and remains steeped in the ways and manners of the old, aristocratic South. However, she does acknowledge that that world has now disappeared for good: "Well, in the South we had so many servants. Gone, gone, gone.

All vestige of gracious living! Gone completely!" (Williams 49). She is not so lost in her rose-tinted view of the past that she is not able to plan for the future, although her efforts fail.

Scientific & Technological Context

The play refers directly to scientific and technological advances of its time through the person of Jim. Jim is studying radio engineering and is wholly enthusiastic about contemporary progress. He speaks in glowing terms of The Hall of Science at the 1934 Chicago Century of Progress Exhibition: 'Gives you an idea of what the future will be in America, even more wonderful than the present time is!' (Williams 56). Such comments come across as being naïve in the extreme; he himself has failed to keep pace with such progress. Moreover, his optimism is wholly misplaced in the world of the play which appears riddled with social and economic problems. Scientific progress, while laudable on its own terms, does not appear to have brought rational enlightenment (Western civilization is on the road to catastrophic war) nor has it brought emotional fulfillment or spiritual nourishment for most people.

Religious Context

Amanda stands up for traditional Christian moral values in the play and attempts to inculcate these values in her children. This leads her to too many clashes with Tom, who drinks, smokes, and seeks excitement and adventure and reads 'filth' (Williams 16) like D. H. Lawrence (one of the first notable twentieth century authors to deal openly with sex in his novels). She reprimands him sharply for wanting to indulge his baser instincts instead of nurturing higher aims as 'Christian adults' (Williams 26) should. Tom, representative of a new and godless generation, pays little heed.

Biographical Context

Perhaps Williams' most lyrical and least sensational play, "The Glass Menagerie" was his attempt to come to terms with his own painful family experiences. When he was growing up, he and his family suffered from the tyrannical ways of his father, who, although he did not literally desert them, was often absent on business after the family moved to a poor neighborhood in St Louis. His mother was very like Amanda in background, character and outlook, while his sister Rose, although not physically crippled like Laura in the play, became mentally unstable in her teens and eventually underwent a lobotomy which did her little good. The playwright himself originally bore the name Tom and like the character in the play, actually worked for a shoe company, a time of acute unhappiness in his life. He uses the play to work through his feelings about his family, especially his sister Rose. They were the best of companions in childhood but thereafter their lives were to take very different paths. He became a writer of some hugely successful plays, like "The Glass Menagerie" and the much more violent "A Streetcar Named Desire" (featuring Blanche DuBois, another faded Southern Belle) and "Cat on a Hot Tin Roof"; his work, like O'Neill before him and Miller after, has had a lasting impact on American theatre. Rose, meanwhile, ended up spending her days in a mental institution. Clearly, he never forgot her, and also looked out for his mother, providing her with financial security after she was separated from her husband. "The Glass Menagerie" is informed by this recollection of the closeness and complexity of family ties. Most of all, Williams' remembrance of the beloved sister whom he was finally unable to help is movingly reflected in Tom's separation from Laura at the end of the play.

Gurdip Panesar, Ph.D.

Works Cited

Siebold, Thomas, ed. Readings on "The Glass Menagerie." San Diego: Greenhaven Press, 1998.

Williams, Tennessee. "The Glass Menagerie." London: Heinemann, 1968.

Discussion Questions

1. Compare and contrast the Wingfields.
2. The film arose from a film script Williams wrote for MGM, entitled "The Gentleman Caller." Do you think this is a more or less appropriate title for the material than "The Glass Menagerie"? Explain your answer.
3. What is the effect of having a character who is also the narrator of the play?
4. Is it fair to describe the Wingfields as being essentially weak characters who attempt to escape into illusions from harsh reality? Explain your answer.
5. Do you agree that Amanda is to be more admired than criticized? Why or why not?
6. Are Tom's actions in leaving the family at the end of the play in any way justifiable? Explain.
7. Discuss the ways in which Williams emphasizes Laura's unusual qualities.
8. Discuss the use of lighting and lights (lamps, candles) in this play.
9. How does Williams create touches of light relief in the play?
10. Is the play to be praised for its pathos or criticized for being overly-sentimental? Explain.

Essay Ideas

1. Examine Williams' use of unusual stage devices in "The Glass Menagerie."
2. Analyze the symbolism in "The Glass Menagerie."
3. Examine the theme of illusion in relation to "The Glass Menagerie."
4. Examine the theme of conflict in "The Glass Menagerie."

The Importance of Being Earnest

by Oscar Wilde

Content Synopsis

The play opens in the "luxuriously and artistically furnished" London flat of Algernon Moncrieff, a fashionable young gentleman who is preparing for a visit from his aunt, Lady Bracknell, and her daughter, Gwendolen (253). He is interrupted by the unexpected arrival of his friend, Jack Worthing, known to Algernon by the name Ernest. When Jack/Ernest confesses that he is in love with Algernon's cousin Gwendolen, Algernon confronts him with a seemingly incriminating inscription on his cigarette case that indicates it was given to him by a young woman named Cecily. After some unsuccessful attempts at evasion, Jack finally admits that Cecily is an eighteen-year-old girl for whom he serves as guardian. Furthermore, he acknowledges that he "is Ernest in town, and Jack in the country" to which Algernon replies, "I may mention that I have always suspected you of being a confirmed and secret Bunburyist; and I am quite sure of it now" (258). It turns out that Jack, in order to get away to the city for excitement, has invented a wicked brother, Ernest, who is always in need of Jack's help in London. This makes Jack a "Bunburyist," in Algernon's words, because Algernon employs a similar ruse, using an invented invalid friend named Bunbury as an excuse to escape to the country in order to get out of social obligations in London.

Lady Bracknell and Gwendolen arrive, and, as soon as Algernon and his aunt leave the room, Jack professes his deep affection for Gwendolen. Unexpectedly, Gwendolen reciprocates and immediately agrees to marry him because, as she says, "my ideal has always been to love someone of the name of Ernest. There is something in that name that inspires absolute confidence. The moment Algernon first mentioned to me that he had a friend called Ernest, I knew I was destined to love you" (263). His counterfeit name turns out not to be the only obstacle; the always status-conscious Lady Bracknell must grant her permission for Gwendolen to marry, something she absolutely refuses to do once she learns that Jack/Ernest has no traceable lineage since he was found as an infant in a leather hand-bag in the cloak-room of Victoria Station. She upbraids the deflated young man: "To be born, or at any rate bred, in a hand-bag, whether it had handles or not, seems to me to display a contempt for the ordinary decencies of family life" (268). When he attempts to press his case, she ends all further discussion of the issue-"You can hardly imagine that I and Lord Bracknell would dream of allowing our only daughter-a girl brought up with the utmost care-to marry into a cloak-room, and form an alliance with a parcel" (269)-before leaving with Gwendolen in tow.

Jack's despair is short-lived, however; Gwendolen sneaks back to reaffirm her vow that they must be together. She asks for Jack's country address, which Algernon overhears and gleefully takes note of, for Jack, worried that Algernon would corrupt Cecily, had always refused to divulge the location of his country house to his friend.

In the second act, the scene shifts to the garden at Jack's country manor. Cecily is being tutored by her uptight and strict governess, Miss Prism, who reveals that once, in her younger days, she wrote a three-volume novel in which the "good ended happily, and the bad unhappily. That is what Fiction means" (275). Unfortunately, she lost the manuscript before it could be published. The appearance of the local Rector, Chasuble, derails their studies, particularly when Cecily suggests that Miss Prism has a headache and should take a walk with Chasuble to relieve it, a suggestion that Miss Prism eagerly takes advantage of. No sooner have they departed than the butler announces the arrival of "Mr. Ernest Worthing." It is Algernon, pretending to be Jack's dissolute brother. In an exchange that distills the larger moral ambiguities of the play, Cecily refers to Algernon as her "wicked cousin Ernest." When he protests that he is "not really wicked at all," she scolds him: "I hope you have not been leading a double life, pretending to be wicked, and being really good all the time. That would be hypocrisy" (277).

As Algernon/Ernest and Cecily retreat into the house, Miss Prism and Chasuble return from their walk and are surprised to see Jack—who is supposed to be in London looking after his "brother"—dressed in mourning clothes. Worried that Cecily has become infatuated by the tales of the incorrigible Ernest, Jack had decided to "kill off" his brother, and pretends to have just received word of his brother's death. Chasuble offers words of comfort, but Jack, remembering Gwendolen's desire to marry a man named Ernest, interrupts him to inquire about being christened right away. The three are shocked when Cecily joins them and tells them that Jack's brother, Ernest, is in the dining room. Jack insists that Algernon return to London immediately, but Algernon manages to steal a moment alone with Cecily, during which he proposes to her. Much to his surprise, Cecily tells him that they have been engaged for three months already; when she heard all of the stories about "wicked Ernest," she had fallen in love with him and carried out an entire courtship in her diary. Furthermore, she tells him, "It had always been a girlish dream of mine to love someone whose name was Ernest. There is something in that name that seems to inspire absolute confidence" (288).

Hearing this, Algernon rushes off to find Chasuble to arrange to be christened Ernest that afternoon. Gwendolen enters, looking for Jack/Ernest. As she and Cecily talk, they are dismayed to discover that they are both engaged to "Ernest Worthing," and they bicker over which of them has the rightful claim. Jack and Algernon both reappear, and Jack is forced to confess: "I will tell you quite frankly that I have no brother Ernest. I have no brother at all. I never had a brother in my life, and I certainly have not the smallest intention of ever having one in the future" (296). Algernon, too, must admit that he is not who he pretended to be. The women run into the house together, and the always-droll Algernon tells his despondent friend that this experience has been the "most wonderful Bunbury I have ever had in my life" (296).

The final act begins with the men following the women into the house to make peace. When they make known that they were both willing to be christened in order to be "Ernest," the women forgive them, and they fall into one another's arms. Into this scene enters Lady Bracknell who has been trying to track down Gwendolen. Confronted by the young lovers' pleas, Lady Bracknell remains unmoved, the circumstances of Jack's birth being an insurmountable barrier in her mind. She also opposes any union between Cecily and Algernon, deeming the girl to be of insignificant birth until she learns that Cecily is going to inherit a great deal of money. She quickly changes her mind, but Jack, as Cecily's guardian, refuses to consider giving his blessing if he is not allowed to marry Gwendolen. The impasse persists until Lady Bracknell recognizes Miss Prism as one of her old family servants and confronts her: "Prism! Where is that baby?" (309). Twenty-eight years earlier, Miss Prism had left with Lady Bracknell's nephew in a perambulator and had never returned. Miss Prism comes clean, admitting that in "a moment of mental abstraction," she had "deposited the manuscript [of her novel] in the bassinette and placed the baby in the hand-bag" that she had brought with her to carry the manuscript in (310). As the facts are unraveled, it becomes clear that Jack is, in fact, Lady Bracknell's nephew and Algernon's brother and that his real name is Ernest. Once he realizes that he is rightfully Ernest and does actually have an unscrupulous brother in London, he proclaims, "Gwendolen, it is a terrible thing for a man to find out suddenly that all his life he has been speaking nothing but the truth. Can you forgive me?" (313). With that, the couples, including Miss Prism and Chasuble, happily embrace. Jack closes the play on a note of supreme irony, telling his aunt, "I've now realized for the first time in my life the vital Importance of Being Earnest" (313).

Historical Context

Near the end of the second act of "The Importance of Being Earnest," Gwendolen, in an attempt to prove her superiority over the country-bred Cecily, says, "The country always bores me to death," to which Cecily retorts, "Ah! This is what the newspapers call agricultural depression, is it not? I believe the aristocracy are suffering very much from it just at present. It is almost an epidemic amongst them, I have been told" (293). On the surface a comic play on words, Cecily's quip has a much more serious meaning that suggests that she is probably winning in the women's trade of insults. Beginning in the 1870s, England suffered a series of poor harvests; simultaneously, foreign sources of cheap agricultural products were becoming more

readily available. From the U.S. and Canada, "railroads and fast steamships brought plentiful wheat that was far cheaper than English grain. Mutton and beef came in cold storage from the grazing lands of Argentina and Australia. English agriculture could no longer compete" (Mitchell 13). While the influx of affordable food may have been a boon for the average consumer, it had far-reaching social effects. The aristocracy, for so long the pinnacle of every aspect of English society, found themselves in difficult straits. Because of the agricultural depression, the landed classes "whose income depended on rent from their land grew less prosperous," and their dominance "in national affairs began slowly to wane" (Mitchell 13).

The financial hardships of the still-proud aristocracy are frequently evident in Wilde's play. Gwendolen can try to intimidate Cecily with her higher hereditary position, but Cecily's vast fortune evens the playing field quite a bit. When wealthy, but middle-class, Jack suggests that he had been considering offering a reward for his lost cigarette case, the aristocratic Algernon says, "Well, I wish you would offer one. I happen to be more than usually hard up" (256). When Lady Bracknell rings the doorbell shortly thereafter, Algernon notes, "Ah! that must be Aunt Augusta. Only relatives, or creditors, ever ring in that Wagnerian manner," indicating that he is accustomed to frequent visits from creditors (260). Immediately after this, he offers to get Jack some time alone with Gwendolen if Jack will treat him to supper. Lady Bracknell's comments perhaps best sum up how the meaning of owning land, once the standard of determining social rank, had changed in light of the agricultural depressions: "land has ceased to be either a profit or a pleasure. It gives one position, and prevents one from keeping it up. That's all that can be said about land" (266–7).

Societal Context

To this day, England maintains more easily recognizable class division than many countries, especially the United States, and this was even more the case in the 1890s when this play is set. In the late Victorian era, society was defined by three broad classes: the working class, the middle class, and the aristocracy. One's social standing was immediately apparent because it "was revealed in manners, speech, clothing, education, and values. The classes lived in separate areas and observed different social customs in everything from religion to courtship to the names and hours of their meals" (Mitchell 17). When bickering with Cecily, Gwendolen does much to exaggerate the class difference between herself and the wealthy, but middle-class, young woman. To Cecily's remark, "When I see a spade I call it a spade," Gwendolen disdainfully replies, "I am glad to say that I have never seen a spade. It is obvious that our social spheres have been widely different" (292).

Of course, when the men's deceit is revealed, the two women are quick to become friends despite the differences in their social situations. This demonstrates one of the odd facts of the class system in the late nineteenth century: class distinctions were rigidly maintained, but alliances of convenience which technically defied social convention were not uncommon, especially when money was involved. By definition, social standing "did not depend on the amount of money people had—although it did rest partly on the source of their income." Oftentimes the wealthier members of the middle class had far more money than did the lower members of the aristocracy (Mitchell 17). This frequently led to carefully orchestrated marriages between the classes; the middle-class family gained respectability and the upper-class family vastly improved their financial situations through such unions. The aristocratic Lady Bracknell shows no inclination towards letting Algernon marry Cecily until she discovers that Cecily is heir to one hundred and thirty thousand pounds. Upon hearing that, she suddenly discovers "distinct social possibilities" in Cecily's profile (305).

The financial troubles of the aristocracy are the source of several jokes in the play. While interrogating Jack about his fortune and background, Lady Bracknell notes that Mr. Cardew, Jack's adopted guardian, "was evidently a man of some wealth." She wonders, "Did he rise from the ranks of the aristocracy?" (267). Algernon likewise associates aristocratic status with a lack of financial resources when, posing as Ernest, he tries to persuade Cecily that Algernon is a better name than Ernest; he argues, "In fact, [Algernon] is rather an aristocratic name. Half of the chaps who get into the Bankruptcy Court are called Algernon" (288).

"The Importance of Being Earnest" pokes fun at the social and moral uselessness of the aristocracy as well. Algernon complains that his servant's "views on marriage seem somewhat lax. Really, if the lower orders don't set us a good example, what on earth is the use of them?" (254). The charity and social work the upper classes participate in does little to help society; instead, they go to meetings of the "Society for the Prevention of Discontent among the Upper Orders" and lectures on "the Influence of a permanent income on Thought" (281, 302). While the aristocrats sat atop the social hierarchy and should, therefore, have been the leaders of society, Wilde's play suggests that they were more likely to be morally and financially bankrupt, unable to manage even their own affairs, much less those of the entire country.

Religious Context

Despite its reputation as an era of the strictest morality, the Victorian Age, under the influence of rapidly developing technological and scientific thought, was a time of decreasing importance for organized religion. For instance, a survey in 1851 found that, in England, "60 percent of the people who were physically able to do so attended church services"; by 1902, however, that number had dropped to just 20 percent (Mitchell 239–41). Just as the nation's religious feelings seemed to be changing, Oscar Wilde's personal views on religion also seemed to fluctuate a great deal. In 1877, during a trip to Rome, Wilde was received in private audience with Pope Pius IX. He was reportedly very moved; yet, merely hours after the meeting, Wilde insisted on stopping at the Protestant Cemetery where, much to the chagrin of his Catholic friends, "he prostrated himself on the grass" before the grave of the great English poet John Keats, offering an even "humbler obeisance than he had offered to the Pope" (Ellmann 74). In addition, though he continued to show interest in religious themes and in the ceremonial aspects of Catholicism, when asked once "what his religion was, Wilde replied, 'I don't think I have any. I am an Irish Protestant.'" (Ellmann 94–5).

If it does not satirize religion directly, "The Importance of Being Earnest" at least satirizes its characters' trivial ideas of religion. The only overtly religious figure is the Reverend Chasuble who is too self-important and boastful, yet ineffectual, to be likeable. Upon hearing about the "death" of Jack's brother, Chasuble offers to recycle once again one of his much-used sermons: "My sermon on the meaning of the manna in the wilderness can be adapted to almost any occasion, joyful, or, as in the present case, distressing. The last time I delivered it was in the Cathedral, as a charity sermon on behalf of the Society for the Prevention of Discontent among the Upper Orders" (280–1). Religious sentiment is further spoofed by Algernon and Jack's attempts to be re-christened in order to be called Ernest. Not only are they ready to employ a sacrament of the Church for devious purposes, but, when the women find out, they are lauded for being willing to "face this fearful ordeal" (301). In the witty and trivial world of the play's character, genuine religious sentiment appears to have no place.

Scientific & Technological Context

The Victorian Age saw the flourishing of the Industrial Revolution and the rise of specialized scientific training and publication. Arguably, one effect of the increased interest in science may have been the decreased commitment to religion mentioned above. Charles Darwin's "On the Origin of Species" was published in 1859, offering an alternative explanation for humans' origins, while, owing to discoveries in fields like geology and archaeology, "the general spread of scientific awareness had cast doubt on the biblical account of creation by revealing the great age of the earth and the late appearance of humankind" (Mitchell 84).

While scientific progress made for ideological changes, technological advances altered everyday life in very explicit ways. The mid-century discovery of the Bessemer process allowed for the cheap production of steel, which, along with advances in steam engines, led to an explosion of railway building in England. As late as the 1820s, "most people never traveled more than ten or twenty miles from home; all their work, shopping, and recreation were done within walking distance" (Mitchell 74). With the expansion of rail travel, however, not only could people travel great distances in short periods, but also so could goods. Farmers, for instance, far from London could sell fresh produce or dairy to city dwellers; Algernon's cucumber sandwiches-all of which he, of course, devours before his aunt arrives-might very likely have been brought to the London market via train.

Much of the plot of "The Importance of Being Earnest," especially the timing of incidents relies on recent technological advances that sped up transportation and communication. Both Jack and Algernon's "Bunburying" is made possible only because of the extensive train lines in and out of London. Even the somewhat older Lady Bracknell has no problem chasing Gwendolen from London to Hertfordshire by means of "a luggage train" (302). Moreover, the particulars of Jack's origins—he was found in a cloakroom at Victoria Station—could not have been the same in the days before rail travel. In addition to trains, telegraphs play an important role in Bunburying. In the 1870s, the postal service had monopolized the telegraph system, connecting it to all post offices, no matter how remote or rural. This enables Algernon to make the excuse to his aunt: "the fact is I have just had a telegram to say that my poor friend Bunbury is very ill again," allowing him to cancel dinner arrangements at the last minute (262).

Biographical Context

Oscar Wilde was born in Dublin, Ireland on October 16, 1854. His family belonged to the middle class but were rather famous and did well financially. His father, William, was a talented ear and eye surgeon who, in honor of his contributions to medicine, was knighted by Queen Victoria in 1864. His mother, Jane, was better known by her pen-name "Speranza." She was a prolific writer who fought for Irish and women's rights.

Wilde proved to be a precocious student, ultimately winning a scholarship to Oxford. While at Oxford, he came under the influence of the writer and scholar Walter Pater. At the height of the influence of Victorian morality-which valorized moral improvement, progress, self-help, and discipline-Pater was arguing that art had no business trying to teach morality. The "Art for Art's Sake" movement, also known as Aestheticism, held that real art need only be beautiful, not useful, and certainly not didactic. These ideas attracted Wilde immediately, so much so that he applied them to his life in general, becoming a dandy famous for his dapper dress and witty conversation and for wearing a green carnation in his lapel and collecting peacock feathers. In the preface to his novel, "The Picture of Dorian Gray," Wilde famously wrote, "We can forgive a man for making a useful thing as long as he does not admire it. The only excuse for making a useless thing is that one admires it intensely. All art is quite useless" (4). Perhaps not surprisingly, many of the harshest criticisms leveled at "The Importance of Being Earnest" have been about its "uselessness." Critics point out that, while it may be clever and entertaining, the play does not ever teach a lesson. By Wilde's standards, this is not criticism; this is what makes the drama an exemplary piece of art.

Oscar Wilde's flamboyant lifestyle finally caught up to him when he sued the Marquess of Queensberry, the father of Wilde's lover, Lord Alfred Douglas, for libel after the Marquess had publicly accused Wilde of sodomy. Wilde not only lost his suit, he was brought up on charges of public indecency, found guilty, and sentenced to two years of hard labor. Though Wilde did manage to write two major works while imprisoned, "De Profundis" and "The Ballad of Reading Gaol," he was a broken man by the time he was released in 1897. He moved to France, using the pseudonym Sebastian Melmoth, where he died in 1900.

Kim Becnel, Ph.D.

Works Cited

Ellmann, Richard. *Oscar Wilde*. New York: Knopf, 1988.

Mitchell, Sally. *Daily Life in Victorian England*. Westport, CT: Greenwood, 1996.

Wilde, Oscar. "The Importance of Being Earnest." The Importance of Being Earnest and Other Plays. New York: Penguin, 1986. 247–314.

____. *The Picture of Dorian Gray*. New York: Norton, 1988.

Discussion Questions

1. Why is the play set both in the city and in the country? What contrasts is the play making between city life and country life?
2. Characters are quick to agree to marriage in this play. What attitudes towards marriage are being revealed?
3. Based on the comments on education in the play, what ideas of education prevail?
4. What distinguishes Algernon from Jack? Is one of them a stronger character?
5. What distinguishes Gwendolen from Cecily? Is one of them a stronger character?
6. Judging from this play, what role did the aristocracy play in Victorian England?
7. What do the women's actions—falling in love with men because of their names and Cecily's writing letters to herself on behalf of "Ernest"—reveal to us about notions of romantic love in this play?
8. Gwendolen says, "Once a man begins to neglect his domestic duties he becomes painfully effeminate" (290). What does this play have to say about gender roles in Victorian society?
9. Assuming that the couples do get married, how do you imagine their lives and relationships playing out?

Essay Ideas

1. With great irony, Jack closes the play by claiming to have learned the "Importance of Being Earnest" when, in fact, he seems to have been richly rewarding for lying about almost everything. Explore what the play has to say about the necessity of honesty, or conversely, the necessity of lying.
2. The play contrasts the highborn, but financially struggling, aristocrats Algernon, Gwendolen, and Lady Bracknell with the middle-class, but wealthy, Jack and Cecily. What is it saying about these groups? Is one group "better" than the other? What makes them different?
3. One of the criticisms most often leveled at this play is that it has no real meaning-it is just silly entertainment with no lesson to teach. Is this a fair criticism or are there lessons to take away from this work? Why do we still read it today?
4. Despite this being a play centered around wealthy and/or aristocratic characters, minor characters from other classes-Miss Prism, Lane, Merriman-do get their chances to speak as well. Why did Wilde include speaking roles for these characters? What purpose do they serve, and what do they tell us?

Twentieth-century Bavarian playwright Bertolt Brecht. He wrote "Galileo," featured opposite. Another Brecht play featured in this work is "Mother Courage and Her Children," on page 125. Photo: Bundesarchiv, Bild 183-W0409-300 / Kolbe, Jörg / CC-BY-SA

Galileo

by Bertolt Brecht

Content Synopsis

Galileo in his study shows the boy Andrea how the earth can move around the sun even though it appears to observers on earth that the sun is moving. He also advises the boy not to speak about his theories because they are not proven and because they rely on a way of thinking based on inquiries motivated by doubt. Faith, not doubt, is what the secular and ecclesiastical princes believe in because faith keeps the people docile, Galileo explains. Doubt in the order of things can lead to rebellion and revolution.

Ludovico, a prospective student comes to Galileo and shows him a small telescope he bought in Holland. Galileo considers that if he improves it, he can offer it to the Venetian senate and receive an honorarium, for, although the senators have no great regard for his pure science, they understand the value of his inventions, like the water pump, and they will find a magnifying instrument useful, especially for warfare. Galileo, particularly because of his great appetite for food and wine, is always in need of money.

Galileo uses the telescope to look at the moon and the Milky Way. He observes that the Milky Way is a vast collection of stars. He also observes that moon's light is reflected and does not emanate from the moon itself. He sees mountains on the moon and concludes that the moon is a body like the earth, a dangerous concept because it challenges the earth's

uniqueness. Ludovico realizes that Galileo has passed off the telescope as his own, is something of a trickster, but Galileo notes that he has improved it.

The senate learns, however, that Galileo has tricked them, but he is not fazed. His attention is focused on the discovery that there are moons moving around Jupiter. That tells him that the accepted belief that there are crystal spheres to which the heavenly bodies are attached and everything circles around the earth is false. Galileo is arguing that the earth moves. His friend, Sagredo, worries that danger lies ahead for Galileo because his discovery of these facts of astronomy takes God out of heaven and replaces faith with doubt.

Galileo writes to Prince Cosimo de Medici, who is a boy of nine, in Florence asking for a position in court and his petition is accepted. In Florence, his discoveries are met with hostility. A philosopher accuses him of disturbing the accepted harmony of the world with his discoveries. The philosopher and a mathematician refuse to look through the telescope at the stars. The authority of the established order is more important than truth and they hint, that what Galileo claims he sees in the heavens is only something painted on the lens of the telescope. They decide to seek the opinion of the papal astronomer.

The papal astronomer confirms Galileo's findings, but that does not override the other churchmen's contempt for Galileo's revision of the cosmos. His discoveries are a matter, they say, not of science but of theological accuracy. But the shipping merchants are interested in his work because of the way it improves navigation.

Galileo, his daughter, and her fiancé Ludovico, who brought Galileo the telescope, and who does not accept Galileo's discoveries, go to Rome. There Cardinals Bellarmin and Barberini argue about Galileo's discoveries. Bellarmin accepts Galileo's findings. Barberini condemns his work as contravening religion, and Bellarmin agrees with Barberini, who argues that the brain is inadequate to know the truth, and condemns Galileo's discoveries. The head of the Inquisition observes the proceedings and his scribes take down Galileo's remarks. The Inquisitor seems to be planning to indict Galileo for heresy.

A Little Monk who visits Galileo, and believes that the cosmic order posited by church doctrine comforts the peasants, is nevertheless drawn to him because of the force of his scientific method and because of his own intellectual curiosity.

Eight years pass during which Galileo keeps out of trouble with the authorities. He does non-controversial experiments regarding water and floating bodies. His daughter, Virginia, a devout churchgoer is engaged to marry Ludovico and even consults an astrologer to determine how she must act.

When Galileo receives a newly published book concerning sunspots, he is tempted to begin again, his research on the relative movement of the heavenly body, especially because the pope is dying and the pope to be is Barberini, who is a mathematician. Galileo naively believes that science will be respected. Hearing that Galileo is resuming his astronomical studies, Ludovico breaks with Virginia, angered that Galileo is threatening the established order and unable to take his daughter into his family, in consequence.

In Rome, despite the Pope's sympathy, Galileo is brought before the Inquisition for his teachings and because they are being popularly used by others to discredit the absolute authority of the Bible on matters of science and, consequently, of faith. Galileo recants before the Inquisition. His students are angry with him and abandon him.

Although his life is spared by the Inquisition, Galileo lives out the rest of his days as a prisoner of the Inquisition, restricted to live in a small house outside Florence and kept under surveillance. Galileo appears to be abiding by the terms of his pardon, not to write any further about his cosmology, but when a former student comes to visit him, reporting how scientific research and thought have languished since his capitulation, Galileo reveals, to Andrea's great joy, that he has finished his "Discourses" and has Andrea smuggle it out of Italy. Galileo explains to Andrea that he feels like a man who sold out his convictions that he capitulated not because he planned to write in secret but because he was afraid of torture. He thinks, however, that if he had defied the Inquisition he would not only have advanced the course of science but of human good, too, because science without human representation can be used by the oppressing rulers to reinforce drudgery.

Andrea does smuggle the book across the border, but at the border, he encounters a group of children looking at an old woman's shadow on the wall and taunting her with being a witch. They see, when they look at the shadow, a broomstick in her hands. Andrea lifts a boy up to see through the window that it is only an old woman stirring soup with a ladle. The boy recognizes the truth when he sees it for himself. Once Andrea has gone some distance, however, the boy calls after him that she is a witch and the children resume taunting her.

Symbols & Motifs

As realistic as it seems to be, "Galileo" is, as a whole, a symbolic work. While the play dramatizes episodes in the great scientist's life, it also uses that life and the events surrounding it to reflect on the problem of rebellion against entrenched, restrictive, and oppressive power. Brecht used astronomy to represent economics and Galileo's scientific formulations, which undermined the cosmology of the Church, to represent Karl Marx's economic formulations, which Brecht saw as undermining the rule of capitalism and the conditions of labor that it established.

A recurring motif occurs when each of the fourteen scenes of the play is introduced by a written panel of several lines of jingling verse that announce the content of that scene. By means of this theatrical technique, part of a technique Brecht called the "alienating effect," Brecht attempted to focus an audience's attention on thinking about the social and political issues the play was presenting rather than responding by identifying emotionally with characters.

Historical Context

Two historical contexts are at work in "Galileo," the seventeenth-century context in which he lived and worked and the twentieth-century context to which Brecht sought to make his life story applicable. By the seventeenth century, the Catholic Church had been considerably shaken by such sixteenth-century defectors as Martin Luther, John Calvin, and England's King Henry VIII. Each founded a new Christian Protestant denomination and a Church independent of Rome.

Galileo's scientific pursuits and particularly his advancing of the destabilizing idea of heliocentricity (that the sun is at the center of the solar system and that the earth is in orbit around it) over the traditional belief in geocentricity (that the earth was still and the sun moved around it) added to the challenge the Roman Catholic Church faced, and it was met with violent repression.

By the time that Brecht wrote "Galileo," the Soviet Union had been established as a state based on the economic ideas of Karl Marx. Marx had, during the latter part of the nineteenth century, written a compendious indictment of capitalism as an economic system and as a system that devitalizes human health and the human spirit as well as supportive community. From its inception, the leadership of the communist state feared it to be under threat of attack from western governments. With the rise of Nazi Germany, that threat became much stronger as Hitler used the specter of communism to mobilize fascist enthusiasm.

With regard to both contexts, "Galileo" considers the interplay of forces that propel and retard historical progress and what role human character itself and individuality contribute to that dialectical struggle.

Societal Context

The vision of society present in "Galileo" is the vision of the use of power by an established group of rulers to keep a relatively impoverished population in its place. The impoverishment is intellectual, emotional, and spiritual, as well as economic. The play shows the attempts of individuals to remove that authority, or to survive despite it. The play also recognizes that a great many people live in comfortable resignation to that authority and find security in its presence.

Brecht presents a description of the social order that applies equally to one that is ecclesiastical, mercantile or industrial capitalist.

Religious Context

The role of religion is fundamental in "Galileo" since the play is an indictment of a major historical role of religion, usurping the intellectual power of the mass of people. While Brecht himself, as a Marxist, was an atheist, "Galileo" is not a play about the existence or non-existence of God. It is about the spiritual and political issue of the conflict between doubt and faith and about the power exercised by the Roman Catholic Church.

Brecht shows religion as it is defined by the Church as a means for some to obtain power and privilege while keeping the many in their place through religious doctrine and thereby protecting their own positions of power.

This seventeenth-century religious context translates into the twentieth-century, for Brecht, by replacing the Church with the capitalist state. For Brecht, the Marxist concept of the dialectic extends Galileo's doctrine of doubt. Each idea was cast in a struggle with its opposite and credence was to be given, not by faith, but by a scientific examination of the results of the struggle.

Scientific & Technological Context

Underpinning the dramatic conflicts in "Galileo" is the philosophical method devised by Marx called "dialectical materialism." Brecht sets competing forces of history against each other and allows each to define itself as best it can. (Brecht allows the churchmen to advance solid arguments against Galileo's revision of the cosmos. He shows Galileo as gluttonously self-indulgent and keeps it unclear which, outright rebellion or apparent capitulation, is the better action.)

The matter of the play, because of its subject, is constituted of several scientific issues. These issues usually involve problems of celestial mechanics and the motion of heavenly bodies. Brecht's explanations and dramatizations of several of Galileo's scientific discoveries and analyses are lucid and simple. Galileo picks up the chair Andrea is sitting on and moves it to explain the importance of point of view; Andrea shows a boy the difference between the shadow a thing casts and the thing itself by lifting him to look through a window at the woman with a ladle the boy had seen as a witch with a broom.

Biographical Context

Brecht was one of the most influential playwrights of the twentieth century and considered by many to be one of its greatest. Others have little regard for him because of his lifelong commitment to Marxism and his apparent support of Stalinist regimes like the Soviet Union and East Germany.

Brecht, despite his collectivist ideology, remained dedicated to himself. Although he collaborated with a number of others in the composition of his plays, he maintained the hierarchical fiction of himself as their author. Although he lived his last years in East Germany, where he was given a theater, the Berliner Ensemble, he had Austrian citizenship, had his money in western banks, and held his copyrights through Switzerland.

Brecht's idea of epic theater, that the drama had a social function and ought not to ensnare audiences but keep them at a distance in order for them to judge the drama, permeated the work of innumerable playmakers and moviemakers. The Berliner Ensemble was the home to his theatrical techniques and conveyed them throughout the world through its tours.

Brecht was born in Bavaria on February 10, 1898. He studied drama at Munich University and his career as a writer began when at eighteen he began writing theater criticism. He spent a few years as a cabaret performer and in 1918 wrote "Baal," his first play. "Drums in the Night, In the Jungle of the Cities," and "Man Is Man," 1926, soon followed. That year, too, Brecht began to study Marxism. During the last years of the 1920s, with the composer Kurt Weill, Brecht wrote several of the century's great musicals including, "The Three Penny Opera," "The Rise and Fall of the City of Mahagonny," and "Happy End."

At Hitler's accession to power in 1933, Brecht left Germany. During the years ending the thirties, Brecht wrote two of his most popular plays, "Mother Courage and Her Children" and "The Good Person of Szechwan." He lived in Hollywood during the war among other exiled German artists and intellectuals. For money, he wrote for the movies, although he despised doing so. In

1948, he was called before the House Un-American Activities Committee for being a communist and double-talked his way to a commendation from the chairman for his cooperation. He already had bought his plane ticket and the next day was on a flight to East Berlin, outraged by the fact that some former Nazis would have a place in the West German government.

Brecht died on August 14, 1956. He wrote criticism, novels, stories, and poetry as well as plays.

Neil Heims, Ph.D.

Work Cited

Brecht, Bertolt. "Galileo." Trans. by Charles Laughton. "Seven Plays by Bertolt Brecht." New York: Grove Press, 1961. Print.

Discussion Questions

1. Discuss the significance and implications of the interaction between Andrea and the boy regarding the "witch" in the last scene of "Galileo."

2. How does Brecht's use of placards at the beginning of each scene affect your reading of the scene?

3. Do you agree with Galileo's proposition that doubt is the foundation of knowledge? Why or why not?

4. Is Galileo as Brecht portrays him a hero? A coward or a sensible man? Explain the reasons for your conclusions.

5. Has the scientific revolution that Galileo began more greatly benefited or harmed mankind? In what ways?

6. Does "Galileo" feel like a propaganda play to you? If so, how? If not, why not?

7. Are the challenges Galileo faces in Brecht's play comparable to challenges people face today? If so, discuss which and how. If not, why not? What has changed? What is responsible for the change? What has not changed? Why not?

8. From your reading of "Galileo," what would you say was Brecht's view of human nature?

9. What idea is Brecht developing when he sets the proverbs "Unhappy is the land that breeds no hero" and "Unhappy is the land that needs a hero" against each other at the end of Scene 12 after Galileo's recantation.

10. How does Brecht depict the churchmen? Are they fully developed human beings?

Essay Ideas

1. Describe and evaluate the kind of man Brecht's Galileo is.

2. Discuss the role of spectacle in "Galileo."

3. Analyze and evaluate the reasons the churchmen feel threatened by Galileo's research and discoveries. Why is inventing a water pump or a telescope rewarded but discovering the moons of Jupiter, for example, deplored?

4. Discuss the importance of self-suppression and the role it plays in "Galileo."

5. After doing the research, write an essay explaining what dialectical materialism is and how the concept of dialectical materialism is used in "Galileo"

Long Day's Journey into Night

by Eugene O'Neill

Content Synopsis

Eugene O'Neill's famous play, "Long Day's Journey into Night" centers on one day in the life of the Tyrone family in August 1912. There are only five characters: the four members of the Tyrone family and Cathleen, their serving girl. Tyrone, a semi-retired actor of Irish ancestry, is a handsome, florid man of sixty-five. Mary, his pretty wife, is fifty-four. They have two sons: Jamie, the elder at thirty-three, and Edmund, who is around ten years younger. The entire play takes place inside the family's summer home in Connecticut.

Act 1

The day begins brightly with Tyrone and Mary chatting with one another as Jamie and Edmund breakfast offstage. Although the tone is light-hearted, there is an undercurrent of unease. Presently, the boys enter, and tensions between Tyrone and Jamie soon become apparent. Edmund's health, too, is giving cause for concern, although Mary lightly tries to dismiss it as a bad cold. Edmund and Mary then exit the room leaving Tyrone and Jamie together. They continue talking of family matters, notably Edmund's illness, which appears to be consumption (tuberculosis). Jamie bitterly blames Tyrone for not hiring the best doctors for Edmund as that would be too expensive. Tyrone, who is frugal to a fault with money, makes the

counter accusation that Jamie is a born waster; he has no proper job, drinks and frequents brothels, and sets a bad example to Edmund. It is clear from these exchanges that father and son are very much at odds with each other. However, when their talk turns to Mary, they are united in their apprehension about her. When she returns to the room, she appears to be in a state of ever-increasing agitation. The other two leave to do some gardening and Edmund comes in. He, too, is worried about his mother. Her behavior now appears to be growing more irrational. She accuses him of spying on her and complains bitterly about her loneliness and the fact that, in all his days touring as an actor, Tyrone has never provided a real home for her. Even when left alone at the end of the act, she is wholly unable to relax.

Act II, Sc. 1

It is now nearing lunchtime. Jamie returns from the garden to share his concerns about Mary, who has briefly retired upstairs, with his brother. When Mary comes down, she is tenser than ever and soon falls to rebuking Jamie for not showing his father more respect. After Tyrone re-enters, Mary's increasing strangeness finally drives him to challenge her directly. This immediately puts her on the defensive. Tyrone, defeated, goes in to lunch.

Act II, Sc. 2

The family has just finished lunch. Mary talks volubly while the other three listen in a kind of grim resignation. When the subject of Edmund's illness crops up again, she suddenly bursts out in a fierce denunciation of all doctors, declaring vehemently that they can ruin your life: "I hate doctors! They'll sell their souls! What's worse, they'll sell yours, and you never know it till one day you find yourself in hell!" (O'Neill 64). Clearly there is a deeper reason underlying this tirade: she is referring to her own experiences. Later, when they are alone together, Tyrone makes an emotional appeal to her, but she is now keeping him wholly at bay and slips back into reminiscing about her past, when she was in the convent, before her marriage. She also remembers her son Eugene who died as a baby, and how her own health failed when she had Edmund. Now, the nature of her affliction is made plain: she has struggled with a morphine addiction ever since she was given the drug to combat her pain when she bore Edmund; a fact that she blames on the "cheap hotel doctor" (O'Neill 75) who attended her at the time. When Edmund comes in, she reveals her very real fear about his illness. Edmund has an appointment in town with the doctor; Jamie and Tyrone also leave. Once more alone, Mary soliloquizes about her one-time religious faith, which no longer sustains her.

Act III

It is the evening. Mary and Cathleen are talking together. Mary again recalls her old convent days and the hopes she then entertained of becoming a musician. Cathleen is slightly disconcerted by her peculiar manner. When Cathleen goes, Mary once more soliloquizes bitterly about her life. Tyrone and Edmund return and the accusations soon begin again. Mary reproaches Tyrone over Jamie, who is not yet returned and is presumably on a drinking binge in town, then abruptly switches back to the sweet memories of her girlhood. Tyrone is both moved and upset. Edmund attempts to tell his mother about the seriousness of his illness but she refuses to acknowledge it. Edmund finally snaps, "it's pretty hard to take at times, having a dope fiend for a mother!" and leaves (O'Neill 105). Mary goes upstairs to take some more morphine, leaving Tyrone sad and bitter.

Act IV

It is now midnight. Edmund returns from town to find Tyrone sitting brooding. Father and son begin the usual litany of mutual recriminations, varying from Edmund's taste in morbid poetry to Tyrone's failure to provide Mary with proper medical treatment from the beginning. Edmund also accuses his father of trying to send him to a cheap state institution for his own treatment. This prompts Tyrone into an impassioned self-defense. He points out that he learnt the value of a dollar the hard way, from having to support his family from the age of ten, after their father walked out on them. Tyrone goes on to bemoan his entire career; being typecast in a commercially successful but artistically unfulfilling play, he has been left with a lifetime of regret for his early thwarted Shakespearean ambitions. Edmund is somewhat mollified and in the new atmosphere of intimate self-confession, reveals his own heartaches and his sense of not belonging in the world. Then they hear Jamie coming back. Tyrone leaves the brothers together for a time. Jamie is utterly drunk and despondent. He expatiates upon his wasted life and admits that he has always desired to take Edmund down with him. Finally, Mary comes down, resplendent in her wedding gown and in a strange exhilaration, talking and behaving as though she were a girl again, and once more recalls what a bright future appeared to lie in front of her before her marriage. Her husband and sons merely sit and listen to her, and on this inconclusive note the play ends.

"Long Day's Journey into Night," based on O'Neill's own family life and winner of the Pulitzer

Prize, is notable for its expressionistic technique; its display of sheer emotion becomes ever more pronounced as the play wears on. Raw feelings and tensions rise to the surface as the four family members interact, and finally overwhelm. Each character has his or her own reasons for guilt, resentment, and a sense of failure: failure not only to achieve their own dreams but also in terms of family duty. They hurt each other, and suffer, and it seems they will continue to do so. Yet the bond that links them all is inextricable: the undying bond of familial love; perhaps the deepest, and most suffocating, love of all.

Historical Context

The emotional force of the play, and its themes, reflect how O'Neill helped to transform American drama in his career as playwright. In the nineteenth-century, and well into the twentieth, American theatre was dominated by European works and the plays performed were often melodramatic, grandiose productions. As well as shaking up theatrical conventions, O'Neill brought a new social and psychological realism to his plays, drawing on such revolutionary dramatists as Ibsen and Strindberg as well as material fashioned from his own experiences. These encompassed the seedier side of life, life on the fringes of mainstream society and included his early days at sea and in the Bohemian environment of Greenwich Village. There was also his association with political radicals, socialists, communists, anarchists; purveyors of doctrines which seemed a real threat to the American way of life in the wake of the 1917 Russian Revolution and America's own economic and social problems: Trade Unionism, increasing immigration, the 1930s Depression, and the growth of modernist ideas in both thought and art. While not directly impinging on the action, these issues are referenced in the play; Tyrone is irked at one point by his sons' "Socialist gabble" (O'Neill 20) and reproves Edmund for reading new and fashionably pessimistic writers instead of sticking to the nobler works of Shakespeare. However, O'Neill's prime concern in this play is with family life and all its attendant problems and complexities. In this, he taps into what became the dominant theme of twentieth-century American playwrights, for example Arthur Miller. (See also Societal Contexts).

Societal Context

The Tyrones' experiences reflect the struggles of working-class immigrants to establish themselves in America in the first half of the twentieth century. Tyrone's early years of financial hardship have permanently colored his attitude towards money, leaving him open to the charge of stinginess, and led him to sacrifice his artistic dreams to his need for financial security. However, he has been less than successful in trying to instill his own work ethic and financial prudence into his sons, particularly Jamie. His relationship with his sons also illustrates generational conflict in other ways. He is intensely suspicious of the authors Edmund reads: decadent writers such as Baudelaire, Dowson, and the philosopher Friedrich Nietzsche. Edmund is receptive to new ideas while Tyrone champions traditional values in the realms of art, politics, and religion. (See also Religious Context).

Turning now to Mary, we can see that her position highlights problems relating to matters of gender. Although cherished by her family, she is isolated as the only woman amongst them, and she feels this even more keenly as she has not managed to build up any social circle of her own. In fact, she has been unable to create a proper domestic establishment owing to the roving nature of her husband's work. Furthermore, it seems she now wholly regrets having given up the possibility of a career of her own, whether as a musician or as a nun, in order to marry Tyrone. As for many other women in the early part of the twentieth century, her opportunities generally appear to have been fairly limited.

Scientific Context

In this play, O'Neill makes extensive use of the ideas underlying the science of psychoanalysis, pioneered in the opening decades of the century by Sigmund Freud. Freud postulated that emotions, desires, and memories of the past may become repressed in the individual, leading to a potentially explosive and damaging situation when such feelings force their way back up from the unconscious. Freud also thought that the family was absolutely crucial to the formation of the individual psyche, as each male infant begins with the desire to eliminate his father and possess the mother; the so-called "Oedipus complex." O'Neill did not necessarily subscribe to this latter idea, but he concurred with Freud in believing in the central importance of family experiences in individual development. As seen in "Long Day's Journey into Night," the influence of parents appears to be lifelong; and even as each character struggles towards the future, there is no escaping the ghosts of the past.

In order to escape this feeling of pain and helplessness, Mary, at the end of the play, appears to have regressed entirely to her younger days, when life still seemed full of hope and promise. The men have spent their energy in self-confession and appear utterly worn out by this stage; any attempts at keeping up normal appearances have been wholly abandoned.

Religious Context

The breakdown of orthodox religious belief, a common theme in early-twentieth century Western thought and art, is reflected in the attitudes of the Tyrone family. Only Tyrone, it appears, has retained the Roman Catholic faith of his upbringing and rebukes his sons sharply for having repudiated it: "You've both flouted the faith that you were born and brought up in; the one true faith of the Catholic Church; and your denial has brought nothing but self-destruction!" (O'Neill 66). Jamie leads a dissolute life while Edmund has rejected the traditional framework of Christianity and morality in favor of new intellectual currents, embracing the often grim and iconoclastic outlook of such writers as Nietzsche, Baudelaire, and Dowson. Mary, too, appears to have lost her religious faith as she has not been able to come to terms with what has happened in her life.

Biographical Context

"Long Day's Journey into Night" remains the play for which O'Neill is most famous, yet he decreed that it should never be published, let alone performed, in his lifetime. Clearly this seems to have been because the material was too close to the bone as regards his own family experiences; writing the play was a painful working through of his feelings and thoughts about his dead loved ones; an attempt to exorcise his demons. He completed it in 1942, over a decade after the deaths of his parents and brother, explaining to his wife that he had written it with "deep pity and understanding and forgiveness for all four haunted Tyrones." Most of the details are true to life: his actor father, like Tyrone, was compelled to relinquish all his acting dreams for the sake of a single role, the lead in a dramatization of Alexander Dumas's swashbuckling novel, "The Count of Monte Cristo." His mother grew depressed with backstage life and turned to morphine; and his elder brother was to die an alcoholic. He even had another brother, called Edmund, who died in infancy, like Eugene in the world of the play. Edmund in the play is a faithful reflection of the author in many instances, from his sea-going days to his bout with tuberculosis (O'Neill almost died of the disease in 1912).

O'Neill found the family theme a fruitful one for his plays; his earlier work, "Mourning Becomes Electra" transposed an ancient Greek tragedy of family strife, murder, and retribution to Civil War America. Other plays released posthumously were about the Melodys, another Irish American family, including "A Touch of the

Poet" (1957). While several of his other plays on different themes, such as "The Iceman Cometh," have also gained critical acclaim, none has had quite the same impact as "Long Day's Journey into Night."

Gurdip Panesar, Ph.D.

Works Cited

O'Neill, Eugene. *Long Day's Journey into Night.* London: Jonathan Cape, 2007.

Manheim, Michael, ed. *The Cambridge Companion to Eugene O'Neill.* Cambridge: Cambridge University Press, 1998.

Discussion Questions

1. Do you think that there is any one Tyrone who deserves more sympathy (or blame) than the others? Explain your answer.
2. Discuss O'Neill's use of symbolism in this play.
3. Discuss the use of poetry quotations in this play.
4. Do you think that the Tyrones indulge their grief and problems too much? Why or why not?
5. Do you find the ending inconclusive? Why or why not?
6. Do you think that the play holds out any hope at all for any or all of the Tyrones? Why or why not?
7. What role do you think that Cathleen (the only non-Tyrone) plays?
8. How does O'Neill set up and maintain tensions between the characters throughout the play?
9. Which of the traditional elements of a play—plot, setting, characterization, dialogue—do you feel are the most important in this work, and why?

Essay Ideas

1. Examine the theme of conflict in "Long Day's Journey into Night."
2. Analyze the usefulness of a psychoanalytical approach to "Night."
3. Examine the theme of sickness in "Night."
4. Consider "Night's" claims to be a tragedy.
5. Analyze the role of gender and/or class in "Night."

Mother Courage and Her Children

by Bertolt Brecht

Content Synopsis

The play begins in 1624; six years after the start of the Thirty Years War, as recruiting sergeants for the king of Sweden are scouring the highways for recruits. Mother Courage, a canteen woman who sells provisions to the army, enters with her three boys, Eilif, Swiss Cheese, and Kattrin. The recruiting sergeant is complaining to another sergeant how difficult it is to find soldiers, and when he sees Eilif, he wants to enlist him. He demands to see their papers and they all begin to banter. Mother Courage reads their fortunes and finds death awaiting them all, including her children. Despite her efforts to protect Eilif, he acquiesces to the sergeant's wishes and joins the army. Mother Courage accepts her son's decision and tells Kattrin that she will have to take Eilif's place pulling the wagon.

Two years later, Mother Courage is in Poland. As the war rages, she is haggling with a general's cook over the price of a chicken. When the general enters, Eilif is with him and is being treated like a hero because he commandeered a herd of oxen from a group of peasants and slaughtered the peasants. As Eilif celebrates with the general by singing a song his mother taught him about a soldier's failure to heed a woman's cautions regarding the risks of war, Mother Courage sings the last verse, revealing herself to her son. Although Eilif thinks she will be proud of him for his heroism, she scolds him for risking his life in the venture.

Three years pass. Mother Courage and Kattrin fold laundry amidst the cannons and Swiss Cheese has become a regimental paymaster, keeping the regiment's moneybox. An officer is trying to sell bullets to Mother Courage, but she is reluctant to buy them, fearing the consequences of being found with army property; however, she ends up buying them at a good price. She warns Swiss Cheese to be careful of the soldiers, not to let his honesty be corrupted. A young prostitute named Yvette is with the family. Mother Courage scolds Yvette for drinking in the morning and references the prostitute's venereal disease. Yvette sings of her trysts with soldiers and while Kattrin is attracted to Yvette's shoes and hat, Mother Courage warns her daughter to stay away from men and from love.

The Cook and the Chaplain enter. The Chaplain says the Cook has fallen for Mother Courage but he says he just wants a drink. The Chaplain says he has come merely as a friend of Eilif's, when he actually intends to get some of the regimental money from Swiss Cheese to take to Eilif. Mother Courage forbids them to corrupt the honest Swiss Cheese and gives the Chaplain some of her own money to give Eilif. When the Chaplain notices Kattrin he takes an interest in her.

The Cook, the Chaplain, and Mother Courage discuss the politics of the war, particularly placing blame on the Germans and the Poles for not appreciating that the king of Sweden has invaded their territories to bring them freedom and has executed those who resisted. The Chaplain notes that the war is a religious war and Mother Courage praises the policy makers because, she says, they are not only making the war for piety but also for profit.

As the Catholics advance, everyone panics. Mother Courage dirties Kattrin's face with ashes to prevent the enemy soldiers from finding her attractive and ravishing her. She reproaches Swiss Cheese for trying to hide the cash box in her wagon. After three days under Catholic control, Swiss Cheese determines to take the cashbox back to his regiment. After he hides it by the river, intending to leave with it at night, Catholic soldiers apprehend him, suspecting he is the keeper of a Protestant regiment's cashbox. When they bring him to Mother Courage, she and her son deny they know each other. In order to save Swiss Cheese by ransoming him, Mother Courage considers selling her wagon to a colonel who is keeping Yvette and wishes to make her a provisioner to the troops. Mother Courage bickers with Yvette over the price of the wagon and Yvette negotiates with the enemy about the cost; however, she fails in the end and Swiss Cheese is executed. When his body is shown to Mother Courage in an attempt to implicate her in his "crime," she denies knowing him.

The year is 1632. As Mother Courage takes inventory and sells soldiers brandy, the Chaplain reassures her that the war will continue and that she will be able to buy more supplies at the same price. The Chaplain proposes to Mother Courage that they become lovers, but she rebuffs him. She is dedicated to the practical matters essential for survival. Kattrin is attacked by soldiers; however, she is still able to bring back provisions to her mother. Mother Courage gives her Yvette's red shoes to console her, but Kattrin crawls into the wagon without taking the shoes. Mother Courage reflects that both her sons are dead and her daughter is ruined.

Mother Courage and Kattrin pull the wagon and Mother Courage sings a song in celebration of the war and of the need for strength to exploit the chances of war.

With the death of the King of Sweden, Mother Courage fears that peace may be declared and ruin her business; however, she is also glad that she has gotten through the war with two of her children, Eilif and Kattrin, still alive. Yvette returns as a wealthy countess, having profited from the war and from her husband's death. Eilif is led in chains, on the way to his execution for breaking into a farmhouse and killing the farmer's wife. He is confused about why he is being punished, for it is the same thing he has been doing during the entire war. The Chaplain goes off with Eilif and his executioners. Mother Courage returns, excited because the peace has been broken and the war is on again. She will profit. The Cook tells her he has seen Eilif but cannot tell her he is being executed. She is happy because she thinks he has survived the war, that she will see him soon, and that she is back in business.

1634: The war has gone on for sixteen years; an innumerable amount of people are dead. Mother Courage and the Cook are in Germany covered in shabby sheepskins. The Cook, whom Mother Courage has supported throughout the war, learns that his mother has died and he has inherited a small tavern. He asks Mother Courage to settle down with him in Utrecht and run the tavern. She agrees and tells Kattrin they are going to live in one place and stop moving around, but the Cook says there is no room for Kattrin, only for himself and Mother Courage. She refuses to go without Kattrin so Mother Courage and Kattrin pull the wagon.

In 1636, Mother Courage and Kattrin are staying with a Protestant family outside of Halle. Mother Courage is in town buying the fleeing citizens' goods. Catholic troops force their way into their farmhouse looking for someone to guide them into the city. They want silence so that their entry can be secretive and, thus, more effective. Kattrin escapes the troops, climbs onto the roof, and furiously beats her drum, warning the city of the soldiers' approach. The soldiers silence her drum by shooting her dead.

Mother Courage sings a lullaby over her dead daughter's body, hitches herself to her wagon, and following the troops, sings the same song she sang in the first scene regarding the unceasing nature of the war.

Symbols & Motifs
Because Brecht is an ideological writer, he uses actualities that have their own representative or symbolic values. Mother Courage represents capitalists, exploiting historical situations and human needs. But she also represents those who are victimized by capitalism and must surrender their lives, and what is dear to them to the demands of markets. Mother Courage's symbolic ambiguity is a result of Brecht's Marxist understanding of dialectical materialism that postulates that its opposite inheres within an event. Mother Courage also embodies the principal motif of the play: survival achieved through the ability to adapt to a variety of circumstances.

Historical Context
As is often the case in Brecht's plays, two historical contexts are simultaneously at work. In "Mother Courage," the Thirty Years War and the Second World War reflect upon each other. Like Mother Courage, Brecht had been transient throughout most of the 1930s, once he was forced to flee Nazi Germany. In addition, Brecht asserts that war itself provides a market for commerce and is good for keeping prices high and profits strong. Lastly, Brecht shows the ravages of war, whether in the seventeenth or the twentieth centuries and the devaluation of human life that can be the result.

Societal Context
The common people and the poor populate "Mother Courage." They are shown scrambling to survive as they carry out the will of a master class as if it were the only reality. They adapt their lives to the roles assigned to them by forces that are seemingly more powerful than they are. The commoners are shown to be living in the grip of circumstances they cannot alter. Having no sense of the possibility of collective power, the downtrodden are in conflict with each other for survival, rather than with their overlords of the ruling class.

Religious Context
The religion of "Mother Courage" is a religion of fatality. It is established in the first song of the play, in both the verse and the repeated chorus. Both Protestantism and Catholicism are shown as oppressive forces in the play, serving as the covers that the powerful use for inciting the people to fight against each other. The war is fought in the name of religion but it is really for the power and profit of the ruling class.

Scientific & Technological Context
The principal technology presented in "Mother Courage" is the weaponry used in the war. Mother Courage's conveyance is a primitive wagon drawn by her children and by herself. Implicit in the play is the idea that life for people caught between combating armies is grim and austere.

Biographical Context
Brecht was one of the most influential playwrights of the twentieth century; however, many people have little regard for him because of his lifelong commitment to Marxism and his apparent support of Stalinist regimes like the Soviet Union and East Germany.

Despite his collectivist ideology, Brecht remained dedicated to himself. Although he collaborated with a number of others in the composition of his plays, he maintained the hierarchical fiction of himself as their author. Although he lived his last years in East Germany, where he was given a theater named the Berliner Ensemble, he had Austrian citizenship, had his money in western banks, and held his copyrights through Switzerland.

Brecht's idea of Epic Theater, that the drama had a social function and ought not to ensnare audiences but keep them at a distance in order for them to judge the drama, permeated the work of innumerable playmakers and moviemakers. The Berliner Ensemble was the home to his theatrical techniques and its tours around the world conveyed Brecht's ideas to many audiences.

Brecht was born in Bavaria on February 10, 1898. He studied drama at Munich University and his career as a writer began at age eighteen when he began writing theater criticism. He spent a few years as a cabaret performer and in 1918 wrote "Baal," his first play. "Drums in the Night, In the Jungle of the Cities," and "Man Is Man," soon followed in 1926. That same year, Brecht began to study Marxism. During the last years of the 1920s, with the composer Kurt Weill, Brecht wrote several of the century's great musical theater pieces including "The Three Penny Opera, The Rise and Fall of the City of Mahagonny, Happy End," and, in the early thirties, "The Seven Deadly Sins."

At Hitler's accession to power in 1933, Brecht left Germany. The final years of the thirties, as the Second World War was being shaped, Brecht wrote two of his most popular and, perhaps, his greatest plays, "Mother Courage and Her Children," an ironic indictment of war, and "The Good Person of Szechwan," an examination of problems of being good in a bad world. He lived in Hollywood during the war among other exiled German artists and intellectuals and wrote an anti-Nazi film, "Hangmen Also Die," directed by Fritz Lang. In 1948, he was called before the House Un-American Activities Committee for being a communist and double-talked his way to a commendation from the chairman for his cooperation. He had already bought his plane ticket and the next day was on a flight to East Berlin, outraged by the fact that some former Nazis would have a place in the West German government.

Brecht died on August 14, 1956. He wrote criticism, novels, stories, and poetry as well as plays.

Neil Heims, Ph.D.

Work Cited

Brecht, Bertolt. "Mother Courage and Her Children." London: Methuen, 1980. Print.

Discussion Questions

1. How is war depicted in "Mother Courage?" It seems to be a force independent of people, a force with a will and a life of its own rather than something that people create and do, can choose to exist or not to exist. Is this an accurate picture of war? Why does Brecht portray war this way? Is "Mother Courage" an anti-war play or is it actually fatalistic?

2. How does Brecht's use of placards at the beginning of each scene affect your reading of the scene?

3. How does Brecht use irony in "Mother Courage"? Give some examples. Does his use of irony serve a dramatic or some other purpose, perhaps a didactic one? Consider the scene in which Mother Courage and the cook haggle over the price of a chicken.

4. Is Mother Courage an admirable character or cynical, heartless, and exploitative? Explain the reasons for your conclusions.

5. In which ways is "Mother Courage" a tragedy? In which ways is it a comedy?

6. Does "Mother Courage" feel like a propaganda play to you? If so, how? If not, why not? If so, does it detract from it or add to it? Explain.

7. How does Brecht depict and criticize religion in "Mother Courage"? What is he criticizing, if he is actually criticizing religion?

8. How does Brecht conceive of the social role of women?

9. How does Brecht define or redefine the nature of vice and virtue in "Mother Courage?"

10. How important is the use of song in "Mother Courage?" Would the removal of the songs from the play strengthen or weaken the play?

Essay Ideas

1. Describe and evaluate the kind of person Mother Courage is.

2. Discuss Kattrin's role in the play. Describe her character. What are the dramatic and didactic effects of her inability to speak?

3. In what way is "Mother Courage" a didactic play? What are the lessons it teaches?

4. Discuss Brecht's use of jokes and songs in "Mother Courage." What purposes do they serve and how do the affect the play?

5. After doing the research, write an essay explaining what dialectical materialism is and how the concept of dialectical materialism is used in "Mother Courage."

American playwright Susan Glaspell, in her living room in Provincetown, 1940. Her play "Trifles" is featured on page 195. Photo: *Life Magazine*, 1940

Oleanna

by David Mamet

Content Synopsis

As is typical of David Mamet's plays, most of the action is in the form of dialogue. In addition, all of "Oleanna's" action takes place in a single setting. The curtain rises to reveal a student, Carol, who is sitting quietly and patiently waiting in the office of her teacher, John, as he carries on a telephone conversation that is already in progress. Telephone conversations occur throughout the play, and each one interrupts one of the meetings between John and Carol. Furthermore, in every case, only John's side of the exchange is heard, which imbues their performance with a greater level of realism, as if the audience were witness to an actual telephone conversation. However, this device also places audience members in a position similar to Carol's. While the intensity of these telephone conversations entices them, like Carol, to eavesdrop, complete access to the content of these conversations is likewise restricted to what they can hear from John's end. Just like Carol, audience members are forced to piece together the meaning and significance of these conversations from mere fragments.

After John concludes this initial telephone conversation, the first words spoken are Carol's inquiry regarding the meaning of a phrase she heard John use while on the phone. "What is a 'term of art'?" (2), she asks. At first, John avoids answering her question and instead attempts to direct the conversation to the reason for Carol's presence in his office. She has simply come to her teacher's office during his office hours looking for assistance with the theoretical material he has been presenting in class. Carol also seems to lack some of the skills that would help her succeed academically and hopes to receive some help in this area, as well.

John's initial demeanor leaves Carol feeling scolded, and she asks if she has done something wrong. John immediately softens his approach. He finally answers Carol's question about the phrase "term of art," saying: "It seems to mean a term, which has come, through its use, to mean something more specific than the words would to someone not acquainted with them. . . indicate. That, I believe, is what a 'term of art,' would mean" (3). Noticing the qualifications in John's definition (e.g., "seems to mean"; "I believe"; "would mean"), Carol then asks, "You don't know what it means . . .?" and John must admit, "I'm not sure I know what it means" (3). Mamet here draws attention to two key features regarding the communication that will make up the rest of the play. First, much of the language used by John in the beginning of the play, and much of the language taken up by Carol toward the end of the play, are essentially "terms of art" specific to a particular environment and usage—higher education and law, respectively. Second, much of the language is employed without a strict understanding of its meaning. It does not seem to matter whether the meaning in question is denotative, connotative, contextual, or individualized to a speaker's delivery. He also changes his persona from that of a busy academician who is reluctant to sacrifice his time for a student struggling with what he considers the "basic" concepts of the course to that of an accessible, patient, and nurturing mentor. In doing so, John will say a variety of things and make a variety of gestures that are inappropriate for a (male) teacher to use with his (female) student or that may be interpreted as such.

The instances of inappropriate behavior serve to foreground the degree of John's commitment to his chosen profession, his level of regard for the system of higher education of which he is a part, and the nature of his relationship with the specific academic institution that provides his livelihood. For instance, John responds to Carol's expression of confusion about his book—the text for the course wherein he is her instructor—with the statement: "Well, perhaps, it's not well written" (11). He then reacts to Carol's fear that she will fail the course with the flippant remark that "it's just a course, it's just a book" (12). Later, John goes so far as to denounce whole facets of education, declaring that to "learn, study, [and] retain" is nothing but "garbage" (16) and that tests are "nonsense" (23). He refers to the committee that is currently reviewing his performance at the university in order to extend him tenure as "a joke," and of its members, he tells Carol flatly, "I wouldn't employ [them] to wax my car" (23).

At this point, John's questionable behavior begins to take a different form. He now becomes too familiar. John offers Carol some "fatherly" advice, but says, "I don't know how to do it, other than to be personal" (19). Carol asks him, "Why would you want to be personal with me?" (19), but the phone rings, and John answers it before answering Carol. Carol learns that the stream of telephone calls are the result of John's efforts—based on the expectation that he will soon receive tenure and a corresponding increase in salary—to

buy a new house. When Carol asks John why he has stayed in his office with her when he clearly has pressing matters to deal with elsewhere, John says, "Because I like you," and the assertion also seems to apply to Carol's previously unanswered question about John's desire to "be personal" with Carol. John then follows this statement with the suggestion that he and Carol "take off the Artificial Stricture, of 'Teacher,' and 'Student'" (21). John then recklessly proposes a "deal" with Carol—he will change her grade for the term to an "A," so long as she agrees to "come back and meet with [him]. A few more times" (25). John retains this unfortunate tone by later speaking of his wish to awaken Carol's interest. To make matters worse, John replies to one of Carol's questions by way of an off-color and opaque analogy about the frequency with which the rich copulate in comparison to the poor.

The first act ends with John's attempt to put his arm around Carol, an act he sees as an avuncular gesture of reassurance for an otherwise inconsolable student. However, the gesture comes too soon after Carol's desperate cry of "what do you want with me?" (36). Carol shouts "no!" and flees to the other side of the room. In fact, during much of the latter part of the first act, John has been trying hard to get Carol to interact with him, as he said, outside the "stricture of teacher and student." He has been pressuring and cajoling her to share with him some aspect of her personal life or her intimate feelings. Yet, as Carol is on the verge of making just such a difficult and personal confession—presumably about her self-image—the phone rings, and John answers it. Carol's confession has been thwarted, and before the conversation can resume, John perfunctorily indicates that he must leave—his wife has planned a surprise party in celebration of his imminent tenure and promotion, and his meeting with Carol has delayed his arrival, causing his wife and the guests to wonder whether he is likely to show up at all.

When the second act begins, John appears seated on the edge of his desk lecturing Carol. In this lengthy opening monologue, John attempts to justify his pursuit of tenure in spite of the persona he chooses to present as a kind of "maverick," to praise the system of tenure he had earlier denigrated, and to urge Carol's withdrawal of a formal complaint. As the act progresses that audience members are given the information that Carol has reported John's unprofessional behavior and charged him with sexual harassment. It also becomes increasingly clear that John's provocative words and actions of the first act represent a mountain of evidence sufficient to demonstrate his unprofessional behavior and to cast doubt on his intentions. The complaint, then, threatens to cost John any chance of receiving tenure and threatens to cost him his job at the university.

In an attempt to salvage his reputation and his promotion, John tries to convince Carol that her claims are ridiculous and that bringing her suit is likely to create more problems for her than for him. He is, after all, a member of the academy, and she is just a student. He argues it would therefore, be in her own best interest to withdraw the complaint. Carol responds with indignation. She underscores the damning nature of the evidence against him and draws John's attention to the advantage she wields as the result of her newly acquired position of power. Carol also refers, for the first time, to the unnamed "group" lending her moral support. She implies that this unnamed group might be supporting Carol in other ways, as well. For instance, the group may have provided her with the arsenal of terms and phrases that enable her to conduct herself with an assurance and a credibility she did not previously possess. In his anxiety, John grows more and more belligerent until, at the end of the second act, he tries to prevent Carol from leaving his office, physically restraining her as Carol cries out for help.

In the third and final act, John has again asked Carol to come to his office, and Carol has agreed despite the recommendations of the "court officers." This mention of "court officers" serves to confuse John. John begins to speak about the complaint she lodged against him, and Carol calls into question his use of the terms "allegations" and "alleged" in reference to it. Carol points out that the Tenure Committee has already met, weighed the evidence, and ruled against John. The "allegations," she says, are "facts"; they are not "alleged" but "proved." John, the audience then learns, has been denied tenure and will be dismissed from his position at the university. Carol's reaction is to insist, "And full well they should. You don't understand? You're angry? What has led you to this place? Not your sex. Not your race. Not your class. YOUR OWN ACTIONS" (64).

By this time, Carol has assumed the role of "teacher" and has begun to lecture John. She accuses him of elitism, sexism, and hypocrisy, and attempts to have John (and the audience) see his past behavior in a different light. Carol correctly assumes that John views her in a singularly unflattering manner. She suggests that he sees her as "a frightened, repressed, confused, I don't know, abandoned young thing of some doubtful sexuality, who wants, power and revenge" (68), and John admits as much. Moreover, Carol recognizes that John will dismiss all of his earlier behavior as "meaningless" and "devoid of sexual content" (70), but tells him, "I say it was not" (70).

Carol finally suggests that there are conditions under which she and her "group" might withdraw the complaint against John and speak to the Tenure Committee on his behalf. The list of conditions turns out to be a list of books that Carol and the "group" wish to have removed from the university's reading lists. When John starts to say something about, "Academic freedom . . ." (74), Carol cuts him off. She says, "Someone chooses the books. If you can choose them, others can" (74), and she admits, "You have an agenda, we have an agenda" (74). John is initially willing to consider these demands, but then sees that his book is on Carol's list of "banned" books. John angrily refuses Carol's terms and orders her out of the office, citing his responsibilities to defend intellectual freedom and defy censorship. Once again, the phone rings, and Carol suggests that John answer it. Something about the telephone conversation makes John very upset and causes him to mutter that he does not understand. When John hangs up, Carol says, "I thought you knew" (77). Then, she explains: during John's earlier attempt at preventing Carol from leaving his office, and according to the letter of the law, he committed battery and rape. He is now subject to charges in a criminal court, beyond the scope of the institution. Exhausted and subdued, John tells Carol that she should leave. However, before she has the opportunity, the phone rings, yet again. This time, it is John's wife calling. John tries to carry on two conversations at once, yelling at Carol to "get out of here," and telling his wife: "It's going to be all right," but "I can't talk now, Baby" (79). As Carol starts to leave, she provocatively tells John, "Don't call your wife 'Baby'" (79). This is the last straw, and it serves as the catalyst for the violence that ends the play. John knocks Carol to the ground, raises a chair ominously over her, and spits, "Rape you . . . ? Are you kidding me . . . ? I would not touch you with a ten-foot pole. You little cunt . . ." (79). With this as the closing vignette, Carol utters the play's final words, saying simply: "Yes. That's right. . . . Yes. That's right" (80).

Symbols & Motifs

The epigraphs and title: Mamet's text is prefaced by two epigraphs, both of which also appeared in the programs for the original production. The first is taken from Samuel Butler's novel, "The Way of All Flesh." The passage selected by Mamet to accompany his play is one discussing the ease with which people are made unaware of the injustices they suffer by means of the familiarity that their suffering engenders, and by means of rhetoric, that assigns blame to the victims for their own misfortunes. The chapter from which the passage is taken is devoted to a discussion of education, a link that should remind us that the play is, after all, about education—a fact frequently overlooked in critical responses to the play. The second epigraph is a verse from a Norwegian folk song and the source of the play's title. In this verse, "Oleanna" is juxtaposed to Norway, the former offering an escape from the bondage, chains, and slavery of the latter. Finally, the play's original subtitle—"A Power Play"—points to the characters' struggle for power and each character's use and abuse of power as (the) fundamental concerns of the play.

Language and power: The latent power of knowledge and, in particular, language has long fascinated Mamet. In fact, Richard Badenhausen argues, "When examined outside the context of the explosive headlines of the early 1990's, the message of "Oleanna" appears to have much less to do with political correctness and sexual harassment and more to do with the difficulties of acquiring and controlling language, especially in the specialized environment of the academy" (1–2). Similar preoccupations with language and power may be seen in other Mamet plays, including the critically acclaimed "American Buffalo" (1976) and the Pulitzer-Prize-winning "Glengarry Glen Ross" (1984).

Sex and violence: Other themes that figure prominently in Mamet's body of work are sex and aggression. In his book "Some Freaks," Mamet writes, "The true nature of the world, as between men and women, is sex, and any other relationship between us is either an elaboration, or an avoidance" (90). Christine MacLeod compares John and Carol's relationship in "Oleanna" with relationships depicted in the all-male world of "Glengarry Glen Ross." She says, "Men do to men in "Glengarry, Glen Ross" much as woman does to man and man to woman in "Oleanna" (206). In other words, struggles over power and violence are the constants in Mamet's canon, whereas sexual harassment and claims of sexual violence are specific to "Oleanna" simply because they are forms of aggression that are limited to members of the opposite sex.

Historical Context

"Oleanna" was written in the wake of the "feminist backlash" of the late 1980's and early 1990's. This was a time when the predominant mindset, mainstream culture, and popular politics of the nation had moved significantly to the right. Feminism was being blamed for societal ills ranging from the breakdown of the traditional family to the nation's increased drug use and higher crime rates. Conservatives espoused an Arcadian return to a time when gender roles were clear and society was better for it. Within this environment, Mamet's play was often held up by the so-called New Right as exemplifying just how far liberals would go in their attempts to force an artificial tolerance of diversity and unhealthy leveling of hierarchies into the various public arenas. Many liberals, for their part, condemned the play as a kind of "feminism bashing," while some accused Mamet of being an apologist for masculine privilege and hegemony.

Furthermore, the play's debut coincided with the highly publicized sexual harassment case involving Clarence Thomas on the eve of his confirmation as United States Supreme Court Justice and a former associate by the name of Anita Hill. During the hearings, the defense focused attention on Hill, painting a portrait of her as an opportunistic female indiscriminately looking to scapegoat, and take revenge on, men for the consequences of her own failures. Using a legal strategy that has since become infamous, Thomas represented himself as the victim in the case by associating Hill's accusations (ironically, those of a black woman) with the discriminations suffered by African Americans throughout U.S. history.

Societal Context

Although written prior to the controversies of the Clarence Thomas case, the concurrence of "Oleanna's" debut with these events made it difficult for audiences and critics to view the play exclusive of those proceedings. As Verna Foster suggests, "Oleanna" "does not in the end center on the issue of sexual harassment . . . . The primary issue in "Oleanna" is not evidentiary—whom to believe. In Mamet's play, we know who said what, though not always with what motive. It is power, not sex, which is of the essence of the relationship between John and Carol" (41).

However, the play did reflect debates that were currently raging over "political correctness" or "PC," and John, in fact, does use the phrase: "You think you can come in here with your political correctness and destroy my life?" (79). The phrase, apparently first used in its contemporary sense during the early 1980's, gained popularity during the 1990's as a catch phrase. It was used for language that was seen by proponents as sensitive to individuals frequently subject to stereotyping and derogatory labeling. Political opponents used this in ridiculous and awkward attempts to monitor speech and control behavior as part of a liberal political agenda. Political correctness became closely associated with colleges and universities in their quests for increased diversity and tolerance. However, the fervor, disingenuousness, and pure silliness of certain attempts to achieve politically correct speech and/or behavior soon caused the phrase's primary usages to be either sardonic or sarcastic. Political correctness is by far the most conspicuously addressed theme in the criticism surrounding the text and its various productions. However, readers should also look past this theme to ones that are not so obvious, but that might prove more significant. Therefore, readers should be reminded that John refers to political correctness only on the last full page of the text. He has a stake in using the phrase—as was commonly done at the time—to avert attention from other issues at hand, and that John refers to political correctness as a means, not as a source or a result, of the conflicts and events of the play.

Religious Context

Religion does not figure into the text. The conflicts, while often dealing with morality and ethics, are secular and kept largely removed from religion and religious connotation.

Scientific & Technological Context

Although science is not given attention in Mamet's play, technology plays a key role in the form of the telephone. This device (the phone as technological device, but also as stage device) allows Mamet to minimize further the communicative content of the play's dialogue. Generally interested in the ways that interpersonal communication can fail to convey meaning accurately (or at all) and result in misinterpretation, in misunderstanding, or in manipulation by the most language-savvy characters, Mamet's plays frequently explore the power inherent in language. This is true whether the language in Mamet's plays is depicted as being purposefully used to accomplish certain ends or is portrayed as a force beyond the control of characters that are, therefore, helplessly subject to the power of language in combination with their own linguistic deficiencies. Moreover, in "Oleanna" the telephone—a tool designed to facilitate communication—is shown to be capable of quite the opposite. Whenever John answers the telephone in his office, he essentially privileges a conversation with an unseen and unknown caller over an ongoing and face-to-face interaction with Carol. During his personal telephone conversations, John also inadvertently shares bits of private information with Carol, an unwilling infiltration into his personal life. While, on the other hand, the one-sided nature of the conversations ensures that Carol will achieve only a partial and inaccurate impression of John. In these ways, at best the incessantly ringing telephone invites one to violate etiquette; at worst,

it invites one to generalize from bits of "information" disconnected from one another and devoid of context while, at the same time, one is invited to feel s/he has managed to glimpse a candid bit of the real person. Mamet, then, invites audience members to reexamine their notions regarding this and similar forms of technology.

Biographical Context

Cecilia Liu writes, "Born on November 30, 1947 in Flossmoor, Illinois, David Mamet studied at Goddard College in Vermont and the Neighborhood school of Theater in New York before venturing into the professional world of the Theatre" (1). Later, after achieving success as a playwright, screenwriter, and director of both stage and film production, he returned to teach at Goddard, as well as at the Yale Drama School and NYU. Mamet's unsatisfying experiences at Goddard—he once quipped that at Goddard he never learned anything of any use—seems to have consistently informed his writing. While "Oleanna" is set in academe and populated by a teacher and a student, Verna Foster notes that there are "several plays written prior to 'Oleanna' in which Mamet depicts some kind of quasi-teacher-student relationship that is also explicitly a power relationship and sometimes . . . involves a reversal of roles" (40).

In his article "'Oleanna,' or, the Play of Pedagogy," Robert Skloot notes that commentary about the play commonly centers Carol and the role she plays in determining John's fate and neglects to weigh John's own contributions to his eventual predicament. Skloot points out that, in doing so, commentators ignore the significance Mamet places on John as teacher. So, while commentators often mention how the play is populated by a teacher and a student, or that the play takes place entirely on campus, few of them mention the characters' very different expectations regarding the nature and purpose of higher education. Fewer still acknowledge that Mamet provides for his audience a detailed account of John's teaching philosophy and its practice in the classroom, nor that Mamet's account of John often serves to highlight a glaring deficiency, inconsistency, or pretense in his teaching.

The play's reception has likewise been colored by Mamet's reputation as a "masculinist" writer. In truth, Mamet's characters are predominantly male and many of the dramatic situations involve male—male relationships and/or male subcultures. This absence of female characters in his plays has been offered as evidence of a disinterest in women on Mamet's part and, in some cases, of an outright misogyny. The degree of violence and profanity (often verisimilar male speech and, therefore, often misogynist speech) in his plays has done nothing to dispel such opinions.

Richard A. Bryan, Ph.D.

Works Cited

Badenhausen, Richard. "The Modern Academy Raging in the Dark: Misreading Mamet's Political Correctness in Oleanna." *College Literature.* 25.3 (Fall 1998): 1–19.

Bechtel, Roger. "P.C. Power Play: Language and Representation in David Mamet's Oleanna." *Theatre Studies.* 41 (1996): 29–48.

Foster, Verna. "Sex, Power, and Pedagogy in David Mamet's Oleanna and Ionesco's The Lesson." *American Drama.* 5.1 (1995): 36–50.

Goggans, Thomas H. "David Mamet's Oleanna." *Modern Drama.* 40 (1997): 433–441.

Heller, Janet Ruth. "David Mamet's Trivialization of Feminism and Sexual Harassment in Oleanna." *MidAmerica.* 27 (2000): 93–105.

Iannone, Carol. "PC on Stage." *Academic Questions.* 6.4 (Fall 1993): 72–86

James, Caryn. "Mamet's Lesson in Sexual Harassment." *New York Times.* 144.49870 (4 Nov.1994): C22.

Kroll, Jack. "A Tough Lesson in Sexual Harassment." *Newsweek.* 120.19 (9 Nov. 1992): 65–67.

Liu, Cecilia. "Mamet: Glengarry Glen Ross." 13 April 2004 <http:// www.eng.fju.edu.tw/ iacd_2001F/asynchrous_drama/ dm_ggr.htm>.

MacLeod, Christine. "The Politics of Gender, Language and Hierarchy in Mamet's Oleanna." *Journal of American Studies.* 29.2 (1995): 199–23.

Mamet, David. "Oleanna." New York: Vintage Books, 1993.

Németh, Lenke. "Miscommunication and Its Implication in David Mamet's Oleanna." *British and American Studies.* (1997): 167–176.

Ryan, Steven. "Oleanna: David Mamet's Power Play." *Modern Drama.* 39 (1996): 392–40.

Silverstein, Marc. "'We're Just Human': Oleanna and Cultural Crisis." *South Atlantic Review.* 60.2 (May 1995): 104–20.

Skloot, Robert. "Oleanna, or, the Play of Pedagogy." *Gender and Genre: Essays on David Mamet.* Eds. Christopher C. Hudgins and Leslie Kane. New York: Palgrave, 2001. 95–107.

Tomc, Sandra. "David Mamet's Oleanna and the Way of the Flesh." *Essays in Theatre/Études thé â trales* 15.2 (May 1997): 163–175.

Discussion Questions

1. Although Mamet indicated that he did not wish to take sides and considered John and Carol equally guilty of a misuse of power, responses to the play have been overwhelmingly sympathetic to John and unsympathetic to Carol. Why might that be? Are these responses unfair, understandable but unfortunate, or completely justified?

2. John's exercise of power is possible because of his membership in the academy. What is the source of the power Carol wields?

3. What do you suppose Mamet means when he says, "The true nature of the world, as between men and women, is sex, and any other relationship between us is either an elaboration or an avoidance" (90)? Do you agree with this assessment?

4. The greater part of Mamet's characters are male, and he has written about some all-male environments. Do you find his female character, Carol, convincing? Why or why not? Based on this play, do see evidence that Mamet is a misogynist as some have claimed?

5. If participation (and membership) in academe requires a highly refined use of language, what responsibility (if any) do professors have in helping students acquire these skills? Does John fulfill his responsibilities?

6. Critics routinely point to Carol's abysmal language skills in the first act. Lenke Németh, however, applies linguistic theory to John and Carol's exchanges in the play and argues that Carol is actually the better communicator and the more successful user of language. He cites her ability to direct the conversation, her ability to complete her thoughts in sentence form, and her ability to effect change in John's demeanor and his approach towards Carol. Can you find examples that support Németh's claims? Whom do you find to be the better communicator, and what are the criteria you find important in determining this?

7. Mamet is often referred to as a "minimalist" for his uses of spare and incomplete uses of language. Where do you find examples of Mamet's "minimalism"? Do you feel that his techniques accurately mimic the speech patterns used by individuals beyond the stage and in real life? How so or how not?

8. Mamet is also known for his fondness for examples of communication that, ultimately, do not communicate. At what points does communication between John and Carol break down? What could one or another of the characters do to remedy these situations?

9. One of the lingering points of contention about "Oleanna" is what exactly Carol means when she utters the words that end the play.

10. When she says, "Yes. That's right." to what is she referring? What leads you to your conclusion?

11. "Oleanna" is, after all, a play with a teacher and a student and set on campus. Do you find any of the material in the play familiar? What portions? What has been your opinion of those facets of the college/university experience? Does having read the play reinforce or alter your impressions of these aspects?

Essay Ideas

1. The play involves an obvious set of conflicts between the two characters. Write an essay in support of John or Carol. Perhaps challenge yourself to write your essay in support of the character you find least sympathetic as a way of better understanding that character's position.

2. Although they have fundamental roles in the play, the members of the Tenure Committee, the members of Carol's "group," and John's wife never make appearances. Write an essay characterizing one of these entities or explaining the function served in Mamet's play by one of these entities. Be sure to include the evidence from which you constructed your characterization or explanation.

3. Read Lenke Németh's article (cited below) and decide whether you accept this interpretation of the first act. Write an essay in which you support or refute Németh's account of John and Carol's relative ability to communicate.

4. Examine John's (or Carol's) opinions regarding education. Write an essay analyzing those notions, looking for strengths and weaknesses, addressing their practicality, considering the effect they might have on the university, the faculty, the students, or the nature and/or quality of instruction should they be adopted.

5. Discussions have been raised about the significance that casting choices might exert on this play. In one production, Mamet insisted that an African-American actor play the role of John, and commentators have occasionally wondered aloud about other potential casting choices (e.g., Carol replaced by a male student or John by a female instructor). You may also think about the age of actors in the two roles and whether the ages are specified are assumed (they have always remained uniform throughout the various productions). Write an essay discussing the fundamental changes in the play's message you believe would be wrought by a particular example of unconventional casting. You may wish to approach the essay with the following question in mind: "What advantages might develop with an unconventional bit of casting?"

Eugene O'Neill, author of "Long Day's Journey into Night." O'Neill completed the play, which is featured on page 119, in 1942. Photo: *New York Times*, Cape Code, 1922

The Piano Lesson

by August Wilson

Content Synopsis

"The Piano Lesson" is set in Berniece's house in the black section of Pittsburg in 1931. It is five in the morning when Boy Willie, Berniece's brother, and his friend, Lymon, arrive driving a truck full of watermelons that they intend to sell. They have come from Mississippi, where both have spent time on a prison farm. Lymon plans to stay up north, but Willie wants to go back south and buy some land, become independent, and have a steady income. Willie is in exuberant spirits and wants to wake the house. Doaker Charles, his uncle, a railroad cook nearing fifty, lets him in and even gets him some whiskey, but Berniece is not enthusiastic to see the brother she has not seen for three years, chides him for his noise, and refuses to wake her eleven year old daughter for him.

Willie has come north not really to see his sister but to convince her to sell their mother's piano, an instrument of considerable monetary value because of its intricately carved legs. He hopes to buy one hundred acres of good land in Mississippi, land that has become available because Sutter, its owner, whose ancestors had owned Boy Willie's family under slavery, died by drowning after falling into his well. The general belief, down south, was that his death was the work of the Ghosts of the Yellow Dog, who, the legend goes, are responsible for other such deaths.

Part of the drama of "The Piano Lesson" involves the revelation of the meaning of that expression, "the Ghosts of the Yellow Dog." The reason for the intricate carvings on the piano is another mystery awaiting explanation, as is the reason for the death, three years before, of Berniece's husband, Crawley, for whom she continues to be in mourning despite the offer of marriage from Avery Brown, who is set on being a preacher with his own congregation. She has also refused Avery's request to sell the piano to help him procure a place to house his church.

The central conflict, however, involves Berniece's refusal to sell the piano and Willie's determination to sell it in spite of her. This drama also symbolizes the conflict between the past and the future played out in the present.

As Doaker and Willie are discussing Willie's plans, they hear Berniece scream upstairs. She reports that she has seen Sutter's ghost. Willie scoffs at her. But she says Sutter's ghost asked for Willie and she thinks that Willie threw him down his well. Willie denies it, calling it a ridiculous idea and reiterates that it was the Ghosts of the Yellow Dog that did. Berniece is not convinced, tells Willie to leave her house, that he brings trouble and that Crawley is dead because of him. Willie denies that he is responsible for Crawley's death. If Sutter's ghost is present, Willie adds, it is not to find him but to find the piano, and she ought to get rid of it.

Despite his plans to sell the watermelons and then load the piano onto the truck and sell it, after three days Willie has done nothing because the truck keeps breaking down before it even gets near the white neighborhoods. As he waits for it to be repaired Boy Willie hangs out with Doaker and Lymon and Doaker's brother, Winning Boy, a rather unsuccessful musician and gambler, drinking, singing, and gossiping, talking about his plans, and listening to Winning Boy talk of the Ghosts of the Yellow Dog.

During the conversation, it is revealed that when Willie and Lymon were gathering wood for a white man three years ago, they were keeping some of the wood for themselves, that when they went to gather it, in order to load it onto a truck, they got Crawley, Berniece's husband, to help them. As they were loading the truck, they were ambushed by some white men. Willie and Lymon fled, but were captured and sent to a prison farm, Lymon wounded. Crawley attempted to fight off the white men and was killed. Berniece blames his death on Boy Willie, who denies any responsibility. After that incident, Berniece moved north.

As the men speak, once again Boy Willie talks about how he is going to take the piano and sell it. Doaker then tells Lymon (and the audience) the story of why Berniece will never sell it.

Doaker explains that their family had been owned by Sutter's grandfather, Robert Sutter, and that Robert Sutter, back then, wished to purchase the piano from its original owner, Joel Nolander, as an anniversary gift for his wife. Having no money, but possessing slaves, Robert Sutter offered to trade some of his slaves for the piano. Nolander insisted on choosing and picked Doaker's grandmother, also named Berniece, and her son, Doaker's father, splitting the family, leaving old Berniece's husband, also named Boy Willie, with Sutter. Sutter's wife, at first, enjoyed playing the piano, but after a while, she began missing Berniece and her son and the way they served her and filled her life.

Berniece not only cooked and cleaned for her, but she also a companion who spoke to her. Sutter's wife actually took sick and became bedridden in her discontent.

When Sutter offered to give back the piano and get Berniece and her son back, Nolander refused. Sutter then summoned the first Boy Willie, Doaker's grandfather to the house. Nolander had offered to buy him in order to keep their family together, but Sutter refused. Willie was valuable. Willie was a master wood worker. Sutter ordered him to carve the faces of Berniece and her son on the piano legs. Willie did that and more, carving images of his entire family and scenes from their lives.

Although Sutter was angry, at first, when he saw the piano, that Willie had so far exceeded his commission, Sutter's wife was delighted. She had the piano and, by Willie's art, her slaves. She recuperated and played the piano again until her death.

Doaker's and Winning Boy's elder brother, Berniece's and Boy Willie's father, Boy Charles, once slavery had been abolished, was obsessed by the piano and determined to have it, particularly because, he said, "it was the story of our whole family and as long as Sutter had it, he had us. [W]e was still in slavery" (p. 45; act 1, scene 2). The three brothers, then, on the fourth of July in 1911, when Sutter was at a picnic, took the piano from his house. Doaker and Winning boy took it to family in another county, but Charles stayed behind. When Sutter found out what had happened, Boy Charles' house was burned down. But Charles was not in it. He was in a boxcar of a train, leaving town. Sutter and several accomplices had the train stopped and set the boxcar with Charles and four hobos on fire and they all died. Soon after that, every one of the men suspected of killing Charles and the hobos was found drowned at the bottom of their wells. The legend grew up that they had been killed by the ghosts of the Yellow Dog. Yellow Dog was the name of that railroad line. The five murdered men were the ghosts.

Consequently, Doaker concludes, Berniece will never sell the piano because her father died for it. Boy Willie argues, however, that it is just for that reason that he will sell the piano. It is the legacy his father died to leave him and for him to build on.

When Berniece returns and sees Willie and Lymon lifting the piano to see how heavy it is, she starts to pound on his chest, accusing him of killing her husband, Crawley. Willie stands perfectly still absorbing her blows and not retaliating. At that moment, the presence of Sutter's ghost is felt in the house and Maretha screams from upstairs the way one does when one sees a ghost.

As the second act begins, things seem to have returned to normal. Nothing has been resolved, but the routine of the household continues. Doaker irons his railroad uniform, Winning Boy cadges five dollars from him and gets another six by selling Lymon an old suit and an old pair of shoes he could not pawn. Willie and Lymon successfully sell the watermelons and prepare to go out on a night on the town to look for women. Berniece continues to resist Willie's intention to sell the piano and Willie remains adamant. Berniece continues, too, to resist Avery's proposal of marriage, but she does ask him to bless the house and exorcise Sutter's ghost, which everyone but Willie believes is haunting the house.

That night when Willie brings Grace, a young woman he has picked up in a bar, back to the house in hopes of seducing her, Berniece throws them out, not allowing such behavior, and they go to her place. When Lymon comes back after an unsuccessful evening, he and Berniece talk shyly. He wonders why she does not marry Avery, and she assures him he will find a woman who is right for him, but that he ought to avoid dissipation. He gives her a bottle of perfume he would have given to a woman if he had found one that night, and they kiss, but part. She goes to her bedroom and he sleeps on the couch.

The action concludes with a series of confrontations. As Boy Willie prepares to move the piano, and Berniece threatens to shoot him if he does, and

Avery tries to bless the house, and Winning Boy plays on the piano in order to keep Willie from moving it, the presence of Sutter's ghost intrudes and becomes apparent to everyone. In a scene where internal, spiritual, historical, and psychological conflicts are externalized, expressed and resolved, Boy Willie wrestles with Sutter's ghost, and Berniece finally sits down, after having long refused to touch it, at the piano, and plays as she sings a song calling upon her forebears, relentlessly repeating the words, "I want you to help me," until hearing the noise of Boy Willie's struggle with Sutter subside, with Willie having driven Sutter out of the house, she begins to chant, "Thank you." Willie takes his leave, going to catch the train back home, and parting tells Berniece that "if you and Maretha don't keep playing on that piano, ain't no telling when me and Sutter both liable to be back." She just chants one more "Thank you."

Symbols & Motifs

Sutter's ghost obtrudes into "The Piano Lesson" as a recurring motif. It is a prominent symbol, emerging at times of family discord, of the lingering, haunting post-slavery-era power of their white oppressors to divide and destroy individual black people, their solidarity, their families, and their sense of community and common purpose.

"The Piano Lesson" is full of ghosts, not just Sutter's. Besides the ghosts of the Yellow Dog, all the family's forebears are ghosts and haunt them, determining their actions and attitudes.

Railroads and railroad trains are also a recurring motif. Boy Charles is murdered in a boxcar. The ghosts of the Yellow Dog, the name of a railroad line, represent the avenging forces of assailed and broken black people. Doaker has worked for the railroad most of his life and is now a cook, a nurturing force, and uses railroad imagery to suggest the journey of life itself. Lymon hopes for work unloading boxcars. Railroads join the idea of constant motion, the possibility of flight, with predetermined routes that nevertheless allow the traveler a choice. As Doaker says, the railroad goes in all directions, but a passenger must know in which direction he or she is going. Doaker adds that if a passenger has taken the wrong direction, all that is needed is to wait for the train to come back, which it always does, and go in another direction. In "The Piano Lesson," the past comes back, and the characters start from where they have gotten (by having gone the wrong way) to travel to a new place.

The piano itself is a recurring motif, a symbol of the past, of the family's history, of their present struggle. But it is not only a symbol but a bearer of symbols since it is the medium through which the images of the past are conveyed to the present through the wood carver's art. The piano is a symbol of the medium of art and of the affective force of art. The piano confirms the power of art itself in the lives of people to serve as a force to join them together, once they accept and understand that art.

Historical Context

"The Piano Lesson" is a play about the power the influence of history has on the present as well as a historical play that is a meditation about history. First presented in 1987, it tells the story of the members of a black family, living in 1931, in Pittsburg, who are grappling with events that occurred in the periods before and after the Civil War. The play shows the way black people lived, and through Wilson's uncanny ear, how they spoke, in 1931, as well as what life was like for people under slavery and how black people were treated in the South at the beginning of the twentieth century.

The piano itself is a vehicle of history as well as a work of art. Boy Charles took it back from the Sutters because his family's history was carved on it. Boy Willie tells Berniece that she ought to celebrate her history rather than making her daughter feel ashamed of being who she is.

Societal Context

The social context in which "The Piano Lesson" occurs is the context of segregation. Segregation was a social system that took two forms. In the American South, it was "de jure" segregation, that is, segregation, or separation of the races by law or by a series of laws. In the North, segregation was "de facto," separation of the races not determined by a set of laws but existing in reality, in fact, because of the social patterns determined by the distribution of wealth, living arrangements, opportunities, secret covenants, etc.

Wilson not only explores the social reality of a black family in America in the early thirties but also provides because of his ear for the black speech of the time, a poetics and a grammar of that speech in the dialogue of his characters.

In addition, Wilson is helping to give black people, in 1987, a sense of pride by showing the complexity of black history and the humanity that endured throughout slavery and afterwards. As such, "The Piano Lesson" is a play that enhances the social consciousness of blacks and whites.

Religious Context

Wilson shows the vital role that religion plays in the lives of his characters and, by extension, in the black community.

Avery Brown represents a positive Christian spiritual center for a disenfranchised people, bringing hope not only of spiritual salvation to the flock he seeks to shepherd but also social redemption. Through a spiritual vision he envisages that he can heal his people of the lingering wounds of slavery. It is Avery, too, who blesses Berniece's house and helps to exorcise Sutter's ghost.

Although not prone to religion or Christianity, Willie, too, is shown to have a spiritual battle to face and go through, which he does when he wrestles with Sutter's ghost—as Jacob in the book of "Genesis" did when he wrestled with the angel

—and emerges from that battle with a renewed and expanded identity.

Scientific & Technological Context

The technology of the railroad is the dominant "mechanical" technology in "The Piano Lesson", given the recurring importance of the railroad to the family.

But automotive technology is also significant, particularly because the truck, which represents such technology, is a means of advancement for Willie. At the same time, the fact of the disproportionate allocation of such technological resources, tied to racial and class status, is made clear by the truck. The only truck available to Lymon is a used one that keeps breaking down.

The play also concerns the metaphysical technology of art as practiced through the craft of wood carving of such a caliber that it is raised to the level of art and thereby becomes a vehicle for conveying the life of the spirit.

Biographical Context

In 1965, after his father's death, Frederick August Kittel, Jr., born on April 27, 1945, in Pittsburg, took his mother's name and became August Wilson. Daisy Wilson was a black cleaning woman whose mother had walked from her home in North Carolina to Pittsburg. Daisy Wilson married Frederick Kittel, a German immigrant and a baker, but raised her six children by herself, after he left her, in a poor black Pittsburg neighborhood, in a two room apartment above a grocery store.

August Wilson had a checkered and insulting education. As the only black student at Central Catholic High School, he bore the brunt of racial taunts. He switched to a vocational high school, but found nothing there to engage him. He dropped out of his last high school in the tenth grade after he was accused of plagiarizing a paper he had written about Napoleon and began to work at menial jobs. For his education, he regularly frequented the Carnegie Library in Pittsburg, where he read voraciously.

In 1965, Wilson began writing, and in 1968, he started the Black Horizon Theater in the black section of Pittsburg. Several of his plays were produced in Pittsburg. In 1978, Wilson moved to Saint Paul, Minnesota. In 1980, he was awarded a fellowship for The Playwrights' Center in Minnesota, where he could work on plays and see them produced.

Wilson's career as a dramatist took fire in 1984, when "Ma Rainey's Black Bottom" was first produced at Yale and then in New York and won the New York Drama Critics Circle Award for the Best Play of 1985. "Ma Rainey's Black Bottom" was the first in a cycle of ten plays he wrote, including "The Piano Lesson", which won the Drama Desk Award for Outstanding New Play, the New York Drama Critics Circle Award for Best Play, and the Pulitzer Prize for Drama in 1990. These ten plays trace the movement and drama of the black experience through the twentieth century, decade by decade. Nine of them are set in Pittsburg. These plays include "Fences," for which Wilson won the New York Drama Critics Circle award for Best Play, the Drama Desk Award for Outstanding New Play, the Tony Award for Best Play, and the Pulitzer Prize for Drama, in 1987, and "Joe Turner's Come and Gone," which also won a Drama critics award in 1986.

Wilson died of liver cancer on October 2, 2005, in Seattle, Washington, where he worked with the Seattle Repertory Theater. He was buried in Pittsburg on October 8th.

Neil Heims, Ph.D.

Work Cited

Wilson, August. "The Piano Lesson." New York: Penguin, 1990. Print.

Discussion Questions

1. Describe the personalities of Berniece and Boy Willie and contrast these two figures particularly with regard to how mature and how responsible each one seems to be. Do they grow during the course of the play? Do they ever surprise you? When? How? How do you account for their differences?

2. How are Boy Willie and Winning Boy alike? How do you account for the recurrence of the "Boy" in each of their names? How does it reflect their social position? Do you think it affects their character? How?

3. The word "nigger" is generally not used in polite speech or in print, and when it is, is usually indicated by the expression "the 'n' word." Wilson uses it profusely in "The Piano Lesson." Explain its use there. Do you find its use objectionable in the play? Explain why or why not. Is it a racist term in the play? Consider it in relation to Berniece's admonition to Maretha in act 1, scene 1, "Don't be going down there showing your color." What does she mean? What kind of effect can that have on Maretha? What does it say about Berniece? Evaluate Willie's response to her warning.

4. Is Sutter the only ghost in "The Piano Lesson"? Who are the others? How do they manifest themselves? What is their role?

5. Did Boy Willie kill Sutter?

6. Is "The Piano Lesson" a feminist play or is it critical of feminism? Explain your answer.

7. Does "The Piano Lesson" exploit racial stereotypes? If so, how? If not, explain and show how it avoids doing so.

8. What is the role of religion in the life of the characters in "The Piano Lesson"?

9. How do Berniece and Boy Willie each change by the end of the play?

10. How significantly have social conditions changed since the time of "The Piano Lesson"? How have they remained the same?

Essay Ideas

1. Examine Winning Boy's attitude towards being a piano player, as he explains it in act 1, scene 2, and discuss its significance as a metaphor for a black man's relation to his own identity in America during the twenties and thirties in America.

2. Analyze Berniece's character.

3. What are the options, according to "The Piano Lesson," that black people living in the United States had during the 1920s and thirties?

4. Discuss the effect that the past has on the present in "The Piano Lesson."

5. What is the lesson of "The Piano Lesson"?

Pygmalion

by George Bernard Shaw

Content Synopsis

"Pygmalion" (1913) is the story of Eliza Doolittle, a young and impoverished flower girl who undergoes a process of social refinement. Act I opens with a scene in the Covent Garden area of London where a group of people, including Clara Eynsford-Hill, her mother and younger brother Freddy, find shelter from the rain. They are a poor but genteel family, scarcely able to afford a cab. Freddy is sent off to find one. Eliza comes on the scene with her wares, and Freddy inadvertently collides with her. Two gentlemen, Colonel Pickering and Professor Henry Higgins, both linguistic experts, also appear. The latter is so intrigued by Eliza's accent as she tries to sell flowers to the Colonel that he writes down what she says, making her nervous. He also claims that he could teach her to speak like a duchess while appearing quite inconsiderate of her as a person, as he rebukes her for being a sniveling "guttersnipe." He however, does, give her some money that she uses to pay for a cab, appropriating the one that Freddy had brought for his family.

Act II follows with Eliza, who comes to call on Higgins at his home the following day. Pickering is already there. Entertaining the hope of social advancement, Eliza takes Higgins up on his offer to give her elocution lessons and reveals she can pay for them. Pickering bets Higgins that he cannot succeed and offers to pay for her lessons if he does.

The housekeeper, Mrs. Pearce, takes charge of Eliza. Another visitor comes: Eliza's father Alfred. He does not care what happens to his daughter, but senses an opportunity to get money out of Higgins by effectively selling her to him. At the end of the scene, Higgins admits to Pickering that a difficult task lies ahead.

In Act III, Higgins' mother is at home entertaining the Eynsford-Hills. Higgins arrives and is less than gracious to the guests. He tells his mother that lessons with Eliza are progressing very well. Eliza then joins the party, conversing in an impeccably refined accent, although the substance of her conversation has not altered from the old days. Freddy is utterly charmed by her. After the guests and Eliza leave, Mrs. Higgins chides her son for what he is doing and asks what will become of Eliza once the "experiment" is over. Neither Higgins nor Pickering understands her concerns; they seem to treat the whole thing in the nature of a game.

It is midnight at Higgins' house during Act IV. Higgins, Pickering, and Eliza have just returned from a high-society ball where Eliza comported herself in such an exquisite manner that she was deemed to be foreign royalty, thus winning Higgins the bet. Pickering congratulates him. Both men scarcely seem to be aware of the tired and despondent Eliza. Pickering retires to bed. Higgins casually asks Eliza for his slippers and is astounded when she flings them at him. It is as Mrs. Higgins had foreseen; Eliza, upon her social transformation, is left lost, confused, and furious with Higgins. She feels she cannot return to her old life, but has no idea what else she can do either. Higgins is disappointed in what he feels is her total lack of gratitude and leaves her alone in the room.

In the following morning, during Act V, a rather agitated Higgins and Pickering arrive at Mrs. Higgins's house with the news that Eliza has disappeared overnight. Mrs. Higgins is very curt with Higgins, castigating him for his cavalier treatment of the girl from the first. Alfred Doolittle then arrives unexpectedly to inform Higgins that he is about to marry his "missus." He blames Higgins bitterly for recommending him to a rich and philanthropic American, who left him a sizeable annual pension upon his death and therefore pressured him into adopting a middle-class, moralistic lifestyle. He leaves, while Mrs. Higgins divulges that Eliza is upstairs. When Eliza comes down, she is quite self-assured and pointedly ignores Higgins. She looks, speaks, and acts as a perfect lady. However, upon seeing her father, she is momentarily startled back into her old speech, giving Higgins a chance to gloat. Eliza, Pickering, and Mrs. Higgins agree to attend the wedding. All leave the stage with the exception of Eliza and Higgins. Now, it becomes clear that Higgins does in fact have some feelings for Eliza, and he asks her to come back. Eliza responds that she will leave to marry Freddy, who loves her. Higgins reproves her lack of ambition, pointing out that, thanks to him, she can now pass for royalty. Indeed, she is now so self-confident that she declares that she can teach phonetics. This stings Higgins, but at the same time, he is pleased at her show of spirit. Eliza is about to depart for the wedding when Higgins gives her a list of errands to run. She refuses, but Higgins remains confident that she will obey him.

Shaw later changed the ending of "Pygmalion" in response to the 1938 film version, in which Eliza returns to Higgins, and it is implied they will get married. In this later ending, Eliza emphatically rejects the notion of marriage with Higgins and wonders what he will do without her. Higgins is left to scoff at the idea of her marrying Freddy. In view of earlier romantic interpretations put upon the ending of the play, Shaw also added a sequel in which he took pains to explain why Higgins and Eliza could not marry and outlined her subsequent life with Freddy. However, even here, Higgins and Eliza appear to retain a fascinating connection, and it is this aspect of the play that continues to exert the most appeal from audiences.

The play's title refers to the classical myth, as told by Ovid, of King "Pygmalion", who built a statue of his ideal woman and fell in love with it. It was a popular myth with nineteenth-century writers, although Shaw's treatment of it remains the best known by far. Higgins, too, attempts to create a perfect woman, but in less-than-romantic terms; rather, he behaves as though he is hardly aware that she is a flesh-and-blood creature from the start, with her own thoughts, feelings, and desires. However, it also seems that he is more drawn to her than he would care to admit.

Historical Context

In "Pygmalion," we have a clear picture of British society on the eve of World War I; the community still harbors fixed notions about class and gender that had persisted for centuries. There is no real hint of continuing social unrest of the era with Trade Union strikes, the high-profile campaign for women's rights, or the political build-up to the cataclysm of war, which would help shake loose some of the old social ideas, norms and conventions. "Pygmalion" presents a society that appears complacent, and set in its ways.

Societal Context

"Pygmalion" features representations of almost every level of society, from the lowly working class in the shape of the Doolittles, to the genteel poor (the Eynsford-Hills), the upper-middle-class (Higgins and Pickering), and the aristocracy (the ball at which Higgins wins his bet is sometimes staged). Class differences are shown to be rife in early twentieth-century Britain. Accent is a vital, distinguishing characteristic of class. The gulf between Eliza's "guttersnipe" speech and "proper" English is deliberately highlighted, for instance in Act I when Shaw makes a point of reproducing what Eliza says in a way that makes it appear quite unintelligible. Although the transformation of Eliza's speech and diction allows her to pass off as foreign royalty at the Ambassador's Ball, it may be questioned whether it really does bestow a new social opportunity upon her. Her attempts to master refinement of speech and behavior often make for comedy. For example, in Act II she talks with an impeccable accent in front of guests, but some substance of her conversation remains unchanged from the old days, though she remains unaware of this discrepancy. Something similar is also present in the person of Higgins. Although obsessed with the niceties of speech and pronunciation, he never seems to realize his own uncouth manners consistently infringe codes of decency and gentility upheld by his class.

On a deeper level, Eliza's social identity becomes confused when, because of Higgins' experiment, she is suddenly elevated from her class and entered into a sort of limbo. Similarly, her father is utterly miserable at the prospect of being sold into middle-class morality when his cause is taken up by a well-meaning, rich American. (Shaw also takes this opportunity to slyly poke fun at the philanthropic societies much in vogue at the time.) Social mobility was slowly increasing during this age, ever since the industrialization that had helped to change the face of British society in the previous century. However, the Doolittle's reaction shows that it was not at all an easy, or maybe even particularly desirable, transition.

Eliza might also be seen to suffer constraints placed upon her due to gender. As a poor flower girl, there would appear to be few avenues open to her until she is literally plucked from the gutter by Higgins. However, there were steadily increasing employment and educational opportunities for women at this time, and such opportunities would only accelerate further during the exigencies of World War I. The vigorous campaign conducted by the Suffragette movement, for instance, resulted in granting women the right to vote after the war. In "Pygmalion," Eliza appears as one of the so-called "New Women," fighting for her own rights by standing up to Higgins. She chooses what to do with her life and whom to marry. Even before her transformation, she takes advantage of her own business opportunity by setting up a flower shop. Though this is a fairly modest feat, it shows nevertheless that she is able to take steps for herself as a woman in order to gain some measure of economic and social independence.

Religious Context

Although Shaw believed in some kind of a "Life Force" that influences human actions (expressed most forcibly in his 1903 play Man and Superman), there is no sense of a god in any of his work. As co-founder of the Fabian society, he was keen to see human beings improve their lot through their own efforts rather than appealing to any external religious agency.

Scientific & Technological Context

"Pygmalion" explores the science of phonetics, an issue dear to Shaw's heart, as is clear in the preface to the work. He also mentions several eminent phoneticians of the century as possible prototypes for Higgins (although he does not intend the resemblance to go very far): for instance, Henry Sweet and Alexander Melville Bell, father of Alexander Graham Bell, inventor of the telephone. However, Shaw is concerned not only with the niceties of proper speech, but with the broader, deeper issues regarding the value and significance of language itself. Higgins, upon first meeting (and hearing) Eliza, chastises her:

> A woman who utters such depressing and disgusting sounds has no right to be anywhere—no right to live. Remember that you are a human being with a soul and the divine gift of articulate speech: that your native language is the language of Shakespeare and Milton and The Bible; and don't sit there crooning like a bilious pigeon. (Shaw 8)

The scientific study of language—principally linguistics (dealing with the more technical aspects) and philology (concentrating more on the historical development and significance)—burgeoned in the nineteenth-century. A noted philologist, Max Muller, held that language was a special distinguishing characteristic of the human race alone. This clashed with the Darwinian view that human speech evolved from animal cries and signs and, although infinitely more sophisticated, does not differ in essence from animal communication. However, both viewpoints did extol the vast superiority of human language as a form of communication. Higgins' observation, quoted above, might raise a laugh, but it also reveals an ingrained snobbery of his class toward the lower orders, mocking their speech and seeing in it a mark of inferiority and even proof that they are at a lower stage of development.

Biographical Context

Shaw was born in Dublin in 1856, and moved to England twenty years later. He started out as an unsuccessful writer of novels, but found his forte as a dramatist, fired by the example of Ibsen. He found in Ibsen a great degree of social realism, which he determined to bring to the English stage (although he did not bother with the deeper psychological and poetical aspects of Ibsen's work). He succeeded in this and dealt openly with thorny social issues such as prostitution in Mrs. Warren's Profession (1893). Other well-known plays include Man and Superman (1903), Major Barbara (1905), and the historical St. Joan (1923). Shaw was active in the socialist Fabian Society, which he co-founded, and he aimed to bring about various social reforms. He was also a vocal music and literature critic.

Shaw remains one of the most-quoted writers in the English language. His humor was of a dry yet scathing kind; his work is full of strictures against his society, as he never missed an opportunity to mock it. His wit is often compared to that of his fellow Irishman and playwright Oscar Wilde; although, wholly unlike Wilde, he insisted on a didactic element to his work. Indeed, in his preface to "Pygmalion," he declares that "art should never be anything else" (Shaw 3). However, "Pygmalion" is lauded for its comedy and romance elements, almost entirely eclipsing whatever didactic aims Shaw may originally have had in writing it.

Gurdip Panesar, Ph.D.

Work Cited
Shaw, George Bernard. "Pygmalion." London: Penguin, 2003.

Discussion Questions

1. Which character do you find most sympathetic? Explain your choice.
2. Do you think Higgins or Freddy would be a better husband for Eliza? Explain.
3. What role does Mrs. Higgins play?
4. The play is subtitled a "romance." How important do you think the romantic element is to the play?
5. Do you think Higgins's treatment of Eliza is unduly harsh? Why or why not?
6. What do you think Shaw is trying to say about the importance of proper speech? Is it merely a mark of social class? Explain.
7. Why is Alfred so miserable at the prospect of middle-class morality? What does this suggest about social class?
8. Do you think Eliza's social prospects have improved very much by the end of the play? Why or why not?
9. What role does profanity take on in the play? Which characters tend to cuss more and why?
10. What sort of social commentary does Shaw present throughout the play?

Essay Ideas

1. Examine the phenomenon of social mobility in "Pygmalion."
2. Consider the role of gender in "Pygmalion."
3. How far does "Pygmalion" succeed in being "didactic," in keeping with Shaw's stated aim?
4. Analyze the importance of language in "Pygmalion."
5. Examine the role of comedy in "Pygmalion."

Irish playwright George Bernard Shaw. He wrote "Pygmalian" in 1913, which is featured on page 147. "St. Joan," another of Shaw's plays, is featured on page 159. Photo: Library of Congress, Prints & Photographs Division, LC-USZ62-25210

A Raisin in the Sun

by Lorraine Hansberry

Content Synopsis

Act One, Scene 1 of this three-act play opens in the living room of the Younger family's small, worn-out apartment at dawn. The setting is the Southside of Chicago sometime between World War II and 1960. Segregation is still in place. Ruth Younger has risen and is trying to rouse her husband and son to get them ready for work and school. She is only thirty, but life has aged her; her once beautiful face appears tired and filled with disappointment. Ruth and her husband, Walter Lee, converse while their son Travis occupies the only bathroom—the one they share with the tenants across the hall. It is clear from their conversation that Ruth and Walter's relationship is strained.

When Travis comes out of the bathroom, he tries to get his mother to give him fifty cents for school. She refuses, claiming they do not have any money. Travis asks her if "the check" is coming tomorrow (Hansberry 28). When Walter Lee comes out of the bathroom, he generously gives Travis more money than he asked for. After Travis heads to school, Walter Lee talks to Ruth about how he wants to open a liquor store with his friends Willy Harris and Bobo. She does not take his friends seriously, but Walter is convinced that this investment will get the family out of poverty and out of their "beat up hole" of an apartment (32). Ruth has no such grand illusions and she reminds her husband that the money is not his to spend.

Walter Lee's sister, Beneatha, enters the room. She is twenty years old, pretty and more educated than the other members of the Younger family. While she waits for the neighbors to get out of the bathroom, Beneatha and Walter argue about Beneatha's dreams of going to medical school. He is bitter that all the others must work while she gets to spend her time in school. Like Ruth, Beneatha tells him that the money is Mama's, not his. He feels like he should have some rights to the insurance money because, "He was my father, too!" (38).

Walter leaves for his job as a driver and Mama enters the scene. She is sixty years old, full-bodied, and strong. She talks to Ruth about Walter Lee and is also not convinced about his investment plans. Ruth tells Mama that she and Walter are having problems connecting. They talk about what Mama should do with the money and she reminisces about her late husband. She contemplates buying a house with the money. Beneatha returns from the bathroom and talks about her guitar lessons. Mama wishes she just settle down and not "flit" from hobby to hobby. Beneatha talks about a man she is dating, George Murchison. He is rich and cultured, but she has no interest in marrying him despite Mama's encouragement. As they continue talking about Beneatha's future, she tells Mama that she does not believe in God. Mama is outraged and returns to thoughts of buying a home and having her own garden. The scene ends when Mama returns from her reverie to find Ruth passed out on the floor.

Scene Two takes place in the Youngers apartment one day later, a Saturday. Mama and Beneatha are cleaning the apartment while Walter Lee talks to Willy on the phone. Everyone is waiting for the mail to arrive, knowing that the check will be there soon. Beneatha complains about the cockroaches. Ruth returns from an appointment and Mama discovers that Ruth is pregnant and contemplating an abortion. The doorbell rings, interrupting their conversation; Beneatha's African friend, Asagai, has arrived for a visit. He has brought her some traditional robes from Nigeria. They discuss identity and Beneatha insists that she is not an assimilationist despite the fact that she straightens her hair in the American fashion. Asagai expresses his fondness for Beneatha, but she does not know how to handle his affection.

Shortly after Asagai leaves, the check for ten thousand dollars arrives in the mail. Walter comes home and is excited over the check and his plans with Willy Harris. Mama tells him that she will not invest in a liquor store. When Ruth tries to talk to him, he shuts her out and she storms off. He cannot control his anger and his dissatisfaction with life has overtaken him. Mama tells him that Ruth is pregnant and considering terminating it. She tells him to be a man and say something encouraging to Ruth, but instead he walks out the door.

Act Two, Scene 1 opens later the same day. Ruth is ironing when Beneatha comes out of her room wearing the Nigerian robes and a headdress. She puts on a record of Nigerian music and begins dancing. Walter comes home drunk and starts moving around the room in a tribal pose. He and Beneatha get caught up in the mood and chant and dance their way around the room. When her date, George Murchison arrives, Walter is on the table with his shirt open wielding an imaginary spear. George urges her to get ready and she takes off her headdress revealing that she has cut her hair short

and it is no longer straightened. George is appalled and Beneatha calls him assimilationist, arguing for the need to honor their African heritage. Ruth intervenes and Beneatha goes to get ready. In the meantime, Walter insults George and after George and Beneatha leave, Walter and Ruth argue over the rift in their marriage. Walter is overflowing with bitterness at his place in life. Mama comes home and tells the family that she just put a down payment on a house. Everyone is happy except Walter who wishes he had to power to make decisions and lead the household. Mama then reveals that the house she has purchased is in a white neighborhood.

Scene Two presents the Younger family a few weeks later. There are packing boxes around the house. George and Beneatha return from a date, and he makes advances on her. She turns away from him and wants to talk. He makes it clear that he wants a woman who is not full of ideas, so Beneatha asks him to leave. Walter's boss calls because he has not been to work in three days. Ruth answers and makes excuses for him. He explains to Mama that he is depressed and has been drinking at the Green Hat for the past few days. Mama says that her dreams are meaningless if they are going to "destroy" her son (106). She explains that she put $3,500 down on the house and that the remaining insurance money will be his responsibility. She hands him the money and asks him to open a bank account and set some aside for Beneatha's school. He can spend the rest as he sees fit. This trust changes Walter and the scene ends with him telling his son he will hand him the world.

Scene Three takes place one week later, on moving day. Ruth and Beneatha are joyfully finishing the family's packing. Walter comes home and dances with Ruth. It is clear that their relationship has improved from the beginning of the play. They are renewed. A man comes to the door. He is from their new neighborhood and, as politely as he can, tells them they are not wanted. He offers to buy their new house back for more than what they paid for it. Walter Lee takes charge and tells the man to leave.

When Mama arrives home, they tell her what happened. She prays for protection. The family gives Mama some gifts to celebrate their new home, a set of gardening tools and a big gardening hat. Everyone is hopeful.

Walter's friend Bobo comes to the door. He is distraught and explains to Walter that Willy Harris took off with their investment money. Walter is destroyed. He confesses to his family that he spent his and Beneatha's school money on this investment and now all the money is gone.

Act Three resumes an hour later. The Youngers are in separate rooms and the house is filled with gloom. Walter Lee is lying on his bed staring at the ceiling. Beneatha is in the living room when the doorbell rings. It is Asagai and she explains to him how the money is gone. She tells him a story about when she was young and realized that she wanted to be a doctor. She wanted to cure people, but now she is not sure if she cares enough, because mankind's problems are much bigger than anything she can cure. They argue about life, and while Beneatha believes it is a circle, Asagai thinks it is a long line that keeps changing. He comes from a place where there are much greater ills than lost money, and he wants to return to bring education and make a difference. Before he leaves, he asks Beneatha to think about returning to Nigeria with him.

Mama enters the room and starts unpacking. Ruth begs her not to and tells her that they can still make it work paying the mortgage on the new house, but Mama has lost faith. When Walter enters the room, he tells them that he has called back Mr. Lindner, the man who offered them money to stay out of his neighborhood. He figures he can get the man to give them lots of money to stay away. Even Mama objects to making money off someone else's prejudice. She tells him, "ain't nobody in my family never let nobody pay 'em no money that

was a way of telling us we wasn't fit to walk the earth. We ain't never been that poor" (143). Walter tells her that he did not make the world this way but he has to live in it, and he storms off. Beneatha tells Mama that he is no brother of hers, but Mama tells her that love does not work that way; "there is always something left to love" (145).

Mr. Lindner arrives at the Younger's apartment ready to make a deal. Walter sits down and tells him that they are proud people, and they do not want his money. He tells Mr. Lindner that they will try to be good neighbors, but they are going to move into their house. Mr. Lindner leaves and the family, renewed, gathers their things and prepares to move. Mama notes to Ruth that Walter Lee "came into his manhood today," takes one last look at the apartment, takes her houseplant and leaves.

Symbols & Motifs

A recurring symbol in "A Raisin in the Sun" is Mama's houseplant. The first thing that Mama does when she enters the scene is tend to her houseplant: "She crosses through the room, goes to the window, opens it, and brings in a feeble little plant growing doggedly in a small pot on the window sill" (39). Throughout the play, Mama takes care of this plant as if it was a child and, in fact, it symbolizes her unconditional love for her children. The plant struggles to survive and despite its "feeble"-ness, Mama is determined to care for the plant and even to take it with her to the new house. Mama dreams of having her own home with a yard so she can have a garden to tend to. At the end of the play, Mama leaves the apartment and then comes back for her plant, a symbol of both her dreams and her children, neither of which she will abandon.

The title of the play references a line from the Langston Hughes poem, "Harlem—A Dream Deferred." The insurance money symbolizes each of the Younger's dreams for the future. What happens when the money is lost and some of those dreams are put on hold is different for each person.

Fortunately, the dream of owning a home is still realized and the family comes together to embrace that dream.

Historical Context

The works of Langston Hughes largely inspired Hansberry. Originally entitled "The Crystal Stair" after a Hughes poem, Hansberry later renamed her first play "A Raisin in the Sun," a quote from a line in the Hughes poem "Harlem—A Dream Deferred." Hansberry, and the play's creative team, was unsure as to whether the play would be a success, but immediately upon its premiere, it became a huge Broadway hit. It was also the first Broadway play to be directed by an African-American since 1907. In 1961, "A Raisin in the Sun" was made into a film starring Sidney Poitier (a member of the original cast) and was nominated for an Oscar for Best Screenplay.

The play focuses on a topic that was influenced by Hansberry's own experience. In 1937, her family moved into an all-white neighborhood outside of Chicago. A mob of people attempted to scare the Hansberrys out of the neighborhood, but rather than move, the family sued.

Societal Context

The play addresses the societal problems of segregation and discrimination that were rampant in the 1950s when the play was written. The Brown vs. the Board of Education decision in 1954 determined that segregated schools were not of equal quality ("Civil Rights Era") and therefore in violation of federal law. Rosa Parks' refusal to sit on the back of a public bus in 1955 led the way to the desegregation of buses. The Civil Rights movement was on its way, but not without much struggle and resistance from the white majority. When the city of Little Rock, Arkansas, decided to desegregate its Central High School in 1957, federal intervention, including the use of paratroopers, was required in order to ensure the African American students, who came to be known as "The Little Rock Nine," could safely attend school ("Civil Rights Era").

Lorraine Hansberry wrote "A Raisin in the Sun" in 1958, just as the movement was gaining steam. Her play addresses the ugliness of racism and the damage it can do to those who have been stifled under its reign. Walter Lee is filled with bitterness and rage at his place in society. He dreams bigger, but does not quite know how to achieve those dreams and thereby becomes his own roadblock. He associates the road to success with money rather than with hard work. It is not until the end of the play that Walter and the rest of the family rise above their circumstances and unite to achieve their dreams.

Biographical Context

Lorraine Hansberry was born in Chicago in 1930, to a successful black family. Her parents were well-educated individuals as well as vocal civil rights activists. Hansberry attended Chicago's public schools, which were segregated at the time. She briefly attended the University of Madison at Wisconsin before moving to New York to pursue a career as a writer. There she met the writer Langston Hughes, who greatly influenced her work ("Biography of an Intellectual"). In 1953, she married Robert Nemiroff, a white Jewish man whom she met at a protest against the exclusion of black athletes from university sports. She worked as an editor for a radical black newspaper "Freedom" before pursuing writing full time ("Lorraine Hansberry").

"A Raisin in the Sun" was Hansberry's first play. Published when she was just 29, it won the New York Drama Critic's Circle Award as Best Play of the Year. She was the youngest American and the first black playwright ever to receive the award ("Lorraine Hansberry"). The success of the play gave Hansberry a voice in the Civil Rights Movement, in which she took an active role. Hansberry and Nemiroff divorced in 1964. She died from cancer in 1965, at the young age of 34, during the run of her second play "The Sign in Sidney Brustein's Window." Nemiroff finished and produced her third play, "Les Blancs," after her death. Her autobiography, "To Be Young, Gifted and Black," was published posthumously, and in 1969, became another hit on Broadway. It was not revealed until many years after her death that Hansberry had identified herself as a lesbian ("Lorraine Hansberry"). Quoted as saying, "I was born black and female," these two roles dominated her life and her brief but enduring career.

Jennifer Bouchard, M.Ed.

Works Cited

"Biography of an Intellectual," *Social Justice Movements*. 13 Jan. 2006. Columbia University. Web. 23 April 2009.

"Civil Rights Era," *African American Odyssey*. 21 Mar. 2008. Library of Congress. Web. 28 Apr. 2009.

Hansberry, Lorraine. "A Raisin in the Sun." New York: Vintage Books, 1958. Print.

"IMDB: Internet Movie Database." Imdb.com, Inc. Web. 23 April 2009.

"Lorraine Hansberry," "Voices from the Gaps: Women Artists and Writers of Color". University of Minnesota, 2006. Web. 23 April 2009.

Discussion Questions

1. Which character do you think is the most sympathetic? The least sympathetic?
2. Outline each character's dream and show how each is systematically destroyed.
3. Discuss the way the characters communicate with one another.
4. Why does Asagai call Beneatha "Alaiyo"? How is his name for her true?
5. What is the significance of Mama's houseplant?
6. How does the content of the play relate to its title?
7. How has Walter become a man by the end of the play?
8. What did you think of the play's ending? Is it a tragedy or a success?
9. What do you think will happen to the Youngers after they move?
10. What is the theme of "A Raisin in the Sun"?

Essay Ideas

1. Develop a formal argument, supported with text evidence, detailing the main statement or theme of the play.
2. Analyze Hansberry's writing style. Examine the dialogue, suspense, supporting characters, and tone.
3. Discuss the role of morality in the play. Evaluate whether you think the characters are redeemed in the end.
4. Compare and contrast the characters of Ruth and Beneatha. Discuss their roles as twentieth-century women and how they approach life.
5. Write an epilogue in which you provide an update on the Youngers one year later.

Saint Joan

by George Bernard Shaw

Content Synopsis

At his castle, Captain Robert de Baudricourt, a handsome, but blustering, military nincompoop is storming angrily at his steward because, according to the steward, the hens have not been laying, nor the cows giving milk, because they are under a spell. Baudricourt scoffs at this explanation, accusing the steward of theft or permitting theft. However, the steward insists that as long as de Baudricourt refuses to see a young woman, Joan, waiting at the gate to be admitted, as he did two days ago, the hens will not lay, and the maid will not leave. In fact, he informs his master, she inspires all the men and fills them with a sense of courage, not with the fear they feel because of de Baudricourt.

In anger, de Baudricourt summons Joan to him. He is determined to get rid of her and believes her wish to be a soldier and command the troops in battle against the English for France is absurd. Nevertheless, her charm is such and her words so innocent and assured that she succeeds in turning him around and getting the horse, armor, and soldiers she is seeking. She intends then to gain an audience with the Dauphin and convince him to lead a siege at Orleans against the English.

The Dauphin is floundering, powerless, and does not inspire the French with awe or a sense of common purpose, but Joan intends to crown him king at Rheims and invest him with the authority of royal and national charisma.

Robert de Baudricourt grants her wishes and sends her off to the Dauphin at Chinon to pursue her mission. The steward enters to announce that "the hens are laying like mad," and de Baudricourt exclaims that Joan "did come from God."

In the throne room at the castle in Chinon, the Archbishop of Rheims and the Lord Chamberlain, Monseigneur de la Trémouille wait impatiently for the Dauphin, complaining about the amount of money he owes them. Instead of the Dauphin, Gilles de Rais ("a historical figure who was to become a brutal serial killer and is thought to be the prototype for the fairy tale character Bluebeard"), and Captain La Hire arrive. They are astonished by La Hire. He tells them of a soldier who has a reputation for no restraint in the coarseness or frequency of his swearing, but who, after another soldier reproached him for swearing, fell down a well. That soldier was not a soldier but an angel, La Hire says. With great reverence, then, he tells them about Joan.

King Charles VII, still called the Dauphin because, although his father has died he has not yet been crowned, enters. The relationship between the Dauphin and the nobles is in shambles. They bicker, taunt, insult, and reproach each other. Charles is fumblingly ineffective as a man and as a ruler.

Learning that Joan is coming to see the king, the Archbishop and Trémouille insist he not see her, but Charles insists that he will, particularly because de Baudricourt writes that she has promised to beat the English at Orleans, where the French have been stymied despite their good generals because their fleet is constrained by a bad wind. Desperate for a miracle, the nobles agree to allow Joan to see the king with her proposal to fight, although the archbishop notes that she must be examined by the Church. As a preliminary test, they decide to pretend that Bluebeard is the king in order to see if they can fool Joan or if she will show her powers by knowing who the king is despite their ruse. With no trouble, and joining in the general merriment, Joan finds the Dauphin and explains her mission: to drive out the English and crown him king at the cathedral at Rheims. She maintains her authority despite the courtiers' mockery, and the Archbishop gives her his approval.

Alone with Joan, Charles reveals his weakness, fear, and lack of authority, as well as his dislike of military exploits and danger. He wants a calm, gentle, comfortable life. She tells him, however, that he must yield to God's plan for him and that he will find he has more strength and authority after he has actually been crowned.

Inspired by her, but not entirely free of his insecurity, Charles makes Joan the commander of his army and she sets off for Orleans.

At Orleans the commander of the army, Dunois is pacing back and forth, trying to compose verses to cajole the west wind, frustrated that the wind is from the east when he needs a west wind for his fleet to sail the Loire and rout the English. Joan arrives, talks strategy with Dunois, and as they are about to go to church to pray for a change of wind, the page notices that the wind has changed, a change they attribute to Joan's arrival. The French force sets off joyously to defeat the English.

In the English camp, after a number of French victories, a Nobleman and a Chaplain talk. The Nobleman laments the fact that men, encouraged by Joan's nationalism, are beginning to think of themselves in national rather than in regional

terms: as Englishmen or Frenchmen rather than as Bretons or Picards; that their loyalties are to the English or French king rather than to their regional, feudal lords. When the Chaplain mentions Joan, the Nobleman assures him that one faction among the French will sell her to the English and that the English will burn her for a witch.

The Bishop of Beauvais, Monseigneur Cauchon, for whom they have been waiting, joins them. He explains that Joan is not a witch, that her victories are not necessarily miracles, but that she is a heretic, leading men to believe that there is another voice and agency of Divine authority beside the Catholic Church. The Archbishop argues that the Church does not wish to burn Joan but to seek her salvation by convincing her to renounce her heresy, and that if a heretic does not repent, then the Church turns the heretic over to the secular authority, which is responsible for the burning.

Joan is disheartened that Charles, now king hopes to stop fighting before the English are entirely expelled from France and not try to capture Paris. When she scolds Charles for calling their victories luck rather than God's work, the Archbishop scolds her for the sin of pride and for thinking she knows better than others what to do regarding military strategy. Innocently, she responds that she does and delivers a lecture on battle strategy. The Archbishop adheres to his rebuke. She is a heretic because she sets herself above the authority of the church, he says. The men tell Joan that if the English or the Burgundians capture her, they will burn her as a witch and that they will not ransom her or fight for her release. The Archbishop repeatedly calls her disobedient and willful.

Joan refuses to heed them and accepts being alone in her godliness, condemning their institutions as separated from God. Joan goes forth to battle even without their support, but a hero to the people.

It is 1431, two years after Joan crowned Charles and nine months after she was captured by the Burgundians and sold to the English. She is now a prisoner of the Inquisition and on trial for heresy in Rouen. The English look forward to her conviction and the churchmen argue they are hoping they can avoid a conviction by convincing Joan to repent and recant what they consider her heretical belief. But, they report, Joan seems unlikely to do so and seems as eager to be burned as the English are to see her burned.

After arguments between the prosecutors of the Inquisition and Joan in which they attempt to win her recantation and she refuses to say that the voices whose instructions she obeyed were not from God, when she is condemned to be burned, she despairs because her voices told her she would not be burned. They have, she fears, betrayed her. In consequence, she is ready to believe they were sent by the devil and not God. She signs a confession of recantation and is declared free from the "danger of excommunication." She escapes burning. The English are furious. But she does not escape punishment. Declared by the Church a sinner, she is sentenced to life imprisonment. Astounded that she is not to be set free, to see the daylight and enjoy the natural world, Joan tears up her recantation and tells them to "[l]ight your fire," that her voices were right, that they are of the devil's party and she, of God's. She is pronounced a heretic and sent to the stake.

The Inquisitor, once the English have Joan, declares that she really was an innocent. The English chaplain, who had so much called for her burning, upon seeing it is horrified and tells of an English soldier who for pity gave the dying Joan two sticks tied together for a cross. In her dying, Joan filled the churchmen and most of the English with a sense that she was of heaven, not of hell. The executioner reports that her heart would not burn.

In 1456, the news that Joan's sentence has been reversed by an ecclesiastical court is brought to Charles, who has now become a strong king. He falls asleep and in a dream, Joan, the members of the court, and the soldier who gave her the makeshift cross appear to him. They reminisce about the trial and reconcile. Into this dream scene steps a man dressed in the style of the 1920s. He announces that Joan has been beatified, made a saint by the Catholic Church. Everyone praises her, but when she wonders if she ought to come back from the dead, everyone withdraws and Joan is left to meditate on the fact that the earth is not yet ready, if ever it will be, to receive God's saints.

Symbols & Motifs

Witty and intellectual debate, designed to reframe and redefine accepted ideas and phenomena, whether about matters of church or state, of religion or nationalism, constitute an ongoing and principal motif of "Saint Joan." Paradox, likewise, defines the dialogue and the thought of the play. The archbishop, for example, discussing whether Joan actually performs miracles explains that "[a] miracle—is an event which creates faith. They may seem very wonderful to the people who witness them, and very simple to those who perform them. That does not matter: if they confirm or create faith they are true miracles." La Trémouille asks, "Even when they are frauds?" The archbishop responds, "Frauds deceive. An event which creates faith does not deceive: therefore it is not a fraud, but a miracle."

The conflict between the authority of individual intelligence and the doctrines of institutions is also an ongoing theme of the play. Joan trusts in herself, that is, she trusts in the authenticity of her experience, that the voices she hears are sacred and from God. The churchmen do not dispute that as much as the principle of individual authority. Joan's experience threatens the authority of the Church as the agency of mediation between God and mankind. Her voices, according to the churchmen are diabolical because they undermine Church authority, not because they go against God. The conflict between the Church and Joan is a conflict between authority and conscience. That conflict symbolically represents the conflict between Catholicism and Protestantism.

In the secular realm, a recurring motif is the conflict between the feudal authority that had characterized the middle ages and the emerging nationalism. Feudalism demanded loyalty to a particular Lord. Nationalism transfers that loyalty to the idea of a country, France or England, for example, and to a central figure, a king who gains ascendancy over the Lords.

Historical Context

"Saint Joan" is a historical play in which Shaw uses historical events to analyze the intellectual and social evolutions of history. The play reflects the emergence of Protestantism in religion and nationalism as secular authority. Protestantism sets the force of individual conscience and direct communication between a person and God over the authority of a church that represents itself as a mediator, through its rules, between persons and God. (Although Martin Luther had not yet formalized this division, the movement had already begun.) Nationalism established the idea of national identity, which Joan advocates, and loyalty to king and country, over a feudal structure composed of many lords and their vassals. Feudalism is a system of decentralized loyalties. Regional lords, nobles, rule a distinct population, and these lords present a counterforce to the king.

In the first scene, Joan argues, "We are all subject to the King of Heaven; and He gave us our countries and our languages, and meant us to keep to them.

Shaw also uses the play to plot the course of Joan's rise, to consider the working of the historical institution of the Catholic Inquisition, and to trace the swerves of historical opinion as Joan moves from being considered a hero, to a heretic, to a saint.

Societal Context

"Saint Joan" Shaw describes the social structure of Feudalism, a confederation of nobles given their land by the king but not socially or politically inferior to the king. He shows, too, the division of authority between the decentralized feudal lords and the monolithic, medieval Catholic Church. Shaw also describes the roles and places of individuals in that system. Joan is as scandalous because she eschews women's clothing and dresses as a man as she is for violating the order established by the Church. Wearing men's clothing disrupts the social order by challenging the social roles that define that order.

Religious Context

"Saint Joan" is less a play about religion or faith than about religious authority. It considers the question, upon what authority is a person's faith based? It is a play that sets a centralized power structure, the Catholic Church, against individual conscience, and formal doctrine against individual experience.

The religious, as well as the secular issue, is clearly expressed by Cauchon, the churchman in Scene IV: "It is the protest of the individual soul against the interference of priest or peer between the private man and his God. I should call it Protestantism if I had to find a name for it."

Joan puts it more pithily in Scene VI when she asks, "What other judgment can I judge by but my own?"

Scientific & Technological Context

"Saint Joan" chronicles a historical moment when the technology of knowing was undergoing a change that set opposing ways of accounting for phenomena against each other. Joan of Arc is a maid who heard voices that she believed were voices of the saints sent to her by God and which enabled her to perform miracles. The idea of causality, then, becomes a central problem of the play. At the root of causality, in the play, is the conflict between divine intervention, miracles, and natural causation linked to coincidence. A soldier falls down a well: is it a miraculous punishment occurring after Joan reproaches him for a foul mouth, or just a coincidence? Similarly, does the wind just happen to change on the Loire, as winds do, or was it Joan's presence? Shaw does not take a side. He presents a conflict in ways of making interpretation.

The technology of war is changing, too, moving from sword and shield combat in heavy armor to the use of gun powder. Attitudes towards war are also undergoing a change. Joan urges the mentality of loyalty to God and country to lead soldiers, not personal gain and self-interest.

Biographical Context

Shaw not only wrote plays, like "Saint Joan," that he intended to be accounts of historical eras and events. He also hoped to insert himself into and affect the flow of events, historical, social, political, aesthetic, and cultural, by his work, and, through his work, by the critical operation of his intellect and the paradoxical keenness and wit of his iconoclastic insights. In his plays as well as the pamphlets, reviews, prefaces, letters, and novels that he wrote, Shaw was, fundamentally, a polemicist and a propagandist. Among the causes he championed were socialism, pacifism, vegetarianism, human improvement through the evolutionary workings of a life force, and a revision of English spelling. As a music critic, he was a champion of the works of the German composer, Richard Wagner, and, as a drama critic, he championed the social drama of the Norwegian playwright, Henrik Ibsen. He favored Ibsen's choosing social issues as the subjects for his plays and Ibsen's use of realism in their construction and presentation.

Shaw was awarded an Academy Award in 1938 for the screenplay of the film version of his play "Pygmalion." "Pygmalion," too, served as the basis for the highly successful Broadway musical of the 1950s, "My Fair Lady," by Alan Jay Lerner and Frederick Loewe. For "Saint Joan," Shaw was awarded the Nobel Prize for Literature in 1925. He accepted the award but refused the monetary award requesting that it be devoted to translating Swedish literature into English.

George Bernard Shaw was born on July 26, 1856 in Dublin, Ireland. His father was a grain merchant and his mother was a singer who abandoned his father in 1872, when Shaw was sixteen, and went to live with her voice teacher in London. Shaw remained in Dublin with his father for another four years and then joined his mother and her lover and his sisters in their household in London. Shaw detested his formal schooling, comparing school to prison and educated himself at public libraries and the reading room of the British Museum.

In 1898, he married Charlotte Payne-Townshend, like himself a socialist and a feminist. They had no children.

Shaw's first literary attempts were rather unsuccessful novels that were published years after he wrote them, once he had become famous, first as a reviewer and critic of music and theater and then as a playwright himself. His first plays, "Mrs. Warren's Profession" (1893), "Arms and the Man" (1894), and "Candida" (1894) were successful from their first appearance and are still produced, as are the plays that followed, "Caesar and Cleopatra" (1898), "Man and Superman" (1903), "Major Barbara" (1905) and "The Doctor's Dilemma" (1906). Shaw continued writing plays, including "Saint Joan," "Heartbreak House," "Androcles and the Lion," "Back to Methusela," and "Pygmalion," as well as a number of others, a total of more than sixty, before his death.

Shaw was a socialist, a founder of the Fabian Socialists, a group dedicated to a non-violent and evolutionary development of socialism, and a founder of the London School of Economics.

Shaw died on November 2, 1950. His ashes were mixed with his wife's and scattered on the paths that wind around a statue of Saint Joan in their garden in Hertfordshire, England.

Neil Heims, Ph.D.

Work Cited

Shaw, George Bernard. "Saint Joan." New York: Penguin Classics, 2001. Print.

Discussion Questions

1. Discuss whether Shaw's characters seem like fully realized people or seem to be determined by the roles the dramatist has assigned them.
2. Consider whether the churchmen are hypocrites? What is their primary interest?
3. Is Joan a fool? Is she a Jesus figure? Do those two terms imply one another?
4. Explore the varieties of authority postulated in "Saint Joan" and the virtues and the faults of each.
5. Is "Saint Joan" actually a play about religion or does it use an event in the history of religion for another purpose? If so, what is that purpose? If the play is about religion, what does it say about religion?
6. Explore the importance of power in "Saint Joan" and the varieties of power explored in the play.
7. Are there, or have there been, any situations in your own life that remind you of Joan's situation in the play?
8. According to the play, what are the differences between Catholicism and Protestantism? In what way is Joan actually a Protestant rather than a Catholic saint?
9. From the way he portrays nearly everyone but Joan, what ideas do you derive regarding Shaw's opinion of mankind as a whole?
10. Analyze Shaw's use of irony. What is its intellectual effect in "Saint Joan?" Consider the effect of how what the characters say and how they act often goes against what you might expect people in their positions to say and do. What effect does that discrepancy have in shaping the intellectual climate of the play?

Essay Ideas

1. In what way is Joan a harbinger of nationalism?
2. Discuss the meaning and the importance of heresy in "Saint Joan."
3. Compare and contrast the attitudes of the churchmen and the English towards Joan.
4. What is the case the churchmen make against Joan and why do they make it?
5. Describe Joan as a character.

She Stoops to Conquer

by Oliver Goldsmith

Content Synopsis

Act I

After the "Prologue," which asks for the audience's favor and proposes to cure the ill and dying muse of comedy from the ailments of ",," the play begins in Mr. and Mrs. Hardcastle's old country house. We are introduced to the main country characters: the Hardcastles, Mrs. Hardcastle's son Tony Lumpkin, her niece Constance Neville, and Mr. Hardcastle's daughter, Kate.

In Act I Scene 2, we are transported to the Three Pigeons Inn, where we meet Marlow and his friend Hastings, whom Constance had earlier described as her town "admirer" ("She Stoops" 241). Hearing that they have lost their way, Tony Lumpkin grabs the opportunity and sets a trap for the visiting gentlemen: he directs them to their destination, the Hardcastle mansion, but says that it is "one of the best inns in the whole county" (247). However unrealistic and contrived this joke might seem, Goldsmith gives good logical basis for it; after all, in Act I Scene 1, Mrs. Hardcastle had already complained about their mansion "that looks for all the world like an inn" (237). Thus, the main plot of the comedy is defined by Tony's plotting (Malek).

Act II

Act II begins with Mr. Hardcastle training his servants so that they can give due reception to the visiting gentlemen. The conversation gives a comically stereotypical view of country life by playing on the dialects of simple folks. Immediately following, Marlow and Hastings arrive "to the comforts of a clean room and a good fire" (251). Marlow confirms the rumors about his shyness among women of rank and his rowdiness among women of lower orders, raising the question of how he should ever think of marrying any lady. He also explains that he has no enthusiasm for the marriage arranged by his father and he has chosen to come only because in this way Hastings may have a chance to meet his sweetheart Constance.

When Mr. Hardcastle enters, he tries to strike up a conversation and soon starts to boast of his military exploits, substantiating Mrs. Hardcastle's earlier complaints. The scene turns into an absurd dialogue of misconception, after which Mr. Hardcastle believes he has met the two worst and rudest city gentlemen, while they, in turn, are partly tired, partly amused by the "innkeeper's philosophy" (256).

When Marlow leaves with Mr. Hardcastle at his back, Constance Neville comes in, surprising Hastings. After he explains his amazement at this chance encounter at an inn, Constance tells him the truth about the place. She sees through it at once, understanding that Tony must have set the guests up. Constance assures Hastings that she is ready to marry him, but she would prefer if her dowry, now in the care of her aunt Mrs. Hardcastle, could be legally theirs. However, Mrs. Hardcastle wants her son Tony to marry Constance, so that her fortune may remain in the family—ignoring the fact that Tony and Constance actually despise each other. We are introduced to the jewel-box subplot, concerning the little treasure of which Mrs. Hardcastle is so protective.

The lovers agree that, for the time being, they should leave Marlow in the dark. Marlow and Kate Hardcastle engage in a dialogue that comically confirms all that we have heard about Marlow's shyness with women of his own rank. Kate states that "I understand you perfectly, sir" (263), but Marlow does not believe her and leaves the room in a state of confusion.

When Mrs. Hardcastle tries to demonstrate how amicably Tony courts Constance, her son retorts rudely, stressing that he has no nice feelings towards his cousin. This highlights the antagonism between the spoilt child and his mother, which is one of the most dramatic elements in the conflicts of the play. Hastings offers to "lecture the young gentleman a little" (268). Instead of instructing Tony in the way of manners, however, he suggests eloping with Constance, with which Tony is eager to assist.

Act III

Mr. Hardcastle and Kate discuss the character of Marlow, who has, in the meantime, continued behaving in his inappropriate behavior. The father cannot understand the daughter's misconception of the suitor's character, but on one thing they seem to agree: "to reject him" (272). Still, Kate has her conditions and sets out plotting to prove Marlow "less impudent" and "more respectful" towards her father and to show that he is "more presuming" and "more importunate" towards her. At this point, she takes over the main plot, and the successful conclusion of the play depends upon her adroitness in orchestrating the outcome.

Meanwhile, Tony has stolen the jewel-box. Constance, however, would prefer to go the lawful way,

which worries Hastings. Mrs. Hardcastle is unwilling to part with the jewels and would rather pretend they have been lost—a fact to which Tony is ready to testify. When Mrs. Hardcastle leaves the stage, Tony explains to Constance that the jewels have, indeed, been stolen, by no one else but himself. His mother's hypocrisy is further revealed as she storms onto the stage once more, furiously shouting about the robbery. Tony continues mocking her, as if they were still play-acting the loss of the jewels, and the scene turns into downright slapstick comedy, as he keeps repeating, "I can bear witness to that" (276–77).

Kate insists on talking to Marlow, and when he finally looks at her, his earlier refusal turns into the wildest confession of infatuation. Immediately, he starts begging Kate for a kiss, first metaphorically (deliberately misunderstood by Kate), and then directly "Attempting to kiss her" (279). Nevertheless, Kate is determined to teach him a lesson and retorts in the most bitingly ironical manner: "Pray, sir, keep your distance. One would think you wanted to know one's age as they do horses, by mark of mouth" (279).

Marlow now goes on to brag of his conquests among the ladies, while speaking of Kate in derogatory words. The eroticism of the scene heightens as Marlow tells about his past exploits and tries to use any pretext to seduce the "barmaid." However, just as he grasps Kate's hand, and she starts struggling to break free, Mr. Hardcastle enters, his arrival driving Marlow off stage. The father is triumphant, convinced of the impudence of the young suitor, but Kate insists that he will be proved just the opposite. The act ends in an agreement: though Mr. Hardcastle was going to send Marlow away immediately, he allows his daughter an hour: "Well, an hour let it be then. But I'll have no trifling with your father" (282).

Act IV

We learn that Marlow's father, Sir Charles, is coming to visit, having set out "a few hours after his son" (283). This makes matters more urgent, since Sir Charles knows Hastings and would spoil his plot to run away with both Constance and the jewel-box, which he has meanwhile entrusted to Marlow. The latter, unaware of Hastings and Constance's plot, sends the casket straight to Mrs. Hardcastle, since it is with her, he thinks, that it is safest. When Hastings asks him about the box, Marlow tells him he deposited it with the "landlady"; no wonder that Hastings parts from him with the double-edged wish: "may you be as successful for yourself as you have been for me" (285).

Marlow gives further demonstration of his impudence by admitting to Mr. Hardcastle that he himself told his servants "to drink freely—for the good of the house" (286). In a comic interlude, a servant of his appears on stage in a state of complete inebriation. At this, the "landlord" loses his temper and—violating his agreement with his daughter—turns Marlow out of doors, mentioning the letter he had received from Sir Charles and passing devastating judgment on the young man, whom he decries as "no better than a coxcomb and a bully" (288).

Kate suspects that Marlow might soon learn about his mistake and turns the plot in yet another direction. She explains that she is a poor relative employed as a keeper of keys in the house, but when Marlow insists that it is an inn, she tells him that it is Mr. Hardcastle's house. This is the moment of recognition, as Marlow exclaims: "My stupidity saw everything the wrong way." This house I no more show my face in!" (289). But it is also the first moment of concord between him and Kate, who exchange words of tenderness. Marlow only regrets that her lack of a fortune makes "an honourable connexion impossible" (290). Having seen his character, however, Kate is now more determined than ever not to let him go.

Tony and Constance do all they can to convince Mrs. Hardcastle of their mutual dedication. When a letter is brought to him, he first wants his mother to read it but the servant explains that it is to him

personally that it must be delivered. We learn, however, that Tony has difficulty in reading. Constance realizes immediately that the letter is written in Hastings' hand and—should it get into Mrs. Hardcastle's hands—it could undo the whole plot. She offers to read the letter for him. She makes up a fake story with false names instead, concluding that the letter is "of no consequence" (293). However, Tony is not satisfied and gives the letter to his mother, who reads what really is on the paper: that Constance should go immediately to the bottom of the garden, and "the hag, your mother" should not be allowed to suspect anything (293). Mrs. Hardcastle now decides to leave the house with Constance, thus hindering Hastings and Constance's plot. Tony closes the act promising that "two hours hence at the bottom of the garden" everything will be corrected and rectified (296).

Act V

In Act V, Sir Charles arrives and heartily laughs at his son's mistake along with Mr. Hardcastle. They are now ready to agree on their children's marriage, provided Marlow and Kate are also to each other's liking. Marlow comes in, begging a thousand pardons and expressing his gratitude for Kate's benevolence. He denies that any communication about personal affairs should have taken place between him and Kate and leaves the stage in a state of distress.

Kate, on the other hand, confirms that they have talked to each other several times and Marlow did express his love for her. When Sir Charles is incredulous, since the "forward, canting, ranting" (300) manners described by Kate do not seem to fit his son, Kate offers to demonstrate Marlow's real character.

In the meantime, Tony takes the ladies on a ride around the Hardcastle house, leaving them off in a horse-pond. Mrs. Hardcastle crawls on stage like a comic "mermaid" "draggled up to the waist" (302). When she says, "I wish we were at home again" (302), Tony spots Mr. Hardcastle approaching and claims it must be a highwayman. He hides Mrs. Hardcastle behind a tree. Unable to bear the tension, however, she rushes forward, only to find that the highwayman is her husband. Frightened to death and humiliated by Tony's tricks, she drives her son off stage among threats and curses.

The scene is now ready for the initiation of Sir Charles and Mr. Hardcastle. Kate accuses Marlow of running after a fortune alone, and in response to this, Marlow confesses the most profound emotions in a way that "amazes" even his father (307). When Kate is about to "cease" their relationship, the fathers step forward and explain the situation to Marlow. He feels very humiliated and wants to take his leave. However, Mr. Hardcastle detains him, and all is set for their final reconciliation.

Constance, due to her prudence, has refused to elope with Hastings and decided to appeal to her aunt's forgiveness instead. Nevertheless, the old lady is unwilling to consent to "the whining end of a modern novel" (310), so Mr. Hardcastle has to step in. He reveals that Tony has, in fact, been of age for some months, so his refusal of Constance's hand means that she finally obtains her own jewels from Mrs. Hardcastle's custody and she is free to marry whomever she likes.

All that remains is for Mr. Hardcastle to provide the formal denouement: "Tomorrow we shall gather all the poor of the parish about us, and the mistakes of a night shall be crowned with a merry morning; so boy, take her; and as you have been mistaken in the mistress, my wish is, that you may never be mistaken in the wife" (311).

Symbols & Motifs

"She Stoops to Conquer" is a classical five-act laughing comedy. It centers on "The Mistakes of a Night," but through a series of misunderstandings, misconstructions, and mischief, it culminates in what seems to be a nearly perfect happy ending, light-hearted and exhilarating.

The first scene initiates the audience into practically all that would happen in the entire play. Tony is presented as a mischievous and spoiled lad. As the farcical antagonism between Mr. and Mrs. Hardcastle about their preference for country and city life, respectively, commences we learn that Kate and her father have a compromise about her dressing style. He allows her in the morning to dress as she likes, but forces her in the evenings to wear a simple "housewife's dress" (239). The curious character of Marlow, Kate's suitor, whom she has never yet met in person, is described by Miss Neville: "Among women of reputation he is the modestest man alive; but his acquaintance give him a very different character among creatures of another stamp," that is, servants, barmaids, and prostitutes (242). All the motifs and main sources of character comedy are presented here, for which reason one often has the impression that subsequent exchanges work based on flashback humor.

Kate, from Act III onwards, holds that she can easily pretend to be the barmaid of the "inn" and "keep up the delusion" of Marlow, to find out more about his real manners. "But my chief aim is to take my gentleman off his guard, and like an invisible champion of romance, examine the giant's force before I offer to combat" (277). This suggests that their love-games are very much like a battle—but fought for one common goal, the mutual happiness of both parties involved.

Historical Context

Complying with the traditions of Restoration comedy, the plot of the play is meant to be nearly contemporaneous with the presentation. This "nearly" is quite marked here, since Mr. Hardcastle keeps referring to his military exploits in the Duke of Marlborough's army, which had taken place roughly 60 years before the composition of the comedy, and although Mr. Hardcastle certainly is not pictured as a young person, to estimate his age over 80 would be quite extravagant. Goldsmith, for his part, comments on the various views of history in connection with Mr. Hardcastle, whose constant reference to his "old stories of Prince Eugene and the Duke of Marlborough" is put down by Mrs. Hardcastle as "old-fashioned trumpery" (237).

"Marlborough's Wars" largely coincided with the land campaign of English and allied troops in the War of the Spanish Succession (1702–13). This followed very soon after the Nine Years War (1689–97) had ended and "decisively established that concerted allied power was able to contain France" (Hoppit 106). In the Treaty of Ryswick, King Louis XIV of France, who had previously sided with King James II, recognized William III as the lawful ruler of Great Britain and Ireland, "renounced James's claims, refused future support to the Jacobites, and acknowledged the success of the Anglo-Dutch alliance as a powerful force in the European balance of power" (Hoppit 107). However, although peace was welcomed by the English population, it could not last.

Both the King of France and the Hapsburg Emperor made claims to the throne of Spain in case King Charles II of Spain should die heirless, which was more or less taken for granted, given his ill health and imbecility. On his deathbed, Charles II bequeathed the throne to Bourbon Philip, Duke of Anjou, and grandson of Louis XIV. The French King therefore revoked the Partition Treaty regarding the domains of Spain, which he had signed in 1699, and accepted Charles's will instead. In order to ensure peace, the English–Dutch alliance also accepted Philip as King of Spain, but Louis attacked the Spanish Netherlands and thereby impinged on the Treaty of Ryswick. Moreover, in 1701, James II died in exile in France, and Louis XIV quite impudently declared his son, James, the "Old Pretender," King of England as James III (Hill 256–7). By this time, however, England, the Netherlands, and the Hapsburg Empire had already "signed a Grand Alliance to ensure that France should not

dominate the Mediterranean or the Netherlands, that the crowns of France and Spain should never be united, and that France should not possess Spanish America" (Hill 257). The London Parliament, which had opted for a more pacific solution before, now also accepted that once again war should be declared on France. This came to be known as the War of the Spanish Succession.

The greatest threat that England and its allies had to face was the possible creation of a "Franco-Spanish behemoth" through the unification of those two thrones (Hoppit 109). During the next decade, the Duke of Marlborough campaigned gloriously in the Netherlands, marching into French territory, and gaining a decisive victory over the French with the help of Prince Eugene of Savoy, the Hapsburg Emperor's military leader, at Blenheim (1704), practically conquering Bavaria (Cannon 109).

Mr. Hardcastle typically alludes to, though in an ambiguous manner, this grand national narrative. Catching up on Marlow's careless mention of an "embroidery to secure a retreat," he aptly misconstrues that last word in order to jump on his hobbyhorse: "Your talking of a retreat, Mr. Marlow, puts me in mind of the Duke of Marlborough, when we went to besiege Denain" ("She Stoops" 254). Ironically, the Battle of Denain (24 July 1712) was the only major French victory in the Netherlands during the War of the Spanish Succession. Moreover, by this time, the Duke of Marlborough had fallen from favor, and the new commander was no other than Prince Eugene, who came too late to relieve the Earl of Albemarle's troops from the French assault (Cannon 285). The defeat at Denain was followed by "the fall of three fortresses, Douai, Le Quesnoy, and Marlborough's last conquest, Bouchain" (Clark 223). The way Mr. Hardcastle seems to misremember crucial facts undermines his credibility and, with discerning audiences, adds to the comic effect of the play.

On the other hand, he also poses as an international hero of Christianity, placing himself at the side of Prince Eugene of Savoy, who, in 1717, recaptured Belgrade from the Turks: "Your generalship puts me in mind of Prince Eugene, when he fought the Turks at the battle of Belgrade" (256). Goldsmith thus both reinforces the national myth of the fundaments of British predominance in Europe and satirizes the country gentleman's obsession with historical events. In fact, the two lines of discourse meet when Mr. Hardcastle cuts both threads short; referring to a fictitious relative, he says: "Your manner, Mr. Hastings, puts me in mind of my uncle, Colonel Wallop. It was a saying of his, that no man was sure of his supper till he had eaten it" (257). This exquisite anti-climax ultimately ridicules Mr. Hardcastle's former babbling about history.

In terms of the history of literature, Oliver Goldsmith can be seen as an author linking two rather distant periods: the Restoration proper, and, more broadly, Neo-Classicism on the one hand, and the later developments of the 19th century on the other. It has often been attempted to place him conclusively among the Neo-Classical, the sentimental, or the "pre-Romantic" poets, but he defies such classification, just like his works. Perhaps Alistair M. Duckworth comes closest to the truth in listing the main characteristics of Goldsmith's writings in this context:

The combination of "utile" and "dulce" in his work puts him closer, perhaps, to his Augustan predecessors than to the Romantics who followed him, though his sentiment and rural subjects give some justification to the label "pre-romantic," which literary historians used to describe him. (238)

From the very beginning, that is, the prologue to the play, Goldsmith makes it clear that, in opposition to the "Sentimentals," who, in John Harrington Smith's conjecture, tried to target "the Ladies" through their "exemplary comedies" including "sentimental elements" (Scouten 61), he is writing a "laughing or low comedy" (Malek). In this respect, he actually draws at least as much on the traditions of Restoration comedy (most notably

Wycherley's and Congreve's comedies of manners) and the decades leading up to the Stage Licensing Act of 1737 (see Farquhart's "The Beaux' Stratagem" cf. Malek) as on sentimental comedy. Even the title of the play alludes to this, cunningly linking the character of Miss Hardcastle and the farcical plot of the "mistakes of a night" with the person of Restoration poet and dramatist John Dryden, to whom the following couplet had been attributed by the Earl of Chesterfield in 1751: "The prostrate lover, when he lowest lies, / But stoops to conquer, and but kneels to rise" (III: 131).

In "On Sentimental Comedy" (1773) Goldsmith puts the question: "[W]hich deserves the preference; the weeping sentimental comedy, so much in fashion at present, or the laughing and even low comedy?" and answers it at once: "If we apply to the authorities, all the great masters in the dramatic art have but one opinion. Their rule is, that as tragedy displays the calamities of the great, so comedy should excite our laughter, by ridiculously displaying the follies of the lower part of mankind" (239). Little wonder that his contemporaries viewed his comedies in this light, and although they criticized his concessions to farcical effects or his assumed inconsistencies, they commended him because of "taking the field against that monster called Sentimental Comedy, to oppose which his comedy was avowedly written" (Rousseau 122).

Of course, the social climate had changed since the rowdy and heavily sexual stage practices of the last decades of the 17th century. As Robert Hume remarks: "By the standards of Wycherley or Congreve, Goldsmith and Sheridan are rather soft-boiled" (326). Still, the drama manages to engage and exhilarate the audience throughout, due mainly to a brilliant combination of consistent plotting and convincing characterization.

Societal Contexts

In Oliver Goldsmith's time, education—public as well as private—was a growing concern all over

Britain. It is telling, in this respect, when Mrs. Hardcastle proudly proclaims, "My son is not to live by his learning" (237). Indeed, he is not; moreover, his relative illiteracy leads to one of the most disastrous comic scenes in the play, when he presents Hastings' letter to his own mother, the last person that should ever see it. We may take this as a hint at Goldsmith's own stance concerning the problem, which he discussed more specifically in his "Enquiry into the Present State of Polite Learning in Europe" (1759).

The play also presents various types of marriage. Mrs. Hardcastle, probably drawing on both her own example and a tendency in Restoration and 18th-century marriages of convenience, makes the telling remark about Tony and Constance's relationship: "They fall in and out ten times a day, as if they were man and wife already" (266). The ultimate resolution of the plot, however, gives us a far more optimistic view of marriage based on self-knowledge and mutual respect than what was generally presented around the turn of the 17th and 18th centuries. Namely, for Wycherley or Congreve, marriage had either been a troublesome burden (see the Pinchwifes in "The Country Wife") or a pretext for conducting love affairs with other men and women (see the Fainalls in "The Way of the World").

In making marriage contracts, social status and financial wealth play a crucial role in his play; Goldsmith shifts focus to a critique of society rather than of individuals and their foibles. Even the distant, impoverished relative of the Hardcastles would not be a suitable match for Marlow, in spite of her nobility. Marlow's bashfulness among ladies of condition, then, may in part follow from a serious indecision based on the dilemma: how to enjoy life optimally while not giving in to external restrictions and limitations?

Tony Lumpkin shows one extreme, rebelling against the mere shadow of anyone else's will imposed on him. The greatest happiness for him is to be "his own man again" (310). Marlow's schizophrenic behavior is the other extreme. It is incredible that he should be such a different man in the company of aristocratic ladies than the spirited rake that he is among lower-class women. This phenomenon can well be explained by the psychological background that is contoured by his father's wanting him to marry the daughter of a dear old friend and thus "make our personal friendships hereditary" (297), on the one hand, and his eagerness for adventure and romance, on the other. In fact, Goldsmith's "tour de force"-ending manages to reconcile the two opposites, leading Marlow into a wedlock that is "both" a marriage of convenience "and" a marriage based on the most passionate love that can be proclaimed on any theatrical stage.

Besides the class-consciousness testified to by "poor relative" Kate's exclamation, "One of the best families in the country keep an inn! Ha, ha, ha, old Mr. Hardcastle's house an inn!" (289), the contrast between the city and the country is as poignant as ever since the comedies of the 1660s and 1670s. There is, nonetheless, a decisive difference. Whereas Wycherley and Congreve presented the city as far superior to the country with its dullness (e.g. Mrs. Pinchwife in "The Country Wife") and tendency to produce blockheads with a propensity towards drunkenness (e.g. Sir Wilfull Witwoud in "The Way of the World"), Goldsmith is more sympathetic towards country life and manners than the fashionable London world. In terms of literary history, this development may be a logical conclusion to the process in whose course Henry Fielding's presentation of London and the country supplied a balanced view based as much on stereotype (e.g. in Squire Western's character in "Tom Jones") as on a well-meaning attention to individual detail (cf. Tom Jones himself).

The favorable presentation of rural life is transparent from several elements in the play. First, the comparison of London and the country is one of the main points introduced in the initial exchange between Mr. and Mrs. Hardcastle. If we consider that in the end it is the husband who gains the upper hand (though both he and his wife are subject to a series of comic situations during the progress of the play), it may indicate Goldsmith's implicit preference for the country.

The same idea is communicated in how Tony rectifies Hastings' fashionable distemper: "Ay, now it's dear friend, noble 'Squire. Just now, it was all idiot, cub, and run me through the guts. Damn your way of fighting, I say. After we take a knock in this part of the country, we kiss and be friends. But, if you had run me through the guts, then I should be dead, and you might go kiss the hangman." (302)

This reveals Tony's rustic foolhardiness as much as the idyllic light-heartedness of rural life, and when Hastings concedes his point, he seems to have learned the lesson: do not take things all too seriously, and, when in the country, leave your city affectation behind you. And this, indeed, is what happens: from gentlemen who "look woundily like Frenchmen" (245)—a feature of city nobility since the days of Charles II—Hastings and Marlow develop into mature men capable of facing up to the facts of reality and surrendering all appearances.

Thirdly, Goldsmith's overall attitude to urbanization and the demise of country life shines through in other of his works as well, notably in "The Deserted Village." If the playwrights and poets of the Restoration and the Augustan Age favored London over the country, the Age of Sensibility—partly, perhaps, due to an escapism triggered by the threat of urban industrialization carried to an extreme—turned the tables and presented rural Britain as a site of blissful idyll. Tony's mischief, however rude, is still seen as harmless trickery that deserves as much hearty laughter as Marlow's series of mistakes.

Still, the presentation of country life does not lack the stereotypes dwelt on by Dryden, Pope, or even Fielding. The compromise between Kate and her father makes her behave half like a mundane lady and half as a typical country maid, plainly clad and demure. It is indicated that she goes on regular afternoon walks (261; cf. Pope's "Epistle to Miss Blount"). The dialect used by the butler and the servants as well as Tony serve a comic purpose. Horseracing, fairs, and other forms of rural entertainment are mentioned to make the plot more realistic. However, all these elements are elaborated in a way that might captivate Goldsmith's primary audience, the city aristocracy. Tony, for instance, promises the fleeing couple "a pair of horses that will fly like Whistlejacket" (291), drawing on the enormous fame of the brilliant racing horse epitomized by the painter George Stubbs (c. 1762).

Biographical Context

To call Oliver Goldsmith a comic author is to do him justice, yet also understates the seriousness of his work. On the one hand, for the best part of his life, he was appreciated in learned circles mostly for his comic abilities and he himself was a comic phenomenon as well, having a rather disadvantageous appearance "marked by a protruding brow, large upper lip, and receding chin" (Duckworth 225). In addition, he usually dressed in a style of inappropriate flamboyance (rather like a Restoration fop or coxcomb) and consciously "sought public applause for his wit" (Duckworth 225).

On the other hand, in his writings, he aimed at a more artistic type of appreciation. He excelled in many comic as well as non-comic genres, composing three most influential works in diverse tones and styles: a pastoral elegy ("The Deserted Village", 1770), a highly controversial sentimental novel ("The Vicar of Wakefield", 1766), which is often read rather as a satire "on" the sentimental novel genre, and "She Stoops to Conquer" (1773), an immensely successful play that attacks the genre of the sentimental comedy at its softest spot: laughter.

No wonder that these achievements earned Samuel Johnson's half-mocking, half-approving aphorism: "No man was more foolish when he had not a pen in his hand, or more wise when he had" (Boswell 28). In his own defense, Goldsmith argued that wit was an essential part of polite culture, and one should not mind "if it is the only property a man sometimes has—we must not underrate him who uses it for subsistence, and flies from the ingratitude of the age, even to a bookseller for redress" ("Enquiry" 104–5). Because of this paradoxical duality, it is perhaps not too far-fetched a proposition that in the comic character of Tony Lumpkin, Goldsmith drew heavily on his own life experiences and personality traits.

Oliver Goldsmith (c.1730–1774), sharing the Anglo-Irish background of his great satirical precursor Jonathan Swift, among others, received both informal and formal education from a very early age. At the school of the Irish village Lissoy, where he spent most of his childhood, he was tutored by Thomas Byrne, a veteran of Marlborough's wars (Duckworth 225), who, with his adventurous recollections of those wars, may well have served as a prototype for the character of Mr. Hardcastle. Byrne was also a great enthusiast for Vergil, inspiring Goldsmith to compose witty verses, which were highly praised (Duckworth 225). Between 1737 and 1745, Goldsmith attended the diocesan school at Elphin; his father intended him to become a businessman. His mother, in contrast, wanted him to go to university, and, indeed, in 1745, he began his studies at Trinity College, Dublin as a sizar (Duckworth 225), "an undergraduate member—receiving an allowance from the college to enable him to study" ("OED" XV: 578). His lower social rank was publicly shown, enhancing his inherent self-consciousness. In Dublin, he also started to develop an addiction to gambling, which would later have a detrimental effect on his fortunes. He only graduated as a Bachelor of Arts in theology and legal studies in February 1750, due to various

problems and clashes with his tutor and others at the college (Duckworth 225).

His subsequent career was also marked by controversy and scandal. At his family's instigation, he studied medicine at Edinburgh, but he also carried on with his social activities. Clearly, his penetrating insight into the manners and fashions of the time, so vividly present in "She Stoops to Conquer," is a result of these experiences. He gained the acquaintance of many high-ranking personages, but his position as a "court jester" actually disheartened him (Duckworth 226).

The year 1754 saw the beginning of Goldsmith's years of European pilgrimage: he visited Switzerland, the Dutch township of Leyden, as well as Paris and Padua, intermittently attending universities. In the winter of 1756–7, he returned to England and settled in London, where he began to work as a regular reviewer for Ralph Griffiths's *Monthly Review*. From 1759, he wrote for Smollett's *Critical Review* and, in the meantime, he also translated from French (Duckworth 227).

His major breakthrough as an author came with the publication of "An Enquiry into the Present State of Polite Learning in Europe," in which he complains precisely about the devastating effect "[c]ritics, sophists, grammarians, rhetoricians, and commentators" have on "the literary commonwealth" of all times (14). He even makes a poignant remark about those who, in his views, perpetuate the destitution of poets.

The poet's poverty is a standing topic of contempt. His writing for bread is an unpardonable offence. We keep him poor, and yet revile his poverty. Like angry parents, who correct their children till they cry, and then correct them for crying, we reproach him for living by his wit, and yet allow him no other means to live. (103–4)

Ironically, it was the publication of the highly vitriolic "Enquiry" that first brought acclaim for him as a full-fledged author. In 1764, this greatly contributed to his eventual participation in founding Samuel Johnson's literary club, together with Edmund Burke and Joshua Reynolds (Oliver-Morden 636). Here he would remain "the butt of jokes," but he did strike back by composing humorous epitaphs for his fellow members (Oliver-Morden 637). It was also in this period that he famously retorted to Johnson's aforementioned aphorism, claiming that "[t]here is no arguing with Johnson; for if his pistol misses fire; he knocks you down with the butt end of it" (Boswell 221).

In the 1760s, Goldsmith continued writing for periodicals, and in effect helped prolong the golden age of literary journalism, which had started in the first decades of the century. His Chinese letters, published in John Newbery's daily "Public Ledger" from 24 January 1760, were later compiled and printed as "The Citizen of the World" (1762) (Duckworth 228). In a mock-documentary form, this work summarizes all those experiences that Goldsmith had accumulated during his early years, and which pervade his literary works, lending them a sense of intense credibility.

At the same time, Goldsmith's funds began seriously to dwindle. He was regularly in debt and not even the critical success of "The Vicar of Wakefield" and "The Deserted Village" could redeem the situation. Although the performances of "The Good Natur'd Man" (1768) and "She Stoops to Conquer" (1773) also meant a significant income for him, he remained in a precarious financial situation, due, according to Duckworth, to "his gambling, his generosity, and his extravagance in dress and hospitality" (235).

Down to the last year of his life, he was working on large-scale books of antique and universal historiography which, though "standard works until well into the Victorian period, are hardly read now" (Duckworth 238). He died of a kidney infection that, according to some, he misdiagnosed and maltreated. His reputation as an author would remain quite high in the decades following his death, and although it has diminished since, his great works of comedy, poetry, and prose are still widely read and, even more importantly, staged in our time.

Boldizsr Fejrvri, Ph.D.

Works Cited

Boswell, James. "The Life of Johnson," I–IV. Ed. George Birkbeck Hill. Charleston: Biblio Life, 2008. Print.

Cannon, John, Ed. "The Oxford Companion to British History," New York: Oxford UP, 1997. Print.

Chesterfield, Philip Dormer. "Letters to His Son." Ed. Eugenia Stanhope. London: J. Dodsley, 1775. Print.

Clark, G. N. "The Later Stuarts 1660–1714." Oxford: Clarendon Press, 1934. Print.

Donoghue, Frank. "The Fame Machine: Book Reviewing and Eighteenth-Century Literary Careers". Stanford: Stanford UP, 1996. Print.

Duckworth, Alistair M. "Oliver Goldsmith." "Dictionary of Literary Biography" 39.1: "British Novelists, 1660–1800." Ed. Martin C. Battestin. Detroit: Gale Research Company, 1985. Part I, 222–39. Print.

Goldsmith, Oliver. "Enquiry into the Present State of Polite Learning in Europe." 2nd edition. London: J. Dodsley, 1774. Print.

————. "On Sentimental Comedy." "Essays and the Bee." Boston: Wells and Lilly, 1820. 238–44. Print.

————. "She Stoops to Conquer," *Four English Comedies*. Ed. J. M. Morrell. London: Penguin, 1950. 233–313. Print.

Hill, Christopher. "The Century of Revolution: 1603-1714." 2nd Ed. London: Routledge, 2002. Print.

Hoppit, Julian. "Land of Liberty? England 1689–1727." Oxford: Oxford UP, 2000. Print.

Hume, Robert D. "Drama and Theatre in the Mid and Later Eighteenth Century." *The Cambridge History of English Literature, 1660–1780*. Ed. John Richetti. Cambridge: Cambridge UP. 316–339. Print.

Jarvis, Simon. "Criticism, Taste, Aesthetics." *The Cambridge Companion to English Literature 1740–1830*. Ed. Thomas Keymer & John Mee. Cambridge: Cambridge UP, 2004. 24–42. Print.

Malek, James S. "She Stoops to Conquer." *Reference Guide to English Literature*. Ed. D. L. Kirkpatrick. 2nd ed. London: St. James Press, 1991. 1845. Print.

"The Oxford English Dictionary." Ed. J. A. Simpson & E. S. C. 2nd ed. Weiner. Oxford: Oxford University Press & Clarendon Press, 1989. Print. 20 vols.

Oliver-Morden, B. C. "Goldsmith, Oliver." *Reference Guide to English Literature*. Ed. D. L. Kirkpatrick. 2nd ed. Vol. 1. Chicago & London: St. James Press, 1991. 636–7. Print.

Rousseau, G. S. (Ed.). "Goldsmith: The Critical Heritage." London and Boston: Routledge and Kegan Paul, 1974. Print.

Scouten, Arthur H. "Restoration and 18th-century Drama." *Reference Guide to English Literature*. Ed. D. L. Kirkpatrick. 2nd ed. Vol. 1. Chicago & London: St. James Press, 1991. 58–66. Print.

Discussion Questions

1. Collect paradoxical or proverbial aphorisms from the play and discuss whether and in what way they may be taken "seriously."

2. How does Goldsmith exploit the advantages of Restoration stagecraft? How are his ideas reflected in the Stage Directions?

3. Which is the "hardest castle?" In other words, who has the most difficult task in conquering which character in the Hardcastle family?

4. Who is the main plotter in the play? Is it Tony Lumpkin, Kate Hardcastle or someone else?

5. How is dialect or linguistic idiosyncrasy used in the play?

6. Give titles to the five acts and identify the main agents in each. How do conflicts, dialogues, and actions emerge and evolve? What is the driving force behind them?

7. Is it plausible that any character should undergo such radical change in such a short period of time?

8. Choose the most comic scene of the play and highlight in what ways it is effective in creating a "laughing comedy." Dare to be subjective in your choice.

9. To what degree does the play's "happy ending" satisfy the different characters of the play?

10. The title refers to Kate Hardcastle's "stooping to conquer." In what ways do other characters "stoop" during the play? Do they choose or are they forced to do so?

Essay Ideas

1. Discuss the types of irony in "She Stoops to Conquer."

2. Examine "She Stoops to Conquer" in light of the comic ideals of the late 17th and 18th centuries.

3. Provide a comparative analysis of "She Stoops to Conquer" with a Restoration comedy of manners. You may focus on character, plot and plotting, the contrast between appearances and reality, gender roles, the views of marriage, or any other aspect of the selected plays.

4. Discuss the use of proper nouns, characterization, and social criticism in "She Stoops to Conquer,"

5. Might appearances lead to a deeper understanding of reality the way Kate Hardcastle's several metamorphoses suggest? Discuss.

Six Characters in Search of an Author

by Luigi Pirandello

Content Synopsis

As an acting company is beginning to rehearse a play, six people who reveal that they are not exactly people, interrupt them. They are characters that an author had begun to create for a play he was writing but stopped writing before he finished it. They have been given existence by having been conceived. However, they were prevented from realizing that existence when the author stopped writing his play, their play now. Consequently, they are looking for an author to finish the job.

They present themselves to the theater manager and the actors and try to convince the company to stage their story. Since it has not been written, The Father character suggests that the Stage Manager become an author and write it for them based on the story they tell him. As they are explaining themselves to the company, elements of their story emerge and the play, of which they are a part, is presented obliquely. The six characters include The Father, The Mother, The Son, the son of The Father and The Mother, who has contempt for his father, a shady affection for his mother, and wishes to have no part in their play, The Step daughter, The Boy, and The Child. The last two do not speak.

It is a family drama of conflict, violation, and betrayal. The Father says that he allowed The Mother to live with her lover after he, The Father, saw how unhappy she was without her lover. The Mother, however, decries The Father for having

abandoned her. They argue about what the truth of their history actually was. With her lover, The Mother had several children, among them, The Stepdaughter, a haughty beauty. When The Father learned of her, he often followed her in the street, observed her, and even gave her gifts. When, after her lover's death, The Mother needed money, she took a job sewing for a dressmaker, Madame Pace. Madame Pace is the seventh Character, who appears later and does not enter with the six. The Stepdaughter and The Father tear at each other as they present themselves to the company. It becomes apparent that there is an incestuous element, a matter of sexual attraction, repulsion, and shame that connects them. The dressmaker for whom The Mother did sewing was, also, a bawd. She introduced the daughters of her workers to men, and she took money from the young women. In her shop, The Father and The Stepdaughter meet under those circumstances. It is not clear how far their contact went, but it is clear that lecherous intention drove The Father and defiant shame drove The Stepdaughter to submit to him.

As the Characters bait each other, the actors watch, amused and irritated by their behavior, their presumption, and their interruption of the actors' rehearsal. The Manager, intrigued by The Father's suggestion that he become the author of their story, calls for a break. He leaves the stage with The Father to write the scene between The Father and

The Stepdaughter. The others leave the stage bare and the actual audience is given a twenty-minute intermission. The usual boundaries that are defined in the theater are displaced. The curtain remains up. Consequently, the intermission merges stage time and real time.

When the actors return, the business of rehearsing the scene in the dress shop is performed. The Father and The Stepdaughter are introduced to each other as client and prostitute in this scene. As the dynamics of their encounter is developed, so, too, is the relationship between characters and the actors who perform them. The Characters are instructed to perform the scene for the benefit of the actors who will perform for the public. The Characters object, seeing no need for the actors because they desire to play their scenes themselves. The actors object, arguing that it is *they* who give life to the characters.

In the midst of this contretemps, the Manager notices that the dress shop owner, Madame Pace, is absent. The Father asks for the women's hats and cloaks and, by hanging them up, draws Madame Pace, as if by theatrical magic, onto the stage. She is a stock comic stage caricature with a fake English/Italian accent. The tension between her and The Mother is terrible, and she quickly leaves, furious, once her bit of business in the scene is achieved. The Stepdaughter, then, proceeds to block the scene, and the Manager protests that she is taking on his function.

After The Father and The Stepdaughter perform part of their scene, the Leading Lady and the Leading Man perform it so entirely differently, from how the Characters did that the two Characters laugh in scorn at them. The Manager silences them and encourages the Actors to continue despite the objections. The Characters are laughing at the distortion of the truth or reality of themselves, that is, at the distortion through pretense of a fiction that masquerades as truth. These two varying representations of the same material show how presentation and interpretation alter and affect the meaning and the appearance of reality.

The Stepdaughter again interrupts the actors and reproaches the Stage Manager turned author when they deviate from the story. She turns something awful into what she calls a sentimental romance because they avoid the sordid reality of the fiction. After the daughter had told The Father when he offered her a hat that she could not wear it because she was wearing a mourning dress for her father, who died two months earlier, his response had been to tell her to take off the dress. The manager objects to this as impossible material for the stage. The Stepdaughter insists on it, but compromises finally as long as her arm can be bare.

The action climaxes as The Mother discovers them in their incipient debauchery and cries out. The Manager, satisfied with the drama, says that this is where the curtain can fall. The stagehand, hearing the word "curtain," drops the actual curtain, leaving the Manager and The Father, in front of the curtain, as the only ones visible now to the actual audience. As they exit, through the curtain, onto the stage, now hidden, the second act of the play that the audience is watching concludes.

When the curtain rises, the Manager is reconstructing the fictional reality the Characters have brought, consolidating the action, and fitting things that happened in several locations into one playing area. The Manager argues it is necessary to promote the illusion that they are creating, and The Father objects to the word "illusion," explaining that the Characters have no other reality but the illusion. That very fact, he argues, makes the Characters more real than the actors do. Reality, for the actors, continually changes because of time. For them, today is not yesterday and what has already occurred no longer exists, whereas for The Characters, everything is eternally fixed.

The final encounter which brings the Characters face to face with each other and with their essential definitions involves playing out a scene in the garden, a run through which the actors follow, even to the extent of following the Characters as they move through the action.

In this final action, the child drowns in the fountain and the boy, seeing her there, shoots himself. Not only is this action performed by the Characters, it is narrated by The Son who has throughout tried to remain aloof from the story, the others, and his own identity. He has been defined only by his desire not to be part of the play and by the hint of an unrealized attachment to The Mother.

The violent and melodramatic ending to the twisted family drama is not the real climax of the play. The climax comes with the theatrical confusion. The actors are unsure whether the character playing The Boy is "really" dead or only "make believe" dead. The problem is left unresolved for the audience. However, a sharp reader may recall that earlier, it was stated that a Character could not die, even if part of his role is that he does die. [Think, for example, of Hamlet, who is eternal even though he dies at the end of his play]. The Father calls what has happened reality. Nevertheless, that, after all, is only from a Character's point of view. The Manager dismisses everything unable to resolve anything. Unable to mediate between pretense and reality, all he is sure of is that the whole series of events that have just passed has been a waste of his time.

Symbols & Motifs

The governing motif in "Six Characters in Search of an Author" is the confused relation illusion and reality bear to each other. The problem the play presents is determining whether what is called fiction is truer than what is called real. What is real may only be what we think is real, and it may be a result of the intersection of several fictions and illusions. What is real to one person, the play argues, when transmitted to another through words, may not be the same reality, to the person who hears the words as it is to the one who speaks

them because words may not have the same meaning to each. Reality, because of the slipperiness of language, is itself unstable. Identity, too, the play repeatedly argues, is unstable because we are not the person we were yesterday nor the one we will be tomorrow. Our circumstances, feelings, and points of view fluctuate. A character, however, is unchanging, but even a character is subject to interpretation by an actor. A character may be true. A person may be false. The authenticity of someone or something depends just as much on how we view that someone or something as that someone or something itself, which, paradoxically, cannot exist by itself but needs to be perceived by others for its existence.

Historical Context

"Six Characters in Search of an Author" is play that marks the separation and builds a bridge between Ibsen and the absurd. At the end of the nineteenth century playwrights like Henrik Ibsen and Anton Checkhov defined theatre. They mastered the art of realism with the well-made play. They assiduously created the illusion that what the audience saw on the stage was life itself, real life, going on before them and that such a perspective was possible because the playwright had permitted it by removing the "fourth wall." The playwright and his craft were hidden behind the illusion that the audience was eavesdropping on "real" people undergoing "real" experiences and dramatic confrontations that were just like the problems and situations the audience itself might face.

Pirandello broke that illusion in "Six Characters" and other plays of his. He brought theatricality to the foreground of the action. He played with the difference between an actor and the character he portrayed and had actors play actors and their characters. He broke the unity of narrative presentation by presenting a story obliquely and in fragments. Perhaps most important for the evolution of theater, he challenged the idea not only that reality could be portrayed and truth rendered, but that there is one reality or that truth exists. Consequently, a play like "Six Characters" is a harbinger of the Theater of the Absurd that was to become so important in the 1960s. Theater of the Absurd is a theater where meaning, perspective, order, illusion, narrative continuity, character definition, and the traditional relationship of audience and actors are challenged by being dramatically and theatrically undermined.

Societal Context

Society in "Six Characters" is represented by the theater. Because of the structure of the play, that social context is disrupted. The Characters undo the conventional social order by undermining the theatrical process, challenge the actors, and proceed, rather than flow from, an author. They do not "know their place" in the order of things, and the order of things is challenged. A reader may see this dislocation and disruption as an oblique reference to the rise of fascism in Italy. "Six Characters" was first performed in 1921. Mussolini consolidated his power in 1922. The establishment of fascism in Italy can be seen, depending on a person's beliefs, as disrupting traditional ideas either of reality and order or as a way of restoring a tradition of order and revising and renewing a reality that had become corrupt.

Religious Context

There is no overt religious context to "Six Characters in Search of an Author." There is no reference to God, religion, the Church, or spirituality. The play's concerns seem to be secular. A reader may, however, interpret a religious meaning if she chooses to read the play as a metaphor and to see the characters, who have been abandoned by their author before they and their story were completed as symbolic of mankind in a world without God. The play may suggest a world where God has hidden himself or died and left mankind unfinished, in search of a creator.

Because of God's absence, mankind, like the unrealized Characters can be seen as unrealized, without meaning, and attempting to create or complete themselves without success.

Scientific & Technological Context

The technology of the theater and of creating illusion is at the heart of "Six Characters in Search of an Author." The play is concerned with how roles are written, illusion created, and the mechanics of stage craft accomplished. Implicitly, and at a time when indeterminacy and relativity were becoming aspects of scientific inquiry, the play calls the practice of traditional science into question through its challenge to the idea of a fixed and knowable reality.

Biographical Context

Considering the way that Pirandello plays with the instability of reality and the power of illusion to influence human perception and challenge a sure sense of what is and what is not, it is almost uncanny to learn that instability and disillusion characterized his early life, especially with regard to his relationship with his father, whom he discovered, by reading some letters he found, was having extra-marital relationships. The disgust and distrust he felt towards his father is suggested in the attitude of The Son to The Father in "Six Characters." An even more provocative fact of Pirandello's life is that his wife's madness was the central fact of his marriage and, thus, brought him face-to-face daily with a conflict of realities.

Pirandello was born on June 28, 1867 in southern Sicily, in a village with the apt name, Caos, given that his family spent vacations at a house called Chaos. His family was wealthy, and his father determined that young Pirandello should study engineering and work alongside him at the sulfur mines that the family owned. Pirandello preferred literature to mining and management.

Although he did spend some time working with his father, he did not enter the business, studied literature, and received his doctorate in literature at the University in Bonn, Germany, in 1891. He began writing seriously, published a collection of stories in 1894, and, in the same year, married Antonietta Portulano. In 1897, he became a teacher of Italian literature at the "Istituto" Superiore di Magistero di Roma. A year later, he began to publish a weekly journal, "Ariel."

When the sulfur mines his family owned were flooded in 1903, Pirandello's family lost their fortune. Upon learning of this, his wife suffered such an intense mental shock that she became insane and remained so for the rest of her life. Pirandello devoted himself to caring for her until 1919, and when she became habitually violent in her insanity, he institutionalized her.

Throughout, he wrote and published stories, novels, and plays extensively. When "Six Characters" was first performed in Rome, it was a failure and caused rioting in the theater and accusations that its author was mad. Nevertheless, a year later it was performed in Milan and acclaimed, as was "Henry IV," 1922, his next play.

Initially, Pirandello supported Mussolini, declaring himself a fascist, and Mussolini supported him, making him the artistic director of the "Teatro" d'Arte di Roma. In 1927, however, Pirandello publicly destroyed his Fascist Party membership card and lived the rest of his life under surveillance.

Pirandello was awarded the Nobel Prize for Literature in 1934. He died in Rome on December 10, 1936.

Neil Heims, Ph.D.

Work Cited

Luigi Pirandello. "Six Characters in Search of an Author." London; New York: Penguin Books, 1995. Print.

Discussion Questions

1. How do the Characters in "Six Characters in Search of an Author" differ from the Actors in that play? Is the difference real or fictional? What distinction is being made between Actors and the Characters they play?

2. When you see a movie, a play, or watch a television program are you watching actors or characters? Consider the popular celebrities of today and consider how any one of them functions as an actor and as a character.

3. Do you agree with the assumptions of Pirandello's play that illusion is stronger than reality?

4. Are there things that you take for granted in your life as real that might just be overwhelming fictions?

5. What role does illusion play in your everyday life? Consider the television programs you watch, the news reports, your perception of others, your beliefs, and your values. To what extent does it matter whether these are "real" or "illusory?"

6. Do you ever have the sense that you are a fictional character? Do you model the way you act and think and feel on characters you have seen on television and in the movies or read about? Do you have a sense about others that they are authentic or inauthentic, actually themselves or trying to be somebody else? What determines these feelings or perceptions?

7. What is the image of the family as a social institution as presented in "Six Characters in Search of an Author"?

8. Is The Father an immoral man or a victim of circumstances?

9. Contrast the roles of The Stepdaughter and The Mother in relation to the way women are expected to behave and how women are treated both inside the play and in the actual world.

10. What happens at the end of "Six Characters in Search of an Author"? How do the two plays that are being presented merge? How does each of these plays affect the way we understand the other?

Essay Ideas

1. Analyze The Stepdaughter's character. Contrast that with her role as a Character.

2. Examine Pirandello's idea of the role of illusion in formulating truth.

3. How does Pirandello dramatize the conflict between illusion and reality?

4. Discuss the way in which The Father becomes the author of "Six Characters in Search of an Author."

5. Compare "Six Characters in Search of an Author" to "The Purple Rose of Cairo."

Speed the Plow

by David Mamet

Content Synopsis

Scene One of this three scene play opens in the office of Hollywood executive Bob Gould. Boxes and painting materials are scattered around the room suggesting that Gould has recently moved into it. His friend and co-worker Charlie Fox enters and tries to talk to Gould who is ranting about the scripts that land on his desk now that he has been promoted. He says they are somewhere between "art" and "entertainment" (Mamet 3). When Fox finally gets a word in, he tells Gould that Doug Brown, a famous actor, came to his house after reading a script that Fox gave him and he wants to make a movie at this studio.

Gould is interested and calls his boss Richard Ross in order to get his approval to green light the picture. Gould assures Fox that he will get a producer credit and Fox thanks Gould and flatters him repeatedly. Gould compliments Fox's loyalty to the studio. Their plans to meet with Ross get postponed until the next day. Fox is nervous because Doug Brown only gave him until 10 am to decide. Gould assures them it is a done deal.

Fox is wired from the thought of making so much money on a big picture deal. Gould tells him that money is not as important as people and this is a "People Business" (22). Fox cannot wait to settle some scores once he gets the respect he feels is due to him.

Gould shows him the book he is reading as a courtesy to some agent. It is called "The Bridge: or Radiation and the Half-Life of Society. A Study of Decay." They read from the book aloud, mocking it. Fox and Gould joke that they are going to drop the Doug Brown picture to make this novel into a film.

Karen, Gould's temporary secretary, brings them coffee. While she is serving them, they half-jokingly call each other "whores" to the movie business (25). Fox reveals his resentment at Gould when they discuss working their way up from the mail room. Gould assures Fox that once he makes it big, people will be out to get him behind his back while sucking up to him in public. Gould tells Karen this business is all "garbage" and people are in it for themselves and everyone thinks they are original. He asks Karen to cancel all his appointments for the rest of the day and make a reservation for him and Fox for lunch.

Once Karen leaves the room, Fox tells Gould that she is not interested in him. Gould says he was not looking to hit on her but Fox does not believe him. Gould is offended that Fox does not think he can get her and Fox bets him five hundred dollars that he cannot get her to go on a date with him and then sleep with her.

Fox leaves and Karen enters to tell Gould that she could not get him a reservation. He tells her that she made a mistake and she realizes she should have told the people at the restaurant who the reservation was for. She apologizes profusely and he tells her there is nothing wrong with being naïve about this business. He starts to tell her about the Doug Brown picture and she asks if it is a good movie. He explains to her that it is a "commodity," a moneymaker and that he is not an artist (41). His job is to find films that will make money for the studio.

Gould uses the book as an example and explains how Ross told its famous author he would read it, but gave it to Gould to read so he could tell the author that is was a good book but will not work as a movie. Karen asks Gould what he would do if there was actually something in the book worth making a movie about. Gould tells her that he prayed to be pure but that the job has turned him into a "Big Fat Whore" (43). Gould asks Karen to read the book for him and report back to him at his house that evening. She is flattered that he is asking for her feedback and agrees. As she exits, Gould asks her to call Fox and tell him he owes Gould five hundred bucks.

Scene Two takes place at Gould's apartment later that evening. Karen is reading from the book. She thinks the book is perfect and has been changed by it. Gould thanks her and offers to help her out with a job at the studio. She asks to work on the film. He thinks she is talking about the Doug Brown film but she means the book adaptation. He tells her that he is not going to make that film. She tries to convince him and tells him that she knew he wanted to sleep with her, but once she read the book she felt like it was her destiny. The scene ends when she tells Gould that she is here to answer his prayers.

Scene Three opens the next morning back in Gould's office. Fox enters and is all excited about the film and wants to ensure that he will get the co-producer credit. Gould tells him that he is not going to make the Doug Brown film. Fox does not believe him and sarcastically tells Gould he should make the radiation film, that it will make a great "summer picture" (62). When Gould finally convinces Fox that he is serious, Fox tells him that this move will ruin his career. Gould tries to explain that the book made him realize that his life is a "sham" and he wants to do something about it (69).

Fox rants and raves at Gould and tries to convince him that Karen has lured him in order to get herself ahead in this business. Gould insists that she understands him. Fox calls Karen in to set things straight. He asks her if she would have slept with Gould had he rejected the book. She says she would not have and Gould is confused. Karen tries to talk to him about making a difference in the world, but Fox pushes her out the door and tells her that he and Gould have to meet with Ross. Karen says, "I don't belong here" and leaves (80). Gould tries to explain how he got caught up in things because she said he was a good man. The play ends as Fox comforts him and tells him not to mope, that they are here to make a movie and if their names go above the title then life cannot be so bad after all.

Symbols & Motifs

A recurring motif in "Speed the Plow" is the concept of loyalty. Fox repeatedly emphasizes his loyalty to Gould and the studio, and Gould agrees to reward Fox for his loyalty, yet it is obvious that each character is in this business for themselves. Gould easily leaves Fox empty-handed when Karen convinced him to make a movie from the book, but then he just as readily goes back to Fox at the end of the play. The fact that Gould and Fox proudly admit that they are "whores" reinforces this motif.

Power is another important motif in the play. Charlie Fox uses the star power in order to get Bobby Gould to help him get a producer credit on a film. He also uses the claims of his loyalty to manipulate Bobby. Karen uses her sexuality to gain power of Gould in order to get him to side with her. Gould has the power to decide which films he will present to his boss, Richard Ross, the man who although never seen on the stage has the ultimate power in the play.

Historical Context

"Speed the Plow" opened on stage at the Royal Theater in New York on May 3, 1988. Ironically, it starred the prominent Hollywood stars Joe Mantegna as Bobby Gould, Ron Silver as Charlie Fox and Madonna as Karen.

Societal Context

The play satirizes the lifestyle of those in the Hollywood filmmaking business. Mamet, himself a screenwriter, director, and producer, has firsthand experience in the business and therefore, understands its nuances. He explores why some movies get made and others, even if they are good, honest stories, get pushed aside. Money is at the heart of the matter, not truth. Mamet is quoted as saying, "We Americans have always considered Hollywood, at best, a sinkhole of depraved venality. And, of course, it is. It is not a protective monastery of aesthetic truth" (imdb.com). Gould explains to Karen in the play that everyone comes into Hollywood thinking he or she is a "maverick" and then end up making a movie that was already made the year before. Nevertheless, Mamet acknowledges the thrill people get out of being in the business. Gould and Fox admit they are sell outs but also get excited at the possibility of making the next big blockbuster due to the money and recognition that comes with it. In the end, the two men are satisfied that even if they do not make the most original, eye opening film, what counts is that their names are above the title.

Religious Context

"Speed the Plow" does not have a specific religious context.

Scientific & Technological Context

"Speed the Plow" does not have a specific scientific or technological context.

Biographical Context

David Mamet was born in Chicago, Illinois on November 30, 1947 (imdb.com). He attended Goddard College in Vermont and the Neighborhood Playhouse School of Theater in New York (filmmakers.com). He is married to actress Rebecca Pidgeon and they have two children. He also has two children from a previous marriage (imdb.com). His first successful play was "Sexual Perversity in Chicago" in 1974. He won the Pulitzer Prize in Drama for "Glengarry Glen Ross" in 1984, and was also nominated for a Tony Award (imdb.com). "Speed the Plow" was nominated for a Tony in 1988 (imdb.com).

In addition to playwriting, Mamet also writes for the screen and occasionally directs. His first big onscreen success was as a screenwriter for the film "The Untouchables" (filmmakers.com). He later received an Oscar nomination for his screenplay "Wag the Dog" (filmmakers.com).

Mamet is known for his unique dialogue in his plays and films. He tries to recreate natural speak and has his characters speak quickly, stutter and not complete their sentences (imdb.com). He uses a metronome during rehearsals to ensure the actors deliver the lines the way in which he intended (imdb.com).

Jennifer Bouchard, M.Ed.

Works Cited

Filmmakers.com. 20 October 2008. <http://www .filmmakers.com/artists/mamet/biography>

IMDB: Internet Movie Database. Imdb.com, Inc. 30 April 2008. <http://www.imdb.com>

Mamet, David. "Speed the Plow." New York: Grove Press, 1985.

Discussion Questions

1. Which character did you most like?
2. Which character did you like the least?
3. What does Gould think of his position?
4. Discuss the way the characters communicate with one another.
5. Why is Fox constantly flattering Gould?
6. Do you detect any resentment between the two men? Why?
7. Do you think Karen is as naïve as she claims to be?
8. What is the significance of the book about radiation in the play?
9. What do you think Karen's motive is for manipulating Gould?
10. What might Mamet be saying about the movie business?

Essay Ideas

1. Develop a formal argument, supporting with text evidence, what you consider to be the main statement or theme of the play.
2. Write a 2–4 page essay in which you analyze Mamet's use of humor in the play.
3. Discuss the role of morality in the play. Evaluate whether you think the characters are immoral or whether the business makes them so.
4. Compare and contrast Bobby Gould to Charlie Fox. Discuss their approach to business as well as their approach to life.

A Streetcar Named Desire

by Tennessee Williams

Content Synopsis

"A Streetcar Named Desire" opens with a view of a two-story corner apartment building in a deprived area of New Orleans called the Elysian Fields. The set is crowded with vendors and passers-by and intermittent jazz music can be heard from the nearby bars. A white woman, Eunice, the owner of the building, is seen talking on the steps to a nameless 'Negro Woman.' Two men come around the corner—Stanley Kowalski and his friend Mitch. Stanley loudly calls out for his wife Stella, and throws a packet of meat to her from the butcher, before going off to bowl. Stanley's wife Stella is gentle and has been brought up in luxury in the South. In this backdrop of rough and coarse charm, Blanche Du Bois, Stella's sister, arrives dressed incongruously in a white suit with a 'fluffy' bodice, pearls, white gloves, and hat.

Blanche announces to Eunice that she took a "streetcar named Desire," and is looking for her sister's address at Elysian Fields. Eunice lets her wait inside while she goes to call Stella. Once inside Stella's place, Blanche is obviously bewildered. She quickly pours herself a drink when she sees a bottle; she rinses the glass and puts it back. When Stella comes they embrace each other with joy, but very soon, Blanche makes disparaging comments about her sister's house. Blanche recalls their own fine house "Belle Reve," where they were brought up in the South. Stella is uncomfortable in

Blanche's presence as Blanche throws her weight about marveling as to how Stella could live in a two-room apartment. Blanche then says she would love to have a drink, "if Stella has any in her flat." Blanche then explains that she was let off before the spring term in her school and that she would love to stay with Stella. Blanche appears nervous and wonders if Stella's husband 'the Polack' will not mind her staying. Soon, Blanche also confesses that she has 'lost' Belle Reve. She gives vague reasons for it. Stella cries softly and goes to the bathroom. Meanwhile Stanley enters and is civil to Blanche.

Scene Two opens the next evening as Stanley and Stella overhear Blanche singing loudly while having a bath. Stanley is furious to hear that Blanche has lost the family mansion, and rummages Blanche's valise in search of a bill of sale. He imagines expensive furs and jewels of Blanche's possessions that Stella refutes, arguing they are old and inexpensive. Stella asks Stanley to be kind to Blanche and to avoid mention of Stella's pregnancy. After bathing, Blanche attempts to seduce Stanley and, sensing that her conversation with Stanley about Belle Reve might upset Stella, sends Stella out on an innocuous errand to the drug store. Blanche retrieves papers from her suitcase that illustrate her honesty in the loss of Belle Reve—the estate was not sold as Stanley suspected. Stanley fishes through her belonging looking for papers, and then comes across some old love letters that Blanche has treasured. After being convinced that no wrong-doing has been done, Stanley lets it slip that Stella is pregnant. Blanche is enlivened by the news of her sister's pregnancy, as she believes it is the only way to preserve their lineage. She and Stella go out for a night on the town.

Scene Three opens on a colorful poker party with Stanley, Steve, Mitch and Pablo. Blanche and Stella return from their night out. Mitch, who is single and lives with his mother, finds Blanche interesting and has a polite conversation with her. Blanche feigns modesty and tells Mitch that she does not drink much and persuades Mitch to put a paper lantern on the naked light bulb that is casting a sinister light on the room. Blanche turns on the radio; an act that enrages Stanley who throws the radio out the window. When Stella protests, she is hit by Stanley. Blanche and Stella subsequently leave the house. Stanley sobs and repeatedly calls Eunice to send Stella home. Stanley then throws the phone on the floor and shouts Stella's name in front of the apartment. Stella comes back to him in an "animal tenderness." Blanche is devastated that Stella has gone back, but Mitch comes round the corner and they enjoy a smoke together.

Scene Four opens as Stella wakes luxuriously on the bed and Blanche comes in looking distraught. Blanche, clearly disturbed by Stanley's behavior, proposes to get in touch with her former paramour Shep Huntleigh who has struck it rich in the oil industry. Stella explains that she is perfectly happy with Stanley as "there are things that happen between a man and a woman in the dark—that sort of make everything else seem—unimportant." Blanche tries to compare their life in Belle Reve to Stella's life with Stanley whom she finds sub-human and brutish. Unfortunately, during Blanche's rant, Stanley is standing outside and overhears it all.

In Scene Five, Blanche frames a letter to Shep that is full of lies about her social engagements.

In the background, Eunice quarrels with her husband Steve about a second woman. Stanley comes in having unearthed secrets about Blanche's past. He mentions a man and a hotel called Flamingo. Blanche goes pale. Stanley and Stella leave to go to the bar. Left alone in the apartment, Blanch flirts with and kisses a young man collecting money for the paper. The boy leaves uncomfortably and Mitch arrives with flowers; Blanche and Mitch go out together.

Mitch drops Blanche home at 2 in the morning. Mitch confesses he has never had a girl before. Blanche plays the modest woman. She reminisces about her husband whom she had loved very much, without the knowledge of his homosexuality. Blanche tells of her husband's suicide; as she sobs softly, Mitch proposes to her.

On Blanche's birthday, Stanley reveals to Stella that Blanche is a fake and that she was known to be a loose character seducing soldiers in Laurel. She had even seduced one of her students, which was what resulted in her dismissal from her job at the school. Because Mitch had been informed about Blanche's past, he does not turn up to the party. Stanley rudely gifts Blanch with a return bus ticket for a birthday present. Stella needs to go to the hospital for delivery.

In the next scene Mitch comes over, and insists on seeing Blanche in the light as he had only seen her in dimly lit places. Mitch tears the paper lantern off of the naked bulb, and solicits Blanche for intimate favors. As he sees her for what she is, Mitch has now lost all respect for Blanche. Blanche confesses that she sought intimacies from strangers after her husband died. Mitch refuses to marry her. Following this, Stanley comes in, insults her, and rapes her.

Some weeks later, Stella is seen crying while packing Blanche's clothes. Eunice comes downstairs and goes over to Stella who asks how her baby is (since Stanley is having another poker night, Eunice is watching Stella's baby). Blanche is in the tub waiting for a call from Shep Huntleigh who she believes is coming to take her on a trip. Stella confides to Eunice that they are sending Blanche to the country for a rest and is not sure if they are doing the right thing. Stella makes an excuse for herself saying, "I couldn't believe [Blanche's] story and go on living with Stanley." A Doctor and a Matron appear and they take Blanche to a lunatic asylum. Stella cries on Stanley's arm and he fingers the button on her blouse.

Historical Context

Tennessee Williams' plays are acknowledged to be substantially constituted of violence and victimization. While Shakespeare, for instance, can directly be read as 'tragedy' highlighting and upholding man's dignity and will, Williams' plays very often end in what seems to be victimization. If characters are interpreted as not tragic but victimized, the onus shifts from individual to society. The response of the audience after the play is often anger and frustration at the prevailing condition of things. In this sense, Williams' plays are directly connected to the historical and social conditions of the day.

The Great Depression in the United States occurred from 1930 to 1939. During this time the stock market fell by 40%. Wages nationwide were decreased by an average of 60%, and around 9,000 banks went out of business. A quarter of the people in the USA were without employment. This feeling of loss and the necessary fight for livelihood and its associated insecurity is customarily highlighted in modern American drama. In "Streetcar," we are made to hear Blanche mention often that she has practically nowhere to go. From a wealthy background she is reduced to penury, and she pitifully misses her financial and social security. The economic concern is also voiced by Stella when she mentions that among all people, only Stanley was likely to reach somewhere. Though not a play directly based on the Depression, the intersection between the Depression and its concomitant angst finds utterance in the play.

Race is a central component in "A Streetcar Named Desire," (The Civil Rights Act of 1964, that would proclaim the end of segregation in public places and institutions, was still some two decades away.) In "Streetcar," Blanche Dubois is perhaps fated to be reviled given her chauvinistic attitude towards Stanley and New Orleans itself (Vlaspolos, 325). Southern women looking back on their 'better days' is a recurrent motif in Williams' plays. In "The Glass Menagerie," Amanda, like Blanche, seems an eluded woman looking back on her life in the South.

In the Civil War (1861-5), freedom of the slaves was a key, if not defining, point which the Confederacy (or the Southern states) did not find conducive to their interests. A century later, Martin Luther King Jr. (1929–1968) was mobilizing demand for Black equality and voting rights, which would eventually win him the Nobel Peace Prize in 1964 for non-violent resistance to end racial prejudice in the US. In "A Streetcar Named Desire," Blanche looks back and misses her lovely childhood bred on Black labor as typical of the old South. The word 'Blanch' itself means 'white,' but in the play she is 'no lily,' and is ruthlessly punished for her race and class reservations.

"Streetcar" was written during the cold war years. This era of Joseph McCarthy was marked by a time during which communism became a persecuted word. The 'First Red Scare' had occurred before the twenties as communism was recognized as a political force. Following World War II and during the writing of "Streetcar," the 'Second Red Scare' occurred, accompanied with an almost paranoid fear of communist influence on American institutions. During this time, thousands of Americans were accused of communism giving rise to the term "McCarthyism." Anti-communist witch-hunts of places and persons took place wherever leftist ideas were perceived. Critics of Williams' plays have suggested that Williams' references to homosexuality could not be direct and forthright, significantly because of the deeply mistrustful and intolerant political atmosphere he was writing in.

Societal Context

The 1940's outlook on life derived significantly from the aftermath of the World War II. Disillusionment was a favorite theme in Europe and America. With its ever-optimistic outlook, the United States reiterated its belief in the age old 'American Dream' through its contemporary literature underscored by its cult of 'success' (Choudhury, 16). The culture clash between Blanche and Stanley, the clash between values of the past, and the new success, shows a society gradual move from old values to new. Stanley and Blanche represent opposing ways of life. Blanch represents the old; Stanley the ruthless new.

The dichotomy between the social values of the American South and those of the North is essential to understanding the play. The South, dominated by countryside, farms, and somewhat parochial living is contrasted with the Northern values of cosmopolitanism and urbanism. In the play, New Orleans' multicultural ambience contributes to Blanche's shock. In this world of the new, Williams' plays disparage the decadent white southern womanhood. The "Southern Belle," beginning with Scarlet O'Hara is often shown to be a butterfly and a bigot. Blanche, proud of her aristocratic blood, warns Stella not to hang around 'prehistoric' apes, such as Stanley. Her aging represents the passing of Old South, with its value system grounded in exploitation.

Even though racism was rife in the 1940's, "Streetcar" is set in a multicultural New Orleans that houses many peoples. Stanley is Polish, while Williams refers to 'A Negro Woman' as one of his characters. Blanche continually refers to her brother in law as 'The Polack.' When Stanley hears, he says:

"I am not a Polack. People from Poland are Poles, not Polacks. But what I am is a one hundred percent American, born and raised in the greatest country on earth and proud as hell of it, so don't ever call me a Polack" (197).

Black presence in the play is validated with the mention of New Orleans as a 'cosmopolitan city' and with specific reference to Eunice as the 'Negro Woman.' Black social and community life is reiterated with the use of blues, jazz, and other black musical forms that provide a constant comment within the play. Possibilities of interpretations of the roles from a Black perspective are numerous in "A Streetcar Named Desire." Racial changes in the cast can cause major changes within the meaning of the play. A Blanche attracted to a Black Stanley would have different meaning, just as a Black Stella and Blanche in the play's cast would have different connotations. "Streetcar's" location and theme makes it especially interesting to experiment in performativity.

The marginalized in society are often victimized. The sexual orientation of men is a constant theme in Williams' plays. "A Cat on a Hot Tin Roof" fictionalizes the complex 'friendship' between two men, and the intersection between homosexuality and identity. It is interesting to note that around the time of "Streetcar's" production, Alfred Kinsey's study concerning 'white American males' on the *Sexual Behavior in the Human Male* (1948) was popular. The study famously recorded how 40 percent of the total male population in question had "at least some overt homosexual experience to the point of orgasm." Kinsey demonstrated the evidence how heterosexual men did not consider being homosexual when they often were. In this regard, Kinsey "singularly dismantled the hetero/homosexual continuum fashioned in Victorian America that had controlled those politics for more than half a century" (Bak, 238). Several of Williams' characters, and perhaps not least Williams himself, testified to this category. It is interesting that Blanche judges her late husband, Allen Grey, by what he did, and not by what he was. She considers his homosexual act as only an act, and not a full identity by repenting her lack of sympathy musing, "He was just a boy." In effect, Williams' extremely sympathetic portrayal of the misfits and non-conformists living on the fringe of society is a powerful indictment of a society mainly devoted to economic prosperity (Choudhuri, 113).

Religious Context

America has historically offered religious freedom. Many peoples emigrated to America because of religious persecution in their homelands. Constituted mostly of Protestants, twentieth century America saw the rise of American Roman Catholicism, Protestant Pentecostalism, Judaism, as well as an increased presence of Buddhists, Hindus and Muslims. Early in the century, in 1908, Pope Pius X declared that America was no longer a missionary territory of Roman Catholicism, as the church of America was well established and required no assistance from Europe. In addition, by the 1920's, the division between liberal and conservative Protestants increased.

In "A Streetcar Named Desire," there is barely any mention of religion. The play mentions class and race, but the characters' religious faiths seem deliberately withheld. America, especially New Orleans, is reflected as a melting pot. Stanley as from Polish origin could have been of the Jewish faith, but there is no mention in the meat he gets from the butcher as 'kosher.' The meat has had many interpretations in the play, but religion seems to have been deliberately overlooked in the play. It is possible that the play poses to focus on an utter absence of religion.

However, Darwinism and its associated controversy vis-à-vis Christianity finds utterance in the play. The question of religion versus science has been keenly contested in the USA and the debate continues on even today. Since the last quarter of the nineteenth century itself, Southern Evangelists fought against evolutionary ideas that originated with Darwin's "On the Origin of Species" (1859). Conservative Protestants in the North defended the Bible, though Southerners opposed evolutionary teachings more stridently. The southern states of Florida, Oklahoma, Texas, and North Carolina attempted to stop the teaching of evolutionary ideas in public schools. Tennessee joined by passing the Butler Act which made it illegal to "teach any theory that denies the Story of Divine Creation of man as taught in the Bible, and to teach instead that man has descended from a lower order of animal." A group of anti-creationists in Tennessee were aided by John Scope, a science teacher, who defied the statute.

Scopes was arrested and the trial received extreme media attention. The Scopes Trial took place in Tennessee in 1925. The "Monkey Trial" was a drama of the day with science vs. religion, village vs. city, North vs. South. In "Streetcar," Tennessee Williams clearly espouses the theory of evolution. Blanche deplores Stanley's lack of progress and evolution saying to Stella, "Don't hang back with the Brutes"—thereby validating Darwinian theory of evolution and negating the Bible's own godly theory of creation of Man. This is especially significant as teaching evolution effectively vanished in the nation's public schools until the 1960's. The debate among religious fundamentalists, humanists, and scientists goes on to this date, and the rise of "Creation Sciences," especially in the eighties, pertains to the same issue.

Scientific & Technological Context

"A Streetcar Named Desire" is as suddenly destructive as has been the possibilities launched by contemporary science. The theory of nuclear force was put forward by Yukawa in 1935. The first half of the twentieth century was a period of rapid advancement in science, particularly the physical sciences. Einstein formulated the Theory of Relativity, special and general in 1905/1915. The discovery of nuclear fission by Meitner and Frisch in 1939 would make possible the use of the nuclear bomb against Japan after the Manhattan Project brought together several highly regarded scientists to develop the nuclear bomb before Germany succeeded in doing so.

Twentieth century interest in the life sciences represented a break from physical sciences and mathematics. The first mapping of a gene to chromosome was done in 1910. The study of heredity and genetics was begun early in the century. It is interesting to explore the issues of heredity and genetics which were common topics of conversation during the writing and staging of the play. In Williams' work, Blanche and Stella are essentially as different from each other as not to be called sisters. The relatively new interest in psychiatry and the changing role of madness and its management—whether beneficial or manipulated to adverse ends—is also highlighted in the play.

The Scopes controversy (referred to in the Religious Contexts above) also brought to fore the peculiar 'scientific' thinking rooted in the Common Sense Realism of Scottish Enlightenment—that true science consisted of plainly observed facts of nature. To look back and to imagine a prehistoric evolution was not in the purview of thinking espoused by 'common sense' realism. The argument went that the evidence in fossils resembled human beings in skeletons, so where was the proof of slow evolution through the ages? Science in the twentieth century overturned earlier theories which would themselves be demolished by the end of the century. Although not directly connected, one civilization giving way helplessly, but inevitably, is one of Williams' themes.

Biographical Context

Thomas Lanier Williams was born in March of 1911 in Columbus, Mississippi. His father was a traveling salesman, while his mother was the daughter of a rector. Cornelius Coffin Williams, Tennessee's father, was violent and aggressive, much unlike his gentle Quaker wife, Edwina. Throughout his life Tennessee remained attached to his grandparents, the Dakins. In childhood, Tennessee had called his Negro nurse as 'Nigger.' Apparently, the girl left her job offended and this left Tennessee with a lifelong hatred of discrimination. Tennessee was also partially paralyzed in the leg as a result of diphtheria, during which time he missed school and led a solitary, introspective life. Shortly afterwards, the family moved to St. Luke's. In this Midwestern city, Tennessee suffered deeply from his nostalgia for the South. This nostalgia and trauma for a lost place would come up time and again in his plays.

In his early youth, he had a brief love affair with Hazel Kramer which was broken up by his father. Tennessee was forced to work in an office during the Depression, and he found it extremely dispiriting. After a nervous breakdown, Williams tried to sort out his life by registering once again to a graduate course. Washington University had dropped him in 1937; Williams got his degree from the University of Iowa in 1938. Meanwhile, his beloved sister Rosie was growing withdrawn and closed, like Laura in "The Glass Menagerie," to be finally diagnosed with Schizophrenia.

Tennessee moved to New Orleans from where he won a play writing competition, which changed his life. The judges included Irwin Shaw and Elia Kazan. Since the competition was for under-twenty-fives, Williams lied about his age—reducing it by four years. With Audrey Wood as his agent, he was offered a plum job as a scriptwriter in Hollywood, but dropped out after a month. However, Wood managed his money well. "The Glass Menagerie" opened in New York and Chicago in December 1944–45, and made Williams an overnight success. Much influenced by the novelist D. H. Lawrence, Tennessee wrote "I Rise in Flame Cried the Phoenix" around 1940 as a tribute to Lawrence and Frieda.

"A Streetcar Named Desire" was earlier called "The Poker Night." Just before its opening in New York during December of 1947, Williams changed it to the name it is known by today. The cast included Vivien Leigh. It was hailed as a masterpiece. His other famous plays are "American Blues" (1945), "Battle of Angels" (1945—revised in 1957 as "Orpheus Descending"), "The Rose Tattoo" (1950), "Camino Real" (1953), "Suddenly Last Summer" (1958), "Sweet Bird of Youth" (1959) and the hugely acclaimed "Cat on a Hot Tin Roof" (1955). Williams wrote countless plays. His world is a world of sex, violence, and frustration. Some of his plays were made into films, including "Cat on a Hot Tin Roof," "A Streetcar Named Desire," "Suddenly Last Summer," "Orpheus Descending," (Renamed "The Fugitive Kind") "Summer and Smoke," "The Roman Spring of Mrs. Stone," and "Sweet Bird of Youth." "Streetcar" won Williams his first Pulitzer Prize in 1948, and his second New York Drama Critics Award.

Williams' plays have consistently reflected a homosexual theme. By 1948, he was openly living in a homosexual relationship with his secretary Frank Merlo. It was a positive and secure relationship until Merlo died of cancer in 1963. In 1979, Williams suffered beatings in an act of anti-gay violence. He died in February, 1983 at a New York hotel after choking on a bottle cap. Some say he was murdered.

Suchitra Choudhury, Ph.D.

Works Cited

John S. Bak. "sneakin' and spyin'" from Broadway to the Beltway: Cold War Masculinity, Brick and Homosexual Existentialism." *Theatre Journal* 56.2 (2004).

Anca Vlasopolos. "Authorizing History: Victimization in 'A Streetcar Named Desire.'" *Theatre Journal* 38.3 (1986).

Choudhuri, A. D. *The Face of Illusion in American Drama*. Atlantic Highlands, NJ: Humanities Press, 1979.

Discussion Questions

1. Imagination and improvisation gives depth to any understanding and performance of a play. What do you think Stanley's earlier love affairs may have been like?

2. Every character on stage has his other own personality as interpreted by the actor. Impersonate Stanley's wife Stella and write a letter to your best friend.

3. Enact the scene of Blanche arriving at her sister's place, as well as Blanche meeting Stanley in your own words.

4. We all have our favorite spaces. In a play the playwright assigns spaces to characters. Attempt to understand each character in A Streetcar Named Desire, and discuss how their space, in your view, relates to the identity of the character.

5. Blanche's first husband was homosexual. Discuss the depiction of homosexuality in "A Streetcar Named Desire."

6. Discuss the presence of fact and illusion in the play. Is Blanche the only person who holds on to her illusions?

7. Discuss the moral shortcomings of the character of Stella.

8. Discuss the effect of the play's violence on the audience.

9. What image do you form of the historical construction of the Southern Belle from the play?

10. Discuss the kind of music you would use for a production of the play.

Essay Ideas

1. Discuss the various stereotypes of women in "A Streetcar Named Desire."

2. Write an essay on the theme of illusion in the play

3. Is there any villain in the play? Who would you think is the 'baddie' in the play and why.

4. If you were to re-write the play, what kind of ending would it have? Write an essay on the effect Williams' ending has comparing it to your own.

5. Write an essay tracing the production history of "A Streetcar Named Desire."

Trifles

by Susan Glaspell

Content Synopsis

Inspired by the true story of Margaret Hossack, an Indianola, Iowa farm wife who was charged with the murder of her husband John in 1900, Susan Glaspell's one-act play still exists as a fascinating hybrid of murder mystery and social commentary on the oppression of women.

The play begins with the immediate introduction of the five characters who make up the play: County Attorney George Henderson; Sheriff Henry Peters and his wife Mrs. Peters; and neighboring farmer Lewis Hale and his wife Mrs. Hale. The two central characters of the drama, Minnie Wright and the husband she is accused of killing, John, never appear on stage. Small details that emerge from Glaspell's stage directions, as well as information communicated before one line is even delivered, develop the play's broader theme of patriarchal oppression. The three male characters are known by their first names as well as their last and are also described in the opening stage directions by their profession (sheriff, attorney, farmer). The female characters, in contrast, are known only by their last names and the prefix "Mrs.," indicating that they are married, and revealing the most significant component of their identity, their marital status. Furthermore, any vocational information, assuming a career outside the home is even a possibility, is not attached to their character names. Even the moniker "farmwife" or "homemaker"

escapes mention and the two female characters, Mrs. Peters and Mrs. Hale, are simply described by their married surnames. Finally, the play is set entirely in the kitchen of the Wright's home, arguably the (only) domain of Mrs. Wright. Glaspell is careful to mention in her early stage directions that unwashed pans are visible under the sink, a loaf of bread resides out of place adjacent to the breadbox, and "other signs of uncompleted work" can be seen by both the women on stage and audience (1763). Placing the entire play in the most domestic of domestic spheres, a home's kitchen, and choosing to reveal an unkempt and thus failing level of housekeeping at the hands of the accused murderer, Glaspell immediately sets the tone for a drama and murder mystery that will have everything to do with women's culturally defined gender roles and issues of domesticity.

As County Attorney Henderson, farmer and neighbor Lewis Hale and Sheriff Peters enter the kitchen, Mr. Hale begins to recount what he discovered when he initially came upon the crime scene. Shortly thereafter, the men make some disparaging remarks about Mrs. Wright's homemaking skills and commence with several patronizing observations to Mrs. Peters and Mrs. Hale. Amid the varying levels of bravado and joking at Mrs. Wright's expense, Henderson looks around and commits what will be several his oversights and failures to notice important facts during his investigation. He declares that the kitchen scene provides "nothing important—nothing that would point to any motive" (1766).

Amid the constant peppering of condescension by the male characters on stage, Sheriff Peters laughs at his wife's remark over Minnie's concern from jail over the status of her glass jars of fruit preserves. As she had worried they would, Minnie's jars have exploded due to the cold of the Wright's kitchen, the fruit and glass violently shattering from frigid temperatures and no protection from a warming fire. (Indeed, the requisite, substantial labor involved in the canning, Minnie's concern for the jars' survival, and the ignorance of both from the male point of view are all noteworthy here.) Hale's and Henderson's patronizing comments follow:

> Sheriff: Well, can you beat the woman! Held for murder and worryin' about her preserves!
> Hale: Well, women are used to worrying over trifles.
> County Attorney: (with the gallantry of a young politician) And yet, for all their worries, what would we do without the ladies?

This pattern of male condescension masking investigatory incompetence during the examination of evidence is continued throughout the play. After the three men leave the scene of the kitchen to explore possible clues upstairs, the two women and the audience discover the real clues that are left behind. There was a killed bird that Mrs. Wright had cherished, an unfinished quilt, a broken and unhinged door), clues that elucidate Minnie's motive and the underlying theme of the play: women's oppression at the hand of patriarchal society and male domination. As the women surreptitiously discover, and then conceal, the evidence that speaks to Minnie's motive, evidence that would certainly aid in her conviction, the audience sees a gendered solidarity among Mrs. Hale, Mrs. Peters, and the incarcerated Mrs.

Wright. In addition to making the final and climactic decision at the plays' conclusion to hide crucial pieces of evidence from the County Attorney and Sheriff, Mrs. Peters and Mrs. Hale consistently assume a quietly defensive stance on behalf of Mrs. Wright as the latter becomes the recipient of castigatory remarks regarding her housekeeping. This invariable defense of Mrs. Wright's inability to keep house alongside a husband who "was a hard man" who would not make a room any cheerier for being in it (1768). Moreover, not to mention a sense of guilt both women express at their failure to visit and provide companionship/assistance to their increasingly isolated comrade-in-need, exposes a theme of gender-specific unity throughout the play.

The delivery of the play's final, crucial line, in which Mrs. Hale responds to County Attorney Henderson's "facetious" quip about what kind of needlework Mrs. Wright may or may not have been utilizing, leaves audiences with an ominous, if slightly melodramatic tone to ponder. As Henderson remarks, "At least we found out that she was not going to quilt it. She was going to-what is it you call it, ladies?" Mrs. Hale, who has just helped conceal potentially damning evidence, replies, "We call it-knot it, Mr. Henderson" (1774). In addition to speaking the last words of the play, Mrs. Hale more importantly refers to the potentially unifying, gendered practice of quilting, an activity which in its least effectual enables women to congregate and talk freely, at its most, served as a mechanism of communication for the underground railroad (specifically-coded quilts and quilt designs were often displayed/hung in public locations around homes and farms to share information without the notice of authorities.) Finally, the "knotting" technique, as the murdered bird and birdcage mentioned before it, surfaces as a metaphorical comment on the lives of women in a culture that allows them fewer rights and privileges than their male counterparts do.

Historical Context

Life in the rural Midwest at the turn of the century was a lonely, difficult, often depressing way of life. The isolation and despondency with which Glaspell characterizes Minnie Wright's existence is not far from the reality that many farmers would have experienced, with no telephones or televisions, miles between the nearest neighbor, and backbreaking work a necessity just to survive. The small networks of sewing circles and churches would have provided some of the few outlets for farmers' wives to connect with others in their community on a social level. Usually living miles from their closest neighbor, more than just the need for human companionship went unfulfilled. For women who suffered domestic abuse at the hands of their husbands or fathers, few if any laws existed to protect them, and many, like Minnie Wright, would have suffered in silence, as the forced isolation resulting from miles between neighbors prevented outsiders from providing help. Finally, even if a woman did have the requisite courage and outsider assistance to leave an abusive situation, earning a living or maintaining custody of her children would have certainly posed a difficult, if not impossible, challenge to overcome.

In addition to being defined by their status as it related to men (daughter or wife), adult women's lives were predominantly defined by their status as mothers in Minnie Wright's culture. Professional lives outside the home for farmwives like Minnie were not an option; bearing and raising children would be seen as an obligation, life's major responsibility, and a given. The fact that Mrs. Hale and Mrs. Peters extend a level of sympathy toward childless Mrs. Wright would not have been insignificant to "Trifle's" original audiences.

Women's "unofficial" role as the subordinate sex in the private sphere (within the home) was not the only facet of gendered inequality at the turn of the century. Officially and publicly, adult women were denied the right to exercise their voice in political elections. Although at the time of "Trifles'" writing, women's suffrage was already a powerful political movement across the Atlantic in England. It had gained a strong foothold throughout the nineteenth century U. S. thanks to suffragists such as Frances Wright, Elizabeth Cady Stanton, and Lucretia Mott. American women would not be granted the right to vote in federal elections until the passing of the nineteenth amendment in 1920. In 1915, a bill legislating women's suffrage was presented to the U.S. House of Representatives but failed to pass because of insufficient votes.

In addition to not having the right to vote, women did not have the right to be on juries at the time of "Trifles'" initial production. In this sense, the title of the play's later adaptation into a short story, "A Jury of Her Peers," takes on added significance. Since by law Margaret Hossack would not have been entitled to a jury of other farm wives or even other women (her peers), a certain irony underscoring the legislated inequality toward women is established before the play even begins.

Although nineteenth century American theater had already witnessed the strong presence of traveling minstrelsies and melodrama, early twentieth century American drama was still considered a kind of bastard sibling to the more established and respected British, French, and Scandinavian drama that largely defined modern canonical theatre of the nineteenth century and in the early decades of the twentieth century. Although Glaspell and her colleague Eugene O'Neill would certainly change that with their contributions to the world stage, largely the playwrights considered "great" (Moliegravere, Ibsen, Strindberg, Wilde, and Shaw) did not originate from the United States.

As the second decade of the twentieth century continued, Susan Glaspell persisted in including experimental components to her work. Her colleague Eugene O'Neill also utilized these components in expressionistic plays such as "The

Emperor Jones" (1920). But the expressionistic techniques of some of her other works, such as "The Verge" (1921), are largely unseen in the mostly realistic "Trifles," which employs a realism of costume, set, and character speech. With regard to the realistic dialogue, Glaspell engages a significant departure from the elite and polished dialect of the salon dramas performed across the Atlantic ocean at the time of "Trifles'" first production; the regional dialect she employs can be found in lines such as Mrs. Hale's description of John Wright: "But he was a hard man, Mrs. Peters. Just to pass the time of day with him— (shivers) like a raw wind that gets to the bone—I should think she would' a wanted a bird."

Another frequent component of early dramatic expressionism for Glaspell and her peers was the incorporation of psychoanalytic themes and concepts. A frequently discussed and increasingly influential discipline, Sigmund Freud's discourses of human psychology and sexuality were also increasingly emerging in American popular culture, as with Glaspell's dramatic satire of psychoanalysis, "Suppressed Desires" (1920).

Societal Context

When Margaret Hossack was charged with the murder of her sixty-year-old husband John, the man she had been married to for thirty-three-years, Indianola, Iowa and the greater public would have been more shocked than today's post-OJ, Court TV-savvy audiences. Killed by two blows to his head with an ax, John Hossack was thought to be a cold mannered and difficult man to be married to, but his murder was surely not regarded as deserved in any way. In a culture that denied women the right to vote or the ability to serve on juries, the community in which the Hossacks resided was not terribly different from the rest of the country: a woman's role was largely defined in terms more domestic than professional. For the typical woman, an unhappy

marriage usually meant a lifetime of difficulty rather than today's possibilities of divorce and a fresh start. Female violence toward husbands, abusive or otherwise, was prohibitive.

In addition to the specific political issue of women's suffrage, Glaspell and her work are also considered more broad criticism of feminist issues arising in and outside the home. For example, the title of the play and the ironic underscoring of any "trivial" nature attributed to women's daily lives and their often labor-intensive-if-tedious work, (Minnie Wright's sewing, cleaning, cooking, etc.), is considered an astute observation on the demeaning, insignificant characterization of women's labor and their lives within domesticity. The nonchalance and frequent condescension with which the male characters address Mrs. Hale and Mrs. Peters, the two characters who in actuality solve the crime, reflects the frustration and powerlessness many feminists felt in early twentieth century America. Women were still denied reproductive control, the vote, the ability to serve as members of the justice system, and in many states, even the ability to be landowners or maintain custody of their children after divorce.

Religious Context

Much of the farming population living in the American Midwest identified themselves with various forms of Protestant Christianity. Although the Village Bohemians' broad agenda of religious freedom and opposition to anti-Semitism would certainly have been a fair description of Glaspell, Cook, and O'Neill, no religious or faith-based specificity resides in "Trifles." On the contrary, many in Glaspell's circle would have publicly identified as Atheists or Agnostics and if anything, the assumed hypocrisies and oppressive hierarchies of organized religion would have been understood as worthy of criticism along with other potentially domineering social organizations (such as patriarchy) of the twentieth century.

Scientific & Technological Context

Today's readers and audiences are more used to the complicated technology and gadget-driven crime solving techniques that perpetuate film and television crime narratives. For "Trifles'" original audience, however, black-light recovered fingerprints, DNA-testing and blood splatter patterns would have sounded like futuristic science fiction rather than the tried and true procedures law enforcement use every day to solve violent crimes.

The technology available to investigators of John Hossack's (and by implication, John Wright's) murder would have involved mostly questions to witnesses and suspects, alibi-verification, and gut hunches based on experience. The fact that the Wright's farm, essentially the scene of the crime, was not kept secure and untouched between the time of the murder and the County Attorney's visit days later reflects more than just poor evidence care. At the turn of the century, inviolable police tape, and scientific data, collection typical to today's investigatory practices was limited to gauging the truthfulness of interviewees and discovering motive, opportunity, and means. The fact that the three male characters are bent on finding clues which suggest motive, clues which of course evade them but not their female counterparts, reflects a more or less accurate modus operandi of forensic science in 1900. Although Glaspell would later encounter criticism for arguably constructing her male characters as overly or simplistically incompetent as they consistently bypass evidence (such as a dead bird) which would help convict Minnie Wright, the fact that pieces of evidence which speak to motive would be of primary concern to authorities is not an oversimplification of the turn-of-the-century forensic procedure.

Of course, Glaspell does not provide any answer as to the outcome of the Wright case, which dramatically highlights the conditions leading up to the violence rather than the eventual verdict of the crime (or the investigation's success/failure in proving guilt). Nevertheless, Attorney Henderson's desperation to find any evidence of motive is not an unfair representation of the methods prosecutors would employ in attempt to "prove their case." (Note: Minnie Wright's real-life counterpart, Margaret Hossack, was initially convicted but later won her freedom under appeal.)

Finally, the technological advances that many of us take for granted in the twenty-first century, including dishwashing machines, laundry and drying machines, wireless computer and telephone services, and of course automobile travel, were not within the reality or even the imagination for most Midwestern farmers such as the Wrights, Peters and Hales. Life on a farm for men and women alike would have involved backbreaking work with no days off and reward arriving merely in the form of survival.

Biographical Context

In her lifetime, Susan Glaspell (1867–1949) worked successfully as a reporter, a novelist, and an essayist, but she is best known as an American playwright and as one of the founders of the Provincetown Players.

Born in Davenport, Iowa, Glaspell graduated from Drake University in 1899 and began work as a reporter for the "Des Moines Daily News" shortly thereafter—although she had successfully worked as a reporter for several years before her graduation. (It was during her work as a reporter that she first became aware of the Hossack case and subsequently became interested in not just the case itself, but the public's strong reaction to it.) Glaspell biographer Linda Ben-Zvi points out that the Hossack murder was unique in the extensive nature of its coverage and the vivid writing style of the reporter who wrote about it. Ben-Zvi also notes that in the 26 total stories Glaspell published on the Hossack case for the "Des Moines Daily News," she also managed to engage a kind of "gonzo journalism" which predates Hunter S. Thompson by some sixty years. (Gonzo journalism, a form of nonfiction writing made famous by Hunter S. Thompson in the 1970s, employs a colorful and dramatic prose style and self-consciously places the reporter and her/his reactions in the story.)

While studying at the University of Iowa Writer's Workshop, Glaspell met her husband, George Cam "Jig" Cook, whom she eventually followed to Chicago, where Cook along with Maurice Brown helped in establishing The Little Theatre and the consequent Little Theatre Movement. After a stint in Europe, Glaspell and Cook returned to the United States, where they made a home for themselves in Cape Cod, Massachusetts. By 1915, Glaspell and her friends, including Eugene O'Neill, started to stage amateur productions in what would eventually be known as the Provincetown Players. In addition to first staging "Trifles" there, Glaspell's "Suppressed Desires" (1914/1915), a satire of Freudian psychoanalysis, was also staged at Provincetown, cementing the Provincetown Players with the critical cachet among New York theatre that it still enjoys today.

Issues concerning patriarchy, unfair labor practices, and racial inequality were all a large part of the leftist ideologies that Glaspell and her Greenwich Village and Provincetown peers were concerned with. Indeed, in addition to socialism and psychoanalysis, feminism was arguably the most frequent discourse to emerge in conversation. Glaspell's husband George, her colleague Eugene O'Neill, and writers and activists such as Max Eastman, John Reed, Emma Goldman, and Louise Bryant, were friends. They comprised the circle of literati and activists with which the playwright surrounded herself in the early decades of the twentieth century, a group of "Village Bohemians" which would also be varying associated with communism, free love, labor rights, racial equality, and reproductive rights.

Glaspell is considered a feminist playwright by today's standards. The large body of critical attention which investigates her work, however, is by no means limited exclusively to feminist critics. As one of the founding members of the Provincetown Players, Glaspell, along with Eugene O'Neill, is considered one of the more important examples of early American drama, as well as a significant voice of American Modernism. As Veronica Makowsky writes in her essay "Susan Glaspell and Modernism," Glaspell can also be read as a transcendentalist writer of sorts, in the tradition of Ralph Waldo Emerson and Henry David Thoreau. Unlike Emerson, however, Glaspell would have preferred that gender be a specifically-mentioned component to the inequalities suffered by man and the larger need for nonconformity.

Although she met with success during her lifetime,—indeed, her 1930 play "Alison's House" earned Glaspell the Pulitzer Prize for drama—in recent decades, Glaspell's work has met with more academic interest and her status as a canonical playwright and novelist has been revived by feminist critics and writers. Nevertheless, while as a peer of O'Neill she has consistently garnered critical attention, unlike the former (who is frequently dubbed as the man who put American drama on the world map) Glaspell is sadly still relegated mostly to inquiries into "feminist drama," while O'Neill enjoys status as the "father of American drama."

L. Bailey McDaniel

Works Cited

Alkalay-Gut, Karen. "Jury of Her Peers: The Importance of Trifles." *Studies in Short Fiction 21.1* (Winter 1984): 1–10.

Ben-Zvi, Linda, ed. *Susan Glaspell: Essays on Her Theater and Fiction*. Ann Arbor: U of Michigan P, 1995.

____. *Susan Glaspell: Her Life and Times*. Oxford: Oxford UP, 2005.

Bigsby, C.W.E. "Introduction." *Susan Glaspell: Plays*. Cambridge: Cambridge UP, 1987. 1–31.

Glaspell, Susan. "Trifles." Boston: Small, 1920. Rpt. In *Understanding Literature: An Introduction to Reading and Writing*. Eds. Walter Kalaidjian,

Judith Roof, Stephen Watt. Boston: Houghton Mifflin Company, 2004. 1763–1774.

Holstein, Suzy Clarkson. "Silent Justice in a Different Key: Glaspell's Trifles." *Midwest Quarterly* 44.3 (Spring 2003): 282–291.

Makowsky, Veronica. "Susan Glaspell and Modernism." *The Cambridge Companion to American Women Playwrights*. Ed. Brenda Murphy. Cambridge [England]; New York: Cambridge UP, 1993.

Noe, Marcia. "Region as Metaphor in the Plays of Susan Glaspell." *Western Illinois Regional Studies*. 4.1 (1981): 77–85.

Russell, Judith Kay. "Glaspell's Trifles." *Explicator* 55.2 (Winter 1997): 88–91.

For Further Study

Carpentier, Martha C. "Susan Glaspell's Fiction: Fidelity as American Romance." *Twentieth Century Literature* 40.1 (Spring 1994): 92–114.

Barlow, Judith, ed. *Plays by American Women: 1900-1930*. New York: Applause Books, 1985.

Dymkowski, Christine. "On the Edge: The Plays of Susan Glaspell." *Modern Drama 31* (March 1988): 91–105.

Friedman, Sharon. "Feminism as Theme in Twentieth-Century American Women's Drama." *American Studies 25* (Spring 1984): 69–89.

Jones, Jennifer. *Medea's Daughters: Forming and Performing the Woman Who Kills*. Columbus: Ohio State UP, 2003.

Kenton, Edna. *The Provincetown Players and the Playwrights' Theatre: 1915–1922*. Jefferson: McFarland, 2004.

Marsh, Kelly A. "Dead Husbands and Other 'Girls' Stuff': The Trifles in Legally Blonde." *Literature/Film Quarterly 33.3* (2005): 201–206.

Rajkowska, Baacutebara Ozieblo. *Susan Glaspell: A Critical Biography*. Chapel Hill: University of North Carolina Press, 2000.

Discussion Questions

1. Do you think that the murder of Mr. Wright is justified in any way? Why or why not? As a crime, would it be any more/less justifiable today? Why or why not?

2. Does the fact that the play is based on a true event change any "message" the play might be trying to impart? Why or why not?

3. What might be some of the symbolism generated by a dead bird which formerly resided in a cage?

4. What dramatic mechanisms does Glaspell utilize to underscore some of the play's themes (for example: dialogue, set, character blocking, costume, mise-en-scene, stage direction)? How are these mechanisms employed and what possible meaning do they generate?

5. Mrs. Hale speaks the last words of the play, when she tells County Attorney George Henderson, "We call it—knot it, Mr. Henderson." What larger importance or concept, if any, does quilting and the name of the technique "knotting" have for the women characters in the play? How might potential significance emerge as a result of Mrs. Hale speaking these words as the last line of the play?

6. What cultural assumptions about women do the male characters reveal in the play? What cultural assumptions about women do the female characters reveal in the play?

7. How and why might this play be different if it were not in a rural Midwest setting? (For example, if it were set in the American south, or in an urban setting, what might be different about the play or its course of action?)

8. Do the constructions of gender (male identity and female identity) come across as too simplistic or as overly exaggerated stereotypes to today's reader/audience? Why or why not?

9. Do you think that any social critique Glaspell's play is attempting to make ends up losing credibility because of an extreme or simplistic way that masculinity and/or femininity is presented? Why or why not?

10. Does the title of the play still have something to say about gender and domesticity in today's culture? Why or why not?

Essay Ideas

1. "Trifles" was later rewritten by Glaspell as the short story, "A Jury of Her Peers." What might be accomplished by the story as drama that cannot be achieved via short story? Why?

2. Analyze the constructions of gender in the play and explore what connotations emerge about turn-of-the-century masculinity and femininity. Does this parallel any of the gender constructions in a play often compared to "Trifles," Sophie Treadwell's 1928 "Machinal?" Why or why not?

3. Glaspell uses different layers of symbolism throughout the play; explore some of the more important instances in which the play employs symbolism and discuss their possible meanings. What might be some of their limitations?

4. Explore Glaspell's role in early American drama and the Provincetown Players. What makes "Trifles" a "typical" play of this time/genre and in what ways does the play "diverge" from the drama being produced in America at the turn of the century?

5. Interrogate the different meanings and connotations of the play's title. On a cultural and historical level, what does it refer to, what does it exclude, and why?

Russian playwright Anton Chekhov. His play, "Uncle Vanya," is featured opposite. Photo: Library of Congress, Prints & Photographs Division, LC-DIG-ppmsca-33710

Uncle Vanya

by Anton Chekhov

Content Synopsis

"Uncle Vanya" is set in Russia, in the last decade of the nineteenth century, on the country estate of Aleksandr Serebryakov. For twenty-five years, Serebryakov has been a professor of art. He appears to be a successful man and scholar. He has married the beautiful Elena, who is far younger than he is, after his first wife's death. The drama of the play is less the product of any action, however, than it is the revelation of the depths of the misery and the degrees of impotence of the characters gathered on the estate as they interact with each other.

In the garden, on a monotonous afternoon, Marina, the old nurse, sits by the samovar knitting. The doctor, Mikhail Lvovich Astrov, a melancholy man, paces back and forth. He has taken to drink and is burdened by a sense of age, loneliness, and overwork. overwork. He is oppressed by guilt: a patient of his recently died as he was operating on him, trying to save his life. He has been called to the estate to see Serebryakov, chronically petulant and full of complaints about his gout and rheumatism. Marina offers him tea, vodka, and consoling words, to no avail.

Ivan Vonitsky (Uncle Vanya) is disheveled after his nap and joins them in the garden. Vanya, the brother of Serebryakov's deceased first wife, is therefore Serebryakov's brother-in-law and Sonia's uncle. He is a man of middle age who has, over the years, cared for the estate and lived frugally, supporting Serebryakov and Sonia with the income produced by the estate. Now, he complains, since Serebryakov's visit, the daily routine of the estate has been disrupted and he (Vanya) has been idling rather than working. Worse, Serebryakov apparently intends to reside on the estate permanently. Elena, his young and beautiful wife, is idle and discontent, but her languorous beauty causes a general discontent on the estate because of the frustrated desire it arouses in Vanya and Astrov. Sonia, Serebryakov's daughter, shows herself devoted to his happiness and anxious to placate his discontent. The pockmarked Telegin, called "Waffles" because of his complexion, is an impoverished neighbor and Serebryakov's sycophant.

In the garden, Telegin speaks enthusiastically about the lovely weather, but Vanya complains: his old mother talks endlessly about the emancipation of women or about her coming death; Serebryakov annoys him with his complaints about his health, his exploitation of the estate, his pomposity, his ignorance, as Vanya sees it, in his field as an art critic. Nevertheless, Vanya confesses that he envies Serebryakov because of his success with women. Vanya's mother adores him; his sister loved him, and his new wife is a jewel Vanya himself covets.

The afternoon passes idly, with hints of discontent arising with each turn of the conversation. The conversation is itself a mix of philosophical and political conjecture and of each character's expression of longing, regret, and remorse. Vanya regrets his own unfulfilled life and his loss of the ideals he once had. He regrets that Elena has remained faithful to Serebryakov when she is not in love with him and has abandoned her own self-development to be with him. Astrov is tired of his life and his profession, going about his rounds as a doctor with no heart. His real passion is forestry and ecology. On his own land he has a seed nursery. He grows plants, cultivates his woods, and he supervises the care of the forests surrounding his property. But even in these pursuits he is disheartened. Rapid deforestation is occurring throughout Russia, he complains. Trees are cut down and forests are destroyed for wood to burn—he suggests using peat instead—and both the ecology and the beauty of nature are being ruined.

When Astrov and Sonia leave, Elena scolds Vanya for his bitterness, but confesses she is lonely. She reproaches Vanya, nevertheless, for his lack of understanding, for his contempt for her marriage, for his disrespect, as she sees it, for things like her fidelity to her husband and self-sacrifice. But all he wishes is for her to listen to his confessions of his love for her, for her to allow him to gaze upon her. She rebuffs him.

The scene changes to the dining-room at night. Serebryakov wakes suddenly from a doze, bothered by his rheumatism. He pities himself for his age, accuses others of finding him repulsive because of it, his wife especially. She tells him she is exhausted by the way he goes on. When she asks what he really wants, he says he wants nothing and continues to pick and complain. In addition, he refuses to see Dr. Astrov, who has been called to the estate especially on his account. Sonia scolds him for such ill-usage, but he keeps up his bitter invective against everyone and his pity for himself.

Vanya enters in his bathrobe, warning of an impending thunderstorm and holding a candle. He sends Sonia and Elena to bed, saying he will sit up with Serebryakov, despite Serebryakov's protest. Finally, the old nurse Marina enters, pities Serebryakov and leads him to the kitchen, with Sonia, to give him some tea and to warm his legs by the fire. Left by themselves, Elena and Vanya remain in their rut. As she complains of the gloom surrounding each of them and the bad feelings they have for each other and asks Vanya to bring some reconciliation between them, he laments about his misspent life, his inexpressible emotions, and his need for her to recognize and accept his love for her: the only way, he says, that he can find release from his own despair. In response, she attempts to leave the room, but he bars her way and kneels in supplication before her. But she leaves nevertheless. He recalls first meeting her ten years earlier, imagines he might have won her then, and wallows in the loss of what has not been. Then his thoughts turn to Serebryakov, how he had idolized him and supported him with his management of the estate, but now, he sees Serebryakov as a failure, a man who has accomplished nothing during his twenty-five year career.

Astrov, drunk, and Telegin, with a guitar, join Vanya. Astrov speaks of his own unhappiness, how he has periods, when drunk, of manic elevation, but is often in a slough. He notices the number of medicine bottles set out for Serebryakov and wonders if he is really ill or faking. Vanya says he really is ill. Astrov has Telegin play on the guitar and rhapsodizes about Elena. Sonia joins them and scolds them for being drunk. Astrov, who is only in his shirt sleeves and without his collar and tie, leaves out of propriety. Sonia reproaches Vanya for being idle and reminds him that the hay is rotting.

Astrov returns, fully dressed, prepared to leave. He complains to Sonia about the oppressiveness of the house, of life itself, of Russia, of Elena, beautiful but idle: the unresponsive but disruptive center of everyone's longing. He complains that he loves no one. Sonia, through a hypothetical question, hints at her love for him and asks him indirectly if he could love the hypothetical person she presents for his consideration. He says he could not. Nevertheless, she feels the vibrancy of her love for him. He leaves her alone. Elena enters, and the two resolve the tension that had separated them. Elena confides to Sonia that when she married Sonia's father, Serebryakov, she was fascinated by him and really believed she married him for love, although she realizes now that it was not really love. Sonia, in turn, hints at her love for Astrov, and Elena praises him highly, noting his ideals and the obstacles that Russia puts in the way of a man of genius and energy. She blesses Sonia's love. In their open-hearted rapture, Elena wishes to play music. Fearing it will disturb Serebryakov, Sonia goes to ask him if he minds. She returns to say that he does, and there is no music.

As the third act begins, Vanya, Sonia, and Elena are gathered in the drawing room waiting for Serebryakov, who has indicated he has something to tell them. They bicker as they wait. Elena complains of boredom and worries about how she will survive spending the winter on the estate. Sonia tells her there is work enough to do on the estate and that she might attend the poor and tutor the peasant children, but Elena responds that such things do not interest her. Vanya once more irritates Elena with his talk of love and leaves to gather flowers for her as a peace offering. When they are alone, Sonia directly confesses her love for Astrov to Elena, which she has borne unrequited for six years, and laments that she is homely and that he does not notice her. Elena volunteers to speak to Astrov to learn if he has reciprocal feelings for Sonia, and if he does not to stop him from coming to the estate. While Sonia has gone to fetch Astrov, Elena considers her own feelings. She is sure that Astrov does not love Sonia, but in considering why Sonia might love Astrov—he is handsome, charming, interesting—she realizes that she herself is attracted to him and offers an inward apology to Sonia for the betrayal she now contemplates.

Astrov tells Elena about the terrible destruction of the countryside and of the natural resources that has been wrought in the area over the past fifty years and how there has been no corresponding improvement in the human condition. When Elena asks him how he feels about Sonia, he confesses that despite his affection for her as a person he has no affection for her as a woman; he then accuses Elena of being coy, saying that she knows he himself desires her. As he embraces and kisses her, despite her objections, Vanya, entering with flowers, sees them. Astrov begins talking about the weather and Elena begs Vanya to convince Serebryakov to take her away from the estate immediately.

Serebryakov enters amidst, again, much bickering, and tells the assembly that he cannot stay at the estate but cannot afford to live in the city unless he sells the estate, invests the principal, and lives off the interest. When Vanya hears Serebryakov's plan, he explodes with bitterness and resentment. Sonia is the rightful heir and owner of the estate, as the property belonged to her mother before she married Serebryakov. Vanya speaks of how he has sacrificed his life for Serebryakov: though he could have made something of himself, he has instead worked to pay off the mortgage that came when his sister, Sonia's mother, bought the estate. Like an honest steward, he has worked on the estate and sent the earnings to Serebryakov, and he and Sonia, to help Serebryakov in his studies, gave much time to research and translations for him. Serebryakov responds by calling Vanya crazy but backing off from his plan. When Vanya leaves in anger, Elena sends Serebryakov after him to apologize. In a rage, however, Vanya fires a pistol twice at Serebryakov, missing both times.

The fourth act begins on an autumn evening with Marina and Telegin sitting in Vanya's room, winding wool into a ball and waiting for Elena and Serebryakov to leave for Karkov, where they will move after the tumult at the estate. Astrov enters with Vanya, whom all are worried may try to kill himself, and accuses him of having stolen a bottle of morphine from him. After several denials, and after complaining of his uselessness, of the burden of living, and of the tedium of his routine, Vanya returns the morphine to him at Sonia's insistence.

As Elena is leaving with her husband, Astrov begs her to stay. She refuses but presses his hand and tells him that although she will not surrender to him, she is in love with him a little. Serebryakov departs showing his characteristic pomposity, saying he has accepted Vanya's apology and bears Vanya no malice. He kisses him goodbye. Vanya and Sonia will continue to manage the estate and to support Serebryakov with the proceeds.

Astrov leaves, too, and Vanya and Sonia sit down to work, doing their accounts. Vanya says how miserable he is. Sonia says there is nothing to do but continue in their work, bearing their misery, smothering their feelings, until death takes them to their bright reward of heavenly rest.

Symbols & Motifs

Medium, regret, longing, unfulfilled possibility, and failure are the related recurring motifs in "Uncle Vanya" expressed repeatedly by nearly all the characters. An air of hopelessness is pervasive throughout the play. Vanya sees his life as a sacrifice, himself as a failure, and his ideals and potentialities unfulfilled. Sonia lives a life of grief, running the estate and longing for a love denied her by her physical unattractiveness. The beautiful but bored and lazy Elena has sacrificed herself and whatever interests she once had in music to a loveless marriage. Serebryakov, at the end of his career, hardly has enough to live on and his work, such as it is, in the field of art criticism, is apparently unvalued by his colleagues. Astrov, the doctor, drinks and reproaches himself for his professional failures and regrets the destruction of the ecology of the Russian landscape. He and Vanya both long fruitlessly for Elena.

The very emotions and desires that the characters have are symbolic of the emptiness of their lives. A sense of privation and loss is communicated through various characters' reactions to external stimuli. For example, Vanya's reaction to a thunderstorm symbolizes his longing for a loving companion with whom to share such a moment; the ecological destruction of Russia and Astrov's horror at deforestation symbolize the loss of anything substantial to give life meaning and purpose.

Historical Context

"Uncle Vanya" was written in the last years of the nineteenth century and reflects a society that is passing away. In fewer than twenty years from the date of its composition, the society it depicts will not exist and the individual explosions it presents will have become national. The social and economic upheavals of the Russian Revolution can be seen as the direct consequences of the class relationships, the human despondency, and the economic exploitation that the play presents. The faults of the revolution, too, can be traced to the kinds of character faults Chekhov presents, among them unfulfilled longing, resentment, greed, and stifled or ungovernable anger.

Societal Context

Social relationships in "Uncle Vanya" are depicted as deteriorating and are governed by the principle of exploitation. The natural environment, as Astrov describes it, represented primarily by Russian forests, is being exploited selfishly—the forests are being cut down—with no thought given to ecology, environment, or the natural world as it will be for future generations. Serebryakov has exploited Vanya and Sonia and in the play is prepared to deprive Sonia of her inheritance. Elena, engaged to act on Sonia's behalf with regard to Astrov, betrays her and considers her own interests.

The Russian peasant class is presented only in its function as servants of the ruling class. The abolition of the serfdom in Russia had occurred some decades earlier, and the play reflects the decline of the Russian landed aristocracy as precipitated by this previous social change. The society of the country gentry themselves is shown to be aimless and empty, their lives to be wasted, unfulfilled, and burdensome.

Religious Context

Religion's place in "Uncle Vanya" is as a sentiment designed to offer consolation for the miseries of a stifled life. Its chief gift to the human spirit is its offer of resignation and eventual reward. Sonia exemplifies the religious attitude of the play: if one bears the misery, tedium, and disappointments of life, rest will come as the spiritual reward brought by death. It is not a sentiment that Chekhov endorses but one he presents as concomitant with the kind of existence he is describing. The spiritual vision he seems to endorse is the one of care and stewardship (the ideals of Astrov, although Astrov despairs of them), of human exploration and achievement (the ideals of Vanya, although Vanya despairs of them), and of service (the actual practice of Sonia, although they bring her no earthly reward). The religion of the play is one of despair, consequently, rather than one of faith.

Scientific & Technological Context

The technology lurking in the background of the play is a destructive technology, not because it is inherently evil in itself but because it is misused by people. It is the technology that destroys the land by cutting down the forests. It is the intellectual technology that advances the selfish pride of a poseur like Serebryakov rather than place itself in the humble service of learning and discovery. Serebryakov is the man who exploits science and learning; Astrov attempts to serve science as a physician and an ecologist, but the tenor of the times and his own weakness thwart him.

Biographical Context

Anton Chekhov lived only forty-four years, the last twenty plagued by the tuberculosis that killed him in 1904, but his life was quite unlike the lives of the desperate and defeated, idle and disconsolate characters of his plays. He was a physician who devoted himself to his profession with long hours of service to people who could not afford to pay him and for whom he provided not only his service, but the medicines they needed without charge. He devoted himself to prison reform and wrote penetratingly about the alarming brutality in Russian prisons and penal colonies. He was a master of the short story and he practiced making the perceptions of a character's consciousness the basis for narrative. He was a precursor to such modern novelists as James Joyce and Virginia Woolf. Additionally, he produced a number of plays, with at least four of them, "The Sea Gull," "The Three Sisters," and "The Cherry Orchard," along with "Uncle Vanya," recognized as undisputed masterpieces not only of Russian drama but also of the theater. In these plays he not only explores the psychology of drama but shows the drama of psychology, turning experience, suffering, and endurance into action, and depicting with great finesse, as he traced the lives of his lost souls, the decaying world of pre-revolutionary tsarist Russia.

Chekhov was born in the southern Russian port city of Taganrog, on January 29, 1860, the son of a grocer and the director of the parish choir, a brutal, tyrannical, ambitious man who had been a serf and who bankrupted his family when he built a house beyond his means. In order to avoid his creditors he fled to Moscow in 1875, followed by his wife and children—save for Chekhov, who remained in Taganrog, lodging with a neighbor. In order to earn money, he tutored and began to write sketches for the local papers. He sent what he could of his earnings to his family in Moscow, read widely, and in 1879, after graduating, moved to Moscow himself, where his father had found work at a clothing warehouse. In Moscow, Chekhov continued to write and to sell his stories as he was attending medical school. By that time he had also written (and destroyed) a play called "Fatherless." But the things he wrote at this time were primarily commercial products, comical satirical pieces without any political or social bite, meant simply to sell. Nevertheless, as he continued to write he grew as a writer and his stories became increasingly serious—so much so that, in 1887, he won the Pushkin Prize for his collection of short stories, "At Dusk."

Chekhov first began coughing up blood, a sign of tuberculosis, in 1884. Despite his illness, he maintained a work load, just as a physician, that would overwhelm a man without his drive. In 1890, Chekhov traveled to a Russian penal colony on the Sakhalin Island, north of Japan. He stayed three months and conducted interviews with thousands of prisoners and observed the brutality of their treatment. In 1894, he published "The Island of Sakhalin," a blistering account of what he learned.

Two years earlier, in 1892, Chekhov bought Melikhovo, a country estate not far from Moscow. With ownership came responsibility for the tenants on his land. Chekhov provided them with free med-

ical treatment, built schools, a clinic, and a fire station. In 1887, he wrote the melodramatic "Ivanov," which, when produced, was a great public success. "The Sea Gull," performed in Petersburg in the fall of 1896, was not a popular success, but it was an artistic and critical success, drawing the attention of Constantin Stanislavski, the great director of the Moscow art Theater, who staged it there in 1898, and later also staged "Uncle Vanya," bringing success to that play to after its initial failure.

In 1898, Chekhov moved to a villa in Yalta for his health. There he wrote "The Three Sisters" and "The Cherry Orchard," also for Stanislavski.

He married Olga Knipper, an actress, in 1901. For most of their marriage, they lived apart. He lived in Yalta and she, in Moscow. He died of tuberculosis on June 15, 1904.

Neil Heims, Ph.D.

Works Cited

Chekhov, Anton. "Chekhov: The Major Plays." Trans. Ann Dunnigan. A Signet Classic, 1964. Print.

Chekhov, Anton. "Uncle Vanya." Gutenberg, 2008. Web.

Contemporary Authors Online, The Gale Group. "Anton Chekhov." Brandeis University, 1999. Web.

Discussion Questions

1. Chekhov gave "Uncle Vanya" the subtitle "Scenes from Country Life," not labeling it comedy or tragedy, as he did with other of his plays. Which do you think it is, a tragedy, a comedy, or something else? Explain.

2. Both Vanya and Astrov blame Serebryakov and Elena for bringing indolence with them to the estate and for sapping everyone else's will to work and to follow the routines that their daily responsibilities require. Is this really so? Do Serebryakov and Elena have such power, or are Vanya and Astrov attributing it to them in order to avoid deeper self-examination or to excuse themselves for their lots?

3. Is Serebryakov an authentic and honorable man or is he a hypocrite and a scoundrel? Is he a sympathetic or an unsympathetic character? How does Chekhov manipulate how we feel about him?

4. Evaluate Vanya as a person. Analyze his problems. What do they indicate about him?

5. The theater critic, Robert Brustein, has written that Chekhov "will not comment on reality; he will permit reality to comment on itself" ("Chekhov: The Major Plays", viii). How does he do that in "Uncle Vanya"?

6. Is Sonia a sympathetic character? What are her qualities? Is she worthy of a reader's pity? Why or why not?

7. Discuss the present-day problems of sustainability and ecological balance in reference to those problems as they are presented in "Uncle Vanya."

8. Do you find any of your own attitudes or problems of your own or that seem familiar reflected in "Uncle Vanya?" Which ones and in what way?

9. What do you imagine each character's life is like after the end of the play?

10. What is the relation between language and action in "Uncle Vanya?"

Essay Ideas

1. Discuss the problem of ambiguity in the way Chekhov presents his characters and influences a reader's way of responding to or understanding them.

2. What is the picture of Russia that Chekhov conveys in "Uncle Vanya"?

3. Describe, analyze, and evaluate Astrov.

4. Compare and contrast Elena and Sonia.

5. Compare and contrast Vanya and Telegin.

"Volpone" by Ben Jonson, featured opposite, was first performed in 1605. It comments on the social and religious attitudes of the time. Photo: Library of Congress, Prints & Photographs Division, WPA Poster Collection, LC-USZC2-5462

Volpone

by Ben Jonson

Content Synopsis

The Argument

The play opens with an acrostic of the name Volpone presenting the theme of the play: that it concerns Volpone, who is without children and convinces several greedy suitors that each will be his heir. To encourage this they all give him gifts of gold and other riches. The tricks will redouble until all is lost.

Prologue

The prologue has little to do with the play but is a message from Jonson to his critics. He tells them that the play was not written in a year, but in five weeks, and that five years would not be enough time for them to find a way to better it. He tells them that it is all new and not re-workings of old writing. He tells them that this is a finely written and funny play.

Act I

As the play opens, Mosca, Volpone's servant, enters and finds his master in bed. Volpone gets out of bed and requests to see his riches, which Mosca reveals for him. He then talks about how much joy his treasure brings him. He compares it to the joy of having children, of beauty or of honor and dismisses all these in favor of money. Mosca comments that riches are better than wisdom and Volpone agrees.

He adds that it is the way he achieves his riches that he prefers to the having of them itself. He is pleased that he does not have to work for them, or make poor people suffer for them. Mosca continues in this vein and then comments that his master is also not the kind of person who looks upon their riches and hoards them without spending them. Volpone agrees with this and gives Mosca some money. He then calls for his fool, his dwarf, and his eunuch to entertain him. Mosca leaves and Volpone talks to the audience, telling them of how he teases a number of greedy suitors who would all like to be his heir, how he pretends to be ill near to death, and how they are encouraged to give him rich gifts in order to win his love. This is how he makes his money.

Nano—a dwarf, Androgyno—a hermaphrodite and fool, and Castrone—a eunuch, enter followed by Mosca. Nano and Androgyno then perform an entertainment in which they discuss the idea that Androgyno possesses the soul of Pythagoras as passed down originally from the god, Apollo. Androgyno concludes that of all the people and animals the soul has inhabited, it is best to be a fool. Volpone asks Mosca if he wrote the entertainment and Mosca admits that he did. Nano and Castrone then sing a song about how good it is to be a fool. This song is ended by a knock on the door and Nano, Androgyno, and Castrone leave. Mosca tells Volpone that the visitor is Signor Voltore, a lawyer, who is one of Volpone's suitors. Mosca laughs at the thought of this visitor hoping for Volpone's death, not knowing he is being gulled (tricked/conned). Volpone dons an old robe and hat and Mosca places ointment on his eyes to make them look like they are weeping some kind of fluid. Mosca leaves to fetch the visitor while Volpone gets into his role as a dying man.

Mosca then shows Voltore in to the bed chamber where he presents Volpone with a large gold plate. Volpone thanks him and tells him to come more often. After a short exchange, Volpone feigns a collapse. Voltore then asks Mosca if he is confirmed as Volpone's heir. Mosca tells him it is so and begs to be kept in employment after Volpone's death. Voltore confirms this and then asks why he has been chosen as heir. Mosca tells him it is because Volpone likes lawyers and their facility with words and arguments. This discussion is interrupted by the knock of another suitor. Mosca tells Voltore that he should look as though he had visited on business and that he will come to Voltore later with the will and a list of Volpone's riches. Voltore leaves and Volpone springs up from his fake swoon to congratulate Mosca. Mosca tells him to lie down again as another suitor has come.

Signor Corbaccio enters, an older and more infirm man than Volpone. As he and Mosca talk, Corbaccio often mishears, believing that Mosca describes his worst fears—that Volpone is improving in health—forcing Mosca to repeat his statements of Volpone's worsening health. Corbaccio says he has brought a drug to help Volpone. In an aside, Mosca comments that it would be more likely to kill him. He then turns away the offer of the drug. Corbaccio then asks if he has been made Volpone's heir. Mosca says that he has not as his master has not yet made a will. Corbaccio asks what Voltore was doing there if not drawing up a will, and Mosca tells him the lawyer had brought the gold plate to secure the inheritance for himself. In response, Corbaccio proffers a bag of money

that Mosca takes from him. Mosca then tells him that when Volpone rises from his latest illness he will show him the money and get him to write his will naming Corbaccio as heir. He adds that to help this, Corbaccio should go home and rewrite his own will naming Volpone as heir, and disinheriting his own son. This gesture, he convinces Corbaccio, will further convince Volpone that Corbaccio is the right man. Then, he says, when Volpone dies before Corbaccio, he can change his will back and his son will inherit all. At the end of the conversation Mosca mocks Corbaccio, but Corbaccio, being deaf, either does not hear or mishears the insults. Corbaccio then leaves and Volpone and Mosca celebrate the hooking of another fish. There is another knock on the door and Volpone retreats to his couch once more.

Signor Corvino enters, bearing a pearl and a diamond for Volpone. Mosca tells him that his master is nearly dead but calls out for Corvino. Volpone does just that and Corvino approaches him. Mosca tells him that he cannot see or hear but can feel, so encourages Corvino to place the diamond in Volpone's hand. Mosca then tells Corvino that other people have been to the house looking to be named heir, but because Volpone kept calling for Corvino, Mosca took the liberty of writing a will for Volpone with Corvino's name as heir and executor. Then, to show Volpone's deteriorated state, he shouts insults in his master's ear and encourages Corvino to do the same. He then offers to smother his master with a pillow and Corvino demurs and leaves. As he goes, Mosca tells him that they are partners in all things except Corvino's wife. Once he has gone, Volpone again rises and celebrates with Mosca. There comes another knock at the door but the person is told to return in three hours after Volpone has had food and entertainment. The visitor was Lady Would-be, the wife of a knight and another one wishing to be heir. Mosca then mentions Corvino's wife to Volpone and describes her wondrous beauty. Volpone determines to see this woman for himself by going in disguise to look at her at her window. They leave the stage.

Act II

Sir Politic Would-be, an English knight, and Peregrine, an English gentleman traveler, enter the stage. They have just met and as they talk, Peregrine finds out that Sir Politic is easily fooled, and believes all kinds of rumors and stories. He feeds more of these to the knight who accepts them all as true.

As they talk, Nano and Mosca enter disguised as zanies, followed by a crowd. They set up a rostrum for a mountebank underneath the window where Celia, Corvino's wife, often looks out. Sir Politic and Peregrine talk about mountebanks. Where Peregrine says they are con men who sell poison for pennies after advertising it as elixirs for crowns, Sir Politic believes them to be true healers and purveyors of wonders. Volpone enters, disguised as Scoto of Mantua, a real mountebank. He proceeds to advertise a potion that will cure all ills. Peregrine shows his disbelief but Sir Politic contradicts him. In between Volpone's long speeches, Nano sings songs to entertain the crowd. During the second song, Celia appears at the window. When Volpone, as the mountebank, asks someone to throw a handkerchief to show he or she wishes to buy his potion, she throws hers down. Volpone looks up at her and offers her a magical powder to go with his healing potion.

At this point Corvino enters and chases away Volpone et al and sends Celia away from her window. Sir Politic also leaves and Peregrine determines to follow him because he is so entertaining.

We see Volpone and Mosca, having escaped from Corvino. Volpone declares he has fallen in love with Celia and must have her. He offers Mosca all his wealth if it can be made to happen. Mosca promises to do it.

Back at Corvino's house, he takes his wife to task for standing at the window and dropping her handkerchief for the mountebank in front of so many onlookers. He brands her a whore and an adulteress and determines to seal up her window, bind her in a chastity belt, refuse her from leaving the house, and that she will only move backwards from them on. At one point, he even draws a knife and threatens to kill her. He sends her away into the deeper parts of the house and then Mosca arrives.

Corvino hopes to hear that Volpone has died, but Mosca tells him that the other suitors have bought the oil that Volpone was selling under the guise of Scoto and this has cured Volpone of some of his ills. He then tells Corvino that in order to make Volpone really well, the others have hired doctors who say that the only cure is to have a young, energetic woman to sleep by him. In order to gain favor with Volpone, Corvino eventually agrees to supply his wife to perform this duty. Mosca leaves to prepare this matter.

Corvino calls Celia back in and tells her that his promises and threats were merely a test and that she should put on her best clothes and jewels as they are going to Volpone's house. They both leave to get ready.

Act III

Mosca enters and delivers a soliloquy about how happy he is to be a parasite on society. He claims, however, to be the most superior kind of parasite.

Bonario, Corbaccio's son, enters and Mosca tries to talk to him. Presuming him a beggar Bonario insults him and tries to leave. Mosca protests his innocence and pretends to cry. This stops Bonario who softens and agrees to listen to Mosca. Mosca proceeds to inform Bonario that his father, Corbaccio, plans to disinherit him. He convinces Bonario to come to Volpone's house to overhear the exchange of the will from Corbaccio to Volpone. They leave together.

At home, bored and waiting for Mosca, Volpone gets his three other servants to entertain him. They are interrupted by the knock of Lady Would-be.

She is brought in by Nano but stops before moving to see Volpone and calls one of her maids to adjust her hair. The first maid is sent to fetch a second and both attend to their mistress's appearance while she berates them for their laxness. Finally, she moves to talk to Volpone. He tries to convince her that he is ill and she should leave. To every comment he makes, she responds with a solution, a comparison, a tale, or other over-riding speech. Volpone starts calling to the heavens to save him from her.

Mosca enters and Volpone begs him to get rid of the Lady Would-be. Mosca tells her that he has seen her husband on the river with a courtesan and she immediately leaves. Volpone is expressing his relief when she comes back in to ask which direction her husband was rowing. Mosca tells her and she leaves again. Mosca then tells Volpone that Corbaccio is due at any moment and leaves. Volpone retires to his bed and draws the curtains.

Mosca re-enters with Bonario and gets the young man to hide himself where he can hear what is going to happen. There is a knock at the door.

Mosca answers the knock to find, not Corbaccio, but Corvino and Celia. Corvino was worried that Mosca would forget to send for them, so came on anyway. Mosca goes to Bonario and asks him to take a walk, as his father will not be arriving for half an hour. Bonario, in an aside, tells us of his distrust of Mosca, and he does not leave. Mosca then goes to talk to Volpone. Meanwhile, Corvino is still trying to convince Celia to lie down with Volpone. She says that he could hurt or maim her in any way he likes, but not ruin her in this way. Corvino tries to tell her that no one outside of Volpone's house would ever know and that Volpone is so old and sick that there is no need to worry. She still is not convinced. Mosca returns to the couple and, seeing that Celia is still resisting, suggests that he and Corvino leave her alone with Volpone, as she may be self-conscious with her husband watching her. The moment they leave,

Volpone leaps up from his bed, claiming that her beauty alone has cured him. He informs her that he was the mountebank and tells her that she should leave her husband—who would have happily given her away—for himself who would prize her more highly. He then shows her his treasure horde and promises it to her. Again, she refuses and Volpone tries to force himself on her. Bonario, who has been listening, emerges from his hiding place and leaves with Celia, threatening to expose Volpone's various plots.

Mosca enters, bleeding, having been struck by Bonario's sword. They both believe that their plots are at an end and when a knock comes at the door, Volpone believes it to be the authorities come to imprison him.

Instead, Corbaccio enters, with Voltore entering behind but unseen by the others. Mosca tells Corbaccio that his son has found out his father's plot to disinherit him and has set out to murder both Corbaccio and Volpone. In response, Corbaccio hands over the new will to Mosca. Voltore then makes himself known and accuses Mosca of double-dealing. Mosca explains how he planned to get Corbaccio's new will and then let the son know about it so that he would attack his father—maybe killing him—and so securing a second inheritance for Voltore. Voltore believes him. Mosca then goes on to claim that Bonario, enraged, has run off with Corvino's wife and has made up a story about Volpone being duplicitous and trying to rape her. Voltore, as a lawyer, vows to stop this. Word is sent for Corvino to meet Voltore and Corbaccio at the Scrutineo (the law courts) and they both leave. Mosca tells Volpone to pray for success and they both leave.

Act IV

Sir Politic Would-be and Peregrine enter, talking. Sir Politic is revealing all the schemes and inventions he has created to make him wealthy in Venice. All of the ideas are unsound or ludicrous in one way or another, but Peregrine, secretly laughing at the knight, encourages him to reveal them, expressing wonder.

As they walk and talk, Lady Would-be arrives with Nano and her two maids. She is looking for her husband with the courtesan Mosca told her of earlier. She spots her husband with Peregrine and presumes that the younger man is really the courtesan dressed in men's clothing. She accosts the two men and starts to accuse Peregrine of being a young woman and Sir Politic of being out in public with such a woman. Sir Politic protests his innocence and starts to believe in his wife's error, and leaves rather than being seen with this harlot dressed as a man.

Mosca enters and sees the confrontation. He informs Lady Would-be that she is mistaken and that Peregrine really is a young man freshly arrived from London. He tells her that the woman has been caught and taken to the courts and that the Lady should come with him to see and accuse her. After they leave, Peregrine assumes that all of this has been a trick at his expense and, as he too leaves, he vows his revenge.

Voltore, Corvino, Corbaccio, and Mosca all arrive at the courts, working on the last aspects of the story they plan to put before the judges. As they do, Mosca is talking to the others individually, convincing them how this plan will benefit each of them. Mosca tells Voltore that he has an additional witness in the shape of Lady Would-be.

The four judges and a clerk enter with Bonario and Celia, as well as with various officers and court officials. They have already heard Bonario and Celia's tale of what occurred and have believed it. Noting his absence, they send for Volpone to attend the court as well. Mosca protests that he is too unwell, but the officers are sent to fetch him anyway. Voltore then starts to tell his concocted version of events wherein Celia is accused of having an affair with Bonario. He says that Corbaccio, having heard of his son's affair, had determined to

disinherit his son. Bonario in turn had planned to murder his father before he could do so. However, having arrived at Volpone's where he expected his father to be, but finding his father not yet arrived, he and Celia determined to accuse Volpone of rape and left, striking Mosca in the face with his sword in passing. The judges do not believe this at first, but then Corbaccio, Corvino, and Mosca all attest that this story is true. As a final addition to the story, Voltore accuses Celia of being a well-known harlot who had been seen on the river earlier with a knight of good reputation. Mosca says he has the knight's wife as a witness and he is sent to fetch her.

Mosca re-enters with Lady Would-be who identifies Celia as the courtesan she supposedly saw with her husband. Bonario and Celia are asked what proof they have to refute these claims and they admit that they have none. At this point, Volpone is brought in looking old and sick. Voltore asks the judges if this looks like a man who could leap from his bed and attempt a rape. The judges agree that Volpone looks too old and sick for that and he is taken away again. The judges order Bonario and Celia taken away and locked up separately. They announce that they will pass judgment before nightfall and the judges and all their attendants leave the court. Mosca then goes between the three other men assuring them how they have done the right thing and this will further ensure their place as Volpone's heir. Corbaccio has been convinced to bring his entire fortune and all his belongings, right down to the curtain rings, to Volpone, to secure the inheritance. They all leave except Lady Would-be who offers to accompany Mosca back to Volpone's house. He puts her off saying that it would not look right if he should try to convince Volpone to make her the sole heir if she was present. She agrees and they leave separately.

Act V

Volpone returns to his house, scared from his encounter in the court. He declares that he was happy pretending to be old and ill in the privacy of his house, but doing so outside of it has taken away the fun. He sits and drinks wine and starts to feel better. He calls for Mosca.

Mosca comes in and the two men talk proudly about how it has all turned out well. Now that their tricks have reached such a level, Volpone decides to cap it all by tricking the suitors some more. He tells Nano and Castrone to go out into the streets and spread the rumor that Volpone is dead. He then takes one of the blank wills that have been used to tempt the suitors and fills it out with Mosca's name. Volpone will hide while all the suitors, learning of Volpone's supposed demise, arrive to claim their inheritance, only to find it has all been left to Mosca.

Shortly Voltore, Corvino, Corbaccio and Lady Politic arrive. Mosca is sitting in fine clothes taking an inventory of Volpone's treasure. They all think they have been made heir and wonder at the presence of the others. Finally, Mosca hands over the will and one by one, they realize they have not been left Volpone's fortune. As each protests in turn, Mosca reminds them of the things they have done to achieve the inheritance and threatens to tell the world if they do not leave. The last one to protest is Voltore, who thinks that this has all been a way of clearing the room for him to inherit, but Mosca does the same thing to him and he also leaves, disappointed. Volpone emerges having enjoyed seeing all the suitors so upset and declares a wish to be able to taunt them himself. Mosca tells him that he looks a lot like a constable of the court and he will get the man's uniform for Volpone so that he can go out and cause more mischief. They both leave to prepare.

Peregrine enters with three other merchants. He is in disguise. They are here to play a trick on Sir Politic. The merchants exit and a woman enters. Peregrine sends her to fetch Sir Politic and he eventually emerges. Peregrine, in disguise, tells Sir Politic that he, Peregrine, is actually a spy and he has passed on one of Sir Politic's foolish plans—a

boast that he had a way to sell Venice to the Turks—to the authorities. Sir Politic panics and tries to hide himself in a model of a tortoise. The two merchants enter pretending to be officials searching for Sir Politic. The three men then cause Sir Politic, inside the model, to crawl across the floor in the manner of a tortoise. Finally, Peregrine reveals himself and he and the merchants inform him that this tale of his humiliation will be spread. Peregrine and the merchants leave. Sir Politic sends a serving woman to see if his wife is around and knows about what has just happened. The woman reports that Lady Would-be has arrived home feeling 'melancholic' and is setting sail back to England. Sir Politic decides to accompany her.

Mosca and Volpone enter. The former is dressed as a nobleman, the latter as the constable he is impersonating. Volpone leaves to taunt his former suitors and Mosca tells us of his plan (now that Volpone has left the house and he has the keys and a will with his name on it) to keep all of Volpone's wealth for himself. He exits the stage.

Corbaccio and Corvino enter together on their way to the court to try and free Bonario and Celia. However, they agree that they need to maintain their original tale in order to keep their good names. Volpone enters, disguised, and wishes them each in turn congratulations on their new-found wealth. They protest that he is teasing them and he pretends not to know that they have not inherited Volpone's wealth. They leave. Voltore enters and Volpone also teases him. He then also leaves.

Volpone then catches up with Corbaccio and Corvino again. Mosca walks past in his finery and Volpone teases the men about what they had to do to get the inheritance, only to be overlooked at the last in favor of a servant. Corvino threatens Volpone and he has to call on Mosca to save him. Mosca approaches and the two former suitors leave.

Voltore enters again and accosts Mosca who remains aloof and leaves. Volpone teases Voltore some more and then leads him toward the court.

The judges and court staff enter with Bonario, Celia, Corvino and Corbaccio. Voltore arrives shortly after, followed by Volpone, still in disguise. Voltore, so upset by Volpone's teasing, starts to tell the court the truth of what happened and hands over a signed confession. The judges send the constable—Volpone in disguise—to fetch Mosca only to discover that he is now rich. Corvino and Corbaccio try to keep to the original story before Voltore incriminates them all.

Volpone enters on a separate part of the stage and bemoans the fact that in teasing Voltore so hard he has undone everything and now the court will find out what he has been up to. He meets with Nano, Androgyno and Castrone who tell him that Mosca has put them out of the house and kept the keys. Volpone asks them to fetch Mosca to the court to help him.

Back with the court, the judges are marveling over Voltore's confession. Volpone enters to announce the imminent arrival of Mosca. The disguised Volpone then tells Voltore that he, Volpone, is still alive and this has all been a trick to test Voltore's loyalty. He gets the lawyer to pretend a fever and sickness which caused him to write the confession. He gets Corvino and Corbaccio to play along. Once recovered from his fit, Voltore retracts his confession. Mosca arrives and Volpone asks for his help, but he refuses to confirm Volpone's story unless Volpone gives him half his fortune. Volpone refuses at first and by the time he relents, Mosca has increased his required fee. In response, Volpone throws off his disguise and reveals that all of Voltore's confession was true. The judges realize the tricks that have been played and the lies told by the greedy suitors. Mosca is sentenced to be whipped and imprisoned for life in a galley ship. Volpone, having pretended to be ill and crippled will be imprisoned and chained until he really is ill and crippled. Voltore is disbarred and banished. Corbaccio is stripped of all his belongings, which are passed to Bonario, and consigned to a monas-

tery. Corvino is sentenced to be paraded around Venice with ass's ears on his head and then taken to the pillory for people to throw things at him and put his eyes out. His wife, Celia, is to be sent home to her father with a trebled dowry.

Epilogue
Volpone talks to the audience and asks them, if they have enjoyed the play, to give a round of applause.

Symbols & Motifs
Volpone, as well as being a comic play about greed, can also be seen as a reworking of the animal fable, in particular the story 'The Fox Who Feigned Death' (Knoll, 83–84). All of the characters are given the names of animals—Volpone means fox, Mosca—fly, Voltore—vulture, Corvino—crow and Corbaccio—raven. Even Sir Politic is shortened to Sir Pol—a parrot, and is menaced by Peregrine, a bird of prey. The allegory is then extended with Volpone clothing himself in furs, Mosca flitting from place to place and person to person, and the various carrion birds gathering around the seeming corpse of Volpone (Enck, 133-135). In this way, the characters themselves act as symbols with their various characters predetermined by their animalistic association.

Historical Context
Ben Jonson is often seen as a being more a man of his times than his contemporary, William Shakespeare. In fact, this is often given as a reason for his relative lack of popularity in the subsequent period, because his work does not translate to a modern audience as easily as the seemingly 'timeless' writing of Shakespeare. But as such, he is a good barometer of what was happening in London society at the turn of the 17th Century.

"Volpone," first performed in 1605, was, in its time, one of Jonson's most popular plays, and remains a firm favorite of audiences today. This came from Jonson's decision to appeal to the public as his audience rather than the plays of Shakespeare, which were often aimed at the court and the nobility. In fact, Jonson was arrested after his play "Eastward Ho" was taken as a criticism of the newly crowned King James.

It is thought that Jonson based his play on the folk tale "The Fox Who Feigned Death," a story that would have been part of the public consciousness at the time (Knoll, 83–89). This would certainly have broadened its appeal to the contemporary audience.

Jonson did claim to be a classical dramatist; a follower of the principles of theatre laid down by the Greeks and Romans, and there is some evidence for this in his plays. However, despite his scathing attitude towards Elizabethan writing conventions, he was equally a product of them, using the concept of 'multiple unity' to create different narrative strands (Kay, 18). It is also clear that "Volpone" is an example of the type of morality play popular in Tudor times.

Societal Context

"Volpone," as with so many of Jonson's plays, is undoubtedly a social satire. The only characters to emerge from the play with an unblemished record are Celia and Bonario. All other characters, including the Judges, are portrayed as either corrupt or corruptible, or at best, foolish.

By the time of this play's first performance, the benefits of travel and education (which are seen as mainstays of the Renaissance) were well established. They had created a new class that had disposable income and spare time that they needed to find ways to fill. "Volpone" is a commentary on the rise of this new middle class suggesting that the lack of a consistent work ethic will only lead to greed and avarice (Knapp, 578-579). Thus, Volpone is depicted at the start to the play as already rich enough to attract the suitors. It is this wealth which has led to his desire to play games with the people around him. In addition, it is their riches

and their greed that make them such suitable marks for Volpone's sport (Redwine, 303–305).

In the final act, all is set to right in the style of a Tudor morality play. The greedy are punished to varying degrees and the righteous are rewarded. Thus, Jonson extends his analysis to show that such sin will always get its just reward.

Religious Context

As a moral satire, "Volpone" acts within the boundaries of Christian morality, extolling the virtues of hard work as opposed to the sins of sloth, greed, lust, envy and pride displayed by the characters. It shows these sins in turn and then shows how they each lead to ruin, thus encouraging the audience to lead a more moral lifestyle. In addition, Jonson puts religious language into Volpone's speeches throughout the play. In the first act, the religious terms are turned towards the worship of money. Later on, they are turned towards the worship of Celia instead. However, this is just another example of how sinful Volpone is as he is seen to worship these false idols even as he engages in greed and lust.

At the time of the writing of "Volpone," James I of England (who had been James VI of Scotland) was on the throne. He, like Elizabeth I before him, was a Protestant, but he was more tolerant of the Catholics than Elizabeth had been. Jonson had become a Catholic while in jail and obviously felt more freedom in such a climate. However, the prevailing religions were still based on an agricultural view of society rather than the increasingly commercial capitalist society which was coming to the fore. In response to this, Jonson created his plays to arrest this moral decline, and to show clearly to his audiences the things they should not do (Knapp, 579).

Scientific & Technological Context

Although the Renaissance was a time of scientific discoveries and advances, very little of this is featured in "Volpone." This is not to say that Jonson was unaware of such things as he made much of the modern ideas of science in plays such as "The Alchemist." The only nod that he makes in "Volpone" is in the character of the mountebank, Scoto. He makes all kinds of claims for his potion which both Jonson and the audience would have known were not possible. Such mountebanks would have been common at the time, but the fact that Jonson feels comfortable in satirizing them suggests that their potions were already being overtaken by other forms of medicine.

Biographical Context

The strongest ties between Jonson himself and the happenings in Volpone come from what is known as the 'Dedicatory Epistle.' This is an extended dedication written by Jonson to the two universities of Oxford and Cambridge. In it he talks about being both a god poet and a good man. He talks about the increasing profanity and blasphemy in contemporary drama and apologizes for any part he may have had in it. He claims to have always hated such styles of writing and to have produced, in "Volpone," a worthy work, which will make up for the mistakes of the past.

When compared to the events of Jonson's own life, this epistle seems to be somewhat hypocritical. Born and raised in London, Jonson grew up in a reasonably prosperous family. An unidentified friend paid for Jonson to attend Westminster School where he met the sons of many important families; contacts who would stand him in good stead in later life. After leaving school for the army and then apprenticing as a bricklayer, Jonson broke his apprenticeship to get married—an action which was greatly frowned upon at a time when a man was supposed to marry only when he had his own economic independence. However, this move coincided with his move into the theatre.

It is widely reported that Jonson was not a good actor and was in many ways disreputable and violent. In 1598 he was imprisoned and threatened with capital punishment after he killed a man in a duel. It is a reaction against this wildness in his youth that many critics have seen as the source for the moral tone of his later plays (Hill, 317). "Volpone," written around 1605, coincided with Jonson's reconciliation with his wife after a separation of about five years and it would seem that this 'settling down' caused him to review his past history and attempt to persuade his audiences against such activities.

Calum A. Kerr, Ph.D.

Works Cited

Counsell, Colin, Introduction. "Volpone," London, Nick Hern Books, 1999.

Danson, Lawrence, "Jonsonian Comedy and the Discovery of the Social Self" *PMLA*, Vol. 99, No. 2. (Mar., 1984), pp. 179–193.

Enck, John J., "From Jonson and the Comic Truth." Jonson: Volpone. A Casebook, London, MacMillan Publishers Ltd, 1985.

Hill, W. Speed, "Biography, Autobiography, and Volpone." *Studies in English Literature*, 1500–1900, Vol. 12, No. 2, Elizabethan and Jacobean Drama. (Spring, 1972), pp. 309–328.

Jonson, Ben, Volpone, London, Nick Hern Books, 1999.

Kay, W. David, "Ben Jonson and Elizabethan Dramatic Convention." *Modern Philology*, Vol. 76, No. 1. (Aug., 1978), pp. 18–28.

Knapp, Peggy, "Ben Jonson and the Publicke Riot." *ELH: English Literary History*, Vol. 46, No. 4. (Winter, 1979), pp. 577–594.

Knoll, Robert E., *Ben Jonson's Plays*. Lincoln, University of Nebraska Press, 1964.

Marchitell, Howard, "Desire and Domination in Volpone." *Studies in English Literature*, 1500–1900, Vol. 31, No. 2, Elizabethan and Jacobean Drama. (Spring, 1991), pp. 287–308.

Redwine, Jr., James D., "Volpone's "Sport" and the Structure of Jonson's Volpone." Studies in English Literature, 1500–1900, Vol. 34, No. 2, Elizabethan and Jacobean Drama. (Spring, 1994), pp. 301–321.

Discussion Questions

1. What purpose do the characters of Nano, Androgyno, and Castrone serve in the play?
2. There are a number of songs in the play, what purpose do they serve?
3. What is the purpose of the sub-plot with Sir Politic and Peregrine?
4. Examine the ways in which the animal names are represented in the characters.
5. The scenes of each suitor coming to Volpone's house are essentially the same. What purpose does this repetition serve in the play?
6. Different types and styles of language are used by different characters in different situations. Identify these and what purpose they might serve.
7. How many of the "seven deadly sins" are featured in the play? In what forms?
8. Volpone's actions can be seen as a "play within a play." Examine the various uses of stage techniques within the play itself.
9. Why is the play set in Venice rather than in Jonson's own city of London?
10. Look at the ending of the play. Do all the characters get exactly what they deserve or are some punishments lighter or heavier than you would expect?

Essay Ideas

1. What insights into Volpone's character are revealed by his interlude as Scoto of Mantua?
2. In what ways can Mosca be seen as the main protagonist of the play, rather than Volpone?
3. Discuss the various uses of disguise and dissembling in the play.
4. In what ways is "Volpone" a morality play?
5. Jonson uses a very different type of comedy from Shakespeare. Compare "Volpone" with one Shakespeare comedy and examine these differences.

Waiting for Godot

by Samuel Beckett

Content Synopsis

Act I

The play opens with two men on stage with only a bare tree on a small mound as setting. One of the characters, Estragon, is sitting on the mound attempting to remove his boot. The other character, Vladimir, is standing nearby and examining his hat. Estragon gives up trying to remove his boot, saying the play's the opening "Nothing to be done" (1).

The two men then start a discussion of their situation. Vladimir removes his hat and tries to dislodge something from it as Estragon finally removes his boot, feels inside, but finds nothing. They start a conversation about the two thieves who were crucified alongside Jesus and how only one of the gospels mentions that one of the two was saved.

Estragon wants to leave the place where they are waiting, but Vladimir says they cannot because they are "waiting for Godot." (5). However they are unsure if they are in the right place or if this is the right day. Estragon then falls asleep but Vladimir wakes him because he is lonely. Estragon starts to tell his companion about his dream but Vladimir gets angry and leaves the stage. He comes back and the two make up. They then discuss hanging themselves, but decide not to because they cannot guarantee that they would both die, and one of them being left alone would be too difficult to cope

with. Instead they decide to do nothing but wait for Godot.

Estragon announces he is hungry, and Vladimir gives him a carrot. This is just a momentary diversion and the waiting continues. There then comes a loud cry offstage, and the character called Lucky enters the stage on the end of a rope, carrying a number of items. Only when he is halfway across the stage does the holder of the rope, a man called Pozzo, appear. He is driving Lucky with a whip. They continue across until Lucky exits the stage, but Pozzo stops him with jerk of the rope and addresses himself to Estragon and Vladimir.

The two men think at first that he might be Godot, but Pozzo corrects them. He tells them that this is his land, but the road is free for all so they are not trespassing. He decides to rest with them for a while. Lucky sets up a seat and lays out food for Pozzo, who eats chicken and drinks wine, casting the chicken bones on the floor. Estragon asks to have the bones, but Pozzo says the bones are for Lucky. Estragon asks Lucky if he wants them, but Lucky hangs his head and says nothing, so Estragon takes this as permission for him to take the bones.

Vladimir then upbraids Pozzo for his treatment of Lucky. He and Estragon try to understand why Lucky does not put his load down on the ground. Pozzo explains that his servant is being especially diligent, because he is trying to persuade him not to sell him. Lucky starts to cry and Pozzo hands Estragon a handkerchief to wipe away the servant's tears. However, when Estragon approaches him, Lucky kicks him in the shins.

Pozzo reveals that Lucky has been serving him for sixty years, and Vladimir gets angry with him for selling the servant. Pozzo then gets upset, and Vladimir gets angry with Lucky for mistreating his master. Pozzo calms down, and Vladimir leaves the stage to urinate. Upon his return, Pozzo talks about the quality of twilight and then offers to have Lucky dance and think for the other two men.

The dance is awkward and underwhelming. Pozzo then tells them that Lucky needs his hat to think. Vladimir puts the hat on the servant's head and Pozzo commands him to think. What comes out of Lucky's mouth is a long stream of seeming philosophy mixed with nonsense. The other three suffer through the torrent of words and then finally tear the hat off Lucky's head, causing him to stop "thinking." Pozzo tramples the hat, while the others help Lucky to his feet. Pozzo then helps his servant gather his burdens before once more picking up the rope and driving his servant from the stage.

After Pozzo and Lucky leave, a boy arrives. He says he has a message from Godot saying that he will not arrive today but will arrive tomorrow and that Estragon and Vladimir should wait for him. Vladimir seems to think the boy has come before with this message, suggesting that the two have been waiting for a while. The boy leaves, and Estragon takes his boots and places them at the front of the stage while the two men continue their conversations about futility. They decide to leave, but as the act ends neither of them do so.

Act II

Act II opens on the same scene on what seems to be the following day; however, the tree now has a few leaves on it, suggesting a greater passage of time. Estragon's boots and Lucky's hat are where they were left the previous day. Vladimir enters

and sings a song about dogs. Estragon enters in fear and tells his companion that he spent the evening in a ditch and that he was beaten by ten men. They talk about splitting up, but decide not to.

Vladimir points out the change in the tree, but Estragon is not interested. Vladimir talks about Pozzo and Lucky, but Estragon claims to not remember them. As an attempt to show that these things happen, Vladimir exposes the wound on Estragon's shin where Lucky kicked him. Estragon still protests, but Vladimir points to the boots. Estragon protests that they are not his.

Vladimir offers Estragon a radish to eat as there are no carrots left. Estragon refuses it because it is black. Vladimir then persuades his companion to try the boots on, which he does and finds to his surprise that they fit. Estragon decides to try and sleep again. He does so as Vladimir sings him a lullaby.

Estragon then wakes suddenly in fright and is comforted by his friend. Vladimir then finds Lucky's hat and tries it on. There then follows a comedic scene of hat swapping back and forth between the two of them. Vladimir tries to get his friend to join him in pretending to be Pozzo and Lucky, but Estragon does not remember the other men and so simply does as his friend suggests.

Estragon leaves the stage and then runs back on believing that someone is coming. Vladimir believes it will be Godot, but no one comes. Their discussion then dissolves into an argument, but eventually they make up. They then attempt some physical jerks and a yoga position called 'the tree'. While they are doing this, Pozzo and Lucky enter and, along with the baggage, fall to the floor.

Pozzo, who is now blind, calls for help, and after some discussion of whether they should ask him for another bone, or for money, the other two try to help him. Vladimir is pulled over while trying to help Pozzo up. He, in turn, pulls Estragon over. Vladimir and Estragon fall asleep, but are awakened by Pozzo's shouting. Vladimir strikes Pozzo, who crawls away. They call for Pozzo but get no response. Then Estragon tries other names. He calls "Abel," to which Pozzo replies. He then wonders if Lucky's name might be "Cain," but Pozzo answers to this too.

Boring of this activity, Vladimir and Estragon climb easily to their feet. They help Pozzo up and quiz him. He does not remember them, and tells them that his blindness came suddenly and that he no longer has any concept of time. He asks about Lucky, who is still lying on the floor. Estragon goes to look at the servant, and exacts revenge for the injury to his shins by kicking him; however he hurts his foot in the process, so he goes to the mound to sit down again.

Pozzo gets Lucky to stand up and makes to leave. Vladimir asks him to have his servant dance and think again, but Pozzo protests that Lucky is now dumb. Pozzo and Lucky leave. Once offstage, they fall down again, and Vladimir mimics the movement.

Vladimir then wakes Estragon, who has fallen asleep again. He talks to his friend about the events of the day and about Pozzo and Lucky. A boy enters. He claims to be a different boy than the previous one, but he carries the same message from Godot. Vladimir scares the boy away and tells Estragon that, once again, Godot is not coming. They discuss hanging themselves again, but when they test the strength of Estragon's trouser cord with the aim of using it as a noose, it snaps. Estragon's trousers fall down.

They talk about separating again, and about hanging themselves again, but decide to carry on waiting. Estragon pulls his trousers up, and the two men decide to leave the spot, but, as the play ends, neither one moves.

Symbols & Motifs

The main motif running through the play is the sense that the characters lack control over their own lives. This is emphasized by the repetition of such phrases as "Nothing to be done" (1), which shows a kind of fatalism, and "We're waiting for Godot" (5), which shows that they have abdicated responsibility for their decisions to this unknown third party. Any and all attempts to better their situation, or simply to change it, are in turn shut down by these kind of phrases.

The various hats and Estragon's boots also work as symbols emphasizing this stasis. Estragon's boots are uncomfortable and, at least in part, rejected by him. Thus the men are prevented from simply walking away from their situation. Likewise, Vladimir continually searches in his hat but does not find what he is looking for. Their inability to complete an action represents their inability to think their way out of their situation. The only hat that does provoke thought, the one belonging to Lucky, only yields useless and random thought, and is stamped upon and shunned.

The tree next to which the play takes place is also symbolic in its function. In the first act, it is bare, like the cross on which Jesus was crucified, tying it in with Vladimir's discussion of the thieves. In the second act it has sprouted a few leaves, suggesting the possibility of change and progress, but these leaves are so few that it seems to reinforce the notion that the possibility will not be realized.

Historical Context

Beckett's work has been seen as straddling the divide between the literary movements of modernism and postmodernism. Modernism emerged at the beginning of the 20th century as a reaction against 19th century realism, and emphasized the subjective over the objective and the internal life of the individual over the external life of a society. As a style of writing, it was characterized by fragmentation and "stream of consciousness," which tried to imitate the random nature of real thought. An example of this is seen in Lucky's "thinking" speech.

Modernism grew in the years before the First World War, but it was the horrors of this conflict which galvanized it as a movement. In the same way, the Second World War is often seen as the event which precipitated the move from modernism to post-modernism. This movement continued many of the features of modernism, but it also introduced greater levels of irony, self-awareness, and play. As such, Waiting for Godot, written in the years immediately following the Second World War, despite containing much that can be classified as typically modernist, can be seen as one of the first works of postmodernism.

The play was performed for the first time in France, in its original French version (En attendant Godot) in 1953. Waiting for Godot, Beckett's own English translation of his play, was first performed in London in 1955, and directed by Peter Hall.

Societal Context

The play itself, existing in no particular place at no particular time, cannot really be seen as being representative of the society from which it emerged. Rather, it is more a product of literary movements, such as modernism and post-modernism, and schools of thought, such as existentialism and psychoanalysis. However, a look at the initial reception of the play does shine some light on its relation to its time period.

The initial French performance in 1953 was unabridged and, despite some ambivalent or unenthusiastic audiences, received a range of reviews that were, on the whole, positive. At the time of its first English production though, UK censorship the meant that some words—"erection," "fartov," and "the clap"—had to be replaced with more "polite" words, and attempts were made to ban the play altogether. The first un-censored version of the play was not performed in London until 1964.

The first English production initially garnered mixed reactions from audiences and critics alike, but eventually the influential critics Harold Hobson and Kenneth Tynan, who lauded the play, made it into a phenomenon. Initially lined up for Best New Play award in the Evening Standard Drama Awards for 1955, it eventually received the specially created award of Most Controversial Play of the Year, a prize that has not been awarded since (Hall).

Religious Context

Beckett was raised in a tradition of Protestantism by his parents, in particular his mother, who "reinforced it with her own values of piety and discipline" (Bryden, 155). However, Beckett as an adult was more ambivalent about religion, and claimed to follow no particular belief system (Bryden, 157-8).

The most immediate religious parallel is drawn between the character of Godot and his seeming namesake, God. Not only is there the similarity of the name, but Godot is also described at the end of the play as having a 'white' beard (80), which would fit with very traditional depictions of God in Christian art. In this context it could be seen that Vladimir and Estragon are either nearing the end of their lives and waiting to die, or have already died and are waiting to go to heaven and to God. Thus the setting of the play could be seen as being a limbo place, such as purgatory, where the dead wait for their judgment.

Another specific religious reference is Vladimir's comments near the beginning of the play regarding the two thieves who are crucified alongside Jesus, one of whom is saved. This would seem to suggest that if Vladimir and Estragon are indeed awaiting judgment; should Godot actually arrive, then only one of them would be saved. Pozzo and Lucky can also be seen as being such a pairing, with one of them marked for salvation the other for damnation.

There is also the specific reference to Cain and Abel made by Estragon when he and Vladimir are trying to attract Pozzo's attention in act 2. Together, these various aspects suggest that, although this play may not have a clear-cut religious message and Beckett may not have followed any particular faith, he was still writing within a Christian tradition.

Scientific & Technological Context

The play takes place in a seemingly bucolic setting at an indeterminate point in history. As such, there are no scientific or cultural allusions in the play. The lack of these references serve the play by reinforcing the dreamlike, un-fixed quality of its existential ponderings.

Biographical Context

Samuel Beckett was born in Dublin, Ireland in 1906. His parents were Church of Ireland Protestants, his father a quantity surveyor and his mother a nurse. As a young boy, he attended Portora Royal School in Enniskillen and later attended Trinity College Dublin, where he studied French and Italian. After graduating, he moved to Paris and took up a post at the École Normale Supriéure. While there, he became a close friend and assistant to James Joyce, and was involved in the research that led to Joyce's Finnegan's Wake. Beckett's first published work, in 1929, was a contribution to a collection of essays on Joyce.

He returned to Dublin and Trinity College as a lecturer in 1930, but became disillusioned with academic life and resigned in 1931. He travelled around Europe, writing and taking an interest in the burgeoning theories of Carl Jung, which are thought to have influenced his later works.

Having finally settled in France, Beckett served as a courier for the French Resistance during the Second World War and continued to live in Paris, more or less continuously, for the remainder of his life.

His most well-known work, "Waiting for Godot" brought Beckett fame and gave him greater scope to write and publish his works. He died in Paris in 1989, just five months after the death of his wife. He is buried in the Cimètire du Montparnasse in Paris.

Calum A. Kerr, Ph.D.

Works Cited

Beckett, Samuel. "Waiting for Godot." London: Samuel French, 1965.

Blue Angel Films. *Beckett on Film*. 16 July 2009 <http://www.beckettonfilm.com/>.

Bryden, Mary. "Beckett and Religion." Samuel Beckett Studies. Basingstoke: Palgrave Macmillan, 2004. 154–171.

Coe, Richard N. Beckett. Edinburgh: Oliver and Boyd, 1964.

Davies, Paul. "Samuel Beckett." The Literary Encyclopedia. 16 July 2009. <http://www.litencyc.com/php/speople.php?rec=true&UID=5161>.

Hall, Peter. "Peter Hall looks back at the original Godot." *The Samuel Beckett On-Line Resources and Links Pages*. 16 July 2009. <http://samuelbeckett.net/PeterHallGodot.html>.

Kalb, J. *Beckett in Performance*. Cambridge: Cambridge University Press, 1989.

Oppenheim, Lois. *Samuel Beckett Studies*. Basingstoke: Palgrave Macmillan, 2004

Discussion Questions

1. In what ways does the setting affect or reflect the tone of the play?
2. In what ways is this play about repetition?
3. Hats play a big role in the play. Discuss their use both as props and as symbols.
4. Examine the role of memory in the play.
5. Can the relationship between Vladimir and Estragon be compared to a marriage?
6. What is the role of the tree in the play?
7. Examine the significance of Estragon's boots.
8. The play is described as a "tragicomedy." What does this term mean, and is it appropriate?
9. What is the role of the boy(s)?
10. What is the significance of the fact that Godot never actually appears?

Essay Ideas

1. In what ways is "Waiting for Godot" a play about religion?
2. Compare and contrast the relationship between Vladimir and Estragon with that between Pozzo and Lucky.
3. What is the significance of Lucky's "thinking" speech in the context of the play as a whole?
4. Examine the similarities and differences between the two acts. How are the differences significant?
5. To what extent is the opening line, "Nothing to be done," a useful synopsis of the play?

The Wild Duck

by Henrik Ibsen

Content Synopsis

Some twenty years before the play begins, Werle and Ekdal were business partners in a lumber mill. When the firm was accused of criminal business practices, a court determined that Ekdal was guilty and that Werle was not. Ekdal was sent to prison and was released after serving his sentence, a broken man. Werle continued in the business and grew prosperous. As the play opens, a gala dinner is being given at Werle's, to which old Werle's son, Gregers, who has been away for many years working at his father's lumber mill, has invited his childhood friend, old Ekdal's son Hjalmar. As they are having dinner, old Ekdal, whom old Werle has taken on as a copyist in his employ as a way of supporting him, is working in the offices attached to the house. In order to leave work, the disgraced Ekdal must pass through the salon in which the guests are enjoying themselves after the banquet. It is an embarrassment for everyone, particularly for his son Hjalmar, who pretends not to notice his father as he passes through the room on his way out.

Gregers and Hjalmar have not met since their childhood. After dinner, among the guests, they talk about how they have fared. Gregers, and the audience, learn that Hjalmar, with old Werle's help, has married Gina Hansen, who had been a servant in the Werle household, and with whom old Werle once had an affair, although Hjalmar does not know that. Gregers learns, as well, that his father has established Hjalmar in business as a photographer and has contributed financially to his household. His father's generosity disturbs him because he thinks its function is to cover his, old Werle's, guilt. The reader gets a sense that old Werle might not have been as innocent as he seemed in the business scandal but managed to transfer all the blame to old Ekdal, and that he paid a debt to Gina for dishonoring her by arranging her marriage. However, whether these are valid suspicions are never made certain. In addition, Werle resents his father, thinking he treated his wife, Gregers' dead mother, badly. She had appeared to Gregers as a highly moral woman, but appeared to his father as overbearingly demanding and censorious. His father repeatedly asserts that Gregers is too stiflingly, much like her.

In conversation with his father after the party, Gregers refuses to become a partner in the business, confronts him with all his resentments, and concludes, without saying what it is, that he has found his purpose in life. What that purpose is, the reader will discover, is to free Hjalmar and his family from the illusion of his father's goodness and from their dependency upon him. Gregers has been a youth who felt called upon to summon others to pursue "the ideal." In addition, he will continue on that mission using Hjalmar. He vows to leave his father's house and to live on his own.

The next morning, he goes to visit Hjalmar, learns that Hjalmar and Gina have a spare room to rent, and becomes their tenant.

Hjalmar, Gina, their daughter Hedvig, and Hjalmar's father, old Ekdal live in an apartment with a large loft that Hjalmar and his father have turned into a kind of indoor forest where they keep birds, rabbits, and a wild duck, and where old Ekdal goes hunting, shooting a rabbit now and then. The duck has survived being shot and winged by old Werle when he was hunting. He gave it to them and they have cared for it, nursing it back to a crippled health. Hedvig adores it and considers it her duck. She is also deeply in love with her father. Hjalmar, ostensibly a photographer, leaves most of the work (taking pictures of people and developing and touching up the photographs) to Gina and even Hedvig while he contemplates a photographic invention that he believes he is developing. Although he seems to be making little progress on it, thinking about it takes up much of his time and shores up his self-esteem. The family is poor; Hjalmar seems to be something of a dreamer; his father lives in a fantasy world in the ersatz forest; and Gina and Hedvig are the responsible ones. A kind of livable balance has been achieved and is maintained.

With his idealistic project of challenging people to free themselves from illusion and transcend themselves, Gregers intrudes into their world and destroys it. He reveals to Hjalmar that Gina once had an affair with his father, arguing that when she admits it and Hjalmar knows it, it will make their devotion to each other stronger because they have been freed from illusions. However, this is not the case. Hjalmar abandons his family, gets drunk with a neighbor, and goes back to his apartment in the morning, not to reconcile with his wife but because he has nowhere else to go. When old Werle settles an annuity upon old Ekdal and Hedvig, as he, Werle, is about to remarry and retire to the countryside where the mill is located, Gregers insinuates that he is doing it because Hedvig is really old Werle's daughter and not Hjalmar's. This suspicion, too, is never confirmed. In this way, Gregers causes Hjalmar to hate his daughter and withdraw from her, causing her grievous pain.

Then Gregers goes to work on Hedvig. She is distraught and confused by her father's fierce rejection of her. Gregers tells her that a sacrifice would show Hjalmar how much she loves him, that she should kill her beloved wild duck to show the extent and depth of her love. However, the sensitive Hedvig offers an even greater sacrifice and shoots herself. Hjalmar realizes how much the child loved him. Gina and Hjalmar are united in their grief. Gregers has learned little and idealizes his own future death, the chaos he has caused being his sacrifice to the ideal.

Symbols & Motifs

The wild duck is the central symbol and motif of the play. Its significance for the play comes from the characteristic it has that when wounded it dives down deep to the river bottom. Hedvig herself becomes the embodiment of the wild duck. When she is wounded by Hjalmar's rejection of her, she dives to the bottom and kills herself.

Hjalmar's dream of inventing something represents the illusion that allows him to live despite his sense of shame for his father's past. Similarly, his father's old army uniform represents his lost respectability. The motive for Gregers' devotion to imposing the ideal upon others is represented symbolically too in his confession that he does not like his own name. The name "Gregers" stands for the person himself. Rather than confront his own self-loathing, however, he projects imperfection onto others and attempts to cure it in them while ignoring his own.

Historical Context

Ibsen wrote "The Wild Duck" as a dialectical variation on his previous play, "An Enemy of the

People," 1882. In that play, he proposed that it was heroic for a man to defend an important truth at all costs. In this play, he tempers that position by taking into account the delicacy of human adjustments and the need to have a sense of the possibilities of life. The pursuit of truth and the imposition of honesty must be weighed against what harms both illusion, truth can bring, and what good they can do.

Societal Context

Once he stopped writing poetic, mythological dramas, in 1877, Ibsen's plays always focused on social conflicts as they played out among members of one or several interconnected families. These conflicts usually centered on the psychological effects of the unequal distribution of power and the struggle among both the powerful and the powerless to survive. Hakon Werle is intent on maintaining his power and his self-image. Hjalmar Ekdal is striving insecurely to gain power and restore his fallen father's honor in society. His father, Old Werle spends his days in an elaborate fantasy world endeavoring to pretend that the restrictions on his social position and self-respect do not exist, even as he bows before them by numbing himself with drink and turning a loft into a hunting ground. Gregers attempts to overcome his father's power by transcending it with his own through the pursuit of the ideal and the denigration of the quotidian.

"The Wild Duck" explores the effect of exclusion from society on the disgraced Ekdal family. It also examines how the scion of the powerful Werle family, Gregers Werle, copes with his uneasy sense of privilege. His revolt attempts to soothe the aches of social marginality that reflects on his own guilt at his privilege, anger at his father, and inability either to join or to defeat him.

Religious Context

There is no overt religious context in "The Wild Duck", but Ibsen is concerned with fanatical beliefs, particularly with the kind of blind idealism that elevates an idea of how people ought to live over the facts of how people are and what they can bear. Gregers Werle destroys the lives of Hjalmar Ekdal's family through a quasi-religious fixation that demands shattering honesty, self-transcendence, and self-sacrifice.

The idea of transcendental sacrifice introduces a Christian resonance, which Ibsen makes explicit as Hjalmar, in the first act, when asked by a guest, denies knowing his own father suggesting Peter's denial of Jesus in John 18:15–18, 25–27.

Scientific & Technological Context

Technology, as the word is commonly understood, meaning machinery derived from scientific investigation and used to facilitate mechanical operations, is hardly the concern of "The Wild Duck." There is a hint of the advantages that the successful invention of new technology can bring to the inventor, as Hjalmar dreams of devising a new photographic invention. Nevertheless, the technology of psychological manipulation is a significant theme in the play. Gregers and Dr. Relling can be considered as rival technicians, each practicing a particular psychological technology. Relling believes in the necessity of obscuring some aspects of the truth of past events and of allowing some present illusions in order to allow people to continue to live with a degree of hope, contentment, and equanimity, in peace with each other, what he calls "the vital lie." Gregers believes in a brutal honesty and a puritanical absence of illusion, in a "summons to the ideal," so that a person can transcend self, and, in that sacrifice, forge with others a higher communion.

Biographical Context

Ibsen was born in Skien, a small port town in Norway, on March 20, 1828. His father was a prosperous merchant until Ibsen was eight, when he lost his fortune. His mother was a painter. Ibsen's childhood was defined by their poverty and by the social ostracism they faced. At fifteen, Ibsen was apprenticed to a pharmacist, and began writing plays. At eighteen, he fathered a child but abandoned both the woman, ten years his senior, and the child. He moved to Oslo, intending to enter the university. He began writing plays instead. His first play, "Catalina," 1850, was published under the pseudonym Brynjulf Bjarme, but not performed. "The Burial Mound," (also 1850), was staged unsuccessfully. Between 1851 and 1863, Ibsen was employed as a stage manager at several Norwegian theaters. In 1866, with "Brandt," he achieved popular success.

Ibsen married Suzannah Thorsen in 1858. Their son, Sigurd, was born in 1859. In 1864, Ibsen received a grant from the Norwegian government to travel and with additional aid from the Norwegian writer, editor, and theater director Bjornstjerne Bjornson (1832–1910), Ibsen left for Italy and remained abroad, living in Rome, Munich, and Dresden over the next twenty-seven years, returning to Norway infrequently.

In 1877, Ibsen stopped writing mythological or historical dramas in verse. With "Pillars of Society," he began to use contemporary social issues, gender, political and psychological conflicts as the material for his plays. One of Ibsen's most well-known plays, "A Doll's House," concerning the birth of a woman's awareness of the demands for self-abnegation that women faced in marriage,

appeared in 1879. In 1882, he wrote "An Enemy of the People." In it he argued against the wisdom of the majority, analyzed the power and the methods of political manipulation, and presented a drama in which one person, guided by his integrity and by his dedication to truth and personal honor rather than by self-interest and financial security, challenges a corrupt status quo and emerges a hero because of his resolve, although vilified by his townsman and defeated in his original mission. In 1884, Ibsen wrote "The Wild Duck," a counter-companion play to "An Enemy of the People." In it, he probed the problem of a heartless exploitation of truth and honesty. Ibsen's subsequent plays include "The Master Builder," 1892, "John Gabriel Borkman," 1896, and a classic of modern psychological dramas, "Hedda Gabler," 1890. In 1899, Ibsen suffered several strokes. The first impaired his ability to walk. The second, a year later, affected his ability to remember words.

Ibsen died in Christiania (Oslo), Norway on May 23, 1906.

Neil Heims, Ph.D.

Works Cited

Beyer, Edvard. "Ibsen: The Man and His Work." Translated by Marie Wells, A Condor Book/ Souvenir Press (E & A) LTD, 1978. Print.

Ibsen, Henrik. "The Wild Duck," Adamant Media Corporation, 2006. Print.

Discussion Questions

1. What does Relling mean when he speaks of "the vital lie? What is its relation to Gregers' dedication to the "summons to the ideal?" Must we choose between them? If so, which is the better choice?

2. What role does the past play in "The Wild Duck"?

3. How are women portrayed in "The Wild Duck," particularly in contrast to the men?

4. Although a principal theme of the play is idealism, does Ibsen show realism in "The Wild Duck"? How is realism portrayed; how valued? In which characters is it embodied?

5. Is Gregers' vision admirable in itself but misapplied, or is it fundamentally a mistaken vision? If so, how? If not, why not?

6. How do you understand the character of Hakon Werle and his motives for offering his son a partnership in his business or for helping the Ekdal family?

7. How important do you think illusion is in your life? What are some of your governing illusions?

8. Have you personally experienced or are you acquainted with the effects of absolute honesty or of a pursuit of an ideal? Discuss and describe. Were the effects damaging or constructive?

9. How does Ibsen establish a sense of foreboding in "The Wild Duck"?

10. What is a "well-made play?" How is "The Wild Duck" an example of the well-made play? What does it derive dramatically from being a well-made play?

Essay Ideas

1. Analyze and compare the characters of Gregers Werle and Hjalmar Ekdal.

2. Discuss Ibsen's use of ambiguity in "The Wild Duck."

3. Contrast Gina and Hjalmar.

4. Compare and contrast the philosophies of Gregers Werle and Dr. Relling.

5. Discuss the importance assigned to the idea of sacrifice in "The Wild Duck."

BIBLIOGRAPHY

Ackroyd, Peter. Dickens. New York: Harper Collins, 1990.

———. *T. S. Eliot: A Life*. New York: Simon & Schuster, 1984.

Adler, Margot. *Drawing Down the Moon: Witches, Druids, Goddess-Worshippers, and Other Pagans in America Today*. Boston: Beacon, 1979.

Alkalay-Gut, Karen. "Jury of Her Peers: The Importance of Trifles." *Studies in Short Fiction 21.1* (Winter 1984): 1–10.

Anca Vlasopolos. "Authorizing History: Victimization in 'A Streetcar Named Desire.'" *Theatre Journal* 38.3 (1986).

Badenhausen, Richard. "The Modern Academy Raging in the Dark: Misreading Mamet's Political Correctness in Oleanna." *College Literature*. 25.3 (Fall 1998): 1–19.

Barlow, Judith, ed. *Plays by American Women: 1900-1930*. New York: Applause Books, 1985.

Barstow, Anne Llewellyn. *Witchcraze: A New History of the European Witch Hunts*. San Francisco and London: Pandora, 1994.

Bechtel, Roger. "P.C. Power Play: Language and Representation in David Mamet's Oleanna." *Theatre Studies*. 41 (1996): 29–48.

Beckett, Samuel. "Waiting for Godot." London: Samuel French, 1965.

Ben-Zvi, Linda, ed. *Susan Glaspell: Essays on Her Theater and Fiction*. Ann Arbor: U of Michigan P, 1995.

———. *Susan Glaspell: Her Life and Times*. Oxford: Oxford UP, 2005.

Beyer, Edvard. "Ibsen: The Man and His Work." Translated by Marie Wells, A Condor Book/Souvenir Press (E & A) LTD, 1978. Print.

"Biography of an Intellectual," *Social Justice Movements*. 13 Jan. 2006. Columbia University. Web. 23 April 2009.

Bigsby, C. W. E. "Introduction." *Susan Glaspell: Plays*. Cambridge: Cambridge UP, 1987. 1–31.

———. "Tom Stoppard," in *British Writers, Supplement I*: 437–454. New York: Charles Scribner's Sons, 1987.

Bigsby, Christopher. *Arthur Miller: A Critical Study*. Cambridge: Cambridge U P, 2005.

Bilson, Fred. "Tom Stoppard's Arcadia," in *British Writers Classics*. Vol. 1: 23-29. Ed. Jay L. Parini. New York: Charles Scribner's Sons, 2003.

Bird, Edward A. "Introduction." *Cyrano de Bergerac*. Toronto: Methuen, 1968.

Bloom, Harold, ed. *Arthur Miller's Death of a Salesman: Contemporary Literary Views*. New York: Chelsea House Publishing, 1995.

Blue Angel Films. *Beckett on Film*. 16 July 2009 <http://www.beckettonfilm.com/>.

Boswell, James. "The Life of Johnson," I–IV. Ed. George Birkbeck Hill. Charleston: Biblio Life, 2008. Print.

Brannan, Robert Louis, ed. *Under the Management of Mr. Charles Dickens: His Production of "The Frozen Deep."* Ithaca: Cornell UP, 1966.

Brecht, Bertolt. "Galileo." Trans. by Charles Laughton. "Seven Plays by Bertolt Brecht." New York: Grove Press, 1961. Print.

———. "Mother Courage and Her Children." London: Methuen, 1980. Print.

Bryden, Mary. "Beckett and Religion." Samuel Beckett Studies. Basingstoke: Palgrave Macmillan, 2004. 154–171.

Butler, Mildred Allen. "The Historical Cyrano de Bergerac as a Basis for Rostand's Play." *Educational Theatre Journal* 6.3 (1954): 231–240. The Johns Hopkins University Press.

Cannon, John, Ed. "The Oxford Companion to British History," New York: Oxford UP, 1997. Print.

Carpentier, Martha C. "Susan Glaspell's Fiction: Fidelity as American Romance." *Twentieth Century Literature* 40.1 (Spring 1994): 92–114.

Cash, Eric W. "Tennessee Williams 1911–1983." 19 Nov. 2007. *The Mississippi Writers' Page*. University of Mississippi English Department. 6 May 2009. <www.olemiss.edu/depts/english/ms-writers/dir/Williams_tennessee>.

"Cat on a Hot Tin Roof: Introduction." *Drama for Students*. Ed. Marie Rose Napierkowski. Vol. 3. Detroit: Gale, 1998.

Chekhov, Anton. "Chekhov: The Major Plays." Trans. Ann Dunnigan. A Signet Classic, 1964. Print.

———. "Uncle Vanya." Gutenberg, 2008. Web.

Chesterfield, Philip Dormer. "Letters to His Son." Ed. Eugenia Stanhope. London: J. Dodsley, 1775. Print.

Choudhuri, A. D. *The Face of Illusion in American Drama*. Atlantic Highlands, NJ: Humanities Press, 1979.

"Civil Rights Era," *African American Odyssey*. 21 Mar. 2008. Library of Congress. Web. 28 Apr. 2009.

Clark, G. N. "The Later Stuarts 1660–1714." Oxford: Clarendon Press, 1934. Print.

Coe, Richard N. Beckett. Edinburgh: Oliver and Boyd, 1964.

Collins, Wilkie. "The Frozen Deep". London: Hesperus, 2004.

Contemporary Authors Online, The Gale Group. "Anton Chekhov." Brandeis University, 1999. Web.

Counsell, Colin, Introduction. "Volpone," London, Nick Hern Books, 1999.

Danson, Lawrence, "Jonsonian Comedy and the Discovery of the Social Self" *PMLA*, Vol. 99, No. 2. (Mar., 1984), pp. 179–193.

"David Mamet." 20th Century Theatre. Theatre Database. 28 May 2009. <www.theatredatabase.com/americanbuffalo.html>.

Davies, Paul. "Samuel Beckett." The Literary Encyclopedia. 16 July 2009. <http://www.litencyc.com/php/speople.php?rec=true&UID=5161>.

Delaney, Paul. *Tom Stoppard: The Moral Vision of the Major Plays*. New York: St. Martin's Press, 1990.

Dietrick, Jon. "Real Classical Money, Naturalism, and Mamet's American Buffalo." *Twentieth Century Literature*. 52.3 (Fall 2006): 330–346. Academic Source Complete. EBSCO. 3 June 2009. <http://search.ebscohost.com/login.aspx?direct=true&db=s8h&AN=24831626&site=ehost-live>.

Donoghue, Frank. "The Fame Machine: Book Reviewing and Eighteenth-Century Literary Careers". Stanford: Stanford UP, 1996. Print.

Duckworth, Alistair M. "Oliver Goldsmith." "Dictionary of Literary Biography" 39.1: "British Novelists, 1660–1800." Ed. Martin C. Battestin. Detroit: Gale Research Company, 1985. Part I, 222–39. Print.

Dymkowski, Christine. "On the Edge: The Plays of Susan Glaspell." *Modern Drama 31* (March 1988): 91–105.

Edwards, Paul. "Science in Hapgood and Arcadia," in *The Cambridge Companion to Stoppard*. Ed. Katherine E. Kelly. New York: Cambridge Univ. Press, 2001.

Effinger, Gove. "Two Mathematical Ideas in Arcadia." http://www.skidmore.edu/academics/theater/productions/arcadia/math.html>.

Eliot, T. S. "Introduction to Shakespeare and the Popular Dramatic Tradition by S. L. Bethell." London: P.S. King and Staples, 1944.

———. *Inventions of the March Hare*. Ed. Christopher Ricks. New York: Harcourt Brace, 1996.

———. "Selected Essays." *Selected Essays: 1917–1932*. New York: Harcourt, Brace and Company, 1932.

———. *The Complete Poems and Plays: 1909–1950*. New York: Harcourt, Brace & World, 1962.

Ellmann, Richard. *Oscar Wilde*. New York: Knopf, 1988.

Enck, John J., "From Jonson and the Comic Truth." Jonson: Volpone. A Casebook, London, MacMillan Publishers Ltd, 1985.

Filmmakers.com. 20 October 2008. <http://www.filmmakers.com/artists/mamet/biography>.

Fleming, John P. *Stoppard's Theatre: Finding Order amid Chaos*. Austin, TX: University of Texas Press, 2001.

Fort, Alice B. and Kates, Herbert S., "Gerhart Hauptmann." *TheatreHistory.com*. 21 Aug 2008. <http://www.theatrehistory.com/german/hauptmann001.html>.

Foster, Verna. "Sex, Power, and Pedagogy in David Mamet's Oleanna and Ionesco's The Lesson." *American Drama*. 5.1 (1995): 36–50.

Friedman, Sharon. "Feminism as Theme in Twentieth-Century American Women's Drama." *American Studies 25* (Spring 1984): 69–89.

Glaspell, Susan. "Trifles." Boston: Small, 1920. Rpt. In *Understanding Literature: An Introduction to Reading and Writing*. Eds. Walter Kalaidjian, Judith Roof, Stephen Watt. Boston: Houghton Mifflin Company, 2004. 1763–1774.

Goethe, Johann Wolfgang von. Faust, Part One. Trans. A.S. Kline. "Poetry in Translation." A.S. Kline. Web. 25 May 2010. <http://tkline.pgcc.net/PITBR/German/Fausthome.htm>.

Goggans, Thomas H. "David Mamet's Oleanna." *Modern Drama*. 40 (1997): 433–441.

Goldsmith, Oliver. "Enquiry into the Present State of Polite Learning in Europe." 2nd edition. London: J. Dodsley, 1774. Print.

———. "On Sentimental Comedy." "Essays and the Bee." Boston: Wells and Lilly, 1820. 238–44. Print.

———. "She Stoops to Conquer," *Four English Comedies*. Ed. J. M. Morrell. London: Penguin, 1950. 233–313. Print.

Gussow, Mel. *Conversations with Miller*. New York: Applause, 2002.

Haley, Darryl E. "'Certain Moral Values': A Rhetoric of Outcasts in the Plays of Tennessee Williams." 1997. East Tennessee State University. 12 May 2009. <http://www.etsu.edu/haleyd/Prospectus.html>.

Hall, Peter. "Peter Hall looks back at the original Godot." *The Samuel Beckett On-Line Resources and Links Pages*. 16 July 2009. <http://samuelbeckett.net/PeterHallGodot.html>.

Hansberry, Lorraine. "A Raisin in the Sun." New York: Vintage Books, 1958. Print.

Heller, Janet Ruth. "David Mamet's Trivialization of Feminism and Sexual Harassment in Oleanna." *MidAmerica*. 27 (2000): 93–105.

Hill, Christopher. "The Century of Revolution: 1603-1714." 2nd Ed. London: Routledge, 2002. Print.

Hill, W. Speed, "Biography, Autobiography, and Volpone." *Studies in English Literature*, 1500–1900, Vol. 12, No. 2, Elizabethan and Jacobean Drama. (Spring, 1972), pp. 309–328.

Holstein, Suzy Clarkson. "Silent Justice in a Different Key: Glaspell's Trifles." *Midwest Quarterly* 44.3 (Spring 2003): 282–291.

Hoppit, Julian. "Land of Liberty? England 1689–1727." Oxford: Oxford UP, 2000. Print.

Hume, Robert D. "Drama and Theatre in the Mid and Later Eighteenth Century." *The Cambridge History of English Literature, 1660–1780*. Ed. John Richetti. Cambridge: Cambridge UP. 316–339. Print.

Iannone, Carol. "PC on Stage." *Academic Questions*. 6.4 (Fall 1993): 72–86.

Ibsen, Henrik. "An Enemy of the People." Chicago: Ivan R. Dee, 2007. Print.

———. "The Wild Duck," Adamant Media Corporation, 2006. Print.

"IMDB: Internet Movie Database." Imdb.com, Inc. Web. 23 April 2009. <http://www.imdb.com>.

Jackson, Allyn. "Love and the Second Law of Thermodynamics: Tom Stoppard's Arcadia." November 1995 <http://plue.sedac.ciesein.org/geocorr/doc/arcadia.html>.

James, Caryn. "Mamet's Lesson in Sexual Harassment." *New York Times*. 144.49870 (4 Nov.1994): C22.

Jarvis, Simon. "Criticism, Taste, Aesthetics." *The Cambridge Companion to English Literature 1740–1830*. Ed. Thomas Keymer & John Mee. Cambridge: Cambridge UP, 2004. 24–42. Print.

John S. Bak. "sneakin' and spyin'" from Broadway to the Beltway: Cold War Masculinity, Brick and Homosexual Existentialism." *Theatre Journal* 56.2 (2004).

Jones, Jennifer. *Medea's Daughters: Forming and Performing the Woman Who Kills*. Columbus: Ohio State UP, 2003.

Jonson, Ben, Volpone, London, Nick Hern Books, 1999.

Kalb, J. *Beckett in Performance*. Cambridge: Cambridge University Press, 1989.

Karlsen, Carol. "The Devil in the Shape of a Woman: Witchcraft in Colonial New England." New York: W. W. Norton, 1987.

Kay, W. David, "Ben Jonson and Elizabethan Dramatic Convention." *Modern Philology*, Vol. 76, No. 1. (Aug., 1978), pp. 18–28.

Keates, Jonathan, "The Paladin of Panache." *Literary Review*. 22 Aug 2008. http://www.literaryreview.co.uk/keates_02_08.html.

Kenton, Edna. *The Provincetown Players and the Playwrights' Theatre: 1915–1922.* Jefferson: McFarland, 2004.

Knapp, Peggy, "Ben Jonson and the Publicke Riot." *ELH: English Literary History*, Vol. 46, No. 4. (Winter, 1979), pp. 577–594.

Knoll, Robert E., *Ben Jonson's Plays*. Lincoln, University of Nebraska Press, 1964.

Kroll, Jack. "A Tough Lesson in Sexual Harassment." *Newsweek*. 120.19 (9 Nov. 1992): 65–67.

Kushner, Tony. "Angels in America". London: Nick Hern Books, 2007. Print.

Lewis, Paul. The Wilkie Collins Pages. 18 April 2006. http://www.wilkiecollins.com.

Liaugminas, Andrew V. "What Is a Simple Definition of the Laws of Thermodynamics?" <http://www.physlink.com/Education/AskExperts/ae280.cfm>.

Liu, Cecilia. "Mamet: Glengarry Glen Ross." 13 April 2004 <http:// www.eng.fju.edu.tw/iacd_2001F/asynchrous_drama/dm_ggr.htm>.

"Lorraine Hansberry," "Voices from the Gaps: Women Artists and Writers of Color". University of Minnesota, 2006. Web. 23 April 2009.

Luigi Pirandello. "Six Characters in Search of an Author." London; New York: Penguin Books, 1995. Print.

MacLeod, Christine. "The Politics of Gender, Language and Hierarchy in Mamet's Oleanna." *Journal of American Studies*. 29.2 (1995): 199–23.

Makowsky, Veronica. "Susan Glaspell and Modernism." *The Cambridge Companion to American Women Playwrights*. Ed. Brenda Murphy. Cambridge [England]; New York: Cambridge UP, 1993.

Malek, James S. "She Stoops to Conquer." *Reference Guide to English Literature*. Ed. D. L. Kirkpatrick. 2nd ed. London: St. James Press, 1991. 1845. Print.

Mamet, David. "American Buffalo." New York: Grove Press, 1976.

_____. "Oleanna." New York: Vintage Books, 1993.

_____. "Speed the Plow." New York: Grove Press, 1985.

Manheim, Michael, ed. *The Cambridge Companion to Eugene O'Neill*. Cambridge: Cambridge University Press, 1998.

Marchitell, Howard, "Desire and Domination in Volpone." *Studies in English Literature*, 1500–1900, Vol. 31, No. 2, Elizabethan and Jacobean Drama. (Spring, 1991), pp. 287–308.

Marsh, Kelly A. "Dead Husbands and Other 'Girls' Stuff': The Trifles in Legally Blonde." *Literature/Film Quarterly 33.3* (2005): 201–206.

McCarthy, Joseph Raymond. *The Columbia Encyclopedia*. 6th ed. 2005. 4 February 2006. <http://www.encyclopedia.com>.

Miller, Arthur. "Death of a Salesman," Harmondsworth, England: Penguin. 1998.

_____. "Introduction." Collected Plays. New York: Viking, 1957. Excerpt rpt. in Miller, The Crucible: Text and Criticism. 161-169.

_____. "The Crucible: Text and Criticism." Ed. Gerald Weales. New York: Viking, 1971.

Mitchell, Sally. *Daily Life in Victorian England*. Westport, CT: Greenwood, 1996.

Moss, Stephen. "The Arcadia Archive." <http://www.cherwell.oxon.sch.uk/arcadia/outlineO.htm>.

Nadel, Ira. Double Act: A Life of Tom Stoppard. London: Methuen, 2002.

Naydor, Lillian. "The Cannibal, The Nurse, and The Cook in Dickens's The Frozen Deep." *Victorian Literature and Culture* 19: 1–24, 1991.

Németh, Lenke. "Miscommunication and Its Implication in David Mamet's Oleanna." *British and American Studies*. (1997): 167–176.

Noe, Marcia. "Region as Metaphor in the Plays of Susan Glaspell." *Western Illinois Regional Studies*. 4.1 (1981): 77–85.

Norton, Mary Beth. *In the Devil's Snare: The Salem Witchcraft Crisis of 1692*. New York: Knopf, 2002.

Novick, Julius. "Theater." Nation 231.16 (15 Nov. 1980): 521–522. Academic Source Complete. EBSCO. 6 June 2009.

O'Neill, Eugene. *Long Day's Journey into Night*. London: Jonathan Cape, 2007.

Oliver-Morden, B. C. "Goldsmith, Oliver." *Reference Guide to English Literature*. Ed. D. L. Kirkpatrick. 2nd ed. Vol. 1. Chicago & London: St. James Press, 1991. 636–7. Print.

Oppenheim, Lois. *Samuel Beckett Studies*. Basingstoke: Palgrave Macmillan, 2004.

Otten, Terry. *The Temptation of Innocence in the Dramas of Arthur Miller*. Columbia and London: University of Missouri P, 2002.

Oulton, Carolyn. "A Vindication of Religion: Wilkie Collins, Charles Dickens, and "The Frozen Deep." *Dickensian* 97(2): 154–158, 2001.

Puritanism. *The Columbia Encyclopedia*. 6th ed. 2005. 4 February 2006. <http://www.encyclopedia.com>.

Rajkowska, Baacutebara Ozieblo. *Susan Glaspell: A Critical Biography*. Chapel Hill: University of North Carolina Press, 2000.

Redwine, Jr., James D., "Volpone's "Sport" and the Structure of Jonson's Volpone." Studies in English Literature, 1500–1900, Vol. 34, No. 2, Elizabethan and Jacobean Drama. (Spring, 1994), pp. 301–321.

Richardson, Katherine W. *The Salem Witchcraft Trials*. Salem, MA: Essex Institute, 1983.

Robinson, Kenneth. *Wilkie Collins, A Biography*. New York: MacMillan, 1952.

Rostand, Edmond. "Cyrano de Bergerac." Toronto: Methuen, 1968.

_____. "Cyrano de Bergerac." Trans. Anthony Burgess. London: Nick Hern Books, 2002.

Rousseau, G. S. (Ed.). "Goldsmith: The Critical Heritage." London and Boston: Routledge and Kegan Paul, 1974. Print.

Russell, Judith Kay. "Glaspell's Trifles." *Explicator* 55.2 (Winter 1997): 88–91.

Ryan, Steven. "Oleanna: David Mamet's Power Play." *Modern Drama.* 39 (1996): 392–40.

Scouten, Arthur H. "Restoration and 18th-century Drama." *Reference Guide to English Literature.* Ed. D. L. Kirkpatrick. 2nd ed. Vol. 1. Chicago & London: St. James Press, 1991. 58–66. Print.

Seymour-Jones, Carol. "Painted Shadow: The Life of Vivienne Eliot." London: Constable, 2001.

Shaw, George Bernard. "Pygmalion." London: Penguin, 2003.

_____. "Saint Joan." New York: Penguin Classics, 2001. Print.

Siebold, Thomas, ed. *Readings on "Death of a Salesman,"* San Diego: Greenhaven Press, 1998.

_____, ed. *Readings on "The Glass Menagerie."* San Diego: Greenhaven Press, 1998.

Silverstein, Marc. "'We're Just Human': Oleanna and Cultural Crisis." *South Atlantic Review.* 60.2 (May 1995): 104–20.

Skloot, Robert. "Oleanna, or, the Play of Pedagogy." *Gender and Genre: Essays on David Mamet.* Eds. Christopher C. Hudgins and Leslie Kane. New York: Palgrave, 2001. 95–107.

Stone, John David. "Arcadia." November 6-14, 1997 <http://www.math.grin.edu/stone/events/arcadia>.

Stoppard, Tom. "Arcadia". London: Faber & Faber, Inc. /New York: Farrar, Straus & Giroux, 1993. (All page references are to this edition.)

"Tennessee Williams 1911–1983." *The Moonstruck Drama Bookstore.* 12 May 2009. <http://www.imagination.com/moonstruck/clsc9.htm>.

"The Oxford English Dictionary." Ed. J. A. Simpson & E. S. C. 2nd ed. Weiner. Oxford: Oxford University Press & Clarendon Press, 1989. Print. 20 vols.

Tomc, Sandra. "David Mamet's Oleanna and the Way of the Flesh." Essays in Theatre/Études thé â trales 15.2 (May 1997): 163–175.

Wilde, Oscar. "The Importance of Being Earnest." The Importance of Being Earnest and Other Plays. New York: Penguin, 1986. 247–314.

———. *The Picture of Dorian Gray.* New York: Norton, 1988.

Williams, Tennessee. "The Glass Menagerie." London: Heinemann, 1968.

Wilson, August. "The Piano Lesson." New York: Penguin, 1990. Print.

INDEX